Y0-BQU-991

945.51
Kl11r

127547

DATE DUE			

WITHDRAWN

THE RISE OF THE MEDICI

The Rise of the Medici

FACTION IN FLORENCE

1426 — 1434

DALE KENT

CARL A. RUDISILL LIBRARY
LENOIR RHYNE COLLEGE

1978

OXFORD UNIVERSITY PRESS

Oxford University Press, Walton Street, Oxford OX2 6DP

OXFORD LONDON GLASGOW
NEW YORK TORONTO MELBOURNE WELLINGTON
KUALA LUMPUR SINGAPORE JAKARTA HONG KONG TOKYO
DELHI BOMBAY CALCUTTA MADRAS KARACHI
IBADAN NAIROBI DAR ES SALAAM CAPE TOWN

© *Oxford University Press 1978*

*All rights reserved. No part of this publication may be reproduced,
stored in a retrieval system, or transmitted, in any form or by any
means, electronic, mechanical, photocopying, recording, or otherwise,
without the prior permission of Oxford University Press*

British Library Cataloguing in Publication Data

Kent, Dale
  The rise of the Medici.
  1. Medici family – History
  I. Title
  945'.51   DG737.42   77–30201
  ISBN 0–19–822520–2

945.51
K41r
127547
Jan. 1984

*Printed in Great Britain
at the University Press, Oxford
by Vivian Ridler
Printer to the University*

ACKNOWLEDGEMENTS

THIS book is based on a doctoral thesis for the University of London, completed in 1971. I am grateful for financial help from several sources during the period of my post-graduate studies. I should like to thank the Victorian Women Graduates' Association of Australia and the Institute of Historical Research in London, for Research Fellowships, and the Italian Institute, London, and the Senate House of the University of London, for assistance with the expenses of microfilm and travel to Italy.

As will be immediately apparent to readers familiar with this field, my greatest intellectual debts are to Professor Nicolai Rubinstein of Westfield College, University of London, and Professor Gene Brucker, of the University of California, Berkeley. My original interest in Florentine history was largely inspired by their work, and it is with the further exploration of questions which they introduced and made central to the study of this area that the present book is essentially concerned. During my years as his student, Nicolai Rubinstein was unfailingly generous with his time and interest, and I was privileged to profit constantly from his incomparable knowledge of the Florentine archives and the myriad problems to which they hold the key; for his friendship and the benefit of his experienced advice I continue to be grateful. My association with Gene Brucker has been largely by correspondence, for which he has a particular gift; his perceptive criticisms of my original thesis formed the essential basis for its revision, in which I was constantly sustained by his generous encouragement and stimulated by the opportunity to exchange ideas with him.

I am also particularly obliged to Professor Gino Corti for his help in breaking down the effects of isolation in working from Australia, remote not only from the archives but even from the great collections of published material; he has given me invaluable aid with many of the small problems and queries which inevitably arise between visits to libraries and archives. I should like to express my appreciation of the friendly assistance which I have received from the staff of the Archivio di Stato and the Biblioteca

Nazionale in Florence, and of the Warburg Institute in London. At the stage of transition from thesis to book I was very grateful for the comments and suggestions of Professor Randolph Starn of the University of California, Berkeley. To many English and American friends I owe less specific debts but am aware how much I have benefited from opportunities for discussion with them and also from their expert advice with particular problems; among these I should like especially to acknowledge Julian and Alison Brown, Bob Black, and Anthony Molho. In Australia I have received help and encouragement from a number of the academic and secretarial staff of La Trobe University; in particular I wish to thank Dr. Paul Rule for his advice on problems of translation, Mrs. Barbara Salmond, whose alertness and forbearance have considerably lightened the burden of preparing the final manuscript, and the Joint Schools Research Committee for several grants for microfilm and travel.

A task as sustained and time-consuming as the completion of a book in concurrence with the ordinary responsibilities of job and family requires more than ordinary support; in the domestic sphere I owe much to my mother-in-law. My debt to my husband in several senses is incalculable. Given the similarity of our research interests, it is impossible to acknowledge or even to identify all obligations, but this book has been shaped from the beginning in the atmosphere of a constant interchange of ideas and information. I am grateful for his specific interest and encouragement with this particular undertaking over the last several years, but perhaps most profoundly for his early recognition and defence of my right to a preoccupation with Italian history equal to his own.

To look forward rather than back, I dedicate the book to my daughter Margaret.

DALE KENT

Melbourne
September 1975

CONTENTS

LIST OF MAPS AND TABLES

ABBREVIATIONS

ARCHIVES

Acqu. e Doni	Acquisti e Doni
Ancisa	Carte dell'Ancisa
A.S.F.	Archivio di Stato, Firenze
B.N.F.	Biblioteca Nazionale, Firenze
C.P.	Consulte e Pratiche
Cap. Pop. Lib. Inquis.	Capitano del Popolo, Liber Inquisitionum
Cat.	Catasto
C.S.	Carte Strozziane
Conv. Soppr.	Conventi Soppressi
Delib. Sig. e Coll.	Deliberazioni degli Signori e Collegi
Giud. Appelli	Giudice degli Appelli
M.A.P.	Medici avanti il Principato
Misc. Rep.	Miscellanea Repubblicana
MSS.	Manoscritti
MSS. Pass.	Manoscritti Passerini
Otto di Guardia	Otto di Guardia e Balìa, periodo repubblicano
Pol. Gar.	Poligrafo Gargani
Provv., Reg.	Provvisioni, Registri

PRINTED WORKS

A.S.I.	*Archivio Storico Italiano*
J.W.C.I.	*Journal of the Warburg and Courtauld Institutes*

INTRODUCTION

(i)

IN the first days of September 1433, after several months of mounting political tension in Florence, Cosimo de' Medici received a request from the newly installed *Signoria* to leave his estates in the Mugello, where he had spent the summer, and return to the city. He was summoned to appear at a meeting in the palace of the Priors on the morning of 7 September, and in his own words,

> when I arrived in the palace, I found the majority of my companions already in the midst of a discussion; after some time I was commanded by the authority of the *Signoria* to go upstairs, where I was taken by the captain of the guard into a cell called the Barberia, and locked in, and when this became known, the whole city was thrown into tumult.[1]

In the course of the succeeding month, Cosimo, seven other members of the Medici family, and several citizens known to be their intimate associates were sentenced to exile, some of them for as long as ten years. The government passed effectively into the hands of an anti-Medicean group led by Rinaldo degli Albizzi, while friends of the Medici were excluded from power as far as was possible.

Precisely twelve months later the situation was completely reversed. In September 1434 a group of largely pro-Medicean Priors was drawn from the electoral purses. After a brief and abortive attempt by the anti-Mediceans to avert the impending crisis by challenging the authority of the *Signoria*, Cosimo, his family, and friends were recalled to Florence, and large numbers of their political enemies were banished in their stead. Many others were deprived of the right to hold office in the future, and Mediceans assumed the key positions in the state. This time there was to be no sudden change of fortune; the return of the Medici from exile marks the beginning of their ascendancy in Florence, an ascendancy

---

[1] Cosimo de' Medici, *Ricordi*, in A. Fabroni, *Magni Cosmi Medicei vita* (Pisa, 1789), ii. 96.

never before approached by any other family in the city's history, and perhaps the most significant single development in the political life of the commune since the end of the thirteenth century.[2]

But despite the importance of these events to the story of the Florentine political experience in the republican period, they have attracted little recent attention from historians.[3] Although great advances over the last few decades in our understanding of the nature and basis of political life in the fourteenth and later fifteenth centuries have made plain the inadequacy of traditional interpretations of the rise of the Medici, no real alternatives have been explored. This may well be due to the complex and ambiguous nature of the events in question. The consensus of Florentine historical opinion in the succeeding century is essentially summed up in the words of Domenico Buoninsegni, writing about 1460; according to him, the exile of Cosimo, and all that followed from it, was due to 'divisions and factions generated previously in Florence by the methods of distributing taxes, and the frequency of their imposition, due to the length of the wars, and by alterations to scrutinies and to the electoral purses'.[4]

However, commentators at the time had stressed that on both occasions the transfer of power to the new regime had been effected by strictly constitutional means; in each case a Parliament of the people was summoned by the *Signoria* to grant power to a special commission to reform the state.[5] Moreover, they had carefully refrained from judgement on either regime, or the circumstances in which it attained power; clearly the political situation was too volatile for citizens to risk open commitment. The private diaries, memoirs, and chronicles in which the Florentine upper classes customarily and characteristically recorded their

[2] For the ways in which the Medici significantly modified the operation of the constitution as essentially established in 1282, see N. Rubinstein, *The Government of Florence under the Medici (1434 to 1494)* (Oxford, 1966).

[3] The latest extensive discussion of the partisan struggles of this period is by C. Gutkind, *Cosimo de' Medici, Pater Patriae, 1389–1464* (Oxford, 1938), Ch. 2.

[4] Domenico Buoninsegni, *Storie della città di Firenze dall'anno 1410 al 1460* (Florence, 1637), p. 47; cf. Benedetto Dei, 'Chronica', MSS. 119, ff. 12r–14r, Archivio di Stato, Florence. All subsequent archival references are to the A.S.F., unless otherwise indicated.

[5] Their composition, deliberations, and acts are recorded in Balìe, 24 (1433) and 25 (1434). See also the account of these events in 'Ricordanze di Guccio di Cino de' Nobili', C.S. 2ª ser. LIX, c. 212, cf. the *Priorista*, C.S. 2ª ser. CII, Sept.–Oct. 1433 (not foliated).

reactions to domestic, business, and political events in which they felt themselves equally personally concerned,[6] are strangely silent regarding the upheavals of 1433 and 1434. Many normally acute and avid observers of the political scene kept their accounts of these years brief, bland, and free from essential comment. One prominent patrician, Domenico Giugni, left the pages of his notebooks blank between these dates.[7] Another, Terrino Manovelli, destined for exile on the Medici return, described their expulsion with obvious satisfaction and repeated with relish the official justification of their condemnation. However, without the subsequent and then unforeseen development of the ultra-violet lamp, his opinions too would have remained unknown to us, as the relevant sections were later heavily scored out by what appears to be the same pen and ink with which they were written.[8]

The result is that most historians, at least since Machiavelli, have relied essentially in their discussion of these events and the years immediately preceding on the only contemporary account which deals with them specifically and at length—the *Istorie Fiorentine* of Giovanni Cavalcanti,[9] whose purpose was expressly

[6] On the form and content of Florentine *Ricordi* see particularly P. J. Jones, 'Florentine families and Florentine diaries in the fourteenth century', *Papers of the British School at Rome*, xxiv (1956), 183–205, and G. Brucker (ed.), *Two Memoirs of Renaissance Florence* (New York, 1967), Introduction.

[7] The family *Priorista* which later in the century came into the possession of Vettorio di Nello, grandson of the Ser Bartolomeo di Ser Nello who was Rinaldo degli Albizzi's son-in-law (C.S. 2ª ser. CV, entries under Sept.–Oct. 1433 and 1434), includes a narrative of events so devoid of any shade of approval or disapproval that it is difficult to believe the writer was not purposely abstaining from comment or commitment. The 'Libro di Domenico di Giovanni Giugni', Biblioteca Laurenziana, Florence, Acqu. e Doni, 103 (not foliated) passes over 1433 without comment on political events and contains no entries at all for 1434. The 'Libro d'Uguccione di Mico Capponi', Conv. Soppr., Monastero di S. Piero a Monticelli, 153, f. 3r, describes how the prospective marriage between the writer's daughter and a member of the Peruzzi family was postponed 'per certe novità furono a Firenze', but does not explain why the events of August and September 1434 made such a marriage undesirable, nor what these events were.

[8] C.S. 2ª ser. XIV, f. 3v. It seems likely that Manovelli erased the entry of 1433 either after the Medici recall or in anticipation of it, in case his private papers should incriminate him as one of their opponents. He made no comment on the events of September 1434, apart from recording that he had been drawn for the *Sedici* on 8 September; the last entry notes the birth of his son on 26 October 1434.

[9] e.g. Machiavelli's account of this period in the *Istorie Fiorentine*, *Opere*, ed. M. Bonfantini (Milan, 1954), Bk. IV, Ch. 6, esp. p. 760, is derived substantially and almost directly from that of Giovanni Cavalcanti, *Istorie Fiorentine*, ed. G. di Pino (Milan, 1944), pp. 56–7. All subsequent references to the *Istorie* are to this edition, unless otherwise indicated.

'to write of the divisions between our citizens and the causes of
Cosimo's exile and his subsequent return'.[10] Particularly in view
of the absence of other evidence on this subject, Cavalcanti is an
invaluable guide to the exploration of the period and its problems.
His original and lively language, far removed from the formal
and conventional style of the professional historian of his time,
mirrors his vivid personal view of his own society which itself
should warn against the uncritical acceptance of his particular
explanations. Cavalcanti regarded these conflicts within the
Florentine ruling class from a peculiar perspective, and his view
of them was obscured by an ambiguous involvement which finds
expression in a multitude of internal contradictions.[11]

He admitted that he embarked on his history partly 'to cool
and give vent to my own passions',[12] but his work was completed
and made public after the Medici victory had made their favour
the essential key to advancement in Florentine society.[13] His history sings the praises of Giovanni and Cosimo de' Medici,[14] but
is shot through with a savage resentment against the exclusion
from participation in politics of the magnate class to which he
belonged,[15] and whose reinstatement into the ruling group had
been part of the programme of the Medici opponents;[16] he detested the populace who, according to his own account, were
their main supporters.[17] He denounced the citizens who embroiled
Florence in the war against Lucca as foolish and immoral,[18] but
named the Mediceans among those who favoured it most strongly.[19]
He hailed the return of the Medici, to whom he was related by

[10] Cavalcanti, *Istorie*, p. 3.

[11] See M. Grendler, *The 'Trattato Politico-Morale' of Giovanni Cavalcanti,
Travaux d'Humanisme et Renaissance*, cxxxv (Geneva, 1973), for a detailed comment
on his life and work, and a much more negative judgement on the value of his
account of these years. Cf. my own forthcoming article, 'Giovanni Cavalcanti and
the social history of fifteenth century Florence'.

[12] *Istorie*, p. 3.

[13] There is no concrete evidence of any hope that the *Istorie* would win Medici
approval; however, in view of his continuing poverty and imprisonment for debt,
he would surely have appreciated some protective patronage. See Grendler (ed.),
Trattato, pp. 14–16; cf. *Istorie*, p. 3.

[14] e.g. ibid., pp. 4, 25, 56–7, 108.

[15] For its most articulate expression, ibid., pp. 10–11, cf. p. 110.

[16] See his own account, ibid., pp. 46–54, and below, pp. 211–21; 296–7.

[17] See the ambiguous but suggestive allegorical passage on this subject, ibid.,
pp. 108–10, also pp. 56–7, 175, 323.

[18] Ibid., pp. 159, 180.

[19] Ibid., pp. 163–5.

marriage,[20] as a triumph of justice,[21] but bemoaned the banishment of their opponents which it necessitated, as the cause of the loss of her greatest citizens.[22] Subsequent writers have ignored these paradoxes and inconsistencies, choosing to accept various elements of his testimony while ignoring the conflicting evidence which he himself provides.

Cavalcanti's history is far too valuable a social document to be discarded. He transcends his own explanations in the acuteness of his observations, in his implicit expression of the structure and attitudes of his society; his value is that of the diarist, or even the novelist, rather than the historian. In attempting to approach this problem afresh, we may best begin perhaps with a reassessment of some general assumptions which have long held the field, in the light of a more critical analysis of Cavalcanti's interpretation of events, of the archival evidence which in the last century has been found to support or refute them, and, most importantly, of the fresh perspectives which the work of the last few decades has opened on to problems concerning the social and political history of Florence.

Perhaps the most notable feature of Cavalcanti's account is his view of the social bases and aims of the two parties; he saw the conflict between the Mediceans and their opponents as part of an eternal opposition 'between the patricians and those less distinguished'.[23] While the anti-Mediceans were encouraged 'by all the worthiest citizens of the *reggimento* and by all the nobles', Cosimo's own party flourished 'because the masses had chosen him as their champion and looked on him as a god'.[24] Cavalcanti's stress on the popular nature of Medici support is retained in most subsequent accounts of the period, even some of the more recent.[25] Indeed it has even on occasion been extended to represent the

[20] He was the nephew of Ginevra Cavalcanti, Lorenzo di Giovanni di Bicci's wife. See R. de Roover, *The Rise and Decline of the Medici Bank* (Cambridge, Mass., 1963), p. 51.

[21] *Istorie*, pp. 280–7, 297–8.

[22] Ibid., pp. 317–31.   [23] Ibid., p. 4.

[24] Ibid., p. 268.

[25] Later in the fifteenth century a Medicean apologist like Benedetto Dei stressed the family's populist sympathies in his account of the events of 1433–4 (MSS. 119, ff. 12r–14r), and referred to Cosimo as 'padre de' poveri' (12v) and 'cholonna e sostegnio del popolo fiorentino' (13r). Among modern writers see, for example, Gutkind, *Cosimo de' Medici*, pp. 78, 85, and A. Dainelli, 'Niccolò da Uzzano nella vita politica di suoi tempi', *A.S.I.* 7th Ser. xvii (1932), 35–86.

Medici themselves as upstarts, though the socially hypersensitive chronicler would himself have been appalled by this error.[26]

Writers and readers of history in the last century or so have naturally been attracted by this popular element in the Medici image, but anachronistic attempts to represent their political outlook as generally democratic have simply served to demonstrate that this was certainly not the ideological basis of their party. According to Cavalcanti, they were largely responsible for the institution of the *catasto*, a more equitable system of taxation which favoured the poor at the expense of the rich,[27] but an examination of the transcripts of the debates dealing with this issue, which Buoninsegni saw as a major precipitant of factional strife, shows that Giovanni de' Medici opposed the tax by which he would be among the hardest hit, and that it was chiefly initiated and established by the aristocratic opponents of the Medici from the upper echelons of the ruling group.[28]

In any case, Cavalcanti is as clear as other contemporaries about the fact that the regimes of 1433 and 1434 were installed, not through popular revolt or even by popular acclaim, but by a constitutional device designed to take power out of the hands of the people and entrust it to a restricted group of prominent patricians.[29] He even admitted, concerning the creation of the pro-Medicean *reggimento* in 1434, that 'although I say "new *reggimento*", there was no clamour of inexperienced voices, and no alteration in either number or quality of men, but some men of integrity were added

---

[26] F. Schevill, *Medieval and Renaissance Florence* (2 vols., New York, 1961; 1st edn. 1936), i. 344, discussing Giovanni di Bicci's new-won prosperity, describes him as 'novus homo', despised as an upstart by men of inherited wealth. In fact, however, the Florentine memory was rather longer, and the Medici enjoyed the considerable social distinction of having been among the earliest of then prosperous families to gain the Priorate in 1291. For a fuller discussion of the criteria of social acceptability, see below, pp. 113–16. G. Brucker, 'The Medici in the Fourteenth Century', *Speculum*, xxxii (1957), 1–26, illuminates the actual social background of Giovanni di Bicci's success, and shows how if anything, the Medici were nearer in spirit to the *magnati* than the *plebe*.

[27] *Istorie*, pp. 116–18, 139–40.

[28] P. Berti (ed.), 'Nuovi documenti intorno al Catasto', *Giornale storico degli archivi toscani*, iv (1860), 40–62.

[29] As S. Bertelli points out in his review of Rubinstein, *The Government of Florence*, in *Rivista Storica Italiana*, lxxviii (1966), 988–96, contrary to Machiavelli's belief that the Medici needed the *popolo* to renew their authority and that the *popolo* did so because the Medici were popular, the 'people' of a *Parlamento* were always coerced by armed force in the *piazza*; the Parliament was not called to gain popular consent, but to take government out of the hands of the people (p. 988).

who had had no place in the previous regime'.[30] As the arrogant and splenetic chronicler habitually referred to most of his own social inferiors as 'the stupid, crazy mob'[31] or 'the brutish masses',[32] whatever their actual position, and as he also observed that Cosimo counted among his supporters some of the most distinguished citizens in all Florence,[33] one begins to wonder, if not about the reality, at least about the relevance of the popular support which he attributes to the Medici cause.

On the other hand, a number of the more convincing episodes in the clashes described by Cavalcanti arise out of substantial social differences between the parties; particularly notable is an alleged meeting in 1426 of the hard core of anti-Mediceans in the church of Santo Stefano, to express the aristocratic fear that the *gente nuova*, supported by Giovanni de' Medici, would eventually oust them from the electoral purses and the leading offices, if nothing were done to prevent them.[34] Like Buoninsegni, Cavalcanti consistently presented the struggle for offices, open only to the patrician class, as the chief ground on which battle was joined between the parties, and the latter's representation in the purses from which offices were drawn as the chief indicator of their comparative strength, and the ultimate cause of the Medici victory.[35]

Viewed as a whole, without allowing the strong strokes of self-conscious polemic to obscure the accuracy of detail carefully drawn from a life-long observation of Florentine society and political life, Cavalcanti's picture confirms rather than conflicts with more recent research, in indicating the direction in which an explanation of these events is to be sought. Since Nicola Ottokar's pioneering work on the Florentine ruling group, it has been clear that a crude conception of class conflict is insufficient to illuminate political events, since almost all politically effective activity took place within the confines of a single class—the patriciate.[36] However, Gene Brucker and Marvin Becker have subsequently drawn attention to the importance of more subtle

[30] *Istorie*, p. 311.

[31] '[la] stolta e pazza plebe', ibid., p. 525, cf. pp. 53, 221, 250.

[32] 'La bestiale moltitudine', ibid., p. 175, cf. pp. 51, 178, 323.

[33] Ibid., p. 263.   [34] Ibid., pp. 46–54.

[35] Ibid., pp. 263–4; cf. Buoninsegni, *Storie*, e.g. p. 47, and the observation of the chronicler Villani in an earlier period that in Florence government was traditionally transformed not by violence, but by obtaining office (cit. B. Dami, *Giovanni Bicci dei Medici*, Florence, 1899, p. 64).

[36] N. Ottokar, *Il comune di Firenze alla fine del dugento* (Florence, 1926).

social and political distinctions within this class, between families established in the governing group shortly after its consolidation in 1282 and those new men—the *gente nuova*—who later rose into its ranks through the operation of social mobility;[37] Lauro Martines, in his study of the Florentine humanists, has demonstrated the practical value of these distinctions in illuminating social attitudes and behaviour.[38] Finally, Nicolai Rubinstein's study of Medici government in Florence after 1434 has shown that the exploitation and manipulation of the electoral system was the major political technique of the victorious Medici after 1434.[39] All this points to the necessity of a more precise social analysis of the partisans of both sides in the late twenties and early thirties, and of a careful consideration of electoral activity in this period.[40]

The second major concern in all accounts of this period is to explain how, when, and by whom the two parties were assembled. According to Cavalcanti, the lines of division between them were becoming clear as early as 1426. The 'popular' group had definitely coalesced under Medici leadership by the end of the Brescian war, although the opposition remained comparatively inchoate until almost the eve of Cosimo's exile; the Lucchese war exacerbated the conflict between them, but was not its essential cause.[41]

Official records enable us to form some independent idea of the membership, aims, and methods of the parties in the last twelve months from September 1433 to September 1434, when

[37] See particularly M. Becker, 'An Essay on the "Novi Cives" and Florentine Politics, 1343–1382', *Mediaeval Studies*, xxiv (1962), 35–82, and G. Brucker, *Florentine Politics and Society 1343–1382* (Princeton, 1962); Brucker explains the development of Florence in this period largely in terms of the dialogue and conflict between these two groups within the ruling class.

[38] L. Martines, *The Social World of the Florentine Humanists* (London, 1963).

[39] Rubinstein, *Government of Florence*.

[40] At the same time there is no need entirely to dismiss the importance of a Medici reputation for popular support, nor the possibility that the latter may have expressed itself in alternative forms as a crucial factor in the Medici victory. The role of armed force, for example, in the events of 1433 and 1434 is not clear (below, pp. 337–8); the mere existence of a large following among the *contadini* (the rural inhabitants of Florentine territory) and the urban artisans could have been exploited as a threat to bring strategic pressure on the governing patriciate. A study of the Medici homeland in the Mugello, and in particular of the nature and terms of land-holding there, could illuminate their local power-base. P. J. Jones, in *The Cambridge Economic History of Europe*, i (Cambridge, 1952–66), 416, 427–9, discusses the amassing of large rural estates by urban patrician families like the Medici, and the various forms of service in men and money which might be exacted from their peasantry.

[41] *Istorie*, pp. 139, 180, 205, 259–60, 264–5.

the factions emerged into the open and fought through the organs of the state for legitimate control of the government. However, our understanding even of this brief period is seriously limited by our ignorance concerning the partisan substructure on which this opposition rested, and the forces which precipitated the battle for power. Concerning the clandestine genesis of parties in the preceding period, the only explicit witness is Cavalcanti, whose testimony on this point historians have been peculiarly reluctant to accept. The central issue is whether or not their party was the direct expression of Medici ambition to establish the ascendancy which they later obtained. According to the chronicler, Giovanni di Bicci de' Medici, despite the great authority he enjoyed in the governing group, was by nature a political quietist who found himself the unwilling focus of the hopes and ambitions of 'the people'; however, he and his sons, Cosimo and Lorenzo, were finally persuaded by his ambitious nephew, Averardo, to exploit the family reputation for popular sympathies to make themselves leaders of a popular party.[42] Most writers, being reluctant to represent Cosimo, the future *pater patriae*, as an opportunistic political operator by their own standards, have preferred to draw out other elements in Cavalcanti's account to the point of distorting his essential picture; thus the general view of Giovanni di Bicci has been that 'despite his unwillingness, a party grew up around him'.[43] Cosimo is represented as a reserved statesman, who showed no signs of political ambition until the urging of his *consorti* and the suspicions of his adversaries forced him to act,[44] and even then, it is suggested, Cosimo and Rinaldo degli Albizzi are not to be considered as 'two willing party leaders, who set themselves at the head of two opposing factions to direct them for their own ends . . .' but 'in fact the instruments of these factions into which they were drawn without any particular wish of their own'.[45] A few voices have been raised in objection against the ingenuousness of this view and the unlikelihood that the party

---

[42] Ibid., pp. 56–8; cf. Gutkind, *Cosimo de' Medici*, p. 83.

[43] G. Capponi, *Storia della repubblica di Firenze* (3 vols., Florence, 1876), ii. 168; also F. C. Pellegrini, *Sulla repubblica fiorentina a tempo di Cosimo il Vecchio* (Pisa, 1880), p. 13, and Schevill, *Medieval and Renaissance Florence*, i. 344. Cf. the near-contemporary judgement of Vespasiano da Bisticci, *Vite di uomini illustri del secolo XV*, ed. L. Frati (3 vols., Bologna, 1892), iii. 214; 'It was recognized that he was aiming at a high position.'

[44] e.g. by Gutkind, *Cosimo de' Medici*, pp. 66, 83.

[45] Pellegrini, *Sulla repubblica*, p. 81.

which was to constitute a stable foundation for Medici government for more than half a century to follow could in fact have
been built up virtually overnight,[46] but as no evidence has
hitherto been found of any private or conspiratorial political
activity in the preceding period, it has proved impossible to explore the implications of Cavalcanti's account.[47]

This failure to find a means of pursuing the problem beyond the
official records of government may partly be due to a failure in the
past to appreciate the peculiar social context of partisan conflict
in fifteenth-century Florence. Historians have, until fairly recently,
tended to see these conflicts in terms defined, and in fact limited,
by the perspectives and preoccupations of their own centuries;
hence the popularity of Cavalcanti's class-based explanation which
can be seen as a conflict between opposing ideologies, and the
apparently paradoxical, but in fact related, tendency to see the
events of 1433 and 1434 as the outcome of a rational opposition
between personalities.[48] If we are to penetrate beyond the external
forms of these crucial events to a fuller understanding of their
essential nature and significance on the basis of new evidence, we
must approach the problem on its own terms. Any attempt to
identify the Medici party, to describe its genesis, membership,
structure, and aims, and to trace the course of its operation in

[46] See particularly Dami, *Giovanni Bicci*, pp. 13–14, 23–39, 83.

[47] Official records, like those of the various judicial authorities, the *Provvisioni*,
Balìe, and *Consulte e Pratiche*, and also material from Milanese and Venetian sources,
have been considerably exploited (e.g. by A. Gelli, 'L'esilio di Cosimo de' Medici',
A.S.I. 4th Ser. x (1882), 53–96, 149–69, and Gutkind, *Cosimo de' Medici*) to throw
some light on the nature of private support for either party inside the city, and on the
extent of Medici contacts and influences outside it.

[48] See particularly Pellegrini, *Sulla repubblica*, and also C. Guasti's comments in
his edition of the *Commissioni di Rinaldo degli Albizzi* (3 vols., Florence, 1867–73),
iii, *passim*. Conversely, within these terms, both are masterly studies of the political
life of this period, based on a formidable command particularly of the private letters
and of the council debates, and must be seen as an essential basis for the exploration
of broader questions concerning the structure of the society and the more fundamental determinants of individual behaviour. Recent studies of urban parties in the
late medieval period have profited from the lessons of sociologists and anthro-
pologists that particular phenomena should be viewed in the context of the
whole society and its culture. Several have concluded that in pre-modern societies,
significant conflict occurred within the governing class, and that while different
social backgrounds and orientations might be important underlying factors, private
interests and associations were more important determinants of allegiance than either
ideological convictions or clashes of personality. See, e.g., C. Petit-Dutaillis, *Les
Communes françaises* (Paris, 1947), pp. 20–2; G. A. Williams, *Medieval London* (London,
1963), pp. 20–5.

Florentine society, must take as its point of departure the question of the complex and subtle relation of parties to the political process in that society.

(ii)

The Italian city communes originated as an uneasy coalition of various relatively distinct corporations, and their development was shaped at every point, as their chroniclers and poets so vividly record, by the constant conflict and shifting combinations of the disparate interests which they sheltered. The theory and practice of politics in Florence was essentially a response to these conditions.[49] Dante and his contemporaries in the later thirteenth and early fourteenth centuries were preoccupied with the problem of factionalism, and saw its solution chiefly in the adoption of the Aristotelian concept of dedication to the common good, neatly equated in this context with 'the good of the commune', as the fundamental aim and ideal of political life.[50] Although in fact these thinkers were among the first to propose that the life of the citizen was a sufficient moral end in itself, they continued to operate within a transcendental Christian framework, and secular political theory gained a new dimension and added authority when it was sanctified by theologians like Remigio de' Girolami, whose formulation of the total view was that

the *summum bonum* of the State consists in *concordia*, the union of all wills in willing the same end; 'la nostra pace' is God, who makes all members of a State to have the same one will, 'la Sua voluntade'.[51]

Thus good government—the maintenance of peace, justice, and concord within the city—is the condition not only of the secular, but also of the spiritual well-being of its citizens. This point is

[49] On the political experience and development of the communes, see J. K. Hyde, *Society and Politics in Medieval Italy* (London, 1973), and D. Waley, *The Italian City Republics* (London, 1969). For the origins and genesis of Florentine political thought and the response of Brunetto Latini, Dante, and the chroniclers Dino Compagni and Giovanni Villani to their intellectual and political environment, see N. Rubinstein, 'The Beginnings of Political Thought in Florence', *J.W.C.I.* v (1942), 198–227; C. T. Davis, *Dante and the Idea of Rome* (Oxford, 1957), Ch. i, ii; *La Cronica di Dino Compagni*, ed. I. del Lungo, *Rerum Italicarum Scriptores*, ix. 2 (Città di Castello, 1916); cf. J. K. Hyde, *Padua in the Age of Dante* (Manchester, 1966).

[50] On the general significance and application of this concept see N. Rubinstein, 'Political Ideas in Sienese Art', *J.W.C.I.* xxi (1958), 179–207.

[51] L. Minio-Paluello, 'Remigio Girolami's "De Bono Communi": Florence at the Time of Dante's Banishment and the Philosopher's Answer to the Crisis', *Italian Studies*, xi (1956), 58.

made explicit in the advice of Giovanni Dominici, a Dominican preacher writing in the early years of the fifteenth century, to the wife of a member of the Alberti family then in exile, concerning the education of her children:

To be rulers of the Republic, children should grow up honourable, with the balance of justice in their hands, separated from all parties, sects, and divisions, because partisans do not rule the Republic but rend, divide, and waste it. Therefore, from an early age one needs to guard against these particular affiliations and to punish a youth severely if he should appear more inclined to one party than to another, so that he will be accustomed to say, 'I am neither Guelph nor Ghibelline, but only Florentine'. And I say this not only for the good of the community, but also for his own corporal and spiritual good; corporal, since only the partisans of the opposite party are exiled, and sometimes it is the turn of one, and sometimes of the other; spiritual, because no partisan enters into heaven, which being divine unity receives none except those united, and lovers of unity.[52]

The Florentine constitution, the essential elements of which were established in 1282 and survived until the fall of the republic in 1533, seems designed to prevent the operation of private interest in government at the expense of the common good by the incorporation of two major features—a high degree of citizen participation on one hand, and an almost total lack of general representation on the other. Of course Florentine government was élitist, or oligarchic; in the fifteenth century, for example, participation was restricted to a group of some 2,000 to 3,000 upper-class men who, along with their wives and children, could not have represented more than a fifth of the total population of about 40,000 in this period. Within this group, however, the governing offices were widely distributed, and most of its members would have had in their lifetimes considerable experience of participation in active political life.[53]

The constitution made elaborate provision for the constant circulation of offices, of which over 3,000 fell vacant in any given year.[54] The system of government incorporated three main groups.

---

[52] *Regola del Governo di Cura Familiare Dal Beato Giovanni Dominici*, ed. D. Salvi (Florence, 1860), pp. 177–8.

[53] See D. Kent, 'The Florentine *reggimento* in the fifteenth century', *Renaissance Quarterly*, iv (1975), 575–638; see esp. 600–1.

[54] A. Molho, 'Politics and the ruling class in Early Renaissance Florence', *Nuova Rivista Storica*, lii (1968), 407.

At its head was an executive consisting of the *Signoria* and its two auxiliary colleges; they initiated legislation which was enacted by a complex of councils and administered by a multitude of special commissions. Membership of most of the more important of these bodies was determined by lot. A scrutiny of guild members occurred at regular intervals, and tickets bearing the names of all those eligible to hold offices were placed in bags from which the appropriate number was drawn when positions fell vacant. Terms of tenure were generally comparatively brief, especially in some of the more powerful magistracies, like the *Signoria*, whose members held office for only two months. The essential intention of this system was to make the elevation of individual citizens to positions of power brief and unpredictable, and thus to minimize the possibility of their using such positions to build up a base for the extension of personal power or the advancement of their private interest.[55]

At the same time the constitution also provided against the expression of such private and particular interests as are represented through parties in a modern parliamentary democracy. Political scientists stress the peculiar position occupied by political parties even in modern democracies, pointing out that they are essentially 'private associations to which the law does not give more rights and duties than to other private organizations, but they are usually seen to fulfil an essential representative function without which such governments could not function'.[56] In the Florentine system this representative element was almost entirely absent. Citizens were to act *ex officio* and when voting in the councils, solely 'according to conscience'.[57] Soliciting of votes, or even prior

[55] For Salutati's statement of the official view of the ideal function of the constitution see P. Herde, 'Politik und Rhetorik in Florenz am Vorabend der Renaissance', *Archiv für Kulturgeschichte*, xlvii (1965), 183, n. 225. The most illuminating study of the elements and operation of the Florentine constitution in any particular period is to be found in Rubinstein, *Government of Florence*. For a literal and exhaustive contemporary description of Florentine institutions see G. Dati, *L'Istoria di Firenze dal 1380 al 1405*, ed. L. Pratesi (Norcia, 1904), pp. 140–70.

[56] J. Blondel, *Voters, Parties and Leaders—the Social Fabric of British Politics* (London, 1963), p. 88.

[57] See the preamble to the *Lex Contra Scandalosos* of 1429 (also below, p. 248): 'quod quilibet eorum dirigendo mentem et intellectum solum in Deum, ad iustam gubernationem, ad bonum, pacificum et honestum regimen civitatis, et non ad aliud, iurabit reddere fabam suam secundum eius conscientiam, etc.' (Pellegrini, *Sulla repubblica*, p. 61). See also N. Rubinstein, 'I primi anni del Consiglio Maggiore di Firenze (1494–99)', *A.S.I.* cxiii (1954), 332–3. The original provision has not come

agreement by interested persons on specific issues, was strictly forbidden. Thus parties in the modern sense, as channels for expression and representation of particular interests in government, had no legitimate place in the Florentine system;[58] the only expression of private interest of which the law took account was the aggregate of individual opinions measured in the totals of 'yes' and 'no' votes on proposals put before the councils, and the numerous private petitions which testify to the need for such expression, and which opened a doorway to the soliciting of support.[59]

For ultimately these provisions of a 'jealous constitution' played an essential role in fostering the very factionalism which they were designed to prevent. A system of government in which such large numbers of private citizens participated could not function in practice without some channels for the representation and expression of the interests of some private individuals and groups, and the lack of continuity in government due to the rapid rotation of key magistracies merely accentuated the weakness of a state still very much in the process of consolidation.[60] As in

to light, but the constitution of 1494/5, laid down with the intention of reviving republican government as it had existed before the Medici ascendancy, established that 'nel fare de' partiti . . . nè si parli nè si chiega favore per persona' (Provv. 185, c. 11, Cap. 11); cf. a sermon of Savonarola in *Prediche italiane*, iii, I, ed. R. Palmarocchi (Florence, 1933), p. 220: 'Ciascuno cittadino . . . debbe andare con questo animo in Consiglio, di rendere le fave a chi lui crederà secondo la sua conscientia che sia la salute della città e prima l'onore di Dio . . .' (Rubinstein, 'I primi anni' 332–3, n. 231).

[58] As the fourteenth-century Italian legist Bartolus of Sassoferrato declared in his treatise *De Guelphis*, parties were unlawful and unreasonable unless government itself was by one party, in which case it was reasonable to have an opposition (E. Emerton (ed.), *Humanism and Tyranny*, Cambridge, Mass., 1925, pp. 277–8).

[59] Legislation to benefit individuals, usually concerned with tax concessions or appointment to communal posts, had to be proposed by another citizen and then receive a majority of affirmative votes in the councils to which it was submitted; see the Libri Fabarum for the content of proposals and the results of voting. The *gonfalone* may have retained some of its representative functions into the fifteenth century; see the forthcoming study of Lion Rosso by myself and F. W. Kent. See also Cavalcanti's claim that the *Signoria* valued the *Consulte e Pratiche* as a forum for the expression of representative opinion (*Istorie*, p. 19).

[60] As Dante bitterly observed (*Purgatorio*, vi. 39–44):

> Athens and Lacedaemon, who made rise
> the ancient laws and civic discipline
> scarce showed at all wherein well-living lies,
> compared with thee, who of a thread so thin
> dost make provisions, that to mid-November
> lasts not what thou dost in October spin.
> (Trans. G. Bickersteth, Oxford, 1972)

most societies in which the state is unwilling or unable adequately to defend the interests of the individual, extra-constitutional and unofficial bodies of a sublegal status tended to assume this function.[61] By the beginning of the fifteenth century elements of the centralized state were gaining ground, and the influence and power of some independent corporate entities, like the *Parte Guelfa* and the guilds, had greatly declined.[62] However, as Gene Brucker has observed, early Renaissance Florence was still very far from being an expression of Burckhardtian individualism;[63] in this highly personalized and face-to-face environment a multitude of concrete loyalties competed with the abstraction of the commune in their claims on every citizen. Florentine society was a complex of interest groups from which very few men in the normal pursuit of their personal and civic concerns could stand entirely apart, and indeed most were entwined from birth to death in a network of associations and relationships from which their individual interests and concerns could not easily be disentangled.[64]

A. Molho, 'The Florentine Oligarchy and the *Balìe* of the Late Trecento', *Speculum*, xliii (1968), 29–58, discusses the increasing resort to government by *Balìe* in an attempt to achieve continuity and to increase efficiency; he also shows that *Balìe* could function as instruments of separatist interests and stresses how far the ascendancy of Maso degli Albizzi was from creating a monolithic regime.

[61] Cf. J. Boissevain, 'Patronage in Sicily', *Man*, i (1966), 30.

[62] How far, by this time, Florence had progressed along the road from medieval commune to centralized modern state, is a complex and controversial issue; for two rather different statements of the problem see M. Becker, *Florence in Transition* (2 vols., Baltimore, 1967–8) and G. Brucker, *The Civic World of Early Renaissance Florence* (Princeton, 1977).

[63] G. Brucker, *Renaissance Florence* (New York, 1969), pp. 100–1.

[64] This view informs the whole approach of Lauro Martines in *The Social World*, and is specifically and progressively expressed in the more recent work of Gene Brucker. For an early formulation see 'The Structure of Patrician Society in Renaissance Florence', *Colloquium: A Journal of Historical and Social Thought*, i (1964), 2–11, which was a major stimulus of my own interest in the nature and function of Florentine social relationships. Cf. *Renaissance Florence*, pp. 89–101, and his relation of social structure to changes in the entire style and tone of government and politics in *The Civic World*, Ch. 1. I am deeply indebted to Professor Brucker for allowing me to read the manuscript of this book in draft, thus enabling me to benefit from his further exploration in this latest work of themes which relate so closely to my concerns in the present study. For a contrasting view of the individual in fifteenth-century Florentine society as 'left exposed and isolated, unencumbered with the old social obligations and loyalties', see R. Goldthwaite, *Private Wealth in Renaissance Florence: A Study of Four Families* (Princeton, 1968), p. 261; also M. Becker, 'An Essay on the Quest for Identity in the Early Renaissance', *Florilegium Historiale: Essays Presented to Wallace K. Ferguson*, ed. J. Rowe and W. Stockdale (Toronto, 1971), esp. 302, 306–7, and 'Individualism in the Early Italian Renaissance: Burden and Blessing', *Studies in the Renaissance*, xix (1972), esp. 276–7, 292–3.

At the logical centre of this network was the kin group,[65] extended further by marriage and by relationships with neighbours, business partners, and other natural associates collectively subsumed under the designation *amici*. Friends, relatives, and neighbours constitute the great trinity of Florentine social bonds, which is constantly invoked throughout the period of the republic.[66] Some rare souls, like Ser Lapo Mazzei in the second half of the fourteenth century, might succeed in avoiding such entanglements, but notably even he was moved to comment on the unusualness of his own situation: 'There can be no one freer than I; I am bound neither to relatives nor to factions, nor is there anyone with whom I would wish to have such ties.'[67] Most would have concurred with Giovanni Rucellai, writing half a century later, when he advised his sons of the great happiness and benefit to be derived 'from enjoying the favour and goodwill of kinsmen and relatives and neighbours and all the rest of the men of your district'.[68] The value of these associations lay in the support which these groups lent to the individual in all his activities. Giovanni Morelli's *Ricordi* of the early fifteenth century, also designed for the instruction of his heirs, advised them never to take any important step without such assistance, but 'with the suitable and sound advice of your good relatives and friends make up your mind about everything that concerns you'; he stressed the folly of those who acted entirely without consulting 'anyone else, either relative or friend'.[69] These imperatives involved citizens

[65] On the structure of the Florentine family and its role in personal and social life, see F. W. Kent, *Household and Lineage in Renaissance Florence: The Family Life of the Capponi, Ginori and Rucellai* (Princeton, 1977).

[66] As yet, no extensive study has been devoted specifically to the general exploration of the precise nature and function of these bonds, but for an analysis of particular groups see below, Ch. 1, and Brucker, *The Civic World*, Ch. 1.

[67] N. Tamassia, *La famiglia italiana nei secoli decimoquinto a decimosesto* (Milan, Palermo, 1910), p. 5.

[68] A. Perosa (ed.), *Giovanni Rucellai ed il suo Zibaldone*, i (London, 1960), 9, also 28. Cf. Donato Velluti's references almost a century earlier to 'nostro vicino, amico e parente', or another 'a noi congiunto d'amore, parentado e vicinanza', *La Cronica domestica di Messer Donato Velluti*, ed. I. del Lungo and G. Volpi, Florence, 1914, pp. 12, 22), and from the 1420s, 'Ricordi di Gino di Neri Capponi', ed. G. Folena, in *Miscellanea di studi offerta a A. Balduino e B. Bianchi* (Padua, 1962), 29-39, XXV.

[69] Giovanni di Pagolo Morelli, *Ricordi*, ed. V. Branca (Florence, 1956), pp. 187-8. He also described the plight of 'il povero pupillo' as 'pelato da' parenti, dagli amici, da vicini' (p. 232); however, elsewhere the ambiguity of his desire for some independence of these associations, together with his acceptance of their force in practice, is more apparent, e.g. pp. 242-3, 351.

in practice in networks of patronage whose role in Florentine society was fundamental, but whose operation and effect on political life have hitherto been insufficiently acknowledged and explored.[70]

The extent to which they potentially conflicted with the interests of the state and the good of the commune is implicit in recommendations such as that of Gino Capponi to his sons in 1420: 'Above all else stick together with your neighbours and kinsmen; assist your friends both within and without the city.'[71] The private letters in which individuals often solicited the aid of their *amici* suggest that the range of problems with which they were expected to assist was as broad as the range of the Florentine patrician's interests and concerns, from the contracting of a marriage or the purchase of a house to the carrying-through of a business deal or the obtaining of a tax concession. However, as most upper-class citizens were closely involved with government, a great many letters contain requests for *amici* to circumvent the restrictive constitutional procedures and to arrange unofficially for the appointment of the writer or one of his friends to a particular public office.[72] There was, moreover, a further sense in which most other concerns were ultimately related to politics. Studies of many aspects of Florentine society have tended to confirm the extent to which the Florentine patrician was a political animal, who regarded political pre-eminence as the crowning reward of economic

[70] Gene Brucker first emphasized the importance of patronage in the web of Florentine social relationships. Its exploration in his own work has occurred particularly within the context of a concern with the contrast of aristocratic and egalitarian impulses in Florentine social ethics ('Structure of Patrician Society, 8) and the transition from corporate to élitist values (*The Civic World*, esp. Ch. 1 I.); the related opposition which he discerns between kinship and patron–client relationships is minimized in his most recent work. The patronage networks explored in the present study closely resemble those which have survived into the modern world in areas of southern Europe. J. Boissevain, 'Patronage', pp. 18–33, delineates in his analysis of modern Sicilian society a model of social relationships which is in many essential respects strikingly similar to that which emerges from the evidence concerning fifteenth-century Florence. Particularly notable are the similarity of terminology, as in the nuances of 'amico' (cf. below, esp. pp. 83–7) and the appropriateness to the Florentine situation of his observation that 'while at the analytical level a distinction can be drawn between patronage, friendship, and kinship, this distinction has little importance at the operational level. The Sicilian uses all three interchangeably to influence the outcome of decisions which concern him' (29); cf. below, Ch. 1 (vi). [71] *Ricordi*, XXV.

[72] Below, Ch. 1 (vi). See also Diane Owen Hughes, 'Toward Historical Ethnography: Notarial Records and Family History in the Middle Ages', *Historical Methods Newsletter* vii (1974) 61–71.

success and social distinction;[73] at the same time, these attributes could seldom successfully be preserved if they were not protected through political influence.[74] No doubt Lorenzo the Magnificent was not in fact the first to observe that 'in Florence a man cannot prosper if he has no share in government'.[75]

Where individual concerns were so powerfully affected by the possession of political influence and the exercise of political office, and the public sphere so intimately related to the private, the interest groups based on non-political associations whose members turned traditionally to each other for support might swiftly be transformed into political action groups or parties in times of crisis. The way in which such groups coalesced along the lines of traditional association is nicely illustrated in a passage from Dino Compagni's account of the genesis of the Black–White feuds in Florence at the beginning of the fourteenth century:

The city was divided anew at every social level—nobles, men of middling condition, and humble folk . . . All the Ghibellines supported the Cerchi, because they hoped to suffer less injury at their hands . . . Also of their party was Guido di Messer Cavalcante Cavalcanti, because he was an enemy of Messer Corso Donati; Naldo Gherardini, because he was an enemy of the Manieri, relatives of Messer Corso; Messer Manetto Scali and his kinsmen, because they were relatives of the Cerchi; Messer Lapo Salterelli, their relative; . . . Messer Goccia Adimari, on account of his disagreement with his kinsmen; Bernardo di Messer Manfredi Adimari, because he was a business partner of theirs; Messer Biligiardo, and Bastiera, and Baldo della Tosa, to annoy Messer Rosso, their kinsman, because owing to him the political honours they received were diminished. Among Messer Corso Donati's party was Messer Rosso, Messer Arrigo, and Messer Nepo, and Pinuccio della Tosa, on account of their great familiarity and friendship with him, Messer Gherardo Ventraia, Messer Geri Spini and his

[73] For example, this general expectation emerges from the evidence presented in recent studies of such diverse periods and problems as Brucker, *Florentine Politics*, Martines, *The Social World*, and Rubinstein, *Government of Florence*.

[74] However, the correlation between political influence on the one hand, and wealth and family status on the other, is general rather than precise; it is immediate only on the level of families rather than individuals, and in the innermost circles of government (Kent, 'The Florentine *reggimento*' 604–8).

[75] In describing how, after the death of his father, the leading citizens begged him to take over the guidance of the city, he observed that 'mal volentieri accettai, e solo per conservazione degli amici e sostanze nostre, perchè a Firenze si può mal vivere senza lo Stato' (*Ricordi*, in W. Roscoe, *The Life of Lorenzo de' Medici*, London, 1902, p. 426).

kinsmen, because of the injury done to them; Messer Gherardo Sgrana and Messer Bindello, through familiarity and friendship . . .[76]

As this example shows, when the barricades went up *amici, parenti*, and *vicini* did not inevitably find themselves on the same side; sometimes the intimate pressures of these relationships led in practice to division instead of unity. There are a number of colourful examples in the history of Florence of feuding neighbours, families riven by internal conflict, companies ruined by dissension. However, regardless of the actual directions in which they were driven, Florentines responded to such situations not simply as individuals, but as members of a group or groups bound together by ties of kinship, marriage, neighbourhood, friendship, and custom.

(iii)

It is clear that the basic principles of political life, and the social conditions which moulded and modified them, had not essentially changed by the beginning of the fifteenth century when the Medici family began its rise to power, except that, as Giovanni Morelli observed in recalling the epic feuds of the Florentine past, 'then they used to persecute one another with sword in hand rather than with their votes as they do today'.[77] Long before the triumph of the Medici in 1434, once seen as the event which put an end to the actuality of republican government,[78] the realities of power had ceased to correspond to the constitutional prescriptions for its distribution, and indeed the question of where ultimate political influence resided at any given time continues to tantalize students of Florentine politics and society.[79] Certainly according to Cavalcanti, the commune in his time 'was governed more from the dinner-table and the study than from the Palace', and he coined the aphorism that 'many were elected to offices but few to government'.[80] In this sense, then, the story of parties in

[76] Del Lungo (ed.), *Cronica*, pp. 69–71.   [77] Morelli, *Ricordi*, pp. 130–1.
[78] This was particularly the view animating the work of nineteenth-century patriots like Gino Capponi, *Storia della repubblica*, or liberal historians like F. T. Perrens, *Histoire de Florence depuis la domination des Médicis jusqu'à la chute de la République (1434–1531)* (3 vols., Paris, 1888–90).
[79] See L. Martines, *Lawyers and Statecraft in Renaissance Florence* (Princeton, 1968), p. 123; Kent, 'The Florentine *reggimento*'.
[80] *Istorie*, p. 20; cf. Capponi, *Ricordi*, IV: 'Li ufici sono in più numero fussono mai: e lo stato in meno.'

our period is the story of conflict, not only, or even most profoundly, between opposing factions, but also between unofficial
government in the private interest and constitutional government
in the public interest; these are the terms in which the problem
was perceived in the mid-twenties when a new drive to extirpate
factionalism was instituted in the name of the common good.

Both personal and official documents of this period reflect the
impression that factionalism, endemic in Florence for reasons
which we have discussed, intensified in a wave of unrest from the
early twenties onwards. About this time the prominent patrician
Buonaccorso Pitti bemoaned in his diary the growth of parties
and divisions between the leading citizens, maintaining that on
account of these 'the welfare and honour of our Commune would
be neglected'.[81] Bouts of legislation in 1421, 1426, and particularly
1429 suggest that his concern was shared by the ruling group in
general;[82] Cavalcanti claimed that Cosimo himself 'always sought
to put the interest of the Commune above everything else and
used to say: Nature teaches us that for the sake of preserving the
whole, the part must consider itself of no importance.'[83]

The extent to which the issue appeared as a conflict between
private and public interest is most clearly seen in the focus of
attention on the role of the *Signoria*, the eight Priors led by the
Gonfalonier of Justice who constituted the chief magistracy of
the state and were virtually its visible embodiment. On appointment to this office, citizens were ideally considered to have shed
their private concerns and transcended their personal limitations.
Immured in the palace of the Priors for the duration of their
two-month term, detached quite literally from their customary
environment and interests, they stood for the commune, and
were 'the principal source of authority and direction for the whole
city'.[84] In accordance with the view that good government was
necessary to the spiritual as well as the secular health of citizens,
its maintenance was a sacred trust; notably amidst the multitude
of sacred places, objects, and times upon which public religious
ritual rested, the only sacred element in the secular sphere was the
communal power. In his study of this subject, Richard Trexler
has compared the Priors of Florence to 'sacred but lay monks

---

[81] Buonaccorso Pitti, *Cronica*, ed. A. B. della Lega (Bologna, 1905), p. 135.
[82] Below, pp. 239–52.   [83] *Istorie*, p. 264.
[84] Fabroni, *Cosmi vita* ii. 75–6.

whose holiness was in their activity', and who 'had acceded to their office . . . through ceremonies resembling rites of passage'.[85]

Certainly in their official capacity they were regarded with a reverence akin to piety. Averardo de' Medici bowed to the authority temporarily vested in his partisan enemies as members of the *Signoria*, while taking the opportunity to make a nice distinction between person and office, when he accepted their sentence of exile with the declaration that he never had and never would deny the authority of that 'honorable, almost divine magistracy, supreme even to the Lord Priors and rulers of the Republic themselves'.[86] The disregard of this deeply held principle in their defiance of the *Signoria* may well have been a significant factor in the downfall of his enemies.[87] Open defiance, however, was not the only, or at all the most characteristic, threat to the supremacy of the *Signoria* as the guardians of government in the interests of the whole, rather than a part of the ruling group. One of the greatest statesmen of his age, Gino di Neri Capponi, put his finger precisely on the problem confronting Florentines in 1420 when he laid down as his first maxim concerning the conduct of the patrician that 'the Commune of Florence will preserve its authority in so far as . . . it does not allow any particular citizen or family or group of conspirators within it to become more powerful than the *Signoria*'.[88] In a series of meetings of the advisory council to the *Signoria*, convened throughout 1429 and in the early months of 1430 to discuss the means of achieving a unified citizenry, the insistence that no one should seek 'to be equal to, or wish to be greater than, the *Signoria*', is a recurring theme.[89] Notably it was on the grounds of their 'wishing to violate the ordinances of the Priorate and Gonfalonier of Justice of the Florentine people' that the Medici were condemned.[90]

Early in the course of these discussions an oath was drawn up to be sworn on the Bible by as many citizens from the *reggimento* as

[85] R. Trexler, 'Ritual Behaviour in Renaissance Florence: The Setting', *Medievalia et Humanistica*, N.S. iv (1973), 132–3.

[86] Cap. Pop. 3175, f. 121r.

[87] As one contemporary commentator observed, 'tentorono e presunsono armarsi contro alla Signoria, la qual chosa non si debba', C.S. 2ª ser. CII, Sept.–Oct.; cf. below, pp. 336, 350.

[88] Capponi, *Ricordi*, I.

[89] C.P. 49, f. 108r.

[90] Fabroni, *Cosmi vita* ii. 75–6. For some other facets of the patrician attitude to the *Signoria* in the preceding decades see Brucker, *The Civic World*, pp. 305–12.

possible. They were required to promise simply 'to divest themselves completely of all partisan and factional loyalties', and 'to consider only the welfare and honour and greatness of the Republic, and of the *Parte Guelfa*, and of the *Signoria*'.[91] Later the tone of discussions in the *Consulte e Pratiche* was to become more intense, and there was a growing emphasis on spiritual sanctions against partisanship and factionalism which divided citizens. In the *Pratica* of 25 January 1429 the opening speaker, Lorenzo Ridolfi, pronounced that: 'Just as we should adore one God, so you, Lord Priors, are to be venerated above all citizens, and those who look to others are setting up idols, and are to be condemned.' Shortly after, Palla Strozzi signified his full agreement with this proposition, and the same theme was later taken up again by Giovanni Morelli who urged the *Signoria* to action with the reminder that 'Our Lord stood in the midst of his disciples, and said, peace be unto you! In the same way you, Lord Priors, etc.... He who creates a party, sells his liberty . . .'[92]

The extent to which moral aims and ideals, generated in both the secular and the spiritual worlds of the Florentine citizen, were fused in his view of the sacred role of the *Signoria* in suppressing private factions in the interests of the public welfare, finds perfect expression in these passages, which vividly evoke the atmosphere in which the struggle for power between the Medici and their opponents took place. They may help us perhaps to understand why citizens steadfastly continued to defend the letter of the constitution against the expression of separatist interests which had patently undermined it, and to explain the secrecy and stealth with which the manœuvres of the latter were executed, and which make the task of the historian in identifying and describing these groups and their activities so particularly difficult.

(iv)

As a consequence of the debates on faction, the office of *Conservatori delle Leggi* was set up early in 1429 with the task of

[91] C.P. 48, f. 54v.

[92] Ibid. f. 51r; cf. a very similar discussion of 1372, in Brucker, *Florentine Politics*, pp. 251–2. As the Florentine new year began on 25 March dates between 1 January and 24 March appear in original manuscripts under the previous year. All dates mentioned below have been altered to conform with the modern calendar but where appropriate the original date is also given in brackets with the abbreviation *s.f.* (*stile fiorentino*).

examining evidence of citizens in official positions violating the laws of the commune, and putting private interest above public duty.[93] An anonymous denunciation to this body in October 1429 describes an illegal association purposely created to perform particularly those services and functions generally expected of friends, neighbours, and relatives; indeed members were invited to regard one another in familial terms. They were encouraged to join the group with the inducement that they would henceforth be assured of guidance and protection: 'You will be told what you have to do day by day . . . for we must do what our superiors, like fathers (*padri maggiori*), command. You yourself need never worry about anything: in every matter you will have many to defend and honour you.' With the observation that 'the Commune must maintain its citizens subject to the laws rather than the laws to the citizens', the informant expressed the hope that God would aid the magistracy in its investigations, so that through the formation of such private associations for mutual aid and protection 'the Commune should not perish'.[94] Nevertheless, an organization such as this represented in fact only a short step further in evolution from the customary associations of friends, neighbours, and relatives whose role and relationships it sought to duplicate in a more formalized way. For as a friend observed, writing to Forese Sacchetti in 1427, 'after all, you can do nothing unless, when the need arises, your friends and relatives are willing to exert themselves in your interest—especially in legitimate and honourable matters'.[95]

Despite these obvious similarities, the leaders of the *reggimento* in the twenties and thirties generally failed to acknowledge that some conflict between the two guiding principles of Florentine life—concern for the public welfare and loyalty to personal associates—was inevitable. No doubt this was partly because they and their friends were so involved in government that they tended to regard their share in the state (*stato* or *reggimento*) as almost a personal possession or attribute,[96] and it was often

[93] Provv. 120, ff. 7v–11r; below, pp. 244–5.

[94] Giud. Appelli 75, f. 724r–v. I have to thank Gene Brucker for bringing this document to my attention, and making available to me his transcription.

[95] Conv. Soppr. 78, 324, c. 76.

[96] Kent, 'The Florentine *reggimento*', esp. 580; see also the observation of Alessandra Macinghi negli Strozzi, *Lettere di una Gentildonna Fiorentina*, ed. C. Guasti (Florence, 1877), p. 3, concerning the Parenti, that 'hanno un po' di stato'.

difficult for them to distinguish effectively between public and private interest.[97] So they continued, somewhat ingenuously, to declare that 'they had never belonged to any faction', nor had any enemies other than those of the *Signoria*' had 'never taken part in discussions outside the Palace', but nevertheless had favoured 'one man more than another according to rank and *parentado*'.[98] However, they soon began to recognize that the best possible hope of eliminating the problem lay in ameliorating those injustices from which parties or groups of *amici* primarily sought to defend their members.[99]

In 1422 and 1426 the main focus of contemporary concern over 'parties' were various permanent but unofficial associations which could be used as a cover for the operation of political groups. Chief of these were the religious confraternities, which bore the main brunt of the early phases of the attack on factions.[100] But by 1429, in discussions of the problem in the *Consulte e Pratiche*, there was less emphasis on wiping out potentially subversive associations, and more on the attempt to define the underlying causes and preconditions of the growth of parties. Like Cavalcanti and Buoninsegni, speakers in the council debates stressed the distribution of political offices and taxes as sources of dissension;[101] most funda-

[97] See, for example below, pp. 204–5, 257–6; cf. Brucker, *The Civic World*, e.g., pp. 310–14. Notably Lippo dall'Antella, asking Forese Sacchetti to ensure that he should not be taxed with unjust severity, threw in his own request as one of a number of 'faccende publiche et private' which would be keeping Sacchetti busy (Conv. Soppr. 78, 324, c. 108).

[98] Giovanni di Rinaldo Gianfigliazzi and Rinaldo degli Albizzi, C.P. 49, ff. 32v–35r (26 Apr. 1430).

[99] Cf. below, pp. 247–52.

[100] See Guasti, *Commissioni* iii. 5–6; Brucker, *The Civic World*, pp. 312–13, 478–80; R. Hatfield, 'The Compagnia de' Magi', *J.W.C.I.* xxxiii (1970), 110–11. Apparently, resolutions of 1419 and 1426 to dissolve the confraternities were not actually implemented; nevertheless, the activity of the *Compagnia de' Magi* seems to have been affected for some years by the anti-confraternity legislation. Certainly, few records survive which enable us to assess the political activity of these groups or to judge how far the fear of them was justified. Notably, legislation against *compagnie* and *intelligenze* continued throughout the fifteenth century (N. Rubinstein, 'Politics and Constitution in Florence at the end of the fifteenth century', *Italian Renaissance Studies*, ed. E. F. Jacob, London, 1960, 167–9).

[101] See, e.g., C.P. 49, f. 126v, 21 Feb. 1431 (1430 *s.f.*), where Gherardo di M. Filippo Corsini declared that 'pro unitate et concordia fiant imbursationes officiorum'; cf. ibid. 48, f. 53v, 26 Jan. 1429 (1428 *s.f.*), when Averardo de' Medici, speaking on unity, called for adherence to the law 'et diligentia circa electiones'. Brucker, *The Civic World*, Ch. 5, iv, comments on the tensions between public and private interests expressed in the *Consulte e Pratiche* some two decades earlier, and their connection with tax assessments.

mentally, the struggle was seen as one between those seeking to increase their status and their share in government, and those at whose expense these gains would be made—the already powerful citizens whose best interests lay in preserving the *status quo*.[102]

The essential argument of the chapters which follow will be that the parties of the Medici and their opponents broadly corresponded in fact to these two sections of the *reggimento*, and that they were basically interest groups which, committed to the defence of their members in this as in other respects, became in the process political action groups,[103] or, as the Florentines pejoratively called them, *sette*,[104] within the ruling élite. Such parties, then, were not so much specifically political organizations, as in the modern sense, but rather natural outgrowths of permanent and fundamental elements in the structure of Florentine society. Thus the most natural approach to our original problems concerning the origins, nature, and membership of parties is through the identification and exploration of these networks of association and patronage.[105]

This process is much easier in the case of the Medici than for their opponents. Given the nature of parties as we have described them, it is hardly surprising that there are no lists of partisans, and only a handful of leading Mediceans are mentioned by name in the few contemporary comments. Attempts to infer that those particularly prominent in government, or notably favoured by the Medici after 1434, were necessarily their partisans in the preceding years, are partly vitiated by the consideration that after 1434, support of the Medici and support of the state and the government was to a large extent one and indistinguishable, and while the Medici undoubtedly advanced their friends, they did not necessarily discriminate against the solid body of the patriotic

---

[102] e.g. C.P. 48, f. 52r (Guasti, *Commissioni* iii. 165); below, pp. 242, 247–52.

[103] Pellegrini, *Sulla repubblica*, p. 28, emphasizes the self-protective function of parties, but does not go beyond the personal interests of a handful of prominent citizens to the larger social entities with which they were connected.

[104] e.g. C.S. 2ª ser. CIII, c. 113r; ibid. XIV, f. 3v; Cavalcanti, *Istorie*, e.g. pp. 4, 264. Velluti, *Cronica*, p. 241, speaking of Florence in 1366, described 'la guerra cittadinesca dentro, tra le pessime sette che ci sono'.

[105] It is to these extra-legal 'parties', or factions based on patronage groups, that the term 'party' henceforth refers; despite the confusion with modern parties which the transliteration 'parte' has previously engendered, the term has been retained for want of an appropriate alternative which conveys the multiple meanings of the Italian 'parte'.

supporters of the constitution and its representatives, whoever these might be.[106] However, the Medici family obviously provide a focal point, and the magnificent collection of their letters relating to the years 1426 to 1434 are the primary means of exploring most of the problems which concern us. Unfortunately no comparable evidence survives to illuminate their opponents, but on the other hand, the list of those exiled by the Medici on their return to Florence in 1434 constitutes a solid if limited definition of the core of that group to serve as a starting-point for our investigation.[107] The personal lives, interests, and associations of both groups are greatly illuminated by the evidence of marriage records, private diaries, letters, genealogical miscellanies, and, above all, tax returns, which are such a mine of information concerning the diverse affairs of every citizen of property after 1427.[108]

(v)

Although the sum of our findings from this evidence enables us to confirm and illustrate the connection between these parties and traditional networks of association and interest, the precise relationship of parties to patronage groups remains a problem of some complexity. At the simplest level, it was natural for an individual to seek assistance with his concerns from kinsmen, and, by extension, from those related to him by marriage. Particularly if the power and influence of these most obvious patrons and supporters were limited, he might seek to extend the range of assistance on which he could call by cultivating other relationships with more powerful citizens; thus Morelli, an orphan from a family of comparatively modest status in the city, recommended his sons 'to acquire at least one friend or more in your *gonfalone*'[109] and to align themselves in business 'with a suitable man, wealthy . . . and especially with political influence, or from a traditionally pre-eminent family'.[110] The latter in return would benefit through his honour and status being increased by the enjoyment of a following

---

[106] See Rubinstein, *Government of Florence*, pp. 8–10, 62–7.

[107] Otto di Guardia 224, ff. 211–71r.

[108] For their recent exploitation as a source of invaluable demographic evidence, see the computerized studies of C. Klapisch, 'Household and family in Tuscany in 1427', *Household and Family in Past Time*, ed. P. Laslett and R. Wall (Cambridge, 1972), 267–81, and also, 'Fiscalité et démographie en Toscane (1427–1430)', *Annales—Économies—Sociétés—Civilisations*, xxiv (1969), 1313–37.

[109] Morelli, *Ricordi*, p. 253. On the role and significance of the *gonfalone* in Florentine social and political life, see below, Ch. I (iv).   [110] Morelli, *Ricordi*, p. 226.

of citizens dependent on his influence, and with obligations to him which might be satisfied by the requirement of general and specific support and service.[111]

Since most citizens were bound above and below by a veritable mass of such reciprocal obligations of aid and service, to social superiors, equals, and inferiors, in any particular case where assistance was needed the appropriate patron or patrons might be sought from a multitude of associates, related either horizontally or laterally on the social scale; hence it is impossible to say where a patronage network began and ended.[112] It was essentially fluid rather than finite, and the links between men involved in the activation of a chain of patronage could either be of long standing, or forged specifically for the occasion, in which case they might either be subsequently neglected or solidify into permanent relationships.

However, such networks did tend to cluster and coalesce around prominent individuals or great familes in a particularly favourable position to dispense patronage, and as Morelli's injunctions imply, citizens regularly sought patronage or service within the general bounds of a particular group, or complex of groups, focused on or led by the greater families.[113] The families of the Medici and their most prominent opponents stood at the centre of such groups, and the evidence relating to the two parties suggests that when clients became partisans, the ties which held the group together were largely the reciprocal obligations of a patronage network.[114] Nevertheless, the precise relationship of patronage

[111] Below, Ch. 1 (vi). [112] Cf. Boissevain, 'Patronage', esp. 31.

[113] In Genoa in the fourteenth and fifteenth centuries the satellites of great families were formally included in the kin group (by contrast with the Florentine *consorterie* based essentially on blood); their members were incorporated into the great houses or *alberghi* through the practice of *aggrégation*, which opened the *albergo* to admit those of appropriate wealth and status. See J. Heers, *Gênes au XVe siècle* (Paris, 1961), pp. 549, 565–90. The build-up of a party by the Medici, who used others to extend the resources of the kin group, is in some ways analogous to this process, but partisans remained essentially separate and retained their own names and traditions.

[114] Below, Ch. 1 (vi). However, not all those to whom the Medici extended patronage were their partisans; like most great Florentine families, they recognized a general solidarity with social equals which obliged them to aid and co-operate with other patricians where possible (below, pp. 266–71). The Medici letters are not the archives of a party but the personal letters of a patrician family, and the absence of comparable collections of material concerning the families who supported them should not encourage us to over-simplify the patronage structure of which they were a part.

network to party within each was rather different, and seems to have been the chief determinant of important differences between the structure and functions of the two parties.

The opposition to the Medici coalesced essentially in response to the threat which the Mediceans offered to the *status quo*; it was based on a fairly selective recruitment from a number of patronage networks only loosely connected with one another, and led by the several prominent families on whom those networks had chiefly focused. While this process, and the party which it created, is essentially similar to that described by Dino Compagni in the early fourteenth century, the Medici letters, the actions of their party, and the nature of its subsequent success all suggest that the growth of the Medici party represented less the natural transformation of interest groups into action groups under the pressure of events, and more the planned and purposeful consolidation of existing social ties, and the creation of new reciprocal obligations, with the express aim of more effective political action. Of course it is impossible to investigate the origin and nature of all the social bonds which cemented the Medici party, and great Florentine families had traditionally cultivated personal followings. The Medici family, however, began the fifteenth century at a peculiar political disadvantage which would, in the natural course of events, have debarred them from acquiring much influence within the ruling group. Thirty years later they exercised an effective ascendancy over it, with the aid of a particularly unified and closely knit group of supporters. In this respect their party differed from those typical of preceding centuries, and of their opponents; it was, apparently, not so much a new style of party, as a necessary modification of the old formula. Based, like its opposition, on a network of patronage which began with kin and extended to incorporate others as necessary and desirable, the Medici party seems to have relied more on friends than family for some essential services because the social and political position of the latter was too weak to provide them.[115] The fact that the Medici party was created mainly by the extension of patronage, and the formation of ties with smaller or newer or politically unpopular families, not solidly entrenched within the ruling group and the social networks which dominated it, made the partisans particularly dependent on their wealthy and socially distinguished

[115] Cf. Brucker, 'The Medici' 25–6.

patrons, and the latter the undisputed leaders of a network of patronage and association which was particularly dense and centralized.[116]

This would seem to have been an important factor in its success, and indeed the Medici party achieved a success quite unique in Florentine history in promoting the interests of its members; the Medici ascendancy represented almost the complete triumph of unofficial government in the private interest over constitutional government in the public interest. Paradoxically, however, Medici government came near in practice to resolving this eternal conflict simply because its dominance precluded the creation of effective opposition parties, and achieved in time the incorporation of virtually the entire ruling group into its own ranks; for the first time a single party embraced the state and was able to define public interest in terms of its own private needs.[117]

It is the party and its activities before 1434 which constitute the essential subject of this study. My intention is not ultimately to explain or to account entirely for the victory of the Medici over those who opposed their aims, and indeed I am not in a position to do so. There is evidence, discussed in later chapters, to suggest that their enormous wealth, the decisive economic influence which it enabled them to exert within the city, the powerful foreign friendships which it brought in its train, made their triumph a diplomatic and financial necessity once their ambitions had been openly declared, and challenged.[118] An

[116] J. Heers, in his lively and suggestive, but very brief review of Florence in *L'Occident aux XIVe et XVe siècles: Aspects économiques et sociaux* (Paris, 1970), pp. 343–5, denies that by comparison with other societies Florentine parties had any particular base of social recruitment, that they corresponded to any topographical division of the city, in the manner of Roman or Byzantine factions, or that they had any defined organization. By contrast, the central argument of this study is that subtle but vital distinctions in the organization, and in the social and geographical composition of the parties of 1426–34, explain much about their conflict and the victory of one over the other.

[117] Cf. F. Gilbert, 'Bernardo Rucellai and the Orti Oricellari: A study on the Origin of Modern Political Thought', *J.W.C.I.* xii (1949), 129; he argues that the Medici created 'a somewhat loose but none the less recognizable one-party state' by sending into exile the leaders of the opposition, and tying its less prominent and less active members to themselves 'by grants of financial advantages and by marriage arrangements so that eventually the entire ruling group was interrelated'.

[118] On the crucial question of Medici wealth, see de Roover's account of the Medici bank, *The Rise and Decline*; A. Molho has explored in some detail the economic ascendancy of the Medici over the remainder of the ruling group in his study of *Florentine Public Finances in the Early Renaissance, 1400–1433* (Cambridge, Mass.,

adequate consideration of these themes would require a study much broader in scope than the present one, which is basically concerned with the means by which the Medici family translated economic success into political predominance in the traditional Florentine fashion, in a virtuoso exploitation of the vital weakness of the republican system—the disjunction between the official structure of government and its effective sources of political power in the social structure of its ruling class.

1971). J. Kirschner, 'Papa Eugenio IV e il Monte Comune', *A.S.I.* cxxvii (1969), 339–82, draws attention to the close involvement of papal with Florentine finance, and G. Holmes, 'How the Medici became the Pope's Bankers', *Florentine Studies,* ed. N. Rubinstein (London, 1968), 357–80, discusses the economic and business links between the Medici and the papacy. He has also shown such connections at work in an intellectual context in *The Florentine Enlightenment 1400–50* (London, 1969).

PART I

THE FACTIONS

I

The Medici Party

IN the collection of private letters and documents known as *Medici avanti il Principato* there are over a thousand relating to the years 1426–34, although very little material prior to these years has survived. While students of the period have long made most effective use of selected material from this collection,[1] there appears to have been no previous attempt to sift through it systematically as a source of information concerning the Medici and their associates. It is of course a gold-mine which would take many years to work out; for the purposes of the present study it has been possible to pick up only the most obvious nuggets, though an effort has been made to cover all the ground in some sense.[2]

Most of the letters are addressed to members of the Medici family, although a number directed to their friends and associates also came into their hands. The letters from our period fall essentially into three main categories. The official exchanges in which the Medici took part as incumbents of various government posts seldom illuminate their private lives unless their correspondents

---

[1] See particularly the use of the Medici letters to supplement those of Rinaldo degli Albizzi in illuminating the personal alignments of the war years by Guasti, *Commissioni*; also the appendix to Pellegrini, *Sulla repubblica*, which contains a number of letters between the Medici leaders and their friends during the same period. These reveal quite a lot about their attitudes to communal policy and military tactics, but relatively little about their private affairs.

[2] A major barrier to the fullest exploitation of this collection is the diversity and difficulty of the hands, especially of these early years, and the personal, idiosyncratic, and complex systems of abbreviation and allusion employed to keep the contents of the letters comparatively secret. Even contemporaries encountered problems in deciphering one another's letters; as Paolo Rucellai once remarked jokingly to Averardo de' Medici: 'I have nothing else to say, except that you write even rougher letters than I do; though you might feel inclined to argue that my letters were harder to read than yours could be, I think we would have to go to some lengths to establish which were worse . . .' (M.A.P. V, 38).

happened also to be their friends, as they sometimes were. The
letters addressed by members of the family to one another are the
frankest and reveal most about their actual attitudes and ultimate
aims. Those exchanged between the Medici and their *amici* help
us most to reconstruct the composition of their party, to outline
its essential structure, and to understand the benefits and obligations accruing to its members.[3]

The political and social circumstances described in the intro-
ductory chapter made the compilation of lists of *amici* practically
unnecessary and politically unwise; certainly none has as yet come
to light. Thus the putative list of Medici partisans which forms
the basis of much of the following analysis of the nature and
characteristics of the Medici party has been reconstructed essentially through the identification of partisans from their letters.[4]
This procedure is obviously preferable to that of inferring back-
wards from official or even personal records after 1434, when
the Medici triumph had altered the essential political framework
within which the party had operated, or of relying on names
selected at random from contemporary rumour and report.[5]

However, the list of partisans based on these letters is necessarily tentative and provisional. The sheer volume of this body of
Medici material, its intensive coverage of many periods of weeks
or even months, and the frequency with which it is possible to
track down letters to which other letters refer and to arrange them
in related groups, do suggest that an astonishing proportion of
the Medici correspondence of this period may have survived.[6]

[3] For a general indication of the nature and scope of this collection see Archivio
di Stato di Firenze, *Archivio Mediceo avanti il Principato, Inventario* (4 vols., Rome,
1951–63).

[4] The only exceptions are those cases in which alternative evidence of partisanship
is unambiguous and overwhelming; e.g. for the Martelli, where Ugolino's *Ricordo*
of 1434 and the activities of other brothers in the Medici bank at this time testify
to their whole-hearted support of the Medici, although I have found no written
declaration of loyalty before 1434.

[5] It is often assumed, for example, that membership of the *Balìa* of 1434, which
established the Medicean regime, was an obvious indication of Medicean affiliations;
however, this body, constituted in haste to re-establish order in the city after the
armed rising of 26 September, automatically included all incumbents of the leading
offices, and in fact originally contained no less than fourteen of the citizens whom it
subsequently exiled.

[6] There is, for example, a series of eighteen letters written by Francesco di
Giuliano de' Medici to his father between October 1433 and March 1434 (M.A.P.
V, 688–95, 697–706). Francesco, acutely conscious that letters sent by messenger

But undoubtedly much has been lost; those *amici* who wrote infrequently and were too obscure to warrant a mention in the letters of others will have been omitted from our list.[7] Conversely, some may have been included who were not really *amici* in a partisan sense; given the close relationship between patronage and party networks, the distinction between clients and partisans is necessarily rather imprecise.[8] In cases where the letters themselves constitute evidence of the close co-operation between the Medici and their *amici* in conspiratorial political manœuvring, no problem arises;[9] where the content of the letters is less specific, the *amici* included in the list of partisans are those whose declarations of loyalty and promises of support imply such total commitment to the Medici that they would almost necessarily have been involved in the political activities which were apparently the chief preoccupation of the family in this period.[10]

Two further considerations affect the value of this list based on the letters as a practical guide to the identification of Medicean supporters between 1426 and 1434. The first is that partisanship cannot necessarily be assumed to have existed beyond or before the dates on which it is revealed in the letters; the activity of many prominent partisans is well documented throughout these years, but others are mentioned only once or twice. Some leading citizens like Niccolò Alessandri and Neri Capponi definitely declared themselves for the Medici only after the family's expulsion in September 1433; quite possibly they did not become partisans of the Medici until the depths of the divisions within the ruling

through the war-ravaged papal states might easily be lost or destroyed, kept check by giving a résumé at the beginning of each of his letters of all those previously sent and received. This practice enables us to establish that apparently only one of his letters, written at intervals of approximately a fortnight during this period, is missing from the series.

[7] By the same token, some correspondents who are obviously partisans have necessarily been excluded where they cannot be certainly identified, even as Florentines—e.g. Piero di Cristofano da Gagliano; below, p. 86.

[8] Cf. above, pp. 26–7.

[9] See, e.g., the exchanges between the Medici and their friends concerning the scrutiny for internal offices in 1427 (below, pp. 246–7).

[10] Any letter addressed to the Medici in exile (dated between September 1433 and September 1434) constitutes fairly definite evidence of partisanship; their correspondents were likely at least to be compromised in the eyes of the prevailing regime, if not actually persecuted by it, like Agnolo Acciaiuoli (see below, p. 321). Cf. the letters of Maso Velluti (M.A.P. XVII, 3), Niccolò Cavalcanti (XVII, 4), and Stefano di Matteo Boni (V, 292).

class forced a choice upon them.[11] However, most of the letters which constitute our evidence concerning the Mediceans were written before or by 1432, and reveal patterns of customary association which were unlikely, save in exceptional circumstances, to have undergone radical alteration before the end of 1433.[12] Notably, with the exception of some formal communications between leading citizens concerning the affairs of the commune, there are virtually no surviving letters from this period between the Medici and those whom they exiled in 1434.

The second problem is the extent to which individuals declaring their support for the Medici can be seen as speaking for the rest of their families. The pattern of family participation in party conflict is a complex one; although it would seem that all else being equal, families were seen and acted as unified political entities, in a number of notable cases they were split between the two parties. For the sake of precision, therefore, only the actual correspondents have been included among the partisans to be examined in detail, but we should be aware of the probability that behind many of them stood all or part of an entire lineage.[13]

The number of ninety or so establishable partisans is therefore in effect a conservative indication of the real strength of the party, but would seem in the light of corroborative evidence to include all its major members and to be fairly representative of the group as a whole. The supporters revealed in the letters correspond very closely to those identified by other obvious and customary, if less satisfactory, means of measuring partisanship. Almost all the *amici* of the letters who were socially qualified to do so, appear in the *Balìa* of 1434,[14] the special commission appointed to reform the government after the return of the Medici from exile. Eight out of the ten *Accoppiatori* chosen by that *Balìa* to carry out the

[11] See below, pp. 203–4, 338–9.

[12] A particular instance of the existence of such cases, however, is Giovanni Guicciardini; see below, pp. 90–1. About a sixth of the letters belong to the late twenties, two-thirds to the years 1430–2, and the remaining sixth were written in 1433 or 1434.

[13] For a fuller discussion of this problem see below, pp. 190–7. Occasionally correspondents specifically included their entire houses in protestations of loyalty (e.g. Alberto degli Alberti, M.A.P. II, 108); however, even in such cases the difficulty of defining the group implied and of meaningfully equivalating it in comparisons with more fully documented individuals precludes its incorporation in the actual sample of partisans.

[14] Balìe, 25, ff. 2r–6v and 34r–38v, published by Rubinstein, *Government of Florence*, pp. 244–53.

new scrutiny appear from the letters as intimate associates.[15] Of
the fifty-one citizens honoured by the *Balìa* with an act of private
legislation in their favour, an honour apparently reserved essentially as a reward for faithful supporters, forty were in correspondence with the Medici leaders.[16] All but a handful of those
mentioned in contemporary or near-contemporary comments as
belonging to the Medici party are included,[17] with the exception
of several named in the confessions extracted under torture in 1433
from the former Medici supporter, Ser Niccolò Tinucci. His is the
most systematic and complete list of Medici partisans made by
any contemporary, but because of the circumstances in which it
was produced, his evidence where uncorroborated must be
treated with some reserve. Even so, of the score of those he
named, two-thirds are included in the letter sample.[18] It would
seem, then, that there were comparatively few unambiguous partisans, or even associates close enough to contribute to their
advancement, who did not at some time between 1427 and
August 1434 write assuring the Medici of their support, or at
least merit a mention in the letters of the leaders of the party.[19]

(ii) THE FAMILY

Like most of the families who played outstanding roles in government in the fifteenth century, the Medici had securely established
themselves in the Florentine patriciate by the end of the thirteenth
century. Already associated with banking, they enjoyed a modest
prosperity, were connected by marriage with some very distinguished families, and were well represented in the Priorate after
1291. By 1400, however, while other families of similar origin and
background, like the Capponi and Albizzi, were prominent in the

---

[15] Ibid., pp. 236–57.

[16] Balìe, 25, *passim*; cf. below, p. 347.

[17] e.g. by Neri Capponi, *Commentarii di Neri di Gino Capponi di cose seguite in Italia dal 1419 al 1456*, in *Rerum Italicarum Scriptores*, xviii (Milan, 1731), col. 1182; Benedetto Dei, 'Chronica', f. 12v; Francesco Guicciardini, *Memorie di Famiglia*, in *Scritti Autobiografici e Rari*, ed. R. Palmarocchi (Bari, 1936), p. 11.

[18] His *Examina* is published as an Appendix to Cavalcanti, *Istorie Fiorentine*, ed. F. Polidori (2 vols., Florence, 1838–9), ii. 399–421; for a discussion of some of his specific evidence, see below, pp. 222–32.

[19] Evidence after 1434 must remain suggestive rather than decisive, but notably the partisans identified in Appendix I figure prominently among those who prospered in the early years of the Medici ascendancy; see Rubinstein, *Government of Florence*, e.g., on the Benci (p. 46), the Del Nero (pp. 44, 86), and the Masi (p. 9).

government of the republic, the Medici had ceased to be an effective political force and seemed destined to decline into that
obscurity which had overtaken so many others before them in the
mobile society of late medieval Florence. Gene Brucker, having
traced their career through the fourteenth century, attributes this
decline largely to the withdrawal by mid-century of most members
of the family from the commercial activity usually so closely associated with political pre-eminence, and to their factiousness, which
divided the house against itself on opposite sides of the many
partisan conflicts of this period. They earned a reputation for
lawlessness and anti-social behaviour which made them generally
unpopular, and identified them after 1382 with the opponents of
the regime then in power, leading naturally to their exclusion
from it.[1]

   In 1373 Foligno di Conte de' Medici wrote the moving passage
in his *Ricordi, in memoriam* of the past glories of his house, then in
the decline which he obviously feared might ultimately result in
its extinction.[2] However, less than ten years later, the first indications of a political and commercial resurrection began to appear
in the activities and achievements of a few isolated individuals.
The line of Medici descending from Cambio had remained in
banking throughout the century,[3] and in its second-last decade
some descendants of another branch, the sons of Bicci, Francesco,
and Giovanni, joined Vieri di Cambio as associates of his organization.[4] In 1382 Francesco di Bicci became the first member of the
family to matriculate in the *Arte del Cambio* for thirty years, followed four years later by his brother Giovanni.[5] That the Medici
in the fifteenth century were able to snatch unparalleled predominance out of the jaws of what had appeared in the fourteenth
to be inevitable oblivion was largely due to the leadership of this
line, later called the Cafaggiolo branch.[6]

   [1] Brucker, 'The Medici'.
   [2] Quoted ibid. 1: 'I urge you . . . to conserve not only the possessions, but also
the status acquired by our ancestors, which is great, and was still greater in the past,
and which began to decline as a result of the lack of valiant men . . . of whom we
always possessed a great number.'
   [3] Ibid. 6, 9–10.   [4] De Roover, *The Rise and Decline*, p. 36.
   [5] Brucker, 'The Medici' 21.
   [6] For the popularization of this genealogical division of the Medici family, see
G. Pieraccini, *La Stirpe de' Medici di Cafaggiolo: Saggio di ricerche sulla trasmissione
ereditaria dei caratteri biologici* (3 vols., Florence, 1924). Pieraccini acknowledged the
importance of the role played by Francesco and his descendants in the political

It is generally accepted that the ascendancy of the Medici in the fifteenth century rested fundamentally upon the foundation of their bank; it is less often observed that many of their business associates were also their partisans. The family first regained an effective voice in politics as the reward of economic success, and it is significant that ultimately the Medici used their influence as financiers to exert pressure on political affairs. Both creations—the financial and the political empires—are recognizable as the expressions of a single style, a particular genius which has long been discerned in the political sphere and to which the historian of their bank, Raymond de Roover, has more recently drawn attention in business; it was expressed, indeed, in an analogous manner in the organization, function, and direction of the bank and of the party.[7] Both were necessarily to some extent the personal achievements of Giovanni di Bicci and his descendants, but in both spheres they depended, in traditional Florentine fashion, on the support, co-operation, and involvement of the extended family or kin group. Where the latter was particularly weak—in numerical strength in the electoral purses to provide a strong block of influence within the major office-holders, in the concentration of wealth which so often brought prestige in its train, in the ability to promote further political and economic success with prestigious marriage alliances[8]—they cast their net of patronage wider to include a group of *amici* who could fulfil these functions.

The Medici family after 1300 is divisible into nine distinct lines.[9] Several essential early contributions to the family's political and economic recovery which have been comparatively ignored are those of the line of Cambio and his son Vieri, and

promotion of the Medici family before 1434, but excluded them from his definition of the Cafaggiolo branch, apparently on the grounds of their obscurity thereafter; see esp. i. 3, 10, 19.

[7] On the Medici as bankers, see de Roover, *The Rise and Decline*, p. 74, and 'Cosimo de' Medici come banchiere e mercante', *A.S.I.* cxxiii (1965), 466–79, in which he suggests that ultimately Cosimo's success in business must be attributed to his own qualities and those of his closest collaborators.

[8] Brucker, 'The Medici' 22, 26.

[9] i.e. the lines of Bonagiunta, Giambono, Bonino, Cambio, Alamanno, Salvestro, Talento, Conte, and Giovenco. This division is mine; it seems the clearest and most effective characterization of the genealogical shape of the family in the early fifteenth century. The standard genealogy for the Medici is that in P. Litta, *Famiglie Celebri Italiane* (15 vols., Turin and Milan, 1819–1902), iii. For a partial genealogical table of the Medici family 1300–*c*. 1434, see Table 1 below.

within the Salvestro or Cafaggiolo line itself, of Giovanni's
nephew, Averardo, and his descendants, who were in fact, until
their effective extinction in 1442, the owners of the estate at
Cafaggiolo which gave the branch its name.[10] Averardo di Salvestro, 'detto Bicci', died in 1363, with nothing to bequeath to his
five sons but equal shares in his modest landholdings in the
mountainous Mugello area north of Florence from which the
Medici family had originated.[11] Giovanni and Francesco got their
first opportunity through their employment in the bank of their
kinsman, Messer Vieri di Cambio, and although Giovanni was in
every sphere the more outstanding of the brothers, the business
and political careers of their two lines ran parallel and were often
closely intertwined.

In 1391 or 1392, shortly before his death, Vieri's bank was dissolved, and split into three new and independent organizations,
one of which, under the pirection of Antonio di Giovanni di
Cambio, was itself dissolved after only a couple of years. The
other two were founded by Giovanni and Francesco, the latter's
in the name of his son, Averardo. This one was established
in Florence, while Giovanni's bank was in Rome, and the two
co-operated to represent each other until 1397, when each established a branch in both cities. However, they continued to co-
operate in areas where their services did not overlap for almost
half a century; for instance, the then gigantic Medici bank under
Cosimo established a branch in Pisa only after the death in 1442 of
Averardo's grandson, and the closure of the bank which had
hitherto acted as its representative there.[12] Giovanni's organization
became of course uniquely successful in Florence, and indeed in

[10] Tradition has it that the primitive 'habituro acto a forteza' at Cafaggiolo (Cat.
60, f. 82v) was the favourite rural residence of the elderly Cosimo because all the
country he could see from its windows was his own (Roscoe, *The Life of Lorenzo*,
p. 282). In fact, however, he inherited these estates only on the death of Averardo's
grandson, Francesco, *c.* 1442. The letters written by Francesco in exile form the
basis of an account of this branch, its role in the Medici party, and its fate after
1434, by D. Kent, 'I Medici in esilio: una vittoria di famiglia ed una disfatta personale', *A.S.I.* cxxxii (1974), 3–63.

[11] The following account of the early history of the Medici banks is taken essentially from de Roover, *The Rise and Decline*, Ch. 3, esp. pp. 35–9.

[12] Ibid., pp. 37, 275–6. The close connection between the two banks was apparent
in various ways; for example, while in 1411 Averardo's Roman branch was managed
by Andrea di Lippaccio de' Bardi, in 1393 Giovanni di Bicci had established a partnership in Rome with his brother Benedetto di Lippaccio. The third brother, Ilarione, was Giovanni's assistant manager in Rome *c.* 1400 (p. 38).

Europe in the fifteenth century, but this should not lead us to ignore the fact that Averardo's was also extremely prosperous by comparison with other firms in the city, and had made him by 1427 one of its richest citizens with a net capital of over 15,000 florins. Nor should it be forgotten that it was not until 1413 that within the Medici family Giovanni's wealth outstripped that of the heirs of Vieri, who were still among the top two hundred tax-payers in Florence in 1427.[13]

The same kinsmen were similarly associated with Giovanni and his sons in the growing political influence which accompanied the economic recovery of a part of the family. Giovanni di Bicci's assumption of the office of Prior in 1402 is often seen as the initial step in his family's dramatic rise to power, but in fact his brother Francesco was the first of their branch to attain the Priorate in 1397.[14] Since he died soon after, Francesco had no opportunity to build up the political reputation which Giovanni was to enjoy in succeeding years. However, about 1409, his son Averardo began to appear in the *Consulte e Pratiche* advising the *Signoria*, and after 1420 he was entrusted with a number of important offices and commissions, such as the prestigious embassy to Ferrara with Palla Strozzi in 1428 to negotiate the peace with Milan. By the mid-twenties not only Giovanni di Bicci but also Averardo and Nicola di Vieri de' Medici were prominent and powerful members of the ruling group.[15]

Recent work has stressed the increase in economic individualism in the later fourteenth and fifteenth centuries, expressed in the decline of the family firms characteristic of Florence before the economic crises of the 1340s, and has emphasized that households were separate economic entities within a wider family which might embrace the extremes of wealth and poverty among its

[13] See the tables compiled from the *catasto* of 1427, published by L. Martines, *The Social World*, pp. 365–78. In 1403 the heirs of Vieri paid the third highest *prestanza* in San Giovanni, which was double the next highest assessment (p. 356). See also de Roover, *The Rise and Decline*, p. 48.

[14] *Priorista Mariani*, i (MSS. 248), f. 234v. Moreover, the family had been regularly represented since 1383 (1384, 1392, 1394) by the lines of Cambio di Vieri and Albizzo-Bonagiunta.

[15] For the participation during the twenties of members of the Medici family in the influential *Consulte e Pratiche* see Dami, *Giovanni Bicci*, pp. 61–2. Between 1424 and 1426 Averardo attended 32 *Consulte*, Giovanni 20, Nicola di Vieri 15, and Niccolò da Uzzano, generally acknowledged leader of the aristocratic conservative group then dominating the regime, only 26.

members.[16] In conformity with this pattern, the profits of the banks directed by Giovanni and Averardo directly enriched only themselves and their own line. It is important to point out, however, that their personal fortunes were partly a legacy from the wider family in the shape of their distant kinsman, Vieri di Cambio, and that a notable feature of the Medici banks was the habit of drawing their associates as far as possible from within the family circle. Between 1400 and 1434 at least thirteen Medici, representing seven of the eight lines still extant by the fifteenth century, were employed by Giovanni di Bicci in his bank, and one or two of these had also served his nephew in that period.[17] Such associations must have represented not only the creation of a common and unifying commercial interest within the Medici family, but also in practice a close and increasing contact in these years between the Salvestro line and the other branches of the family, however dissimilar in wealth and status.

Contemporary testimony confirms that Giovanni di Bicci was certainly regarded as 'the head of the entire family';[18] this is about as much, however, as we can establish about his relationship to the family at large. Unfortunately, by 1427 when a sudden increase in the volume of surviving letters makes possible for the first time a detailed study of Medici activities, Giovanni had ceased to be an active figure. He held his last public office in 1424, and had retired from the management of the bank in favour of his eldest son, Cosimo, as early as 1420.[19] The popular belief that Giovanni held aloof from politics would seem to be belied by the rapidity of his own rise to power and by the existence of an active Medici party as early as 1426 or 1427. However, we do have some posthumous evidence concerning his influence on family, friends, and in Florence, which maintained its strength until his death and beyond it. When he died in February 1429 twenty-six male members of the Medici clan attended the funeral, and six of the seven lines of

[16] See particularly Goldthwaite, *Private Wealth*, esp. pp. 253–9. Conversely, Kent, *Household and Lineage*, Ch. 3, cf. Ch. 2, has shown that the members of a lineage co-operated to a considerable extent in economic matters, and that extremes of wealth and poverty among *consorti* were by no means necessarily divisive.

[17] De Roover, *The Rise and Decline*, pp. 45–6, 383–5, and his Appendix I.

[18] Cavalcanti, *Istorie*, p. 54. According to Sacchetti, 'i maggiori della casa' Medici had acted together as a *consorteria* in the fourteenth century under the leadership of M. Francesco (F. Sacchetti, *Il Trecentonovelle*, ed. V. Pernicone, Florence, 1946, Novella lxxxviii, pp. 203–51).

[19] De Roover, 'Cosimo de' Medici' 470.

the family still flourishing at this date were represented among the mourners.[20] After his death the *amici* continued to invoke 'the blessed memory of Giovanni de' Medici',[21] and to refer to him as having 'departed this life with a good name and an excellent reputation'.[22]

The mantle of his authority passed indisputably to Cosimo, of whom a Milanese chronicler observed in 1430 that 'by virtue of his achievements and his generosity and the influence of his father's name, he was able to accomplish a great deal in the city'.[23] However, friends wrote in consolation not only to his sons, but also to his nephew, Averardo;[24] that he too was enveloped by Giovanni's aura is clearly apparent from a letter of congratulation which he received from Vanni d'Andrea de' Medici in 1427: 'I have heard that you have been made an ambassador, which pleases me greatly, as does any honour you may receive, as much as if you were Giovanni di Bicci himself.'[25] It is obvious from the Medici correspondence that Cosimo saw himself, Lorenzo, and Averardo as joint caretakers of the family's political position; as he remarked in his *Ricordi* concerning the events of 1433, it was fortunate that while he himself was imprisoned in the Palazzo del Popolo, the *Signoria* was unable to detain either Averardo or Lorenzo: 'If they had managed to take all three of us, they could have done us great harm.'[26] While Cosimo became the family's leading representative in the ruling group, its symbolic head, and the chief architect of family and party policy,[27] Cavalcanti saw in Averardo the chief instrument of its driving political ambition.[28] As we shall see, he does indeed seem to have taken most of the responsibility for the day-to-day business of cultivating,

[20] The names of those who attended are noted by Rosso de' Medici in his *Libro di ricordi*, M.A.P. CLIV, f. 94v.

[21] M.A.P. II, 167 (Bartolomeo Orlandini to Averardo).

[22] Ibid. II, 92 (Luigi di Manetto Davanzati to Averardo).

[23] Biglia's *History of Milan*, quoted by Gutkind, *Cosimo de' Medici*, p. 70.

[24] M.A.P. II, 92.   [25] Ibid. II, 78.

[26] Fabroni, *Ricordi*, p. 97; cf. the similar implication of M.A.P. II, 371 (Cosimo to Averardo, 21 Oct. 1430).

[27] Cosimo adopted a tone of familiar authority in his correspondence with Averardo; e.g. in the letters published by Fabroni, *Cosmi vita* i., 31–2, and by Pellegrini, *Sulla repubblica*, Appendix; see also M.A.P. II, 101, 371; IV, 246. Cf. Giuliano's letter (5 Sept. 1431, IV, 144) announcing that Averardo had been appointed to a particular office; he advised him to refuse, and concluded 'e di medesimo parere è Chosimo; se da voi non n'ò riposta in fra 2 dì rifiuterò'.

[28] *Istorie*, p. 57; also pp. 207, 303.

co-ordinating, and communicating with the Medici partisans,[29] and his in-laws formed the nucleus of the party's organizers and advisers.[30] Cavalcanti described him as 'an evil man, hostile, and very much a prey to worldly ambitions';[31] he claimed that Averardo was so universally disliked that in 1433 many of the citizens of Florence were unwilling to protest at the exile of Cosimo because Averardo's welcome expulsion was also involved: 'Many men would have refused to tolerate Cosimo's exile, had it not been associated with Averardo's, but as people were saying throughout the city, Averardo's wickedness made Cosimo's misfortune almost inevitable.'[32]

The involvement of the Medici family as a whole in the activities and aspirations of the party is clearly reflected in these proscriptions of 1433; the first to be banished were Cosimo and Averardo, followed closely by Lorenzo di Giovanni, Averardo's son Giuliano, and Orlando di Guccio de' Medici. Some time later Vanni d'Andrea and the brothers Bernardo and Gregorio di Alamanno di Salvestro were added to the list, comprising altogether eight members of the family, representing three separate lines within it. The entire house, with the exception of one household, was politically disfranchised by permanent relegation to the magnate class.[33] Of course these sentences were revoked after the recall of the Medici exiles a year later, and after September 1434 the family as a whole shared with Cosimo and his sons in the rewards of political ascendancy; indeed numerous members of the other five surviving branches of the family regularly occupied the most prestigious magistracies.[34] Where only one Medici gained a majority in the scrutiny of 1433, no less than twenty-one became eligible to hold the highest offices in 1440.[35]

The absence of Averardo's descendants from these rolls may partly account for a general tendency on the part of historians to overlook his contribution to the establishment of the Medici as a political force in Florence before 1434, but the history of this household comes to an effective end at this date precisely because its members suffered in exile the ruin which the enemies of the

---

[29] See below, Ch. 1 (vi), and M.A.P. *Inventario*, esp. Filze I–V.
[30] Below, pp. 55–6.   [31] *Istorie*, p. 57.   [32] Ibid., p. 282.
[33] Balìe, 24, ff. 10v–11r, 22r (9 Sept.), 66r–v (16 Dec.).
[34] See Tratte, 80, *passim*, cf. MSS. 248, ff. 234v–235r.
[35] MSS. 555; cf. Tratte, 1150; on the nature and political significance of the scrutinies, see below, pp. 107–9.

Medici had hoped might destroy the entire house. Giuliano died in Rome in 1434, followed within five months by his father; his eighteen-year-old son Francesco survived for less than eight years to preside over a business essentially undermined by their exile, and which he was quite unfitted either by education or by temperament to repair.[36]

However, the politically prominent members of the Medici after 1434 did include the heirs of Nicola di Vieri, who along with Cosimo and Averardo had prospered in business and had won a place in the inner circle of the city's ruling group as early as the 1420s. It has often been assumed that Nicola's exemption from the proscriptions of 1433 indicated aloofness or even opposition to the aspirations of his kinsmen and their party;[37] in fact, his correspondence with Averardo in the years immediately preceding demonstrates a strong sense of family unity, which found concrete expression in the marriage of his numerous daughters to various Medici partisans.[38] Cosimo himself in his *Ricordi* explained that Nicola was excepted from the general condemnation of the Medici family 'because he was *Gonfaloniere*';[39] the actual removal from a major post of a citizen as wealthy and influential as he would presumably have caused more embarrassment than the Medici opponents were willing to risk. Indeed, according to Cavalcanti, it was Nicola who stipulated that he would remain in office only on condition

that I need not be present when the fate of my kinsmen is put to the vote, so that among future generations of Medici no one can say that I lent my support to the ruin of my house, since this would be a matter for great reproach, and there would be little to say in my defence.[40]

The consorterial solidarity asserted in these words is typical of the attitude to the achievements of the Cafaggiolo Medici which other branches of the family revealed in their letters and expressed in their various activities.

---

[36] Kent, 'I Medici in esilio'.

[37] For example, most recently by M. Mallett, *The Florentine Galleys in the Fifteenth Century* (Oxford, 1967), p. 198.

[38] M.A.P. V, 65 (22 Nov. 1431, to Averardo), and below, pp. 38–9.

[39] *Ricordi*, p. 98. The same explanation is offered by the anti-Medicean Terrino Manovelli in his *Ricordanze* (C.S. 2ª ser. XIV, f. iiii). Cavalcanti expressed the general surprise in Florence at Nicola's exemption from the proscriptions of 1433, observing that he was by no means 'de' meno propinqui che abbia Cosimo cavatone Averardo, e i figliuoli' (p. 277).   [40] *Istorie*, p. 277.

Their cohesion had a definite geographical and physical foundation; the entire family inhabited adjacent areas in three of the
gonfaloni of the quarter of San Giovanni—Lion d'oro, Drago, and
Vaio, which covered the district between the Mercato Vecchio
and the Duomo, then stretched on beyond it to the north.[41]
Though the concentration of the family as a whole on extensive
investment in land during the fourteenth century had helped to
keep them out of commerce and politics, it had made them a
powerful and consolidated force in their ancestral homeland in
the Mugello, where many lines held neighbouring estates to
which they accompanied one another on their frequent visits.[42]
When physically separated, they were not out of touch; of the six
other lines extant in 1427 five were in correspondence with
Cosimo and Averardo, and the affairs of the sixth were mentioned
in their letters. The death of distant relatives revealed the closeness of their relationships to the Cafaggiolo branch. A letter of
Bernardo, of the Alamanno line, to Giuliano, Averardo's son,
records the death in November 1431 of Messer Amerigo, his
cousin, who had nominated as his executors 'Averardo, Cosimo,
Nicola, Lorenzo, Orlando and you, and also me', representing
four different lines of the family.[43] Less than a month after their
flight from Florence in 1433, Giuliano's son Francesco was not
too preoccupied with immediate problems to write to his grandfather Averardo of the death of Antonio, of Talento's line, and to
record a similar list of executors.[44] In the event of death several
lines would also co-operate to aid those still living; on one occasion Nicola di Vieri de' Medici wrote to Averardo that he had
heard from Bernardo d'Alamanno of the death of his aunt Tita,
'and because as you know, she and her household are without
a protector and in a very bad way, I beg you as a favour to see
that by some means her affairs may be otherwise arranged'.[45]

As we have already observed, the honorary extension of immediate family relationships to embrace more distant kin, and even

[41] On Medici patterns of residence, see below, Ch. 1 (iv).

[42] See, e.g., Averardo's tax report listing his estates and their neighbours in 1427
(Cat. 60, ff. 82r, ff.); also M.A.P. II, 283; IV, 87. Those of the Medici family with
properties adjacent to Cafaggiolo included Papi di Bartolomeo de' Medici, Antonio
and Albizzo, Giovanni di Bartolomeo, Monna Filippa, widow of Paolo di Messer
Forese, Antonio di Talento de' Medici, and the estates of the deceased Niccolò di
Francesco de' Medici.

[43] M.A.P. VI, 5.   [44] Ibid. V, 245.   [45] Ibid. V, 65

amici outside the kinship circle, is characteristic of a patronage network in a traditional society. Members of other lines of the Medici family often addressed Cosimo and Averardo in these terms. Guccio di Orlando once informed the latter that 'you and your family are as much my fathers as Orlando',[46] and Vanni d'Andrea, in writing to Averardo, expressed the wish 'to do your bidding more faithfully than a son';[47] in a letter to Giuliano he referred to 'our father Averardo'.[48] As we shall see, they were very much part of the patronage network, which operated for their benefit as well as that of the main branch. There is one desperate letter from Bernardo d'Antonio, of the Giovenco line, explaining to Averardo that he was being held responsible for payment of another's debts; he felt it unjust that the commune should take from him by this device

that little which I have, and which after twenty-two years away from home I have only recently succeeded in acquiring by much hard work and at great risk . . . Thus I beg you for God's sake, along with Cosimo and Antonio di Salvestro [a wealthy and influential friend of the Medici], to help me.[49]

Orlando di Guccio, wanting a position directing the communal galleys, once invoked Averardo's aid, begging him 'to arrange it as best you can, either with money or favours or promises'.[50] Although no evidence remains concerning Averardo's *modus operandi*, Orlando did indeed get the job,[51] like Bernardo d'Alamanno who wrote on one occasion to acknowledge Averardo's assistance: 'I see that through your favour the *Dieci* have appointed me to a most profitable position.'[52]

Along with the benefits, they recognized the obligations of patronage, and family letters, like those of the *amici*, contain assurances that 'I am always yours', 'I have always done my best to serve you',[53] or more explicitly, 'I am even more committed to you than I told you above, and as I shall prove to you when the opportunity occurs. If there is anything I should do, I beg you to

[46] Ibid. II, 234.   [47] Ibid. II, 104.   [48] Ibid. LXVI, 25.
[49] Ibid. II, 142.   [50] Ibid. V, 159.
[51] A month later Averardo received a letter from Guccio's brother, Piero, announcing the latter's appointment and thanking Averardo for his co-operation (ibid. III, 20).
[52] Ibid. V, 133.
[53] For the general tone of the family letters of recommendation see, e.g., ibid. II, 111, 114, 142, 173, 234, 332, 337.

let me know.'[54] Lacking as most of them were in wealth and political influence, the ways in which they might reciprocate such aid were limited; indeed mainly confined, it seems, to the contraction of advantageous marriage alliances, one of the fundamental means of extending a patronage network or party to include wealthier or more influential members. This, as we shall see, was the great contribution of the lineage as a whole to the growth of Medici influence after 1400, and a major practical factor in drawing it closer together.[55]

A detailed study of the Medici marriage patterns and their relation to the party of the late twenties and early thirties leaves little doubt that these contributions were consciously made, especially in the light of the family's conception of corporate honour apparent in their letters. When Guccio requested his job on the galleys he promised that 'I shall do you great honour',[56] and Vanni, in asking Averardo to procure him a position in one of the northern courts added 'and if I get it, it will be a source both of honour and profit to me and to the entire house'.[57] In December 1431 Bernardo d'Alamanno wrote to Averardo on the subject of his own participation in the war effort, expressing the hope that 'with God's pleasure I may contribute to the exaltation of the commune, and to the happiness and the honour of us all'.[58] Averardo was equally aware that Bernardo's honour reflected on his own, and had written somewhat apprehensively to his son Giuliano shortly before that in fact 'Bernardo is in a very perilous position and he will need all his skill';[59] in a later letter Bernardo assured him once more that his only concern was 'to do honour to you and to myself with God's help, as I am sure you well know'.[60]

The other lines of the Medici family associated themselves in turn with the Cafaggiolo branch in its triumphs. When Averardo was involved in the peace negotiations of 1428, after the Florentine war with Milan, Vanni d'Andrea, of the line of Alamanno, had written to him asking to be recommended to Giuliano 'and all your immediate family (*brigata*)' and hoping 'that God will give you victory as each of us desires, for your own honour and that

[54] M.A.P. II, 104.   [55] Below, pp. 55–60.   [56] M.A.P. V, 112.
[57] Ibid. II, 78.   [58] Ibid. V, 140.   [59] Ibid. V, 682.
[60] Ibid. V, 162, cf. Piero di Orlando de' Medici, who in a letter to Averardo concerning the recent appointment of his brother Guccio to an important office, hoped 'che senpre sia rigraziato Iddio cho' speranza che questi vi farìa onore' (III, 20).

of the commune'.[61] On another occasion he had written of his
pleasure at hearing 'how you, who are like a father to us, have
returned safe and victorious, for I am no less joyful and content
at the honour and benefit you have earned than Giuliano himself'.
He went on to speak of 'the faith which I have in you, which has
always been rewarded in so many ways',[62] and indeed his words
express vividly the hope vested by the remainder of the family in
Giovanni and his line, as the sole effective contenders for the
Medici family stake in the wealth, influence, and political power
which Florence could offer to her leading citizens. The outstanding successes of that single branch did not divide it from the rest
of the family; on the contrary, they justified its leadership of the
Medici lineage and endowed it with the responsibility of re-
establishing the greatness of the house, of raising its members up
again, and winning for them a position of honour and influence
in the city. The tone of their family letters betrays, perhaps unconsciously, but with peculiar clarity, the extent of Medici ambitions
in this respect, as when Bernardo d'Alamanno declared his faith
in Averardo thus: 'I commend myself to you with all my heart,
for my only hope is in you and in God . . . You are my God on
earth and all that I crave in this world is the honour and prosperity
which I am confident I will receive by your favour.'[63]

(iii) MARRIAGE

The most obvious beginning for the leaders of a house bent on
reviving its fortunes was to cultivate advantageous marriage
alliances. As we have already observed, Florentines generally
assumed that *parenti* constituted a group of natural allies and
associates, and we shall see how in the operation of networks of
patronage and partisanship a considerable proportion of requests
for assistance were made on behalf of the writer's *parenti*, or
requiring the co-operation of his patron's relatives.[1] The view of

[61] Ibid. II, 111.   [62] Ibid. II, 104.
[63] Ibid. V, 133, cf. Vanni d'Andrea, who had written to Averardo in 1427 (25
Dec.) that 'la mia speranza in llui [Giovanni di Bicci] e in voi si riposa' (II, 78).

[1] In general, see below, Ch. 1 (vi), and particularly such examples as M.A.P. V,
13, in which Niccolò Cocco-Donati begged Averardo to help Niccolò del Benino
'per amore di mme e del detto Nichold col qual'è parentado e amicizia'; Andrea
Bardi's advice to Averardo over a financial crisis that they urgently needed help
from 'Gianozo e altri e tuoi parenti e miei' (ibid. III, 382); Giuliano's remark to his

parentado as an extension of *consorteria* is exemplified in the use of familial terms to describe relations by marriage; thus Stefano di Francesco di Ser Segna could observe of his betrothal to the daughter of Filippo di Messer Biagio Guasconi that it 'seems to me to have given another father to me and to my brothers'.[2]

The corollary of the assumption that *parenti* had a natural obligation to assist one another was that the choice of individual marriage partners became a matter of crucial importance to families, who sought to ensure that they would derive maximum benefit and minimum danger or inconvenience from the formation of these associations which, since they involved the interests of the family in general, were rather a matter of family policy than individual preference.[3] Giovanni Morelli makes no mention of the bride, but enjoins his sons to ensure if possible that a prospective father-in-law 'should be in trade, rich, from a family long established in Florence, Guelf, and active and influential in political life'. He cautioned them particularly against being drawn out on a political limb: 'In making marriages you should incline towards citizens who are in the *reggimento* . . . You should always attach yourself to those who have influence in the halls of government and in the *Signoria*.'[4] The correspondence of Alessandra Strozzi and her family, who in considering suitable marriages for her children weighed at length the comparative advantages of alliances in terms of the wealth, size, antiquity, political influence, and general social standing of the families involved, constitute not only a particularly subtle exposition of the importance of these factors in the making of marriages, but also indicate how in evaluating potential *parenti* their own *parentado* was an explicit preoccupation.

father (ibid. III, 367), that 'troppo ci perseguitano per gli amici e parenti', and Benedetto Masi's observations concerning the effect on his friend Filippo Scolari of his *parentado* with the Aldobrandini (below, p. 103). Similar attitudes emerge from other private letter collections like those of the Strozzi (cf. below, pp. 183–5), the Sacchetti (Conv. Soppr. 78, 324), and *Ricordanze* like that of Manno di Tano di Cambio Petrucci (C.S. 2ª ser. XII), who excused himself concerning a slightly suspect business arrangement with the explanation that 'mi fu adoso molti parenti e diso[n]mi mi farebono fare il dovere' (f. 22r).

[2] M.A.P. II, 161.

[3] This is not to say that the personal qualities of individuals were considered entirely irrelevant (cf. Alessandra Strozzi, *Lettere*, pp. 449, 450, 459), nor that love did not occur in marriage; as Giuliano on one occasion observed to Averardo, 'Simone Tornabuoni avea tolta la figliuola di Nichola ed è ne s'inamorato; non se ne parte'. [4] *Ricordi*, pp. 264, 274.

For example, in seeking a wife for her son Filippo, her first consideration after 'what was available' and 'what we considered ourselves able to run to', was 'which seemed to constitute the best set of marriage connections';[5] a letter reporting to her on the possibilities in these terms from her son-in-law, Marco Parenti, himself the subject of similar calculations twenty years before, speculated at some length on the possible ramifications of *parentado*, once the candidates had been pronounced 'much of a muchness in their personal qualities'. The Adimari he judged

more noble that the Tanagli, but there is no *parentado*, neither father nor brothers; there are plenty of uncles and cousins, but they are very ill-bred, and all their relatives by marriage are men of the same type; but with this defect, there is also the advantage that there will be no bother or obligation involved there. The other girl is quite the opposite. If they are not of really distinguished stock, nevertheless they are a sound and well-established family . . . and this branch is of knightly descent. The father of the girl is the same age as I; a nice enough sort of man, well mannered, well-spoken, sociable, and he has the admirable advantages of a small share in politics and sufficient relatives, all of them good men.

Marco then went on to specify the marriage connections of the bride's father's siblings, his wife, and her siblings, with the Alessandri, Guidetti, and Ridolfi, concluding that they had in addition 'many other fine and honourable associations by marriage', and thus between the two girls, 'weighing one against the other, there is not much to choose, and I will leave the decision up to you'.[6]

Just what proportion in general of the whole extended family was affected by the marriage of one of its members, within what degree of relationship the pull of *parentado* was effective, is not entirely clear. It seems that marriages were usually arranged between households, although distant kinsmen might assist in these arrangements. As the Strozzi letters suggest, and an investigation below into the role of *parentado* in determining partisanship would tend to confirm, it was essentially the immediate families of the protagonists who acknowledged the obligations involved in consenting to the formation of the alliance; where conflicting claims rose from the tangled web of associations spun by any relatively large *consorteria*, only the closest *parenti* commanded automatic loyalty. However, the reputation and prestige of any household clearly depended to some extent on those of the lineage of which it formed a part. The appeal of alliances with individuals was affected by their family traditions and correspondingly, it appears, as when Alessandra Strozzi wrote to her son Filippo of the betrothal of Benedetto Strozzi's daughter with the announcement that 'the Strozzi have made an alliance with the Pitti', that a single marriage might be seen as creating a meaningful link between two great lineages.[7] The interests of a *consorteria* and its *parenti* were certainly assumed to be coincident in a suggestion of Niccolò da Uzzano's in a *Pratica* of 1430, that the growth of factions might be stemmed by guaranteeing a more judicious distribution of offices, 'which should be given according to the virtues and merits of each house and its *parenti*'.[8] As indicated in the Strozzi letters and in Giuliano Davanzati's request to Averardo de' Medici that Antonio di Lorenzo degli Albizzi should be appointed to a certain position, 'and that since he is born of us through his mother you would give great pleasure and be performing a service to him and to me and to all our house and his *consorti*',[9] the connections established by marriage were not restricted to the male line, but also operated through the female; thus the *parentado* was potentially an extremely extensive interest group.

Moreover, the practical relevance of *parentado* depended partly on the nature of the particular case; that quite distant relationships might be invoked to claim identification with an entire house if this seemed desirable and convenient is apparent from a letter of Antonio Corbinelli to Averardo de' Medici in 1431. Antonio's brother Giovanni was certainly a Medici partisan, and his first cousin's daughter had just married Bernardo d'Antonio de' Medici, Cosimo's third cousin; in consequence of the marriage Antonio wrote recommending himself to Averardo. He took pains to stress the tie, however remote, which now linked

---

[7] Strozzi, *Lettere*, p. 267; cf. in general the observations on marriage connections between houses by Martines, *The Social World*, pp. 57–62.

[8] C.P. 49 f. 33r (26 Apr. 1430).

[9] M.A.P. III, 42 (2 Feb. 1432; 1431 *s.f.*).

him to what he obviously felt to be a coming family in Florence, and expressed the 'frank and confident hopes' which he had in the Medici, 'which have risen even higher now that we enjoy the status of relatives by marriage'.[10]

Indeed, given that profitable negotiation in the marriage market depended on the possession of some substantial asset with which to bargain, and for which others could be exchanged, in terms of the criteria articulated above, the Medici were comparatively favourably situated. Despite their general lack of wealth and political influence, they had strength in their size; obviously a large force of *parenti* was usually desirable, and the Medici numbered thirty-two separate households in 1427. Sheer age, and at least a few impressive marriage alliances early in the century, as well as the memory of former prosperity and power, conferred on them considerable social distinction, not to mention the promise of possible future greatness, which may have seemed increasingly near fulfilment as the century progressed.[11]

Precisely because the interests of *parenti* were so inextricably associated in Florence, it is difficult to establish in most individual cases whether the Medici in-laws simply found themselves in time naturally and necessarily involved in the operations of the party, or whether the Medici purposely contracted marriages with their partisans in order to create even closer bonds between them. However, a study of the marriages of members of the Medici family between 1400 and 1434 does suggest some sort of consorterial 'policy', reflected in the nature and qualities of those they attached to themselves as *parenti* and in the degree of

[10] Ibid. III, 151.

[11] As the Medici became an increasingly defined force in Florentine political life the contraction of an association with them by marriage must increasingly have represented the conscious choice to identify with their position and ambitions. An extreme example is that of the Corsini. Cavalcanti described Giovanni Corsini and his father in the twenties as 'so sunk in the overflowing depths of misery that even their own *consorti* despised them' (*Istorie*, ed. Polidori, ii. 195). The information from an entry in the *Ricordi* of Giovanni's son, Matteo (A. Petrucci (ed.), *Il Libro di Ricordanze dei Corsini (1362–1457)*, Rome, 1965, p. 144) that he had betrothed himself to Tita, daughter of Orlando di Guccio de' Medici, then in exile in Ancona, suggests that in order to revive his waning fortunes with a handsome dowry, and to profit in general by association with prosperous *parenti*, he was prepared to take a gamble on their political prospects. Notably, however, he did wait until the day after the unsuccessful attempt of the anti-Mediceans to prevent their recall, before actually consummating the marriage negotiations by taking the bride to his own house.

their coincidence with the partisans of the late twenties and early thirties. Clearly the Medici in 1400 were in need of allies with the attributes of power and influence which they lacked, and the entire *consorteria* stood to benefit by co-operating in their attachment, and by assisting in the efforts of those lines and households in the best position to attract such associates. Certainly almost all of those who became *parenti* in this period were from families with a social position and status equal or superior to their own; conversely a detailed analysis of their *parenti* suggests strongly that these were more than a random selection from the ranks of their peers.

What follows does not purport to be a complete picture of Medici marriages in this period; there are gaps in the evidence, which cannot easily be quantified, and due to the problems involved in the effective definition of *parenti* only the marriages of partisans themselves, or of their mothers, siblings, and children have been considered here. A number of marriages certainly occurred between the Medici and families who cannot be shown to be their partisans, and may even have been their enemies, though apart from the example of the Strozzi, whose political stance was until the last moment ambiguous, there is hardly a Medici marriage, in the whole of the fifteenth century, with a house which came out against them in 1433–4.[12]

What is significant, however, is the overwhelming preponderance of unions with partisans and their families. Benedetto Dei, that astute and informed observer of the Florentine scene, in describing the scrutiny drawn up by the triumphant anti-Mediceans after Cosimo's exile in September, remarked upon their folly in having failed, once the Medici were exiled, to reform the purses more thoroughly. 'They had put into the purses or allowed to remain there the names of many of their enemies, who were all related to one another, especially the leaders . . .'[13] This is not entirely or literally true, but it is true that some twenty-two or twenty-three marriages between members of the Medici family and the immediate families of their supporters occurred in the period between 1400 and 1434, the three decades which saw the

---

[12] An obvious and important exception was Bernardo di Antonio di Giovenco de' Medici's marriage, *c.* 1425, to Costanza, daughter of Tinoro di Niccolò Guasconi, exiled in 1434 (MSS. Pass. 1884⁴, B.N.F.).

[13] Dei, 'Chronica', f. 13r.

rise of the Medici from comparative obscurity to ascendancy in Florence.[14] Four of the leading Medicean partisans were actually married themselves to a member of the Medici family;[15] over a quarter of the group was closely related by the marriages of sons, daughters, brothers, sisters, or cousins, many of them more than once.

There is evidence that the leaders of the Medici party took a keen interest in the marriages of quite distant kinsmen and may also have taken a directive hand in the arrangements. A letter of Cosimo to Averardo at the beginning of 1428 announces the marriage of Giovenco d'Antonio, who had last shared a common ancestor with Cosimo five generations previously, to the daughter of Filippo Giugni. The Giugni were among the most important and influential *amici* of the Medici,[16] and Cosimo's letter suggests that he had himself been involved in the choice of Giovenco's bride, and in the marriage negotiations. Certainly he remarked with some satisfaction on the fact that the Giugni were 'excellent in-laws, and of old stock'.[17]

However, a planned policy is most clearly implied in the unions of those lines which enjoyed both wealth and political influence throughout most of the period 1400 to 1434, and were thus best fitted to contract advantageous alliances. Information survives concerning the marriages of five of Averardo's children before 1434; it can hardly be coincidence that three of the party's leaders and key supporters within the governing élite were Averardo's sons-in-law—Alamanno Salviati, Antonio di Salvestro Serristori, and Giannozzo di Stoldo Gianfigliazzi. His own son Giuliano married Sandra di Filippo Tornabuoni, niece of Francesco di Simone Tornabuoni, who completed the quartet of lieutenants to Cosimo and Averardo drawn from the upper social echelons of the party. In the last months before the Medici exile Piero di M. Luigi Guicciardini was to make a most distinguished fifth, drawn into the Medici family circle by the marriage of his

---

[14] Given the nature of the evidence, this list of *parenti* cannot be assumed to be exhaustive. It is based largely on the Carte dell'Ancisa and the Poligrafo Gargani (B.N.F.). The compilers of both made substantial use of the Gabelle records; they may sometimes have erred in noting the earliest date of marriages.

[15] Luca di Maso degli Albizzi, Giannozzo di Stoldo Gianfigliazzi, Francesco Tornabuoni, and Alamanno Salviati.

[16] Cf. Cavalcanti, *Istorie*, p. 263.

[17] M.A.P. II, 26.

C

daughter, Costanza, to Averardo's grandson, Francesco, in June 1433.[18]

In so far as marriage was a means of procuring useful allies, Florentine lore was ambiguous about the desirability of multiple marriages.[19] Sometimes it expressed the view that to marry into the same house twice was to waste an opportunity to widen one's circle of influential *parenti*; on other occasions it obviously seemed desirable to duplicate ties in order to cement existing bonds. The operation of both principles is apparent in Medici marriages; if Averardo's descendants included a range of key partisans, those of Cosimo and Lorenzo represented the reinforcement of what were apparently conceived as strategic traditional alliances with the *consorterie* of the Bardi and Tornaquinci.

Like a number of those families with whom the Medici allied themselves, the latter lacked current political power and influence—in fact, both were largely, though not entirely, magnate houses specifically excluded from office-holding. However, the Bardi in particular were extremely wealthy; probably the several fifteenth-century *parentadi* with this house were a corollary of the key role which they played in that period in the establishment of the Medici financial empire. Just as, until 1434, both Averardo's and Giovanni di Bicci's banks pursued a policy of recruiting their staff as far as possible from either the Medici or the Bardi families,[20] so Cosimo's marriage to Contessina di Giovanni de' Bardi about 1413[21] had been preceded by that of Lodovico di Mari di Talento de' Medici (a line of the family associated with Giovanni's bank) to Antonia di Piero de' Bardi,[22] and followed up with the union in 1423 between Cambio di M. Vieri and Cammilla di Gerozzo de' Bardi.[23] These lines of Bardi were heavily involved in Medici ambitions and affairs during this period, although other branches of the family were to take a leading role in opposition to them.

The Medici relationship with the magnate house of Tornaquinci and its *popolano* off-shoots of the late fourteenth century,

---

[18] Litta, *Famiglie Celebri* iii, Tav. III. Francesco's own 'Ricordi relativi alle feste e spese fatte in occasione delle nozze di Francesco di Giuliano d'Averardo de' Medici con Costanza di Piero Guicciardini' (M.A.P. CXLVIII) are a vivid illustration of the extent to which these leading Medici partisans were integrated into the family. [19] Cf. Kent, *Household and Lineage*, pp. 95–7.
[20] De Roover, *The Rise and Decline*, esp. p. 386. [21] Ibid., p. 386.
[22] Ancisa, BB, f. 18r. [23] Ibid., f. 46r.

the Tornabuoni and the Popoleschi, may similarly be seen as an intentional alliance, operating in more than one sphere of activity. A member of the Tornaquinci family was prominent in Giovanni's bank in its early days, and although his service proved far from satisfactory, he was treated with conspicuous consideration.[24] In the first three decades of the fifteenth century there were four marriages involving the Medici and this clan; Gregorio d'Alamanno, one of the eight members of the family exiled in 1433, married Lisa di Bernardo Tornaquinci; Giuliano d'Averardo married the daughter of Filippo Tornabuoni, and while one of Nicola di Vieri's daughters wed Niccolò Popoleschi, another became the wife of Simone di Filippo Tornabuoni, thus creating a further link with his uncle, Francesco di Simone, perhaps the most intimate of the quartet of leading partisans mentioned above.[25] When the latter referred to the marriage in a note to Averardo in 1428, he spoke of his nephew as 'your Simone', though Simone and his widowed mother had been living in Francesco's own house since his brother Filippo's death.[26] Certainly the boy's relationship to Averardo was almost as close as to himself; Simone's elder sister had married Averardo's son Giuliano, and at the wedding in June 1433 of their son Francesco, who lived until his marriage with his father and grandfather in a three-generation household, Simone di Filippo Tornabuoni was one of the three 'very closest relatives'[27] to accompany the bridegroom to the ceremonial dinner in the traditional manner. In this case the multiplicity of bonds between the two houses operated to ensure a continuing union; the Tornabuoni remained the faithful partisans and allies of the Medici to the end of the fifteenth century and the status of this union is indicated after 1434 in its ultimate marital consummation—the wedding of Cosimo's eldest son Piero to Francesco's daughter Lucrezia.[28]

In addition to the Bardi, their major financial partners before 1434, and the Tornabuoni, their surest partisans, there were

[24] The brothers Neri and Adovardo di Cipriano Tornaquinci were respectively factors in Rome and Naples in 1402, when the Venetian branch was established, and Neri became its manager. In April 1406 he was recalled and replaced because of incompetence, but in 1424, on hearing that he was living in poverty in Cracow, Giovanni di Bicci sent him a remittance of 36 florins (de Roover, *The Rise and Decline*, p. 41).

[25] Litta, *Famiglie Celebri* iii, Tav. III, VI, VII; Ancisa, BB, f. 45v.

[26] M.A.P. II, 24, 26; Cat. 77, ff. 383r–390r.   [27] M.A.P. CXLVIII.

[28] Litta, *Famiglie Celebri* iii, Tav. III.

several other houses whom the Medici may particularly have
striven to bind to themselves with the ties of multiple marriages.
In contracting an intimate association with Giannozzo Gianfigliazzi through his marriage with Averardo's daughter Tita, the
Medici may have been building on an existing relationship; his
father's wife had also been a Gianfigliazzi.[29] Where another of
Averardo's daughters, Caterina, married Alamanno Salviati, the
sister of Nicola di Veri also married into that house, and while the
marriage of Averardo's grandson Francesco joined to the Medici
perhaps the most distinguished representative of the Guicciardini family, Nicola's brother Cambio had formed a link with its
other major line through his marriage to the daughter of Niccolò
Guicciardini.[30]

Most other lines of the Medici family, and particularly those
closely associated with the Cafaggiolo branch in its financial and
political operations, contracted marriages in accord with the
general policy which we have discerned in the unions of the main
branch.[31] However, the role of the family's second most successful
line, that of M. Vieri, whose bank had served as a foundation for
the organizations of Averardo and Giovanni di Bicci, and whose
heirs had maintained his prosperity into the fifteenth century, and
gained considerable influence in the governing councils, is particularly prominent. Although in the multiple alliances which we
have been examining the key marriages, and the most prestigious,
were those of the Cafaggiolo branch, they were solidly backed up
by the heirs of Vieri, who were in the next most favourable
position to attract desirable allies.[32] Notably the marriages of this
line also linked the Medici with two houses which were later to
furnish them with supporters who may not have been partisans in
the rather conspiratorial activities of the late twenties and early

[29] Litta, *Famiglie Celebri* iii, Tav. III.
[30] Ibid., Tav. VII.
[31] e.g. Orlando di Guccio de' Medici married Francesca di Tommaso Fioravanti
in 1422 (ibid. i, Tav. IV); her uncle, Neri di Francesco, was a Medici partisan. Angela
di Giovanni di Conte de' Medici was the wife of Ugone Vecchietti (ibid., Tav. III),
whose cousin Luigi di Raimondo was one of the *amici*. Corrado di Iacopo Vecchietti
was favoured by the pro-Medicean *Balìa* of 1434 (Balìe, 25, f. 34r–v).
[32] Nicola di Vieri's daughters linked the Medici with the Albizzi, Popoleschi,
Barbadori, Tornabuoni, and Nerli; the latter were favoured by an act of the 1434
Balìa (Balìe 25, f. 76r–v). Nicola and his siblings married into the Acciaiuoli, Salviati,
Guicciardini, and Bardi (Litta, *Famiglie Celebri* iii, Tav. VII). In the political divisions
of these latter houses, Nicola's *parenti* generally favoured the Medici.

thirties, but were certainly instrumental in outwitting their opponents and bringing about their recall in 1434.

The first of these was the Acciaiuoli who, like the Medici, had fallen foul of the prevailing regime in the nineties; although they gave the commune some outstanding statesmen in the early fifteenth century, the family as a whole was not really in the favour of the predominant clique, and had some reason to make common cause with the Medici in their attempt to unseat it. Nicola di Vieri di Cambio married the daughter of Donato Acciaiuoli some time before 1420; some years later Agnolo di Iacopo Acciaiuoli, of another, but closely connected line, gave his support to the Medici and was exiled in their wake.[33] A union with a powerful and prominent supporter probably forged on more immediately strategic grounds was that of Nicola di Vieri's daughter Aurelia, in 1426, with Luca degli Albizzi. While the latter's brother Rinaldo was to be responsible for the exile of Cosimo in 1433 and henceforth assumed the leadership of the anti-Medicean faction, Luca himself was among the leading citizens who helped to bring about Cosimo's recall and subsequently to establish the Medicean ascendancy.[34]

Even the less-favoured lines of the Medici house were sometimes responsible for the creation of connections later to prove of great importance; one such was the marriage of Rosso di Giovanni de' Medici, of the line of Foligno di Conte, to Maddalena, daughter of Buonaccorso Pitti, whose brother, like Agnolo Acciaiuoli, was eventually to turn against the future rulers of Florence, but not before he had promoted their triumph with several decades of strong and crucial support.[35] In a similar category is the marriage in 1431 of Lazzero di Tommaso de' Medici to Albiera di Paolo di Bartolomeo Ridolfi, possibly an earnest of the commitment about this time of the distinguished patrician statesman, Bartolomeo di Iacopo Ridolfi, to the Medici cause.[36] This was one of several marriages which created not only a direct bond between the Medici family and the house of one of its supporters, but also an indirect link with others, thus reinforcing

[33] Below, p. 321.   [34] Below, p. 197.

[35] Litta, *Famiglie Celebri* iii, Tav. IV. Maddalena's brother, Luca, and their cousin Giannozzo were among those most favoured by the Medici immediately after their recall (Balìe, 25, ff. 23r, 28v). On the anti-Medicean movement of 1466, led by Luca Pitti, Agnolo Acciaiuoli, and Nerone Dietisalvi-Neroni, see Rubinstein, *Government of Florence*, Pt. II, esp. pp. 157–66.   [36] Ancisa, BB, f. 47r.

the structure of the party as a network of interrelated individuals and families bound to one another by a number of ties which crossed and re-crossed between them.

For while Paolo di Bartolomeo's daughter married a Medici, his brother Pagnozzo married the sister of Francesco di M. Simone Tornabuoni, that leading partisan with whom the Medici established such a complex web of ties by *parentado*.[37] Similarly, while Averardo's daughter Caterina married another of the 'big four' —Alamanno Salviati—Alamanno's sister, Caterina di Iacopo d'Alamanno Salviati, was the wife of Andrea Pazzi, the manager of Averardo's bank in Rome, and one of the wealthiest and most influential of Medici *amici*.[38] Giovanni Giugni was a Medici partisan related to the family twice over, through the marriage of Cosimo's sister and that of Giovenco d'Antonio de' Medici to the daughter of Filippo di Niccolò (whose brother was also a partisan); when he himself wed a daughter of Francesco Boscoli, Averardo's second-in-command at Rome, Agnolo di Filippo Pandolfini, yet another distinguished partisan, was the go-between who arranged the terms. Pandolfini's own sons married into the Giugni and Valori families.[39] The Valori also boasted a leading Medicean, Niccolò di Bartolomeo, whose sister Giovanna was the second wife of Piero Guicciardini, whose daughter was to marry Averardo's grandson. Piero's first wife was Laudamia di Donato Acciaiuoli, sister of the Bartolomea who married Nicola di Vieri di Cambio de' Medici; Nicola's brother, Cambio, married the daughter of Niccolò Guicciardini, Piero's brother.[40]

This forming and reinforcing of bonds by marriage occurred also among the *amici*, although they too were circumscribed by the natural restrictions of social status. Wealthy partisans of distinguished families, with some standing in the ruling circles, such as those whose links with the Medici are described above, generally married into families with similar attributes. Concerning the marriages of the more plebeian supporters of the family no

---

[37] C.S. 2ª ser. LVI, c. 644. [38] Litta, *Famiglie Celebri* iv, Tav. VII.

[39] Vespasiano da Bisticci, *Vite* iii. 139, cf. the marriage of Tommaso di Bartolomeo Barbadori to Caterina di Filippo di Giovanni Carducci (Pol. Gar. 186).

[40] Litta, *Famiglie Celebri* iii, Tav. II, VII. Cf. the marriage not later than 1425 of Bernardo d'Alamanno di Salvestro de' Medici to Francesca di Iacopo di Latino di Primerano de' Pigli; one of Francesca's sisters was married to Piero di Matteo de' Tedaldi, a small and ancient house in which the Medici had at least two partisans, and another sister was the wife of Matteo di Domenico Corsi, brother of Bartolomeo di Domenico, a declared Medicean (Pol. Gar. 1989).

evidence remains. In between these two strata there was a group of families who at this time were particularly mobile, partly through their association with the Medici. Within this group there do seem to be a few examples of marriages uniting the friends of the Medici across the bounds of social class and tradition, including the alliances of the old and distinguished Davanzati house with a new man, a son of Giovanni Orlandini, in 1424, and with the artisan Salvestro di Michele Lapi in 1427.[41] The Martelli, descended in the mid-fourteenth century from a blacksmith of San Giovanni, made several marriages 'above their station' with other Medici supporters in the early fifteenth century; possibly these were the reward of their comparatively early association with the Medici in political activity against the oligarchic regime in the nineties.[42] However, perhaps the most interesting of these 'mixed' marriages is that which united the Dietisalvi and the Ginori, one a very old and prestigious house, the other a very new and brash one, but both equally committed to the Medici cause in the early challenges of the mid-twenties, and both living under the shadow of their patrons' power in Giovanni di Bicci's home *gonfalone* of Lion d'oro.[43]

(iv) NEIGHBOURHOOD

Perhaps the most notable feature of the Medici party, as an active manifestation of Florentine social patterns, was the solidity of its local base, and the proportion of partisans included in it through another great extension by association of the kin group—*vicinanza*. The strength and practical force of neighbourhood ties is implicit in resolutions in the *Pratiche* of about 1420 by Iacopo Vecchietti and Giuliano Davanzati, to consider the good of the commune above their personal feelings, and thus to suppress 'all partisan bias and affection for one's *gonfalone* and quarter'.[1] Morelli, whose family had risen only recently into the patriciate, and lacked security there, naturally urged his sons to 'try to

---

[41] Ancisa, AA, f. 655v; MSS. Pass. (B.N.F.), 187, Ins. 36.

[42] Below, pp. ooo. For early marriages with the Dall'Antella and Bartolini, see Litta, *Famiglie Celebri* iii, Tav. I, and L. Martines, 'La famiglia Martelli e un documento sulla vigilia del ritorno dall'esilio di Cosimo de' Medici (1434)', *A.S.I.* cxvii (1959), 29–43.

[43] Dietisalvi di Nerone Dietisalvi, *Ricordi*, MSS. 85, f. 97r.

[1] C.P. 44, ff. 54r, 136v, quoted Brucker, *The Civic World*, p. 311.

acquire one friend or more in your *gonfalone*'; Giovanni Rucellai also stressed to his the advantages 'of enjoying the favour and good will of kinsmen and relatives and neighbours and all the rest of the men of your district'.[2] Both Morelli and Rucellai notably tended to equate neighbourhood with *gonfalone*—the four smaller units into which each quarter of the city was divided. Obviously these administrative boundaries were partly arbitrary; there is on the one hand some evidence of a feeling of particular solidarity within quarters of the city,[3] and on the other of neighbourhood association based on geographical proximity which cut across such formal boundaries. However, the *gonfalone* was perhaps the most meaningful social unit because it was a basic administrative unit in several important respects.

Chief of these were the collection of taxes and the determination of eligibility for office-holding. Citizens continued in the fifteenth century to assume that officials who were also neighbours would be moved by pleas for particular consideration, often through the intercession of other influential neighbours to whom they looked for assistance. Although Palla Strozzi's request of 1422 to his kinsman, Simone di Filippo, to intervene on his behalf 'with those who assess the tax for the *gonfalone*', since 'everyone seems to have tried to outdo his neighbour in degrading my standing with the men of the *gonfalone* . . . and disgracing me in their eyes',[4] reflects the importance of local opinion before the institution of the *catasto* put an end to the collective responsibility of the *gonfalone* for the *prestanze*, yet Rucellai's remarks to his sons some thirty years later with reference to their own future testify to the continuing importance of a secure local base. For even in the financial sphere the *gonfalone* retained major responsibilities in the

---

[2] Morelli, *Ricordi*, p. 253; Perosa (ed.), *Rucellai, il Zibaldone*, p. 9.

[3] See, e.g., Del Lungo and Volpi (eds.), *La Cronica domestica di Messer Donato Velluti*, pp. 164–5; Velluti describes how in 1343 the citizens of Oltrarno, feeling themselves unjustly treated in the distribution of offices and taxes, responded 'con minacciature alcuna volta di tagliare i ponti e fare città per noi'.

[4] C.S. 3ª ser. CXXXII, cc. 60, 61. Other collections of letters illuminating the nature of neighbourhood ties, unfortunately restricted mainly to the earlier fifteenth century, are those of the Strozzi family, in various *filze* of the Carte Strozziane, and those to the Sacchetti from their friends and neighbours (Conv. Soppr. 78, 324); from the latter, see the example quoted by Brucker, *The Civic World*, p. 480, of Luca di Matteo da Panzano, who wrote to his neighbour, Forese Sacchetti, promising to favour the Sacchetti if he should be made a *sgravatore* to review the tax assessments (*prestanze*), in return for the latter's support in an imminent *rimbotto*, or revision of the electoral purses.

collection and deployment of local taxes, and in the administration of the communal levies; the *catasto* continued to be described, assessed, and taxed according to *gonfaloni*, and local officials were still concerned with appeals for clemency in the assessment, and with the treatment of defaulters.[5]

In the sphere of political life the compilation of raw lists of eligibles to be voted on by the city-wide scrutiny councils was chiefly the responsibility of the local representatives—the sixteen *Gonfalonieri di Compagnia* who collectively formed one of the two major advisory councils to the *Signoria*. Thus Francesco Tornabuoni wrote to Averardo de' Medici in December 1430, when the Gonfaloniers of Company were due to list the nominations for the *Tre Maggiori*, that 'if there should happen to be any one with whom you or Cosimo or any of your friends have influence . . . he should be written to, and enjoined to name me';[6] conversely, in November 1433 Mariotto Davanzati complained to Matteo Strozzi that 'our Gonfalonier is doing me an injustice', and asked him to see that when the names came to the vote under the Gonfalonier's direction, 'I should not be wronged just because I am not there'.[7]

The success of such pleas obviously depended to some extent on the local reputation and traditions of the supplicants, and certainly a citizen's political standing in the commune was materially affected by these factors; even after inclusion in the lists of eligibles, a man's chances of obtaining a majority of votes from the wider council depended heavily on the political record of his ancestors in the *gonfalone*. Those whose predecessors had been

---

[5] Molho, *Florentine Public Finances*, pp. 85–6, discusses change in the financial role of the *gonfalone* after 1427, while Brucker, *The Civic World*, pp. 484–5, observes that spokesmen for the *gonfaloni* opposed that change (Libri Fabarum 53, ff. 180v–181r).

[6] M.A.P. II, 397.

[7] C.S. 3ª ser. CXII, 142. The Davanzati were also *amici* of the Medici; perhaps their strong connection with the Strozzi expressed a need for some local support. The continuing importance of the *gonfalone* into the third quarter of the fifteenth century is discussed in a forthcoming article by myself and F. W. Kent based on the notarized records of meetings of the *gonfalone* of Lion Rosso between 1423 and 1463. Although this evidence mainly concerns the fiscal competence of the *gonfalone*, it suggests that the social and political role of the neighbourhood unit requires further investigation. F. W. Kent's examination of family residence patterns (*Household and Lineage*, Chs. 4, 5) incidentally throws much light on neighbourhood relationships. See also J. Heers, *Le clan familial au moyen âge* (Paris, 1974), Ch. 4, and Diane Owen Hughes, 'Urban Growth and Family Structure in Medieval Genoa', *Past and Present* lxvi (1975), 3–28.

solidly entrenched in major offices were placed in a favourable position at the top of the lists to be voted on; very few families moved from one *gonfalone* to another in the fifteenth century, and few of those who did ever began to match the political successes of the majority who remained.[8] As his relationship with neighbours in his *gonfalone* could thus significantly affect the economic and political well-being of the individual and his family, it is hardly surprising that powerful neighbours became natural centres of patronage and that this tendency could in turn increase the cohesion of the neighbourhood.

The original urban home of the Medici family was a small area of San Giovanni in the heart of the old centre of Florence, at the north-east corner of the Piazza di Mercato Vecchio, opposite the church of San Tommaso, and among the ancient towers, loggias, and houses belonging to the older of the city's nobility. However, from the mid-fourteenth century on several lines of the family, including that of Bicci, began to move out from the centre into the almost suburban area north of the Via Cerretani; their preferred parish became San Lorenzo, in the *gonfalone* of Lion d'oro, where they systematically built up their property-holdings over the next century or so.[9]

By 1427 the Medici neighbourhood was an extensive one—they were well distributed over three of the *gonfaloni* of San Giovanni— Lion d'oro, centred on the parish of San Lorenzo, Drago, stretching to the west and north of San Lorenzo and including the parishes of Santa Maria Maggiore and San Michele Berteldi, and Vaio, east of San Lorenzo, including the parishes of S. Michele

---

[8] With very few exceptions, those members of families most successful in the scrutinies belonged to the same *gonfalone*; see Kent, 'The Florentine *reggimento*' 589–93. Cf. the case of Giovanni Morelli, *Ricordi*, pp. 338–40. In 1394 he and his family moved from Borgo Santa Croce in the *gonfalone* of Lion Nero to rent a house owned by the Castellani in the district of Carro; although normally citizens were assessed for taxes in the area to which they traditionally belonged and where most of their property was situated, Morelli petitioned for an assessment in Carro, because, as he explained, owing to the influence of the Castellani and other *parenti* and *amici*, his tax burden there would be much lighter. However, in 1404 Morelli recorded his return to Lion Nero and the discrimination he experienced in the scrutinies there as a consequence of his move (*Ricordi*, pp. 428–9).

[9] See Isabelle Hyman's *Fifteenth Century Florentine Studies: The Palazzo Medici and a ledger for the Church of San Lorenzo* (New York, 1977), pp. 44–61. I am most grateful for her permission to read it before publication. See also Isabelle Hyman 'Notes and Speculations on S. Lorenzo, Palazzo Medici, and an Urban Project by Brunelleschi', *Journal of the Society of Architectural Historians*, xxiv (1975), 98–120.

Visdomini and San Michele in Orto. The borders of these *gon-faloni* were generally contiguous and constituted the three-quarters of San Giovanni stretching north and west.[10] Chiavi, the most easterly of the *gonfaloni* of San Giovanni and centred on the old parish of San Piero Scheraggio, contained according to the *catasto* of 1427 only one minor member of the Medici family;[11] the remaining thirty-one who submitted tax returns were more or less evenly distributed between the other three *gonfaloni*. The branch of Alamanno belonged to Drago, as did the minor members of the Cambio branches, the branch of Giambono, and part of those of Talento and Giovenco. In Vaio one-half of the Salvestro or main Cafaggiolo branch was established, represented by Averardo, his son, and grandson. The Bonino branch was also established here, along with sundry members of the Talento, Giovenco, and Alamanno branches. In Lion d'oro, in the parish of San Lorenzo, were the comparatively wealthy and powerful heirs of Cambio, and the most distinguished of the Medici households—that of Giovanni di Bicci himself and his sons, Cosimo and Lorenzo.[12]

The Medici appear as leaders of a local faction in this area as early as the 1340s. Villani described how in this period, when the *grandi* were up in arms,

the *popolo* of the quarter of San Giovanni, who chose as their leaders the Medici and the Rondinelli and Messer Ugo della Stufa, a judge, and the *popolani* of Borgo San Lorenzo, with the butchers and other artisans, without the permission of the commune, and being altogether about a thousand men without the addition of any other company or force of troops, launched an attack from several quarters on those partisans of the Adimari called the Cavicciuli.[13]

By the late 1420s their target had altered, and a few of the families who had supported them eighty years before were on the opposing

[10] On the boundaries of the *gonfaloni* see G. Carocci, *L'Illustratore fiorentino; calendario storico compilato da Guido Carocci* (1909), pp. 81–9; cf. the tentative and partial eighteenth-century reconstruction, Acqu. e Doni, 326. I owe the former reference to Miss Caroline Elam.

[11] Andrea di Lamberto de' Medici; there were also two Medici widows in this neighbourhood.

[12] Cat. 78, 79, 80, 81.

[13] Giovanni Villani, *Cronica*, ed. F. G. Dragomanni (4 vols., Florence, 1844–5), iv. 45.

side; nevertheless, the Medici reappear at this time as the leaders of a neighbourhood party of essentially similar composition.

In this society where families particularly of the second rank, politically and socially, depended to a considerable extent for the maintenance and improvement of their position in the ruling group on the patronage and protection of greater families preponderant in their local world, citizens in the area of San Giovanni and especially in Lion d'oro clustered under the lengthening shadow of the Medici house. In so far as the Medici demonstrably acted as a magnet for the hopes and ambitions of the lesser families in their *gonfalone*, it seems quite likely that their push to the newer residential areas north of the Duomo, which gathered impetus as the fourteenth century progressed, was the result of a considered determination to establish a local base from which to build up their influence in a promising district where they had already found support, and where, in contrast to the ancient area around the Mercato Vecchio, competition from other great and old-established houses with strong spheres of established influence would be minimized.

Of the 93 Medici partisans who can be identified as belonging to a particular *gonfalone*, it appears that 45 (about half) lived in San Giovanni, and 20 of those 45 were established in Lion d'oro.[14] The Mediceans of San Giovanni were not merely numerous; they also included many of the keenest and most irrevocably committed partisans. However, by contrast with the Medici *parenti*, they were not, on the whole, men comparable in wealth, reputation, and status to the Medici family, choosing to support

[14] Those resident in Lion d'oro were Francesco di Lorenzo Benintendi, Antonio di Ser Lodovico della Casa, Nerone di Nigi Dietisalvi and his son Dietisalvi, Giuliano, Simone and Piero di Francesco Ginori, the eight Martelli brothers (sons of Niccolò di Ugolino), Antonio di Ser Tommaso Masi, Luigi, Giovanni and Lorenzo di Ugo della Stufa (Cat. 497).

Those in Drago were Neri di Domenico Bartolini-Scodellari, Bernardo di Cristofano Carnesecchi, Matteo di Niccolò Cerretani, Ser Martino di Ser Luca Martini, Messer Bartolomeo di Giovanni Orlandini, Daddo di Simone Pecori (ibid. 498).

In Vaio were Battista di Doffo Arnolfi, Ser Ciao di Ser Pagolo Ciai, Salvestro di Michele Lapi, Nofri Parenti, Pagolo di Folco Portinari, Piero Ricci, Bartolomeo di Bartolomeo and Tedaldo Tedaldi, Ser Niccolò Tinucci, Giovanni, Piero, and Puccio d'Antonio Pucci (ibid. 500).

In Chiavi were Luca di Maso degli Albizzi, Neri di Francesco Fioravanti, Andrea di Guglielmino Pazzi, Niccolò di Bartolomeo Valori, Agnolo di Filippo Pandolfini, Papi Villani (ibid. 499). Although they cannot be personally located, it is probable, since all their *consorti* appear in these *gonfaloni*, that Papi Tedaldi also lived in Vaio, and Benedetto di Ser Guido di Messen Tommaso Masi in Lion d'oro.

them in the inevitable divisions of oligarchic society and contracting their alliances with the Medici in conscious preference to
others with whom they might have associated themselves. They
were the smaller men, dependent upon the patronage of their
social superiors, or the newer men, joined indissolubly with the
Medici at an essential point in the progress of their social ascent,
or the survivors of older families who had retained their traditions into the fifteenth century, but not their political influence
and social importance, which they needed to build up anew.[15]

Neighbourhood proved a firm foundation on which to build
a personal party; within the Medici orbit *parentado*, *vicinanza*, and
amicizia were clearly mutually reinforcing. There were several
marriages between Mediceans of the same *gonfalone*, including
those of the Dietisalvi–Ginori and the Ginori–Ciai mentioned
above, and others between partisans within the Medici group of
gonfaloni like those of the Pucci and the Orlandini, and the Medici
and Pecori.[16] Opportunities for close association were fostered
by the physical intimacy of the Medici and their partisans with
one another. Giovanni di Bicci, and later Cosimo and Lorenzo,
lived literally next door to the Ginori; the Della Stufa and the
Dietisalvi were similarly close.[17] Clustered as they were in what
is now the Via Cerretani, and its continuation bordering the
Duomo, the streets which fanned northwards from it, and those
which intersected them, the modern Borgo San Lorenzo, and Vie

[15] Cf. below, pp. 116–26. Among them were members of the Bartolini-
Scodellari, Carnesecchi, Cerretani, and Orlandini families in Drago; the Lapi,
Portinari, Ricci, and Pucci in Vaio, and in Lion d'oro the Dietisalvi, Ginori, Della
Stufa, and Martelli.

[16] Litta, *Famiglie Celebri* x, Tav. I; Ancisa, BB, f. 33r. When Dietisalvi di Nerone
married the orphan Margherita, 'figliuola che fu di Benvenuto di Zanobi di Ser
Gino' (*Ricordi*, MSS. 85, f. 97r), her dowry was provided by Piero, Simone, and
Giuliano di Francesco di Ser Gino; a daughter of the latter married Bernardo di
Iacopo di Ser Francesco Ciai (L. Passerini, *Genealogia e storia della famiglia Ginori*,
Florence, 1876, Tav. VIII).

[17] Cat. 78, ff. 159r–161r, 164r–167r. Among the other Mediceans with neighbouring properties were Francesco Benintendi and Giovanni di Bicci (ibid., ff. 19v–
21r); the Martelli brothers and Nicola di Vieri de' Medici (ff. 70v–72r); Andrea di
Niccolò Giugni and the Corbinelli (73, ff. 383r–384r); Bartolomeo Orlandini and
Salvestro and Piero Pucci (79, ff. 151r, ff.); Averardo de' Medici and Nofri Tedaldi
(ibid. 82r); Averardo also rented a house to Bardo di Ser Bardo near to his own.
Many Mediceans also had adjacent holdings in the *contado*, e.g. Simone Ginori and
the sons of Vieri de' Medici (Cat. 78, ff. 493v–496r). These precise observations on
residence are based on the location of the 'house of habitation' given in the *catasto*
reports of 1427 and 1433; obviously when the house was a rented one, the writer's
residence in that particular area of the *gonfalone* might be comparatively temporary.

Faenza, Della Stufa, Ginori, Martelli, Cavour, Ricasoli, Servi, and Pucci, whose very names bear witness to the predominance of Mediceans in this area, most would have lived within a comparatively short distance of one another and would undoubtedly have met constantly in the pursuit of their everyday affairs.[18]

A comparison of the geographical distribution of Mediceans and exiles suggests that the Medici and their friends effectively dominated these *gonfaloni* and that their neighbours were probably either drawn into the orbit of their influence, or forced into opposition against it. Not only did these three *gonfaloni* of San Giovanni contain half the Medici party—they also contained a disproportionately high, though lesser number of Medici opponents when compared with the remainder of the city. Most of the leading families in this area who were not Medici partisans appear among those exiled by the victorious Mediceans in 1434.[19] Local residents may well have been faced with the choice either of joining the Mediceans or seeking powerful protection elsewhere.

That such a high proportion of partisans was drawn from the Medici neighbourhood was undoubtedly partly due to the fact that the party was essentially the personal creation of the Medici family, whose dominating leadership appears to have been unchallenged. The centripetal dynamics of the Medici party are apparent in the residential patterns of the remainder of the partisans who were not also their neighbours in San Giovanni. Of those who lived outside this area almost half were men of outstanding importance in the city in their own right; notably only

[18] Most citizens in their *catasto* reports identified the street in which they actually resided; this is the essential information illuminating the face-to-face element of neighbourhood relationships, and with the aid of works of topographical reference like the *Stradario Storico e Amministrativo della Città e del Comune di Firenze* (Florence, 1913), and W. Limburger, *Die Gebäude von Florenz* (Leipzig, 1910), it is possible to identify most ancient streets and therefore to outline the approximate anatomy of the Medici neighbourhood. However, as a number named only their parish of residence and very few actual houses can be precisely reconstructed in their relation to others, it has proved impossible to construct a map indicating patterns and density of residence which is sufficiently accurate to be suitable for reproduction.

[19] Among those residents of Lion d'oro who were exiled or otherwise punished in 1434 were Piero Ciampegli, the three exiles of the Guasconi family, the Rondinelli family, and Nuccio di Benintendi Solosmei. Rinaldo degli Albizzi's son-in-law, Bartolomeo Nelli, also lived in Lion d'oro. The exiles in Drago included Michele di Alessandro Arrigucci, Michele di Galeotto Baronci, Lorenzo di Giovanni del Bulletta, the Della Casa family, Terrino Manovelli, and Piero Panciatichi, who was fined. Residents of Vaio exiled were Bartolomeo di Nofri Bischeri, Cristofano d'Agnolo da Pino, and Richoldo di Ser Paolo Richoldi.

two of the Medici neighbours can be classified in this category.[20] However, in marked contrast to many leading families opposed to the Medici, and in contravention of a common Florentine social pattern, there is no evidence that they themselves in their turn drew the less-distinguished Medici sympathizers in their own *gonfaloni* under a private protective shadow. Mediceans of all social classes throughout the city seem to have looked directly to the Medici in San Giovanni for leadership and patronage, so that while on the one hand the Medici exploited the strength of local ties and traditions in the creation of the party, on the other the party acted as a centralizing force cutting across the traditional tendencies to association within the *gonfalone* and providing a particular alternative to local separatism.[21]

The Medici building programme in the parish of San Lorenzo from the late twenties on may be seen as a tangible expression of their growing power and influence, and its relationship to the party. In this period the Medici were the leaders of a group of patrons planning to rebuild the church of San Lorenzo, while their consolidation at the same time of the Medici land-holdings on the Via Larga implies that they may already have formed the intention of erecting the present palace on the site just opposite the church.[22] Isabelle Hyman, after assembling the scanty but suggestive evidence concerning the early plans for the Medici palace, has suggested that the tradition that Cosimo rejected Brunelleschi's original design as too sumptuous may well have been accurate, not because its decoration was too elaborate but because it presented the palace facing towards the church of San Lorenzo. Cosimo was not in fact sufficiently bold to unify his palace with San Lorenzo and the square, and thus as a private citizen to rival the great religious and civic centres of the city.[23] According to

[20] Apart from Cosimo and Averardo de' Medici, 17 of the total of 96 Mediceans belonged to the inner *reggimento*, but only 2 (Nerone di Nigi Dietisalvi and Giovanni di Lorenzo della Stufa) were from the three Medicean *gonfaloni* of San Giovanni.

[21] This impression may be due to the lack of evidence concerning the associations of the *amici* comparable to that available for the Medici (cf. above, pp. 60–1); on the other hand, it may be a glimpse of a more centralized social and patronage orientation which could well have resulted from the Medici ascendancy.

[22] However, the 1443 Ginori land trade was the first concrete evidence of building plans (Hyman, *Fifteenth Century Florentine Studies*, pp. 95–6).

[23] Ibid., pp. 113–21. For a later hint of Medici preference in this matter, see Carol Herselle Krinsky, 'A view of the Palazzo Medici and the Church of San Lorenzo', *Journal of the Society of Architectural Historians* xxviii (1969) 133–5.

Richard Trexler, even the Medici tendency in the 1420s and 1430s
to inflate the number of dignitaries in San Lorenzo, their own
parish church, was 'a sign that the family sought to challenge
the charisma of the commune';[24] notably, as Hyman observes,
it was in March 1434, while the Medici were away in exile, that
the *Signoria* took the initiative of entrusting to Brunelleschi the
task of enlarging the Piazza San Lorenzo as part of a general
scheme for the beautification of the city.

Certainly in their building programme, as in their bid for
political power, the Medici expressed their ambitions in a local
context and received considerable support from their friends and
neighbours; the clearing of the site for the palace would have been
impossible without the co-operation of their ardent partisans and
next-door neighbours, the Ginori, who not only sold land to them
as requested, but even took part in an exchange of property to
enable the Medici to consolidate their holding.[25] In both spheres
they proceeded cautiously in the realization of ambitions which
may well have been boldly conceived from the very beginning.
For any one family to embark ostentatiously upon the rebuilding
of San Lorenzo single-handed would certainly have been unac-
ceptable to its fellows and rivals in the ruling group; although the
construction of a new sacristy was completed in 1428 under the
patronage of Giovanni di Bicci, the larger conception of a whole
new church was, ostensibly, linked in the twenties not with the
Medici alone, but with eight other families of the *gonfalone* of Lion
d'oro—the Rondinelli, Ginori, Della Stufa, Neroni, Ciai, Marig-
nolli, Martelli, and the family of Marco di Luca.[26] Most, if not

---

[24] Trexler, 'Ritual Behaviour', pp. 128–9.

[25] Hyman, *Fifteenth Century Florentine Studies*, esp. pp. 115–116, 54–87. Apart from
the fact that the Medici appear to have offered a house for rent at a very cheap rate as
an inducement to the artist Donatello to come from Rome to work for them (Hyman,
64–5), while they also rented houses to Michelozzo, the eventual architect of the
palace, and less affluent political partisans like Battista Arnolfi and Niccolò
Cocco-Donati (below, pp. 78, 127–8), the close analogy between their artistic and
political patronage is apparent in their relationship with Michelozzo. The latter was
employed by the commune on military construction during the war with Lucca
but when his supplies failed to arrive he wrote to Averardo soliciting his help in the
name of the *amici*: 'Vi priegho per utile e onore del comune e nostro vi piaccia
aiutarci' (M.A.P. II, 354, 3 May 1430). He asked Averardo at the same time, as his
friend and neighbour, '[di] mandare insino a chasa e fate loro sapere siano tutti sani'
(II, 352, 1 May 1430), and added that he also had some profitable information for
Averardo but that 'vorrei potervi parlare a bocha'.

[26] P. Ginori-Conti, *La Basilica di San Lorenzo e la famiglia Ginori* (Florence, 1940),
pp. 50–1. According to E. Gombrich, in his discussion of Medici self-expression in

indeed all, of these were partisans so closely identified with the interests of the Medici family that the project may in fact be seen as primarily their personal undertaking, though it is at the same time an expression of the breadth and strength and unity of the Medici party in Lion d'oro.[27]

Not inappropriately, then, the subsequent history of the rebuilding of San Lorenzo in a sense mirrors that of the Medici party. A beginning had been made under Giovanni's direction by a small group of his earlier and more established adherents; its completion on a substantial scale had to await the definitive triumph of the Medici in 1434. When finally in 1441 Cosimo took up once more the plan to subsidize the construction of a *cappella maggiore* he received the support of no less than sixty-three of his fellow citizens of Lion d'oro, many of whom by that time were well established as leading figures in the ruling group under the ascendancy of the Medici.[28]

(v) THE BANK

We have seen how the Medici set about compensating for the inherent disabilities of their kin group in the struggle for political power by extending it along the natural lines of *parentado* and *vicinanza*. The strength and cohesion of the party thus created was one of the pillars which supported the family in its rise to power and after; the other was the Medici bank.[1] It is notable then that in

patronage, 'The Early Medici as Patrons of Art', in *Italian Renaissance Studies*, 279–311, the Medici before 1434 participated essentially in traditional and collective, rather than private enterprises, with a generosity which was finely calculated to express superiority but not to flaunt it (281–2).

[27] It has recently been suggested by F. A. D'Accone, 'The Singers of S. Giovanni in Florence during the 15th Century', *American Musicological Society*, xiv (1961), 307–58, esp. 308 ff. and 351, that the Medici family had private control in the twenties over an important area of supposedly public patronage—that of the provision of polyphonic singers attached to the Baptistery. Though the evidence for this is suggestive rather than conclusive, it may add a new dimension to our view of the Medici as patrons before 1434, which is particularly important in the light of Gombrich's suggestion that after that date patronage was 'one of the chief instruments of Medici policy' ('The Early Medici' 280), and of the close parallels between the political and the artistic in the progressively changing style of Medici patronage.

[28] Ginori-Conti, *La Basilica*, pp. 236–40.

[1] Below, pp. 303–5, 335; cf. de Roover, *The Rise and Decline*, p. 5, and L. Marks, 'The Financial Oligarchy in Florence under Lorenzo', *Italian Renaissance Studies*, 123–47.

the selection of partners and factors in the bank Giovanni and Cosimo drew on a pool of associates which extended outwards from their kinsmen, who outnumbered the members of any other house involved,[2] to include a considerable proportion of their relatives, neighbours, and friends. The characteristics desirable in business associates, particularly in partners as distinct from factors, were very similar to those preferred in *parenti, vicini,* and *amici*;[3] obviously their social and personal attributes could materially affect the success or failure of an enterprise, and absolute trustworthiness was also a vital consideration. Many Florentines operating in small two or three-man businesses seem to have preferred kinsmen as *compagni*;[4] in the Medici organization, a mammoth for its day,[5] the latter were almost invariably men closely bound to the family in some way, often through a multiplicity of ties, which helped to bolster the security of their crucial economic base while further consolidating the party through its association with the commercial as well as the political enterprises of the family.[6] The close analogy between the bank and the party created by Giovanni di Bicci and his sons is also evident in the highly centralized structure of both, and the same firm direction which Cosimo gave his branch managers is apparent in his letters to Averardo concerning the family and the party role in political activity and events.[7]

The Medici association with the Bardi exemplifies the business alliance with partisans and *parenti,* though ironically it failed in the crisis of 1433–4 where others more recent and less solidly cemented endured. Ever since the foundation of the bank, Gio-

---

[2] De Roover, *The Rise and Decline,* pp. 383–5.

[3] See Morelli, *Ricordi,* p. 226; cf. pp. 161, 264.

[4] See Cat. 74–85 (1427) *passim*; cf. R. Goldthwaite, *Private Wealth*; his specific family studies contain many such examples, despite his general comments on economic individualism (esp. pp. 253–7).

[5] Cf. de Roover, *The Rise and Decline,* p. 3.

[6] One of the more obvious concrete contributions of *parenti* and *amici* to the Medici banking enterprise was made by the Cavalcanti; part of Lorenzo di Giovanni's dowry for his bride Ginevra Cavalcanti was a property in Porta Rossa which became the Medici *tavola* (ibid., p. 19). The Medici view of the close connection between friends and business associates is apparent in a *Ricordo* instructing Bartolomeo de' Bardi on his departure in 1420 to take up a position as manager of the Rome branch. Bartolomeo was cautioned against giving credit without discrimination on the grounds that 'a creditor who had to put pressure on his debtors ran the danger of losing friends as well as money' (ibid., p. 90); cf. M.A.P. LXVIII, 402.

[7] De Roover, 'Cosimo de' Medici' 473; *The Rise and Decline,* pp. 78–9.

vanni and his sons had made a practice of choosing their associates as far as possible from either the Medici or the Bardi
families, and the same policy was pursued by Averardo and his
heirs in the staffing of their bank. More than a dozen Bardi were
occupied in one or sometimes both of the Medici organizations
between 1393, when they were created out of the dissolution of
Vieri di Cambio's bank, and 1434.[8] When Giovanni di Bicci took
over Messer Vieri's Rome branch he established a partnership
with Benedetto di Lippaccio de' Bardi.[9] Benedetto di Lippaccio
later became general manager of the entire firm, and on his death
in 1420 was succeeded in the position by his brother Ilarione.[10]
When he in turn died in 1433 his temporary replacement was his
nephew Lippaccio di Benedetto.[11] A third brother, Andrea di
Lippaccio, had been in the service of Averardo since 1402 or
before, and was Averardo's general manager for fifteen years or
so until his death in 1434.[12] Other members of the Bardi house
were employed in less responsible positions in the Medici bank,
or associated with them in some other way; among these was
Bardo di Francesco di M. Alessandro de' Bardi, with whom
Averardo's bank had *accomandite*, or limited partnerships, in
Barcelona and Valencia.[13] Bardo was one of those exiled on the
return of the Medici in 1434, and Raymond de Roover observes
that in the reorganization of the bank which took place subsequently, the long and close connection with the Bardi family was
severed. He suggests in explanation that its members may have
wavered in their political allegiance or failed sufficiently to support the Medici during the difficult and crucial period of their

[8] *The Rise and Decline*, p. 39, cf. Table, p. 396. De Roover observes that by the
1430s 'the importance of family ties in business was on the wane' (p. 52); this is
obviously true in comparison with the thirteenth and fourteenth centuries, but his
own evidence (pp. 383–5) testifies to the continuing participation of members of the
wider family in Cosimo's bank.

[9] Ibid., p. 38.

[10] De Roover, 'Cosimo de' Medici' 470. Ilarione had until then directed the Rome
branch.

[11] *The Rise and Decline*, pp. 36, 38.

[12] Ibid., p. 38, gives his date of death as 1433. In fact he was probably still alive
in September 1434 (M.A.P. XCIV, 116), and possibly even in early December (ibid.
29), but was certainly dead by the end of that year (LXXXVII, 20).

[13] Cf. Bartolomeo d'Andrea de' Bardi (*c.* 1397–1429), who was put at the head of
Giovanni di Bicci's Rome branch in 1420 (de Roover, *The Rise and Decline*, p. 49).
The clerical staff of the *tavola* in 1414 included Agnolo di Zanobi de' Bardi and Vieri
di Bartolomeo (p. 232).

exile from Florence. Although the matter remains obscure, there is some evidence from the Medici letters to support this assumption.[14]

Of course the Bardi were not the only *parenti* and *amici* to be fundamentally incorporated into the operations of the bank. Among the more favoured families were the Portinari; they were related to the Medici by the marriage to Nanna Portinari of Giovanni di Niccolò de' Medici, whose son Rosso was also with the *accomanda* of Naples between 1415 and 1425.[15] In an earlier reorganization of 1420 Giovanni di Adovardo Portinari was made manager of the Venice branch,[16] while his brother Folco became the new local manager in Florence.[17] On Folco's death in 1431 Cosimo assumed responsibility for his children and had them brought up in his own household;[18] not surprisingly, then, the name of Pigello di Folco Portinari appears on the list of Medici partisans in this period.[19] Folco's brothers Accerito and Giovanni were also associated with the bank in the thirties, and the connection with the Portinari continued for several decades until it too

[14] De Roover, *The Rise and Decline*, pp. 54–6, 234. De Roover suggests that Lippaccio di Benedetto, son of the first *socio* of Giovanni di Bicci, and director of the Florentine *tavola*, behaved particularly ambiguously; nevertheless, his letter to Piero di Cosimo, written 30 Sept. 1433 (M.A.P. XVI, 346), is profuse enough in its expressions of sympathy for the Medici misfortune. Conversely, the last extant letter of Averardo's manager, Andrea di Lippaccio, written shortly before his death and addressed to Giuliano di Averardo in Rome in July 1434 (ibid. V, 707), strongly suggests a breakdown in his relations with the Medici and their friends. He was clearly piqued by what he considered to be the Medici failure to consult with him on various issues of importance : 'Diciesti anche quando fosse tenpo mi parleresti più largho. Non so questo tenpo quando sia.' His sense of grievance seems to have been exacerbated by the conviction that other *amici*, more in the Medici favour and confidence, were refusing to co-operate with him; he mentioned particularly Francesco Tornabuoni, Andrea Pazzi (Giuliano's partner in Rome since 1422), Antonio da Pescia, soon to replace his own nephew Lippaccio di Benedetto Bardi as one of the bank's general managers, and most virulently various members of the Gianfigliazzi family, whom he claimed had failed in their obligations and duties, and to whom he disparagingly referred as 'questi tuoi Gianfigliazzi'. Since all of these remained as the trusted intimates of the Medici family and were subsequently to enjoy all the prestige and promotion which accompanied their victory, it would seem clear that Andrea himself was the 'odd man out' and that by this time the *amici* may have been acting for the Medici in contriving to squeeze him out of the charmed circle.

[15] De Roover, *The Rise and Decline*, pp. 50, 387.   [16] Ibid., p. 49.

[17] Ibid., pp. 49–50.   [18] Ibid., pp. 75–6.

[19] Conversely, a kinsman, Bernardo Portinari, was alleged in 1429 to be a prominent member of an illegal society whose other leaders were three citizens subsequently exiled for their opposition to the Medici—Roberto di Lionardo dall'Antella, Bernarba di Bartolo Bischeri, and Francesco di Giovanni Bucelli (Giud. Appelli 75, f. 724r–v); Brucker, *The Civic World*, pp. 492–3.

was cut by Lorenzo de' Medici in 1478 when the extent of their responsibility for the bank's disastrous losses at that time became clear.[20]

After the dismissal of Lippaccio di Benedetto de' Bardi as general manager of the bank, his duties were jointly shared by Antonio di M. Francesco Salutati [da Pescia] and Giovanni d'Amerigo Benci, previously managers in Rome and Geneva. The former had been in the Medici service since 1416 and was active and prominent in sustaining the Medici enterprises from Venice during the period of the exile;[21] the latter was to become Cosimo's chief and most trusted adviser in business matters,[22] and was certainly one of the *amici* in the years before 1434. Others who were both political partisans and major figures in the Medici bank in the late twenties and early thirties included Giuntino di Guido Giuntini, a managing partner of the wool-shop in Florence since 1431 and whose kinsman Andrea was also associated with it by 1433,[23] Francesco di Francesco Berlinghieri, manager of the silk-shop in Florence from 1433 onwards,[24] and Andrea Pazzi, manager of Averardo's bank in Rome.[25]

A number of those who were *amici* before 1434 were given a major share in the operations of the bank only after that date; the most striking example is that of the Martelli family mentioned above as neighbours of the Medici in San Giovanni and among their most ardent political supporters since the 1390s. One of the brothers, Roberto di Niccolò, had been a factor in Rome since 1424, but became head of that branch in 1439;[26] Antonio di Niccolò, who as a factor in Venice had also been instrumental in keeping the bank afloat between 1433 and 1434, was made assistant manager there in the reorganization of 1435.[27] Altogether five of the nine sons of Niccolò served in the Medici bank and three of the heirs of the eldest, Ugolino, followed in their footsteps.[28] The Sassetti family is a similar case. Rosso was a partisan of the Medici before 1434; after that date several Sassetti

---

[20] De Roover, *The Rise and Decline*, p. 350.
[21] De Roover, 'Cosimo de' Medici' 471. See also *The Rise and Decline*, pp. 53, 55-7.
[22] De Roover, *The Rise and Decline*, p. 57.
[23] Ibid., pp. 54, 60.
[24] Ibid., p. 378; see also p. 60. The co-manager was Piero di Domenico Corsi (p. 68); Banco Corsi was a Medici partisan before 1434.
[25] Ibid., p. 37.
[26] Ibid., pp. 58, 66.
[27] Ibid., pp. 56, 82, 247.
[28] e.g. ibid., pp. 218, 276-7; Table, p. 388.

appear in the Medici service, including Francesco, who was
general manager of the Medici bank from 1459 to 1490.[29] In
other instances the kinsmen of pre-1434 political partisans of the
Medici, like Banco Corsi and Giovanni d'Antonio da Panzano,
are later found holding positions in the bank.[30]

Seldom, it would appear, did the Medici fail to utilize a relationship or to turn it to advantage in their business dealings. An
aide-mémoire of Cosimo to Marco Spinellini, concerning the
latter's trip to Bruges and London in 1430, instructs Spinellini
to greet and brief Antonio di Francesco and Giovanni Ginori on
the progress of Medici business matters, and 'to recommend to
them our affairs and those of all our companies'.[31] In Lübeck their
correspondents *c.* 1413 were Gherardo Bueri and his partners;
Gherardo was the first cousin once removed of Piccarda Bueri,
the wife of Giovanni di Bicci. His partner was Lodovico Baglioni,
of the Perugian dynasty with whom the Medici cultivated good
relations, and who during the Medici exile were a strong source
of the extra-Florentine diplomatic pressure which helped to
bring about their recall.[32]

As with the Medici practice of making marriages with their
amici where possible, it is difficult to know which of the multiple
ties binding them to their banking associates was forged first. It
is obvious however, that given the nature and extent of Medici
political ambitions, and the essential role which the bank played
in their fulfilment, that even more than most Florentine merchants the Medici had to be able to trust their business associates;
in areas where the administration of the bank and the interests of
the party affected each other directly, they could not afford to put
the care of their affairs in the hands of other than their *amici*.
This was notably demonstrated when the crisis came with the
exile of the leaders of the family in 1433; it seems clear, as Cosimo
himself observed in his *Ricordi*, that one of the major aims of this

[29] Cf. Fruosino da Panzano, who became assistant to the manager of the Florentine wool-shop in 1440 (ibid., p. 60).

[30] Another such partisan, Antonio di Ser Lodovico della Casa, who had been in
the Medici employ since 1420 and was in the Roman office by the end of the decade,
became manager there when Salutati was sent to Florence in 1435. Benci, also called
to Florence, was succeeded by Antonio's brother, Ruggieri, as manager of the
accomanda (limited partnership) at Geneva (ibid., pp. 56, 205).

[31] M.A.P. LXVIII, 2.

[32] *The Rise and Decline*, p. 63. Bueri had previously been in the service of the Medici
at Venice. See also below, p. 304.

action was to disrupt the function of the Medici banking enterprise 'and by . . . preventing me from availing myself of my assets,
to bankrupt us'.[33] In fact the Florentine branch, under Bardi
management, nearly did go under, but in the end Giovanni Benci
pulled it through, and was able to write to Cosimo and Lorenzo
in August 1434 that despite 'the numerous impediments existing
. . . it seems more profitable to keep the bank open'.[34] Indeed the
correspondence of this period suggests that *amici* like the Pazzi,
Gianfigliazzi, and Tornabuoni, remaining in Florence, and the
Martelli and Antonio da Pescia, who seem to have formed themselves as a liaison between Cosimo directing strategy in Venice and
the *amici* who were able to operate at home, were heavily occupied
in these months with protecting and defending the financial as
well as the political interests of their friends and patrons.[35] The
most concrete example of this is the decision of Cosimo and
Averardo to transfer as much as possible of their business in
Florence into the name of Averardo's son-in-law, the wealthy
banker Antonio di Salvestro Serristori, thus turning aside some
of the force of the economic discrimination to which their position as exiles made them so particularly vulnerable; various
members of the Medici family and their *amici* were instructed 'to
secretly transfer everything into Antonio di Salvestro's name'.[36]

Although this particular strategy was an emergency measure,
it was not uncommon for Florentines to register companies and
hold credits in the *Monte*, the commune's funded debt, in the
names of heirs or associates rather than of the principal investors
themselves.[37] This is a habit which makes it very difficult in many
cases to disentangle the financial affairs of the Medici from those
of their friends with whom they were closely connected in
business, and it has some bearing on any attempt to assess how
much truth is involved in the almost traditional belief that the
Medici fortune was the basis of their political success in the most
immediate sense—that they essentially bought their partisans by
enriching them wholesale from the coffers of the bank.[38] Cavalcanti's comments on the prosperity of some of the *amici* are
partly responsible for this view. For instance, he described

[33] *Ricordi*, p. 97.
[34] M.A.P. XIII, 48; cf. de Roover, 'Cosimo de' Medici' 470.
[35] Kent, 'I Medici in esilio' 34–9.   [36] M.A.P. V, 699, 702.
[37] De Roover, *The Rise and Decline, passim*.
[38] Cf. also Martines, *The Social World*, p. 19.

Domenico di Zanobi Frasca as 'an *amico* of Cosimo, and more-over, although virtually a nobody, he acquired great wealth under Cosimo's sponsorship'.[39] He also referred to Cosimo's fabled generosity and declared that 'because he was a great benefactor to those who became his friends, many of the Buondelmonti, and particularly the sons of Messer Andrea, became enthusiastic supporters of Cosimo and his interests'.[40]

Ser Niccolò Tinucci, an *amico* of the Medici who, under torture in 1433 by the anti-Mediceans, made a denunciation which repre-sented the Medici as conspirators against the authority of law and the commune in every possible respect, accused them of bribing officials to aid them in various ways.[41] From what we know of current political conditions and practice, they almost certainly did so as a matter of course; this is undoubtedly implied in Cosimo's description of how he induced his captors with 800 florins and 500 florins apiece to ensure his safety in 1433, and his observation that in this respect 'they were not very bold, for if they had wanted money, they could have had ten thousand or more for my safety'.[42]

However, Medicean financial aid to the *amici* may customarily have assumed more modest and more natural forms. They rented houses to some of their friends at apparently favourable rates;[43] it was also taken for granted that if the *amici* fell into arrears in the payment of their tax debts to the commune, these would be settled for them by the Medici.[44] In fact this was essentially money spent in their own self-interest in order to keep their followers off the *specchio*, the list of communal debtors ineligible to hold office, and thus to avoid their disqualification for the positions through which they were expected to promote the Medici interests. This

[39] *Istorie*, p. 306; the Della Frasca were very new men, having had their first Prior only in 1417.

[40] Ibid., p. 263. The *catasto* of 1427 (Cat. 74, f. 88v) does indeed record loans totalling 3,500 florins from Cosimo de' Medici and co. to M. Simone di Andrea Buondelmonti.

[41] *Examina*, p. 400.   [42] *Ricordi*, p. 97.

[43] In 1427 Giovanni di Bicci was renting houses to two other of the leading Medici partisans, Battista Arnolfi and Niccolò Cocco-Donati (Cat. 49, f. 1157v); Hyman, *Fifteenth Century Florentine Studies*, p. 65, notes that they were the landlords of Michelozzo and Donatello. There was also the charity normally extended by patricians to the poor; see the report of Cosimo and Lorenzo in 1433 (Cat. 497, f. 177r). Some poor persons were allowed to live rent free in their houses 'per l'amore d'Iddio'.

[44] See, e.g., M.A.P. III, 8, 122.

connection is made quite clear in a letter from Bartolomeo Orlandini, asking Averardo to settle his taxes so that his name would not be entered on the debtors' rolls, 'and therefore I beg you to get me out of this shameful situation in order that God may grant you the honour which you and your friends desire'.[45] The Medici were by no means the only patrons to indulge in this practice;[46] there is, moreover, some indication that such payments were regarded as loans rather than as gifts or bribes.[47] Of course, it is hardly to be expected that evidence concerning actual bribery, particularly on a large scale, would survive, so the question must necessarily to some extent remain an open one. However, a general examination of the business affairs and assets of their leading partisans gives us no reason to believe that the Medici distributed indiscriminate largesse to their followers. Several of the Medici *amici*, including those as closely identified with the family and party interests as the Pucci and the Cocco-Donati, submitted tax declarations which indicate that they were in modest, and in some cases quite straitened, financial circumstances.[48]

The only real light which their *catasto* reports throw on financial relations between the Medici and their friends concerns the number of *amici* who were the recipients of generous loans from the company of Cosimo and Lorenzo in the twenties and thirties. In the period between 1427 and 1433 thirty-nine of the *amici* named the Medici as their personal creditors, often for quite substantial sums.[49] In the case of those associated with the

---

[45] Ibid. V, 14.

[46] Rinaldo degli Albizzi apparently did the same for Bernardo Guadagni, and with similar motives (Cavalcanti, *Istorie*, p. 266); cf. M.A.P. III, 122.

[47] See, e.g., a letter from the Medici partisan Ser Ciao to Averardo (M.A.P. LXVI, 31) with a message to 'Piero, al bancho . . . ricordategli che paghi quelli miei catasti e che m'avisi se niente a d'avere da me e io gli le manderò prestamente'. Cf. Guasti, *Commissioni* iii. 326, Ciao di Pagolo to Giuliano (27 Jan. 1430; 1429 *s.f.*): 'Prega'vi pagassi non so che miei catasti che io resto da luglio in qua, e mi avisassi il chi, e prestamente per lo primo ve gli manderò.'

[48] Twenty-five of the *amici* whose financial status can be clearly established had deductions and obligations exceeding their assets.

[49] Among those in 1427 or 1433 were Niccolò del Benino (Cat. 489, ff. 201r–203v); Ser Ciao di Pagolo (81, f. 223r–v); Piero Ginori (497, ff. 613r–615v); Piero Guicciardini (488, ff. 318v–322v); Ugolino Martelli (497, ff. 758r–760v). Their creditors included not only Giovanni di Bicci and his sons, but also Orlando di Guccio, Vieri di Nicola, Bernardo d'Antonio, and Bernardo d'Alamanno de' Medici. Concerning the information given below on loans and on the membership of business companies, it should be noted that although the general business

bank, this money may well have represented their own investments in Medici transactions, subsumed under personal accounts because of their informal nature.[50] A percentage of the loans would presumably have been made as part of the normal banking business of a family who were among the greatest financiers, not only of Florence, but of all Europe at this time, and the Medici indeed lent freely to Florentines of various political inclinations, including a number of their opponents. However, once these provisos have been made, it is nevertheless notable that a considerable proportion of the Medici personal debtors within Florence were also their *amici*, or the immediate relatives of these friends, and by the same token, most of the Medici *amici* who obtained large personal loans during this period borrowed from their patrons.[51]

These facts suggest that the financial advantage of friendship with the Medici may have been more typically the ready availability of generous financial backing and support than the likelihood of whole-sale enrichment, which even the resources of the Medici bank would not have permitted on a significant scale, and which would have been quite out of keeping with what we know about the Medici methods of operation in both the business and the political spheres. Large sums such as those to the Martelli, Ginori, and Cocco-Donati suggest investment in or support for

environment of most citizens would not appear to have changed radically over the six years between the *catasti* of 1427 and 1433, which may provide either consecutive or alternative sources of information in this section, both loans and companies in Florence could be of short duration, and statements about them may well apply only to a part of the period under dicussion.

[50] Although a broad picture of the general financial position of a large group of citizens can be illuminating and suggestive, the precise financial situation of individuals cannot be clarified entirely from the *catasto* reports, isolated from the context of private financial documents necessary to interpret the real meaning of debts and credits. Cf. J. Kirschner's observations with reference to legal texts, 'Some problems in the Interpretation of Legal Texts *re* the Italian City-States', *Archiv für Begriffgeschichte* xix (1975), pp. 17–27; Professor Kirschner kindly allowed me to read his article before publication. Most of the Medici *debitori* were not in fact their associates in the bank; those who were included members of the Bardi, Benci, Portinari, and Pazzi families (Cat. 487, ff. 287r–294r; 81, 479r, ff.)

[51] The tax report submitted by Cosimo and Lorenzo di Giovanni de' Medici in 1433 lists among the 'debitori de' lor libro proprio' (Cat. 497, f. 192r), Antonio di Cocco Donati, Giovanni di Lorenzo della Stufa, Tommaso di Bartolomeo Barbadori, Fruosino di Cece da Verazzano, Baldinaccio Cavalcanti, Niccolò di Cocco Donati, Giovacchino de' Ricci, and Monna Tommasa di Guidaccio Pecori. A notable feature of Medici loans to the *amici* was the length of their terms.

a business enterprise; smaller amounts may well have been disbursed to help partisans over crises in their financial affairs.[52]

If it is not accurate or appropriate to represent the Medici as using their wealth to buy support, it is nevertheless surely true that their wealth made them attractive patrons, and helped to draw supporters to them. Of the several surviving letters containing requests for loans in this period, most offer pledges of support in return which amount to declarations of partisanship. For instance, in July 1434 Matteo di Niccolò Cerretani requested a loan from Cosimo because he had a daughter to marry but could not himself raise the sum required for a suitable dowry. He observed that 'it is appropriate that I should turn to those whom I can rely on to help me' and he concluded his request to help with the promise that 'my sons and I will pledge ourselves in any way you wish . . . to serve you . . . For the moment there is nothing more to say, except that if ever I can do anything to please you, you may put this to the proof'.[53]

In general, the lists of debtors and creditors in the *catasto* reports reflect the wide range of the Florentine patrician's business dealings, and those of the Medici and their friends were no exception. Any analysis of these lists must take into account a variety of determining factors, such as the nature of the business in which the citizen concerned was involved, and the extent to which debtors and creditors, along with the business itself, were inheritances from his father, reflecting the past rather than the present. Nevertheless, on balance, the *catasto* reports of Mediceans create a strong general impression that in business, as in other areas, they preferred to co-operate and to deal with one another where possible. An entry in the 1427 return of Averardo's wealthy son-in-law Antonio Serristori may imply that Florentines were inclined occasionally, at least in a small way, to favour their friends and relations even if this proved to be bad business; he classified a number of debtors for small sums as 'my relatives and friends, who don't have the means, and so I don't expect to be able to get anything back from them'.[54] However, most of the

[52] For example, in 1433 the Martelli brothers owed Cosimo and co. 1,540 florins, and another 220 to the company in Venice (Cat. 497, ff. 758r–760v).
[53] M.A.P. V, 642, 31 July 1434. Cf. Giovacchino de' Ricci, who asked Giovanni di Cosimo for a loan of 10 florins (ibid. VII, 265), with the apologetic observation that this was the first time he had asked for such help since Giovanni came to manhood.   [54] Cat. 72, ff. 26r–39r; cf. below, pp. 125–6.

evidence concerning the business affairs of the Medici and their friends suggests that this was not usually the case and that in business, as in politics, co-operation was considered as redounding to the general benefit.

Not only Cosimo and Lorenzo, but several other members of the Medici family, including Orlando di Guccio, Vieri di Nicola, Bernardo d'Antonio, and Bernardo d'Alamanno, are mentioned frequently as creditors of the *amici*. Partisans also borrowed from others associated with the Medici bank, like the Bardi, and later Francesco da Pescia. Although the connections involved are much less material, and therefore less significant, the patterns of lending and borrowing reveal a network embracing a number of the *amici*, similar to that formed by marriages. Tommaso Barbadori borrowed from Piero di Giovanni Ginori as well as Cosimo;[55] Banco di Niccolò Bencivenni lent money to Battista Arnolfi and borrowed from Niccolò d'Andrea Carducci and Andrea de' Pazzi.[56] Neri di Francesco Fioravanti received loans from the Corbinelli, the Giugni, and Antonio di Salvestro Serristori.[57] Agnolo Pandolfini's creditors were a perfect set of Mediceans, including Giovanni di Bicci, Cosimo and Lorenzo, Francesco Tornabuoni, the Martelli, and Andrea de' Pazzi.[58]

A number of partnerships must also have helped to cement the solidarity between members of the Medici party. Several of the Medici friends were in business with one another; Giuntino di Guido Giuntini was the *compagno* in a cloth-making establishment of Simone Carnesecchi, who was closely related to that Bernardo di Cristofano Carnesecchi who had himself been a partner in the firm of Vieri de' Medici and co. in 1422.[59] Before he took over the management of the Medici silk-shop in 1433 Francesco Berlinghieri had been the partner of Piero de' Bardi, another *setaiuolo*.[60] From 1418 to 1421 Nerone di Nigi Dietisalvi shared a business with Piero di Francesco Ginori;[61] by 1427 his son

---

[55] Cat. 488, ff. 403r–404r.   [56] Ibid. 67, ff. 19r–20r.   [57] Ibid. 80, ff. 87r–93r.
[58] Ibid. 80, ff. 36r–38r; 499, ff. 738r–739v. Cf. Bartolomeo Orlandini, whose personal creditors were almost exclusively Mediceans, including Giovanni di Bicci, Cosimo, Piero Ginori, and members of the Davanzati, Carnesecchi, and Alberti families (ibid. 79, ff. 151, ff.; 498, ff. 75v–78r), or Alamanno Salviati, who borrowed from Cosimo and Lorenzo, Averardo de' Medici, and Antonio di Salvestro Serristori (ibid. 493, ff. 35r–37r).
[59] Ibid. 75, ff. 316v–317v; cf. Mallett, *The Florentine Galleys*, p. 203.
[60] Cat. 69, ff. 513v–514r; cf. de Roover, *The Rise and Decline*, p. 79.
[61] Cat. 78, ff. 159r–161r.

Dietisalvi was the *compagno* of Bartolomeo Corbinelli, brother of Giovanni.[62]

It would seem then that ties arising from association in business, as well as those created by neighbourhood and intermarriage, played a role in binding their partisans more closely to the Medici and to one another. However, it is important to stress that although the wealth which the Medici derived from their bank must have been a major factor in attracting partisans, and the bank itself a means of reinforcing their commitment by associating them economically as well as politically with the Medici interests, banking was essentially the foundation of Medici power for the far more fundamental reason that it made them a major financial force, not only in Florence, but throughout Italy. We shall trace in later chapters the circumstances in which the enormous wealth of the Medici family gave them a controlling influence in communal finances, and perhaps, in consequence, in politics and government.[63] We shall also observe how their exile proved the occasion for the revelation of the extent to which their position as financiers to the pope and other major powers had made them an element in pan-Italian diplomatic manœuvring transcending the considerations of purely Florentine pressures and conditions.[64]

(vi) AMICIZIA[1]

Having traced out the lines along which links between the Medici and their partisans were forged, we must turn now to examine

---

[62] MSS. 85, f. 101v.

[63] Below, pp. 285–8. See also M. Becker, 'Problemi della finanza pubblica fiorentina della seconda metà del Trecento e dei primi del Quattrocento', *A.S.I.* cxxiii (1965), esp. 466.

[64] Below, pp. 303–8, cf. de Roover, *The Rise and Decline*, p. 198. The pope favoured the Medici bank in this period and usually appointed the manager of its Rome branch as Depository General. Most of these were *amici* or their close relatives—Bartolomeo Bardi (1420–9), Antonio da Pescia (1429–35), and Roberto Martelli (1438–45).

[1] The discussion which follows is concerned with 'instrumental' friendship, distinguished by Boissevain ('Patronage' 22) from 'emotional' friendship as the foundation of the patronage relationship. Many of its distinctive features are apparent both in fifteenth-century Florence and modern Sicily; e.g. reciprocity of services (23), chains of contact (24–6), means of expanding the group (23), and the use of *raccomandazioni* (25). Marvin Becker, 'An Essay on the Quest for Identity', esp. 299–300, fails to consider instrumental friendship when he argues that by the fifteenth century in Florence, *amicitia* and *amore* were no longer 'elevated to the level of an ideal' and therefore personal loyalties no longer constituted an effective social

the specific ties of obligation and service which bound them in patronage and partisanship to one another. These are most clearly articulated in the letters of *raccomandazione* to the Medici from their *amici*—those essential instruments of the Florentine system of patronage in which assistance of various kinds was sought or offered.[2]

The very form of these letters is highly illuminating, and the relationship between writer and receiver is expressed even in the address and concluding signature. While common among forms of polite address between citizens of similar social status were 'my most esteemed superior' (*honorevole maggiore*),[3] or 'admirable sir' (*spectabilis vir*),[4] the incorporation of the *amici* into an extension of the kin group is more often explicitly reflected in their references to members of the Medici family as 'honoured as an elder brother',[5] or to one older and more distinguished than the writer as 'noble, and honoured, almost a father' or 'most dear, and like a father to me'.[6] This equivalation of *parenti* and *amici* is elabora-

---

cement. Conversely, there is also evidence in the Medici letters of personal tenderness, as in the relationship between the leaders of the Cafaggiolo branch and Piero Guicciardini, most evident in his moving letters of consolation to them after the death of Giuliano (esp. M.A.P. XXI, 560, 14 Aug. 1434), and those between Francesco di Giuliano and Iacopo Donado; see Kent, 'I Medici in esilio' 52–3.

[2] The Medici family's patronage group is probably the best documented in this general period. However, the letters of families like the Strozzi, Del Bene, Sacchetti, Capponi, and Albizzi show that, aside from the frequent, extreme, and rather self-conscious expressions of loyalty, the faint but unmistakable air of conspiracy which pervades the Medici correspondence, the scale of the aims and ambitions which as a whole it reveals, and which a small but vital proportion of letters explicitly betray, the group who clustered round the Medici did so in search of assistance generally similar to that sought by the friends of a number of other prominent patrician families in a comparable position to dispense patronage, and the phraseology and content of their letters is almost identical with those analysed below.

[3] M.A.P. II, 190, Banco di Niccolò Bencivenni to Averardo, 8 Feb. 1430 (1429 *s.f.*). All subsequent archival references in this section are to M.A.P., unless otherwise indicated. The authors and dates of letters are given where they contribute to the identification and definition of the personnel of the party and the period of its activity.

[4] Guasti, *Commissioni* iii. 446, Alamanno Salviati to Rinaldo degli Albizzi, 5 Mar. 1430 (1429 *s.f.*); cf. M.A.P. I, 291, Rosso Sassetti to Francesco Tornabuoni and Averardo de' Medici, 15 May 1432.

[5] II, 154, Fruosino da Verazzano to Averardo, 27 Jan. 1430 (1429 *s.f.*).

[6] II, 167, Bartolomeo Orlandini to Averardo, 31 Jan. 1430 (1429 *s.f.*); 246, Benedetto di Ser Guido [Masi] to Averardo, 27 Feb. 1430 (1429 *s.f.*); cf. 198, Papi Tedaldi to Averardo, 10 Feb. 1430 (1429 *s.f.*). Conversely, forms of address and signature depend also on other factors, like the relative age and social or official status of the writer and the addressee.

ted in the assurance of Bartolomeo Orlandini to Averardo de' Medici that 'I turn to you as the one I consider my most intimate friend, indeed as to a father',[7] and of Giannozzo di Francesco Pitti that 'I will obey you as a father always'.[8] Alternatively, the address may stress the patronage nexus in the relationship with phrases like 'friend, neighbour, and benefactor'[9] or 'my greatest benefactor'.[10]

Apart from the formality of the pious consignment of the receiver to Christ's care, the signatures of letters between *amici* usually incorporate some expression of commitment and request for consideration; these vary according to the needs and nature of the writer. Sometimes the statement of obligation is comparatively vague and formal, as in the common expressions 'I am eager to do your bidding'[11] or '[I am] always ready to obey your commands';[12] often it is more explicit, as in the assurance that 'I am quite committed to you, and if there is anything I should do, let me know and I shall do it willingly'.[13] Sometimes the mutual nature of obligation is emphasized, as in a concluding request to 'give Cosimo this message from me, and recommend me to him and to Lorenzo, and if I can do anything, I am at your disposal'.[14] Elsewhere, the stress is mainly on service. Some friends of the Medici were austere in their assurances of support, like Niccolò Soderini, who declared simply that 'I am yours in everything and recommend myself to you';[15] others described themselves more humbly as 'your lowliest servant',[16] or even 'your creature'.[17] Some stressed the importance of deeds rather than words; in 1434 an *amico* from a comparatively powerful and distinguished patrician family sent word to Cosimo and Lorenzo that he would be

[7] II, 242; cf. Giovanni Niccolini to Averardo, III, 116.
[8] II, 380. The Medici were often requested to treat their partisans as they would their own family; for example, Papi Tedaldi asked Averardo to try as hard to procure him a job on the galleys 'chome se vostro figliuolo fossi', II, 198, 10 Feb. 1430 (1429 *s.f.*); cf. III, 151, Antonio Corbinelli to Averardo, 29 Jan. 1432 (1431 *s.f.*).
[9] V, 260. [10] II, 207.
[11] II, 108, Alberto degli Alberti to Averardo de' Medici, 28 July 1428.
[12] III, 110; cf. VI, 3, Nerone di Nigi Dietisalvi to Lorenzo, 5 May 1431; II, 92, Luigi di Manetto Davanzati, 21 Feb. 1429 (1428 *s.f.*).
[13] II, 154, Fruosino da Verazzano to Averardo, 27 Jan. 1430 (1429 *s.f.*).
[14] CXXXVII, 27, Domenico di Giovanni Giugni to Piero di Cosimo, 19 Dec. 1433. [15] II, 311, to Averardo, 1 Mar. 1431 (1430 *s.f.*).
[16] II, 207, Astore di Niccolò Gianni, 13 Feb. 1430 (1429 *s.f.*); cf. V, 289, Lorenzo di Giovanni (Carducci) to Giovanni di Cosimo, 14 April 1434.
[17] II, 382, Sandro di Bardo to Averardo, 23 Nov. 1430.

ready to do all he could for them when the time was ripe, and
'that when my turn comes, I'll seize my opportunity'.[18]

There is some partial correlation between the social status of
the *amico* and the degree of his verbal commitment; a partisan
with comparatively less dignity of his own to preserve and less
obviously substantial resources to pledge might write, like Maso
Velluti to Piero di Cosimo in 1434, that 'I belong more to you
than to myself and shall do so as long as I live',[19] but it was
unusual for any but the humblest clients to indulge in such declarations of utter devotion as that of Piero di Cristofano da Gagliano, an unknown artisan, to Cosimo:

Never have I wished for anything more in life than to take shelter
under the wing of your power and authority . . . I shall say no more
except that while I live, as I have been, so shall I always be completely
faithful to you.[20]

However, a letter from Carlo Biliotti, whose family was an old
and distinguished one, requesting Averardo de' Medici's assistance in retaining a post in 1431, does provide a rare example
from this earlier, more egalitarian period of the highly elaborate
and hyperbolic style which became quite common later in the
century when the Medici ascendancy was firmly established. 'I
beg you', he wrote,

from the innermost depths of my heart, that not in accordance with
my abilities, but in accordance with your own infinite virtues, that you
employ your luminous intelligence and your keen, discerning, and
indeed sublime ingenuity, in arranging that I should remain here as
castellan and commissioner.[21]

The element of reciprocity in the relationship between the
Medici and the authors of these letters of recommendation is
apparent not only in the address and signature, but also in the
content of those which show them functioning as a patronage
network. For example, a certain Piero, writing to Giuliano to

---

[18] C, 16, Bartolomeo Carducci to Giovanni di Cosimo, 17 July 1434. Cf. II, 104,
Vanni de' Medici to Averardo, 7 June 1428.

[19] XVII, 3, 21 May 1434.

[20] XIII, 27, 31 July 1434.

[21] III, 13, 21 Jan. 1432 (1431 *s.f.*). Similarly, Donato Adimari, whose family was one
of the oldest and most distinguished in Florence, wrote to Lorenzo (XX, 8, 24 Feb.
1432 (1431 *s. f.*) that 'io farò mio debito intorn'al fatto chon quella fede e amore che
deba fare nell'un servo per suo signiore'.

request some money which he needed, concluded: 'I beg you to send it to me; don't fail me, my fine Giuliano, do it for love of me . . . serve me as I have served, and will continue to serve you.'[22]

The activation and co-ordination of the whole system of patronage, over which Cosimo and Lorenzo, Averardo, and his son Giuliano particularly presided, required an outlay of considerable time and energy. The following account in a letter from Giuliano to Averardo of operations in hand is fairly typical:

Yesterday I wrote two lines in favour of the son of Lambertino di Goggio and this morning I wrote off on behalf of a labourer of Bivigliano de' Medici . . . I am keeping in mind Ser Ciao's business . . .[23]

It is not surprising then that when one Ugolino wrote to Averardo that he had been elected to the office of the *Mercanzia* 'which as many people have told me, was obtained through your aid, zeal, and diligence in pursuing my interests', but that later, for pressing personal reasons, he had had to resign it, he was profuse in his apologies and expressed the somewhat anxious hope that Averardo would not take his action amiss.[24]

If they seemed to be neglecting the interests of certain *amici*, or attending to them with insufficient speed and success, members of the Medici family might find themselves reproved and reminded of their obligations by other *amici* and *parenti*. On one occasion Cosimo wrote to Averardo on a friend's behalf 'because many of our friends have entreated me to do so; I beg you to recommend him to the captain';[25] on another, Averardo received quite a sharp rebuke from a friend who declared that 'I am astonished that in two letters now you have made no mention of Ser Ciao's affairs, for in my opinion you should have looked after them with a little more solicitude'.[26] Perhaps this letter prompted his own to Giuliano some time later, criticizing his son for ignoring the affairs of Ser Ciao, and asking him to do something about the matter before he incurred the grave displeasure of both Ser Ciao and himself.[27] Once Bartolomeo Carducci and Andrea Bardi, when it seems Averardo had been slow to act, each wrote to

---

[22] V, 712, n.d., to Giuliano (d. July 1434).   [23] II, 159; cf. II, 238.
[24] III, 113, Ugolinus to Averardo, 29 Mar. 1432.
[25] III, 71, 17 Feb. 1432 (1431 *s.f.*).
[26] III, 247, from Averardo (no surname) to Averardo de' Medici, 14 July 1431.
[27] V, 682, Averardo to Giuliano, 2 Nov. 1431.

suggest that he had neglected the affairs of Bartolomeo del Nero, and that the Neri were offended because 'it seems to them that you ought to be more considerate of your friends than you are'.[28] In a final letter on the subject Carducci concluded: 'As I have had no reply, I don't know what has happened about it; I am sure you would have done and will do as much as you are accustomed to do for your friends, and so I recommend you should do.'[29]

However, the most extreme example of the involvement of the whole group of party leaders in response to the persistent importunings of their partisans was in a case concerning Filippo dall'Antella. As papal bankers, the Medici had considerable influence in the *Curia*, where Lorenzo was currently situated. Filippo dall'Antella had asked him to arrange with the pope that he should be granted the office of senator. Subsequently, both the Medici and the Dall'Antella had inundated Lorenzo with requests to exert himself more forcefully in the matter. As he himself wrote to Averardo:

In the last few days I have had one letter from you and now another . . . and in each of them you charge me with the case of Filippo dall'Antella . . . and Cosimo has also written to me about it and similarly . . . Taddeo dall'Antella and Filippo himself.

He explained that he had indeed spoken to the pope, but the latter was not yet ready to make a decision, especially in view of the importance of certain diplomatic conditions which were not yet clear. There is a certain overtone of exasperation in Lorenzo's concluding words:

Averardo, you may rest assured, because it is clear to me that I must do it for your sake and for the others who have written to me about it, and above all for Filippo, to whom I consider myself as a brother, that I have done and will do everything possible, and thus I beg you will be good enough to tell Filippo that I won't write again, because first I want to know certainly whether it is yes or no, and would you please do likewise to Taddeo.[30]

---

[28] II, 206, 13 Feb. 1430 (1429 *s.f.*).
[29] II, 260, 4 Mar. 1430 (1429 *s.f.*); cf. II, 214, 16 Feb. 1430 (1429 *s.f.*), from Neri di Filippo del Nero to Averardo, asking, 'per amore di noi', his help in avoiding an unjust imposition; this may be the incident to which the letters refer.
[30] II, 289, Lorenzo to Averardo, 16 Apr. 1429.

It would be a difficult and lengthy task to follow up all these requests for assistance in order to see in what proportion of cases the Medici were successful in fulfilling the needs of their friends. However, some particular evidence does survive in letters such as that above of Ugolino, who eventually refused the job obtained for him, in general statements of satisfaction like that of Vanni de' Medici, who declared to Averardo that

I see by experience both now and on other occasions that the faith which I have had in you has always been rewarded and in many different ways . . . [and] concerning the election which you brought my way I won't begin to thank you, because I wouldn't be able to stop,[31]

or more explicitly, of one Antonio di Mannato da Villa, notary to the *Signoria*, who expressed his great gratitude to Averardo, 'however little I have deserved or could ever deserve the things you have managed to get done for me, your servant, and for my sons and nephews and the least important of our relatives'.[32] Indeed the effectiveness of Medici patronage is most clearly evident in the extent to which their circle flourished and grew; the nature of this process is suggested in letters of the *amici*, like that from Bartolomeo Ridolfi recommending to Averardo the interests of a certain Benedetto di San Miniato because 'he is a friend and relative of your and my own dearest friends',[33] or of Niccolò di Giovanni Carducci asking for help for someone else, 'because he is a friend to whom I am very well disposed'.[34] Sometimes the incorporation of the client into the circle of the *amici* is more explicit, as when Bernardo di Domenico Giugni underwrote the claims of a man to be 'as much our friend as it is possible to be'.[35] Sometimes the chain of patronage is glimpsed from the other point of view, as in the note from a certain Rinaldo

[31] II, 104, 7 June 1428.
[32] II, 107, 27 July 1428; cf. V, 133, 6 Dec. 1431, Bernardo d'Alamanno de' Medici to Averardo: 'Io vegho qua per vostra grazia ò avuto da' Dieci che mi fia utile.'
[33] III, 126, 14 May 1431; cf. Conv. Soppr. 314, c. 251, Cederni's reference to 'amicho degli amici'.
[34] IV, 79, 24 Aug. 1431.
[35] V, 13, to Averardo, 4 Nov. 1431; cf. III, 299 and 313. Niccolò del Benino, an established *amico* of the Medici, arranged for two other Medici *amici*, Giuliano di Tommaso, and Niccolò di Cocco Donati, to write separately to Averardo to beg him, in Niccolò's words, 'per amore di mme e del detto Nicholò col qual' è parentado e amicizia', to have the latter and his goods granted a safe conduct to Livorno (III, 313).

to Averardo recommending himself and explaining: 'the cause which impels me to write to you is the great confidence I have in you via Antonio di Salvestro di Ser Ristoro, who is my god-father.'[36]

Of course the Medici were not always successful in satisfying the needs of their *amici* and maintaining and extending their allegiance; Giovanni Guicciardini may have been an illustrious example of a disappointed or disillusioned associate. A letter of his to Averardo in June 1427 leaves no doubt that he was a friend of the Medici at that time, but suggests that he was perhaps becoming dissatisfied with what he considered to be insufficient concern with his problems and inadequate protection of his interests. His tone throughout is thus appropriately ambiguous. He wrote from the Florentine camp at Casalmaiore, where he was a commissioner in the war against Milan; a lengthy account of his own discomforts and frustrations was the preliminary to the declaration that

I really do believe that over there [in Florence] there are envious souls who are jealous and displeased by seeing others doing better than they through suffering hardships, and thus I advise you that you should diligently and skilfully strive to maintain and increase the honour of your house and your friends as you do and have done through Messer Giuliano and me, and when the time comes, I shall be with you, for what I am worth, until the death.[37]

He seems to have been particularly put out by the presence, apparently due to their patronage, of another of the Medici *amici*, the ubiquitous Ser Ciao, and complained that he found him lazy and untrustworthy, 'a man of evil and wicked condition', and admitted that in this whole matter he felt himself offended at Averardo and Nerone Dietisalvi, another of the leading partisans, observing that 'it appears that you do not pay any attention to the honour or the profit of your friends'. He also went out of his way to emphasize the duties and obligations owed him by the Medici in a request for help with his taxes:

Concerning the matter of the *catasto*, I must put a good case, since your friends are making me very rich through the taxes, but not enough to take a wife. And when the occasion arises, I will trouble you on my behalf with confidence, since I know you have friends involved with

<hr />

[36] III, 206, 12 July 1431.   [37] II, 50, 28 June 1427.

the assessment. And as in this, so in all my affairs and needs I will give
you some work to do, for one ought to ask help from those men who
can and do get things done, and who are true friends.

Probably Giovanni's tone in these letters was sincere rather than
ironic, but it is notable that in fact when the time did come, he
was not with the Medici to the death; in 1433 he chose instead
to support and to co-operate with their opponents, and according
to his descendant, the historian Francesco, he was saved from
harsh reprisals in 1434 only by the intervention of his brother
Piero, the close relative, partisan, and personal friend of the
leaders of the Medici house. His volte-face, and the split which it
caused in the allegiances of the rather small Guicciardini family,
were unusual; in the absence of a satisfactory alternative explanation we might reasonably suggest that Giovanni was one *amico*
who found Medici patronage unrewarding, and sought a substi-
tute from their opponents.[38]

Although one of the problems here would appear to have been
an unavoidable clash between the conflicting interests of one
amico with those of another, in general the *amici*, like the wider
Medici family, appear to have recognized corporate interests and
a collective honour. They also identified themselves with the successes and failures of its leaders; as Vanni de' Medici had done, so
too Giovanni di Cocco Donati wrote to congratulate Averardo
on his appointment as commissioner to the captian of war in
1427, and declared himself personally delighted by this distinction, as he was by every honour which fell to Averardo.[39]
Another *amico* even wrote encouraging Averardo to exert himself
more forcefully to bring the war to an end by capturing the
strategic tower of Aquila in order to win greater honour:

Listen, Averardo, I know of no more remarkable feat in this world than
the acquiring of renown and virtue. Your servants would like to be
able to say, 'In Averardo's time, he did such and such, and he had such
and such done'.[40]

His impulse was similar to that which prompted Cosimo to
encourage his cousin to greater achievement during the later war

[38] Cf. also below, pp. 196–7, 273–4.
[39] III, 144, 27 June 1431; cf. II, 78, and II, 72, Donato 'de' frati de' servi di
Firenze' to Averardo, 19 Dec. 1427; 'Meglio voglio che voi pensiate per voi per
la fede e amore che io vi porto . . . più e meglio desidero per la vostra persona che
per la propria.' [40] V, 79, Carlo Biliotti, 22 Nov. 1431.

with Lucca.[41] By the same token, and like several of the Medici themselves, Fruosino da Verazzano was aware that his execution of the office procured for him by Averardo would reflect on his patron's honour and that of the group as a whole, and in thanking Averardo for his aid he also expressed the fervent hope that through it he would be enabled to do 'honour to the friends'.[42]

Conversely, patrons felt their own honour diminished by the failure of their *amici* to assist them and one another, and the Medici interpreted the harassment of their friends as an attack on themselves. During the early months of the war with Lucca, when the Florentine practice of eliminating enemies by publicly discrediting them was at its height, and the Medici leaders a prime target, Giuliano observed to Averardo that 'they pursue us too closely through our relatives and friends'.[43]

Indeed, as we have seen, the whole patronage system depended upon a complex of relationships; the leaders of the most powerful Florentine families functioned as brokers of patronage to which they had the greatest access, but the fulfilment of most requests required the participation of a whole chain of *amici* who clustered round them. The most successful patrons were those who managed most often to satisfy the needs of their friends; consequently, successful patrons tended to be those who could attract and maintain a large number of followers who constituted a pool of potential resources for each other's mutual aid.[44]

Their friends sought the help of the Medici with a wide variety of matters, but most of them can be subsumed under several general categories of assistance.[45] The need for financial support was common, and was apparently often met with direct personal loans from the Medici themselves, or occasionally, perhaps, with the provision of opportunities for participation in the lucrative enterprises of the Medici and their more prosperous *amici*. A considerable proportion of the surviving letters of *raccomandazione* are requests for assistance in obtaining various political offices; they also provide some insight into the channels through

---

[41] Below, pp. 275–6.   [42] II, 154, 27 Jan. 1430 (1429 *s.f.*).
[43] II, 367, 12 Oct. 1430.
[44] This point is well demonstrated by Brucker's descriptions of particular patronage groups (*The Civic World*, esp. Ch. I.)
[45] Some of the *amici*, of course, had particular needs; their clerical friend Donato 'de frati de' servi di Firenze' asked Averardo 'di raccommandarmi al padre nostro generale, el quale sta costì a Ferrara' (II, 72, 19 Dec. 1427).

which patronage groups pursued the private interest of their members.

Many of these posts were appointive and thus effectively in the gift of the Medici themselves, or their more politically influential *amici*. For example, thanks to the numerous embassies and commissions in which he participated after 1427, Averardo de' Medici in particular was personally responsible for a large number of appointments auxiliary to the major magistracies. This was especially true during the period of the Lucchese war, when he was closely involved with such tasks as the manning and operation of the Florentine galleys at Pisa.[46] There are a great many letters to Averardo concerning these jobs, including those from several members of the Bonino branch of the family—represented by Orlando di Guccio and his two sons, Piero and Guccio—enjoining him to confer some position of authority on the latter; they show how several friends or relatives would combine to bring more intense pressure on the patron to put pressure in turn on his friends. In December 1431 Guccio wrote begging Averardo 'to exert yourself in Florence with the help of the *amici* to procure for me the galley, for I promise that I will do you great honour'.[47] Guccio's father, Orlando, sent a note about the same time supporting and reinforcing his son's request,[48] and a further reminder from Orlando in the same month gives some insight into the way in which patronage networks operated to secure offices for their members: 'I beg you to arrange it as best you can, either with money or with favours or with promises.'[49] These methods proved effective, for the following month Averardo received a letter of thanks for his assistance from Guccio's brother, Piero, assuring him that Guccio would use his position as far as possible to promote the honour and reputation of his family and friends.[50] When one of the *amici*, Tedaldo Tedaldi, wanted to obtain a similar position for his son, Papi, he also sought to activate the network on several fronts at once; he spoke to Giovanni Pucci, brother of Cosimo's right-hand man, in Florence, and wrote to Averardo in Pisa, asking if anything further should be done by the *amici* at the Florentine end. Tedaldi's offer to do something in return for Averardo in Florence is

---

[46] Cf. below, pp. 270–2.
[48] V, 106, 29 Nov. 1431.
[50] III, 20, 24 Jan. 1432 (1431 *s.f.*).

[47] V, 112, 1 Dec. 1431.
[49] V, 159, 14 Dec. 1431.

a particularly immediate illustration of the reciprocal nature of patronage obligations, while his bald concluding observation: 'You know how great my need is', is a powerful expression of the force of the expectations behind many requests for aid.[51]

Moreover, the greater Florentine families, like the Medici, often came to command, through their private activities as international businessmen, and their long experience as ambassadors and external magistrates in the service of the Florentine commune, a semi-permanent network of association and obligation stretching far beyond the city of Florence; one which could be activated when the occasion arose to serve themselves and their *amici*. In December 1427 while *Podestà* at Ancona, Vanni, of the Alamanno branch of the family, seems to have decided to cultivate a career in foreign service. Thus he wrote to Averardo:

I entreat you to do what you can to beg for a position for me from the Marchese of Ferrara or the Marchese of Modena, for I am sure you will be successful, and if I get it, it will bring a great deal of honour and profit to me and to the whole house.[52]

He suggested that Averardo might begin by calling on Ser Pieragnolo da Foligno, 'chancellor of the magnificent Lord Marchese, who is a great friend of mine', while in conclusion he indicated that another of the Medici friends, one of the more outstanding *condottieri* of the age, had already begun to act on his behalf: 'By your advice I already had great hopes of the job at Mantua through the influence of Niccolò da Tolentino.'[53] Such connections seem to have maintained Vanni in office in the general area of the Papal States for quite some time; several years later he received another position as *Podestà* at Rimini through the influence of a friend whose own interests in that area had been previously promoted by the Medici.[54]

Where the fulfilment of requests depended upon collective action, the corporate nature of the network's operations is even

---

[51] II, 185, 7 Feb. 1430 (1429 *s.f.*)   [52] II, 78, 25 Dec. 1427.
[53] Cosimo considered Niccolò 'a very great friend' (*Ricordi*, p. 97).
[54] Filippo dall'Antella (cf. above, p. 88, and II, 294, Vanni to Averardo, 9 Oct. 1429) lived permanently in Pesaro (Cat. 68, f. 205r–v); he paid his taxes to the Malatesta who were his friends and employers, and fostered the friendship between them and the Medici. For example, as Malatesta de' Malatesti wrote in 1429 to Averardo (II, 295), 'Filippo del'Antella mi ha riportato che con grandissima affectione havete rasionato con lui di mei facti de la quale cosa vi so' sommamente obligato e desidero sempre fare cosa a voi grata'; cf. II, 301, 303.

more clearly apparent, and the consequent transgressions of the constitutional principles of voting and acting in office in accord with individual conscience lead logically to the transformation of patronage network into political party. When Francesco Tornabuoni wrote to Averardo pointing out that the Gonfaloniers of Company for each of the sixteen *gonfaloni* were about to draw up the initial lists for the scrutiny of the internal offices, he asked 'if there should happen to be any one with whom you or Cosimo or any of your friends have influence, that he should be written to and enjoined to name me if possible', though he acknowledged there might be problems involved, with the admission that 'I don't know if that can be arranged'.[55] A brief *polizza*, addressed to Giuliano de' Medici and signed simply Giovanni Carnesecchi, unfortunately undated but on internal evidence almost certainly belonging to the pre-1434 period,[56] gives invaluable insight into the way in which, at a later stage in the process, when the final lists came to the vote, the Medici and their friends formed a lobby to promote the success of their *amici*:

It is essential that when the election of the officials takes place in the presence of the councils, you should have your friends and relatives immediately informed that you need their help, and of my business with the treasurer, so that it is understood that you want to oblige them to serve our interests, and the same should be commended to your Lorenzo ... and if it seems to you advisable, when they attend with the Colleges in the council hall, to examine closely those people who ought to succeed, and put pressure on them to act if it falls to their lot.[57]

Sometimes the Medici cleared the ground by obtaining the prior support of a member of the *Signoria* or one of the leading specialist magistracies concerned with the issue in hand, to promote their case and prepare the way for the main body of the

[55] II, 397, 23 Dec. 1430; cf. V, 266, Amerigo di M. Francesco to Averardo, n.d.
[56] LXVI, 523. The note is undated and without any formal address; though classified as directed to Giuliano di Averardo in the *Inventario*, III, it could be to Giuliano di Piero (1453-78). This, however, is unlikely, on circumstantial and internal grounds, and while there was a Giovanni Carnesecchi roughly the contemporary of Averardo's son, I know of no Giovanni Carnesecchi active in the seventies; we do know that Bernardo di Cristofano di Berto Carnesecchi was a Medici partisan in business with Vieri de' Medici. Cf. the role of the *amici* in the scrutiny of 1427/8, below, pp. 223-34.
[57] II, 184, 6 Feb. 1430 (1429 *s.f.*); cf. III, 298, 19 July 1431, Andrea de' Pazzi to Averardo.

amici who would then try to push through their interest with their votes. There is a series of letters relating to such a case in February 1430. On the sixth of the month Banco di Niccolò Bencivenni, a leading partisan who was currently one of Averardo's companions in the office of the Pisan Consuls, wrote to the latter concerning the promotion of an undefined Medici concern, to assure him that his *compagno*, Rinieri Lotti, 'will act exactly as I should have done, so that we shall keep ourselves alert, and when any of our friends is proposed by the *Signoria* we will be able to put it to the test, putting pressure on our other friends by any means that are honest.'[58] Averardo replied immediately that he had already heard from Giuliano, who was hoping with the aid of Ser Filippo and the Priors to get through a petition for a council with the aid of the *Dieci*—the Ten of War: Bencivenni promised in his rejoinder that 'I will be able to remain here on your behalf, and I believe that with the aid of our friends it will get through, and I will keep you informed day by day'.[59] It seems likely that it was with reference to the same incident that Andrea Bardi reported to Averardo a week later: 'I believe that at least a part of those friends who were requested to do so will assist us.'[60]

Although the *amici* clearly recognized an obligation to support the party on such occasions, they did not invariably do so; indeed it was not always possible for individuals to respond to the Medici calls for support, as we can see from two letters of Neri di Domenico Bartolini-Scodellari, one to Averardo, and the second to Antonio Masi, apparently a leading proponent of the action in question. Both had obviously written to Neri asking him to return immediately to Florence. He explained to Masi that although 'this morning I received your letter in which you proposed me for the job of coming over there to Florence, since some comrades are needed for the making of the *Ten of War*',[61]

[58] II, 183, 8 Feb. 1430 (1429 *s.f.*).
[59] II, 190, 8 Feb. 1430 (1429 *s.f.*); cf. the similar assurance to Averardo from Fruosino da Verazzano (II, 154, 27 Jan. 1430, 1429 *s.f.*) that 'si deba sperare gli amici vostri chol fare bene ogni ora s'otterà; io sono quello senpre fui'.
[60] II, 206, 13 Feb. 1430 (1429 *s.f.*)
[61] II, 373, 22 Oct. 1430, to Averardo; II, 508. 22 Oct. 1430, to Antonio di Tommaso Masi. Cf. a similar apology from Luigi Vecchietti to Averardo, II, 316, 27 Mar. 1439; 'In questa ora riceveti tua lettera la quale viddi così volentieri come di qualunche altro che costì dimori. E inteso vorresti ch'io fussi subito costà volentieri lo fare[i] ma io sono istato malato circha di 2 mesi . . .'

this was impossible; he could not leave Cascina as his partner in the bank had just died and it was imperative that their affairs be settled immediately; he was, however, profuse in his apologies.

If sometimes there were uncertainties and hitches along the way, nevertheless it appears that the Mediceans did get measures through; for instance, as Giuliano was able to report to Averardo in Pisa in 1428:

This afternoon the petition was proposed, and tomorrow morning we should be sure of our position since things are resolving themselves in the way we discussed. Yesterday afternoon the petitions of Piero and Niccolò Valori were put to the vote; Niccolò had 14 votes against and Piero 16, and they will be dealt with again, according to what Niccolò told me today; they have Bartolomeo Ridolfi to thank for that, for he has served us very well.[62]

The measures for which the Medici solicited support among the *amici* did not always concern the promotion of partisans to political offices; the 'petitions' to which the letters obliquely refer might be anything from commercial cases before the merchants' court to private legislation before the *Signoria* and councils, concerned with anything from tax concessions—the most popular problem—to business deals.[63] In the first weeks of 1430 Averardo received several letters from Giuliano and from Andrea de' Bardi concerning a petition involving the affairs of the Covoni. The situation is not clear; the participation of Bardi and Covoni suggests that it was a business matter, but the procedure adopted was similar to that which we have seen operating to influence the outcome of purely political problems; as Andrea had observed with some concern, 'our enemies have been around the Palace of the Priors a great deal'.[64] In the circumstances the Medici had concluded that 'it would be a good idea to do as you say, as long as we have someone in the *Signoria* who will have the necessary regard for our interests'.[65] On this occasion they had in mind Bartolomeo Ridolfi, who had served them well before, 'because he is always ready to do anything that lies within his

---

[62] II, 145, 22 Jan. 1430 (1429 *s.f.*).
[63] Note, e.g. the obscurity concerning the nature of the petition which Banco di Niccolò Bencivenni hoped to have passed 'choll'aiuto degli amici', II, 190, 8 Feb. 1430 (1429 *s.f.*). [64] II, 157, 28 Jan. 1430 (1429 *s.f.*).
[65] II, 159, Giuliano to Averardo, 28 Jan. 1430 (1429 *s.f.*), cf. II, 164, Giuliano to Averardo, 30 Jan. 1430 (1429 *s.f.*); II, 189, Andrea de' Bardi to Averardo, 8 Feb. 1430 (1429 *s.f.*).

power to really oblige you'.[66] When another partisan, Amerigo di M. Francesco di Ser Segna, found that someone had filed against him 'a very unjust petition in the Palace', he wrote to Averardo that 'it seems to me necessary to seek the help of the *amici*, and so I beg you to write a note to the Gonfalonier of Company'. He also suggested Averardo should contact a friend of the Medici then Gonfalonier of Justice, 'and recommend me to him in whatever terms seem appropriate'.[67]

However, from what we have seen of the nature and function of their patronage network, it is clear that it operated largely to promote the political interests of its members, whether in contravention of the letter and spirit of the constitution or not. We shall observe in later chapters how as early as 1426 the Mediceans were interfering with the electoral processes, not simply as an *ad hoc* response to the needs and demands of those who sought their patronage, but in a systematic attempt to increase the representation of their supporters in the governing group. It is at this point that the circle of patronage shades into the party groomed for political action; when the scale and success of the Medici patronage and the consequent swelling of the ranks of their supporters began significantly to change the balance of power within the ruling group and the Medici interest to cut across that of the political establishment, then a private interest group had become a partisan challenge to the state. This was the burden of their opponents' charges against them in 1433; that the Medici had tried to make themselves greater than the Priors by offering to defend their friends' interests better than a government designed to represent the common good;[68] because the *amici* resorted to their friends as the primary source of aid and defence and owed to them their first and strongest loyalty, the allegiance of citizens to Priors and commune was being effectively undermined.

Of course the same might be said of any other Florentine patronage group whose activities and structure were essentially similar to those of the Medicean group which we have been describing,[69] and by no means all of these became embroiled in

[66] II, 145, Giuliano to Averardo, 22 Jan. 1430 (1429 *s.f.*).

[67] V, 266, n.d.   [68] Cf. below, pp. 245–6.

[69] See, e.g., Brucker, *Renaissance Florence*, pp. 99–100, concerning Franco Sacchetti; 'Sacchetti's correspondence . . . reveals that his circle of *raccomandati*, of men who made claims upon him, was quite large. . . . These clients petitioned Sacchetti for tax relief, they were seeking a government post, or an ecclesiastical

the partisan struggles of the decade preceding the crises of 1433 and 1434. Unfortunately, the documentation does not exist to make a meaningful comparison, but the course of subsequent events, and the weight of the evidence concerning the Medici group, suggest at least that the Medici patronage network saw itself with peculiar clarity as a party opposing the interests of others for some years before 1433.

The fact that Medicean letters of *raccomandazione* were often used to convey and renew assurances of loyalty in a peculiarly explicit way may reflect a particular consciousness of the extent to which the patronage network was actually, or at least potentially, a partisan group. While the former might be fluid and infinitely extensible, the latter were illegal and necessarily secret associations whose existence depended upon the discretion and trustworthiness of their members. Consequently, many of these letters have a distinctly conspiratorial flavour. The use of proper names is limited and discreet, the group being customarily known collectively as *gli amici*, an ambiguous term which implies obligation rather than emotional attachment but does not inevitably betray partisanship; the actual obligations involved are seldom too precisely defined. Stefano di Francesco di Ser Segnia wrote to Averardo in 1429 as one seeking almost formal admission to a select band: 'Please include us in the number of your most intimate friends, even though this may prove harmful to us.'[70]

Notably the leaders of the group were quick to discern the signs of disaffection, and then to tread warily. In November 1427 Cosimo wrote of an unidentified associate to Averardo: 'Our friend is not what I thought him; enough said.'[71] He seems to have kept a very watchful eye on his friends, for only a few weeks later he found it necessary to warn his cousin again, possibly of the same man:

Francesco has come over here; I don't know why. He is so cunning that he makes me wonder about his intentions. I know you will find

benefice, or (in one case) a university chair in Perugia. They sought release from prison, or they merely wanted Sacchetti's assurance that he would protect their interests.' Cf. his observation concerning Sacchetti patronage in *The Civic World*, p. 481, that promises of mutual aid in reducing tax assessment and obtaining nomination for political office 'could hardly be described as a conspiracy. But it was one strand in a complex network of private relationships that existed alongside the state and encroached upon its jurisdiction.'

[70] II, 147, 23 Jan. 1430 (1429 *s.f.*).　　　　[71] II, 57, 19 Nov. 1427.

this difficult, but if you hear anything I would be very glad if you would let me know; he is not the friend he ought to be, but rather the opposite; be warned.[72]

It is clear that the obligations incurred by the recipients of Medici patronage were seen by all parties as being of a particularly serious and specific nature. Carlo Biliotti, writing to Averardo, acknowledged himself 'as beholden to you as if you had taken the rope from round my neck';[73] Bartolomeo Orlandini remarked of two other members of the group whom Averardo had recommended to him, that 'this I know; you expect them to fulfil their obligations, otherwise they will be neither your friends nor mine',[74] and Cosimo felt surprised and betrayed by his incarceration at the instigation of the *Signoria* of November 1433 because it contained men like Giovanni dello Scelto, 'whom I considered to be a great friend of mine, and he was obliged to me, and the same with the others'.[75] A number of the pledges offered to the Medici in return for particular assistance could, as we have seen, appear to imply anticipation of some major future enterprise in which the *amici* would find a supreme opportunity to demonstrate their loyalty, as in the promise to give proof of it when the occasion should arise.[76]

Whether or not the Medici were systematically preparing themselves and their party for a *coup d'état* as some contemporaries suggested,[77] their very success as patrons and the consequent growth in their following were bound, in the prevailing social and political circumstances, to bring them into headlong collision with competing and conflicting interests, and the groups which promoted them, and these conflicts could only be resolved by the more or less decisive victory of one or other of the groups involved. That this was indeed the case is most strongly suggested in the fact that various citizens seem to have begun to exercise some

---

[72] II, 18, 31 Jan. 1428 (1427 *s.f.*)   [73] III, 13, 21 Jan. 1432 (1431 *s.f.*).
[74] II, 167, 31 Jan. 1430 (1429 *s.f.*).
[75] *Ricordi*, p. 97. Certainly the Medici relied on Giovanni dello Scelto for assistance on at least one occasion (III, 298, Andrea Pazzi to Averardo, 24 July 1431).
[76] e.g. II, 104, Vanni de' Medici to Averardo, 7 June 1428; C, 16, Bartolomeo Carducci to Giovanni di Cosimo, 17 July 1434; cf. II, 191, Bartolomeo Orlandini to Averardo de' Medici, 8 Feb. 1430 (1429 *s.f.*): 'Bene veggo in ogni cosa avete riguardo sì all'onore e sì alla conservatione della mia, perchè a Dio piaccia qualche volta ve ne possa rendere degno merito.'
[77] Tinucci, *Examina*.

choice by joining the Medicean circle, not merely for the sake of the political promotion which the patronage network might procure for them, but more probably for the protection which identification with this increasingly powerful party might afford against the rapidly coalescing groups of their opponents.

In 1426 Rinaldo degli Albizzi's brother, Luca, made a formal partition of the divisible property the two held in common, and married the daughter of Nicola di Vieri de' Medici; 1426 appears to have been the year in which the profound and unbridgeable gulf between the Mediceans and the aristocratic inner circle of the ruling group, led by Rinaldo, first became entirely obvious.[78] Luca's diary of 1429–30 suggests that by then he was largely estranged from his own family, and that his friends were almost all men who later supported the Mediceans against Rinaldo.[79] It seems very likely that all these things were related, and that Luca's strategy was twofold; to cultivate Medicean connections quickly to replace those he had lost by cutting himself off from his family, and to assure himself of protection in the forthcoming conflict against the wrath, or even merely the indifference, which might be equally fatal in certain situations, of those he had rejected.

The Pitti family may well have found themselves similarly in need of protection. In 1422 Buonaccorso concluded peace after a twenty-year feud with Fibindacci Ricasoli. Up till then, as he explained, 'I didn't see what defence could be sustained against such might as that of the Gianfigliazzi, the Castellani, the Peruzzi, and of the other relatives and friends of the supporters of the Ricasoli, and their followers and henchmen'.[80] However, even despite the conclusion of a formal peace, it is unlikely that after twenty years of hostility the Pitti felt entirely secure; no doubt

[78] C.S. 1ª ser. CCCLII, 3; Litta, *Famiglie Celebri* xi, Tav. VII. Cf. below, 197, 211–22.

[79] Mallett, *The Florentine Galleys*, pp. 195–201. On a voyage to England in this period he wrote four to five letters each to his father-in-law, and to several others subsequently revealed as Mediceans, but only one to his brother Rinaldo; he chose as one of his companions on the galley his brother-in-law, Carlo di Nicola de' Medici. In his youth Luca had belonged to an intellectual circle in which Cosimo and his friends were prominent, and in October 1430 Cosimo, in a letter to Averardo, linked his name with that of Niccolò Valori as one on whom they could rely; certainly, Cavalcanti's comment on the subject suggests that contemporaries remarked upon the open enmity between the two Albizzi brothers (*Istorie*, p. 310).

[80] *Cronica* pp. 172, 241.

CARL A. RUDISILL LIBRARY
LENOIR RHYNE COLLEGE

they continued to fear discrimination from this extremely powerful sector of the supporters of the oligarchical *reggimento*, who
later became the hard core of the extremist wing of the anti-
Medicean party. Already by this time the Medici were exceedingly
wealthy, and beginning to acquire such significant power in the
government that they threatened to become a challenge to the
status quo; thus the marriage of Buonaccorso's daughter to Rosso
di Giovanni de' Medici in 1423 looks very much like an attempt
by the Pitti to obtain protection from their enemies by allying
themselves with a rival group. There is evidence that by the end
of the twenties Giannozzo di Francesco Pitti was a Medici partisan, and in the events of 1434 Buonaccorso's son Luca was among
the family's leading supporters.[81]

The hardening of the networks of association, the need to
choose between various associative loyalties, and the preparation
of the Medici *amici* for a future decisive conflict are most vividly
illustrated in two letters addressed to Averardo in January–
February 1430 by Benedetto di Ser Guido di Tommaso Masi;
these embody a number of the themes which have emerged from
our exploration of patronage and partisanship. The first of the
letters began with an assurance of 'that fine and perfect love which
should exist between father and son, and which I am certain you
have for me',[82] and went on to ask for aid in a case currently
before the commercial court, between himself and Francesco
Guadagni, a prominent member of a family exiled *en masse* by
the Mediceans in 1434. Although in accordance with the volatile
nature of politics in this period, a few of Benedetto's enemies were
eventually to emerge on the Medici side in the political confronta-
tions of 1433–4, it soon became clear that in general Benedetto
was asking the Mediceans to defend his business interests from
the hostile operations of a group which was fairly solidly anti-
Medicean in its political stance.

It appears that Benedetto had secured a relatively favourable
ruling on his case from the guild consuls whose term ended in
December, but when the new consuls took office in January they
included Ridolfo Peruzzi and Bartolomeo d'Ugo Alessandri, who
according to Benedetto 'had never ceased to perpetrate corrupt

---

[81] II, 380, Giannozzo to Averardo, 14 Nov. 1430; cf. above, pp. 59n.,85; below,
p. 328.

[82] II, 166, 31 Jan. 1430 (1429 *s.f.*).

and shameless tricks . . . It was enough for them to see some way to do me harm and injustice, and in truth the cause and instigators of all this were Ridolfo [and] Bartolomeo di Verano.' These were the leaders of the Peruzzi family, from which came perhaps the largest and most consistently anti-Medicean group in Florence.[83] Benedetto complained that despite the ties of *parentado* which he had with the Peruzzi, they had done nothing to help him, but on the contrary had done all they could to turn against him a prominent associate of the anti-Mediceans with whom he had previously been on friendly, indeed intimate, terms—a certain Filippo Scolari, 'who in his times of need I had assisted for a good three years as faithfully as if he had been my father'. Benedetto went on to assert that 'in accordance with the inclinations and desires of others . . . they aroused his hostility against me, and they induced him to take as his wife the daughter of Luigi di Giovanni Aldobrandini'.

Since Scolari had made this *parentado* with Luigi Aldobrandini, 'he considers he has attached himself to a Colossus, and it seems to me that really he can't help himself'. Benedetto could only console himself with the reflection that

I also have him by the short hairs, since if he dies and they try to deny what he promised me, your Niccolò Valori is well informed about it all, because he is one of those commissioners of the merchants' guild concerning these affairs . . . and if I were his brother or his son he could not be more sympathetic, and he is very willing to help me, and I am only too grateful to him; he is too kind, and a man of great integrity.

With one leading member of the Medici party already a strategic figure in the affair, his purpose in this letter was to

ask you to continue to exert yourself on my behalf until this business is concluded, and to advise me as to what you think I should do about it, and I beg you as fervently as I can, for it is evident that you are well disposed towards me.

It seems that the Medici were indeed very willing to take up this cause against his enemies, and theirs, as Benedetto began his second letter with an expression of gratitude for their acknowledgement of his place in the party and its obligations to him:

[83] Below, pp. 153–6.

'I received your reply to my letter, which delighted me, considering that henceforth I know myself to be included with the others
in your friendship and your favour, and nothing could please me
more.'[84] As he observed,

I will never get out of it, if not now, during the term of these Priors
who are an excellent crowd for me, since their leader is a good friend
of Piero Bonciani and I know you will hear everything from him, and
therefore I beg you to write about it to whoever you think necessary,
so that I can put an honorable end to this affair, settle my account, and
exact my due from them.

He expressed some regret that Averardo at the time should be in
Pisa and not on the spot in Florence, but added that 'I am sure
that you will arrange things over there in the same way, and I beg
you to advise me as to what I should do, although I shall also
consult Cosimo and your Giuliano.' He concluded his last letter
with an eloquent plea

that you should assist me and defend me from these furious foes, for
I know they will do me harm if they can, but it seems to me that it is not
God's will that their unbridled fury should have free rein; thus it may
please him that in the future you and the others should flourish and
increase in strength in order to save us from them.

These phrases were echoed by other of the Medici *amici* as
they sought to increase their influence in the ruling group at the
expense of the prevailing regime.[85] Indeed Benedetto's letters are
in many ways a perfect illustration of the way in which patronage
operated, private interest groups were formed and coalesced
along various basic and traditional social lines, and eventually
and almost inevitably, in the defence of their members, turned into
political action groups, consolidating themselves on opposite
sides of a chasm becoming steadily deeper and increasingly more
unbridgeable with each divisive incident.

(vii) THE AMICI

The Medici partisans included a fairly wide range of citizens from
varying social levels, and linked to the family in a variety of ways.
The question arises at this point whether they and their rival
patronage groups cum parties can be seen as something more

---

[84] II, 246, 27 Feb. 1430 (1429 *s.f.*).   [85] Cf. below, p. 234.

than the personal followings of several of the greater Florentine families, if they indeed represented a particular social group or ideology, or whether the interests they promoted were purely personal.

This is a question of particular importance in view of the fact that Cavalcanti, the only contemporary to attempt to analyse the parties in these terms, saw the clash between the Medici and their opponents as a conflict of class interests. His analysis has since formed the basis of most general accounts, until recent work on Florentine politics and society has shown it to be extremely implausible.[1] Felix Gilbert has observed *en passant* that the struggle between Medici and Albizzi in the thirties can most appropriately be seen as essentially personal faction-fighting within the patrician class;[2] however, a close examination of the precise status and social position of Medici partisans does reveal distinctive features which suggest that the Medici attracted partisans concerned with the defence of certain social interests, and who were united by these concerns.

According to Cavalcanti, and the tradition he fostered, the anti-Mediceans were encouraged 'by all the worthiest citizens of the *reggimento* and by all the nobles'; Cosimo's party flourished 'because the masses had chosen him as their champion and looked on him as a god'. The Medici were often called in disparagement 'valacchi' (presumably after the despised Flemish woollen-workers brought in by Florentine merchant entrepreneurs), or alternatively 'Puccini', after Puccio Pucci, a minor guildsman prominent in the party leadership and highly esteemed by Cosimo and his partisans.[3] They drew their chief support then from 'the lower classes',[4] or at the best from 'the minor guilds',[5] and following this tradition, later writers have tended to represent the Mediceans as men 'without political influence, or with very little'.[6] However, as Cavalcanti himself admitted, Cosimo also had a significant number of supporters among the powerful patricians in the inner circles of the ruling group; indeed the observation of the author of a contemporary *Priorista* that the members of 'Cosimo's faction' whom 'some called louts and others the Puccini . . . in

---

[1] Cf. above, pp. 3–10. [2] F. Gilbert, 'Bernardo Rucellai' 128–9.
[3] *Istorie*, p. 4. [4] Ibid. [5] Ibid.
[6] Pellegrini, *Sulla repubblica*, p. 16; cf. Capponi, *Storia della Repubblica*, ii. 160; according to Capponi, the Mediceans expressed 'le ire popolari . . . e ordivansi trame contro allo stato'.

fact were almost all merchants and artisans and sound men'[7] proves on closer examination of the group to be far more accurate.

In no sense does the evidence support the picture of the Mediceans as a popular party, representing the interests of 'the common people (*la plebe*)'. Of course the combination of private letters and public archives on which this study of Medici partisans is chiefly based does not really allow us accurately to assess the degree of popular support enjoyed by the Medici; true plebeians did not appear in the records of a government monopolized by patricians, nor would they have been likely to communicate with their patrons naturally or habitually in writing. However, there are in fact among those whose letters reveal them as Medici partisans a handful of humbler citizens; men from families of no social or political standing or influence, like Giovanni Cirioni, 'stone-mason and carpenter',[8] some others even without distinguishable surnames by which their traditions or activities might be identified. None of them, however, played a prominent or even identifiable part in the organization or activities of the party in the twenties and thirties, and indeed it is impossible to say more about their role in the party structure or their possible part in the crisis of 1434 than that they may well have formed part of the crowds whose physical presence constituted an effective political pressure on the anti-Mediceans attempting to defy the *Signoria* at the dénouement on Sunday, 26 September.[9]

Most of the Medici partisans, and certainly all those who took a notable part in the factional activities of this period, were associated with the guilds which gave citizens entrée to the governing class, and all but a handful of them were attached, not to the minor, but to the major guilds for which the greatest number and the most important of the official posts were reserved, and from which the ruling class was effectively drawn. Those few who were *minori* were often, like the Pucci and the Del Nero, exceptional, being already by the late twenties men of some power and influence in the city; thus by this time they were practically dissociated from the artisans and identified with the major guildsmen whose ranks they were soon to join.[10]

[7] C.S. 2ª ser. CIII, cc. 112v–113r; cf. MSS. 229, p. 167 (Sept.–Oct. 1434).
[8] M.A.P. III, 74.   [9] Cf. below, pp. 337–8.
[10] At the beginning of our period seven or eight of the Medici *amici* were apparently still closely associated with the minor guilds; they included the Pucci and Del Nero brothers, Salvestro Lapi, and Giovanni Cirioni. However, several appear to

Beyond this point, the attempt to measure the share of *stato* enjoyed by the Medici partisans becomes more complex. The *reggimento* or ruling group which effectively governed the city at any particular time is itself an elusive entity, constantly mentioned by contemporaries, but never concretely defined; we may, however, infer from their comments that the essential and most basic criterion would seem to have been qualification in the scrutiny for the republic's trilogy of leading magistracies—the *Signoria* and its auxiliary colleges, the *Dodici* and the *Sedici*, collectively known as the *Tre Maggiori*. Groups habitually excluded from these offices, like the magnates, were described as 'excluded from the city's ruling group';[11] on the other hand, when a family like Giovanni Morelli's gained its first representative in the Priorate, he considered that it had at last made its entrée 'into government, and the ruling group'.[12]

The only available scrutiny for this period is that carried out by the reforming *Balìa* at the time of Cosimo's exile in September 1433, in which only a third of the Miceans were included among the 1,757 major guildsmen whose names were placed in the bags from which the *Tre Maggiori* would subsequently be drawn. Given that the total number of citizens with majorities may have constituted almost as much as a third of the eligible adult male population of the city at that time, the Micean representation and their share in the *stato* would appear to be rather limited.[13]

have been currently in the process of moving up into the major guilds; see, e.g., the Pucci, below, pp. 122–3, and Neri del Nero who, though enrolled since 1409 as a *rigattiere* and nominated for the scrutiny of 1433 among the *minori*, matriculated in the *Lana* guild in 1427 (Ancisa, E.E., f. 49r). He occupied half a dozen major offices between 1429 and 1434 (MSS. 252, f. 1088r), and was appointed to the crucially responsible position of *Accoppiatore* for the scrutiny of 1434. His family had held the Priorate since 1382.

[11] Cavalcanti, *Istorie*, p. 10.

[12] Morelli, *Ricordi*, pp. 157–8. The following observations on the definition and composition of the ruling group are based on a more extensive exploration of these problems in Kent, 'The Florentine *reggimento*'.

[13] The population of Florence in this period is estimated at about 40,000 by E. Fiumi, 'Fioritura e decadenza dell'economia fiorentina', *A.S.I.* cxvi (1958), 466, of which 1,757 major guildsmen plus 327 *minori* would represent only about one-twentieth. However, given the findings of D. Herlihy, 'Vieillir à Florence au Quattrocento', *Annales — Économies — Sociétés — Civilisations*, xxiv (1969), 1338–52, that in 1427 over half the population was under 22 years of age, and when allowances are made for women, and men under 30, the age at which citizens became eligible for the *Signoria* (Rubinstein, *Government of Florence*, p. 219), and the fact that the average male life expectancy would appear to have been about 27 (Herlihy, 1,350), the realistic

Obviously the possibility of discrimination against the Mediceans by their victorious enemies presents itself. As no other scrutinies for the years immediately before and after survive, discrimination can only effectively be measured in terms of families, and on this level appears to have been relatively slight.[14] Indeed, when we look at the representation of Medicean families as distinct from individuals, the picture is rather different: 75 of the 96 partisans belonged to families who were successful in the scrutiny of 1433. Of the remaining 21, half a dozen were minor guildsmen (the Pucci were exiles as well), one belonged to a magnate clan, and two of the others had at least been successful in previous scrutinies.[15] Of the 44 Mediceans whose families were represented in the scrutiny, but not by themselves, half a dozen were members of houses which mainly supported their opponents, and the fact of their dissociation from the political stance of their *consorti* may well help to explain their individual lack of electoral success.[16] Another four were probably dead by September 1433.[17]

However, in any case the appearance of the family is probably more significant than the omission of the individual. There are observable patterns in fifteenth-century scrutinies which suggest certain general principles underlying their compilation; the number of members of any one family qualified was usually roughly proportionate to its total size, and although some families were clearly more favoured than others, it would seem that scrutiny councils were unwilling to qualify more than a certain percentage of the total membership of any one lineage; for instance, a study of the scrutiny representation of the most prominent citizens in government in this period shows that while these leading citizens normally belonged to the most highly represented of all houses in the scrutiny, they often failed personally to obtain majorities.[18] These observations would suggest that representation in the scrutiny was envisaged primarily in terms of families

ratio of eligibles for the *Tre Maggiori* to total population, though incalculable precisely, would certainly be much higher.

[14] Kent, 'The Florentine *reggimento*' 586.

[15] They had been *veduti*, or 'seen' to be drawn from the bags for these offices.

[16] This would probably be true of the Bardi, Gianozzo Gianfigliazzi, Maso Velluti, Filippo dall'Antella, and possibly several others.

[17] Their sons appear in the scrutinies, while they are absent. It is extremely unusual for living fathers to be passed over for sons; note the special circumstances of a rare example quoted by Kent, *Household and Lineage*, p. 191, n. 94.

[18] Kent, 'The Florentine *reggimento*' 606.

rather than individuals, and that the omission of particular citizens in particular years has no great significance. Certainly individual success depended heavily, and indeed primarily, on previous family record, and by the same token, while individual failure to gain a majority in a particular scrutiny meant that a man had less name tickets in the purses and less immediate chance of being drawn for office, the family representation in the *reggimento*, both past and present, lent the individual much of his general standing in political circles.[19]

This was an important factor in the determination of the smaller and more informal group which seems to have represented an alternative contemporary understanding of the term *reggimento*. Naturally, not all of those 2,000 citizens whose qualification to serve on the leading magistracies gave them a claim to membership in the ruling group were equally influential in affecting the policies and procedures by which Florence was governed; indeed contemporary comments stress the crucial and determining influence of unofficial groups existing within the wider *reggimento* or acting on it.[20] Certainly the findings of this study imply that the city was effectively governed in accordance with the wishes and interests of a relatively small group of citizens who exercised their influence by bringing pressure to bear on the official organs of government through their friends and adherents in office, or by simply making known to them preferences which their power in the city made it impossible for the elected officials directed from the palace of the Priors to ignore.

Obviously, given its informal and extralegal nature, this group cannot be completely and reliably identified with any one body, but there is some reason to believe that it may have been largely coincident with the group of citizens regularly invited to attend the *Consulte e Pratiche*. These were informal councils without any specific or necessary role in the procedure of legislation and government. Although they were not compulsory, being constituted and summoned according to the pleasure of the Priors, the latter notably felt the need for such consultation on most major matters of government, either internal or external, and particularly those in which questions of principle or policy arose.

---

[19] Ibid. 590–2.

[20] See, e.g., Gino Capponi's observation in 1420 that 'li uffici sono in più numero fussono mai, e lo stato in meno' (*Ricordi*, IV); cf. Cavalcanti, *Istorie*, p. 20.

Moreover, as Brucker has observed of the fourteenth century, 'rarely, if ever, did the priors flout the consensus of opinion expressed in these consultative assemblies'.[21] Several historians have noted how closely in various periods their membership coincided with the leadership of the current ruling junta as identified by other means.[22] It would appear likely then that the convention of these councils represented a customary means of bypassing the constitutional provisions which kept official posts circulating within a relatively large sector of Florentine society, and of ascertaining and effecting instead the wishes of those known to have the greatest talent for government and the real power to enforce their mandates.

The number of citizens invited to participate in these councils was considerably smaller than the body of 1,800 or so members of the major guilds who constituted the *reggimento* in its widest sense. Between January 1429 (1428 *s.f.*) and December 1434, the registers of the *Consulte e Pratiche* record, in addition to meetings of the colleges to initiate and conclude deliberations, some 245 general sessions attended usually by between 15 and 40 citizens. About half a dozen of these on any occasion were representatives of various interested offices, like the *Dieci di Balìa* or the *Ufficiali del Banco*, depending upon the nature of the matter under discussion.[23] In those six years more than 700 citizens participated in these meetings; of these, 264 appeared only once or twice, or else only as spokesmen for various offices customarily represented there. About 450 were consulted with some regularity and could be said to have constituted an élite of experienced and respected statesmen with an effective hand in the government of the city,[24]

---

[21] *Florentine Politics*, p. 76, also p. 71.

[22] On the use of the *Consulte e Pratiche* as a means of defining the ruling élite and its inner circles, see Kent, 'The Florentine *reggimento*' 601–8; on their importance as a means of exploring more profoundly its values and general view, see Brucker, *The Civic World*. See also F. Gilbert, *Machiavelli and Guicciardini: Politics and History in Sixteenth Century Florence* (Princeton, 1965), Pt. I, Ch. 1, iii, and Rubinstein, *Government of Florence*, p. 133.

[23] For the nature and function of these offices, see below, Ch. 4, esp. pp. 260–6, 284–8.

[24] These figures are necessarily approximate; the surnames of the better-known statesmen were often not recorded, and although most can be fairly confidently identified from the combination of their Christian names and patronymics, some errors and omissions are unavoidable. As an indicator of political prominence, the tabulating of simple attendance at the *Consulte e Pratiche* has the obvious disadvantage of failing to take account of the nature and quality of contributions to the discussion, or to allow for the frequent absences from Florence of citizens on public or private business.

and about half of those identified as Medicean partisans came into this privileged category.

Moreover, according to Cavalcanti, there remained a yet smaller and more select group to whom belonged the ultimate privilege and responsibility of determining the destinies of the republic; these he described as the 'inner circle of government'[25] or the 'very innermost circle of the ruling group'.[26] According to him, this inner, inner circle was very small indeed, consisting of about seventy leading citizens 'experienced, and long accustomed to governing the city',[27] who wielded a decisive influence over others invited to the *Pratiche*. For example, he tells the story of how Niccolò da Uzzano, a 'highly esteemed and most experienced statesman', would sleep through debates, then suddenly awake and 'get up on the rostrum still half asleep', to prevail over the meeting with the decision that he 'with other powerful citizens' had previously agreed upon 'privately and in secret'.[28] It may be that these *potenti* stood altogether outside the whole governing system, even in its more informal manifestations such as the *Consulte e Pratiche*, but Cavalcanti implies the contrary. Certainly even the comparatively random method of defining the hard core of citizens consulted in the *Pratiche* as those who attended between 30 and 70 meetings in our period, reveals a correlation between this group, notably numbering almost the 70 or so nominated by Cavalcanti, and the other attributes of power in Florence— wealth, tradition, and political prominence; this furnishes strong reason for regarding them, if not precisely as constituting, then at least as generally representative of the innermost circle of the Florentine ruling group.[29] It is of the greatest significance therefore, in our attempt to characterize the political composition and representation of the Medici party, to observe that over the period 1429–34, nineteen, or almost a fifth of identifiable Medicean partisans, qualify for inclusion in this group of sixty-four and represent almost a third of its total composition.[30]

The use of the technical criterion of success in the scrutiny, and the employment of the *Consulte* as an unofficial index, are

[25] *Istorie*, pp. 39, 75.

[26] Cavalcanti, *Trattato*, in Polidori (ed.) *Istorie Fiorentine* ii, 515.

[27] *Istorie*, p. 47; cf. Cosimo de' Medici's reference in a letter of 7 Feb. 1428 (1427 *s.f.*) to '[gli] uomini antichi a regimenti' (M.A.P. II, 22).

[28] *Istorie*, pp. 19–20.   [29] Kent, 'The Florentine *reggimento*' 604–8.

[30] This figure includes Cosimo and Averardo de' Medici themselves.

complementary methods of defining the *reggimento* best used in conjunction with one another and indeed with as many alternative
criteria as seem appropriate; the complex realities of Florentine
political authority are bound to elude any single definition. Thus
it is not necessarily surprising that the Mediceans were almost as
well represented in the élite of the inner *reggimento* as in the much
larger proportion of the citizenry embraced by the eligibles for
the scrutiny, nor that a number of those who appeared in the
first group failed to gain a place in the second. However, these
figures could also indicate that in this period the party's *de facto*
influence, measured by attendance at the *Consulte*, tended to out-
strip the share in government officially allotted through the
scrutinies, as might indeed be expected in the case of a group
currently occupied in a concentrated effort to increase its share in
the *stato*.[31] Those who were partisans of the Medici in the late
twenties and thirties, though relatively successful in the scrutinies
of the preceding half-century,[32] were not on the whole prominent
among the greatest names in the direction of the republic before
the late twenties.[33] Although the situation remains far from clear,
these observations suggest the Mediceans played a dynamic role
within the ruling group at this time. This accords with elements
in Cavalcanti's view of the party, and with its own self-image,
portrayed by several partisans in their letters to the Medici, as
a rising force destined to curb the hitherto unbridled power of

[31] Conversely, the Mediceans enjoyed a reasonable share of the offices to which
the scrutinies gave access, and as they were well represented there in terms of family
membership, the observation that families made eligible in the scrutiny of 1433 had
a virtual monopoly over the three top magistracies applied to them; the latter held
647 of the 660 places available to members of the major guilds between 1429 and
1434. See Tratte, 93, ff. 14r–106r; Kent, 'The Florentine *reggimento*' 600–1.

[32] The Mediceans had done fairly well between 1382 and 1411, especially considering the fact that many of them were from newer families (see below, pp. 116–
26), still making their way in governing circles. The majority kept pace with other
families in the *reggimento*, most of whom doubled their representation in the scrutinies for the *Tre Maggiori* between 1411 and 1433, in accordance with the general
increase ('The Florentine *reggimento*' 613–14). For the scrutinies of 1382, 1391, 1411,
and 1433 see *Delizie degli eruditi toscani*, ed. P. Ildefonso di San Luigi, xiv (Florence,
1784), 125–260; Tratte, 397, and MSS. 555.

[33] Compare Brucker's descriptions of the élite in *The Civic World*, Ch. 5, esp.
pp. 265–82, with the list of Medicean partisans; the only ones really prominent between
1411 and 1426 were Agnolo Pandolfini and Bartolomeo Ridolfi. Those 7 of the 65
houses with more than one representative in the élite of 76 men were all families
with one or more exiles in 1434, and who in general represented the anti-Medicean
position.

'those . . . who have governed us in the past' and which it might please God to prosper 'so that you may save us from them'.[34]

The image of a group in the ascendant is, however, more clearly appropriate in relation to a description of the party in general social, as distinct from specifically political, terms. Conversely, this very distinction between the two should immediately be qualified by the observation that a basic reason for the confusion and contradiction apparent in Cavalcanti's account of the composition of the Medici party is the difficulty of distinguishing, as Lauro Martines has observed, between political and social pre-eminence in a society so obsessed with politics and participation in office.[35] The involvement of the Florentine ruling class in government was unusually direct, intimate, and widespread, and since the majority of its members devoted a considerable portion of their time to the business of the numerous offices in which they were involved over a lifetime, office-holding itself tended naturally to become a major factor in the definition of that class.[36]

The precise measurement of status was an extremely subtle matter, which involved the weighing-up of a number of related but distinct factors. The well-known letters of Alessandra Strozzi, concerned with the choice of marriage partners for her children, illustrate the care with which Florentines classifying their fellows in social terms balanced the possession of really noble blood against a share in the *stato*, assessed the precise degree of this share by various particular calculations, and arrived at the judgement that the individual in question was of 'a great and noble family' or one of those merely 'established and sound', as the case might be.[37] Attempting to articulate and to define these criteria more precisely, the humanist Poggio Bracciolini, writing in the early fifteenth century, concluded that social eminence depended in fact upon a combination of old wealth, distinguished birth, and experience in political life.[38]

[34] M.A.P. II, 32, Battista di Doffo Arnolfi to Averardo, 19 Feb. 1428 (1427 *s.f.*); cf. Benedetto Masi, ibid. 246; see above, p. 104.

[35] *The Social World*, p. 47. His study was the first to construct a standard from contemporary criteria determining social place in Florence, and then to measure individuals in terms of them.

[36] A. Molho, 'Politics and the ruling class' 407, has calculated that there were 3,000 or so governmental posts available per annum; for many of the 2,000 odd citizens eligible to fill them, communal politics must virtually have constituted a full-time occupation.

[37] *Lettere*, pp. 3, 11, 313, 395, 449.   [38] Martines, *The Social World*, p. 45.

However, participation in politics does not enter into the measurement of social status simply as one of several important factors—in fact it subtly pervades all the rest. Wealth was important, but it had to be old—that is, dignified by the accompaniment of that political recognition which was in time the natural reward of affluence and the necessary condition of its ultimate maintenance and defence. The coincidence in practice between wealth and social pre-eminence was thus far from complete; just as the latter was often denied the *nouveaux riches*, so alternatively it might long outlast the actual economic decline and failure of a once rich and powerful house.[39]

The idea of distinguished birth came to be similarly associated with a family tradition of service in political office. Of course the very noblest citizens were those who could trace their family's contribution to business and political life in Florence back to the twelfth and thirteenth centuries or beyond, and this view is reflected in the habit of preserving details of the family past and genealogy in personal *ricordi*.[40] These multiplied apace in the later fourteenth and fifteenth centuries, when many families were seeking to establish their eminence over others more newly risen; indeed, as Giovanni Morelli observed in the opening passage of his own *Ricordi*: 'Today everyone lays claim to ancient origins', concluding somewhat ingenuously that 'therefore I want to demonstrate that ours are genuine'.[41] Suspicious of the value of genealogies flaunted by many of their fellow citizens, contemporaries came in practice to measure the social distinction of a family essentially from the appearance of the first of its members in the Priorate, which became the chief executive magistracy at the time when the republic broadly assumed what was to be its definitive shape and organization for the succeeding 250 years. The *Prioriste*, lists of all those who had held the city's highest office since its inception in 1282, were civic genealogies kept and consulted constantly, not only by government officials, but also

[39] Cf. Lorenzo de' Medici's comment, quoted above, p. 18. In fact, however, roughly two-thirds of the wealthiest citizens in 1427 failed to gain a majority in the scrutiny for the *Tre Maggiori* in 1433, and many, though by no means all, were from new and obscure families. Measured as *consorterie*, some half of the ruling group were outstandingly wealthy, but a number of old and influential families, still well represented in the scrutiny, were relatively poor. (See Kent, 'The Florentine *reggimento*' 596–600.) On the traditional Florentine attitudes to honourable wealth, see Martines, *The Social World*, pp. 18–39.

[40] Above, pp. 2–3.   [41] p. 81.

by many socially conscious private citizens as a guide to the precise credentials of prospective marriage or business partners.[42]

If a family's social distinction depended on the possession of wealth and political power persisting long enough to earn it an established position in the ruling class, yet socially mobile individuals and families like the Morelli continued to enter the *reggimento* or ruling group via the scrutinies,[43] then the two could never be quite equivalent, and social and political pre-eminence, despite their close relationship, were nevertheless distinguishable. A perfect illustration of this fact is provided in a unique classifica tion of the *reggimento* on the occasion of the scrutiny of 1484 by Piero Guicciardini, father of the historian Francesco. He distinguished five layers of social status within the ranks of those successful in the current scrutiny. At the top of the pile were the men from great old noble families like the Bardi and the Rossi, on the bottom the plebeian group from the lowest strata of the minor guilds. Above these were the more elevated artisans, and those of the major guilds who had only recently attained the Priorate. A little below the very noblest families were the ancient and distinguished *popolani* houses like the Albizzi, Peruzzi, Corsini, Ricci, and Alberti, and in the very middle were those not yet noble, but no longer base; fully fledged, but only recently established members of the *reggimento* like the Serristori. He went on to explain how those on the lowest level, having once gained the Priorate in a scrutiny,

in another gain something better, according to their ability, or their wealth, and in a short time . . . they ascend from the lowest level and proceed to the next, always rising, and in their place are succeeded by even newer men to fill up the lowest ranks, and thus continually new men make the grade, and in order to give them a place in the governing class it is necessary to eliminate from it long-established citizens; and that is what is actually done.[44]

In view of the focus by Florentines on family traditions of political service, whether explicit, as in the Strozzi calculations, or implicit, as in the Guicciardinian schema, historians, lacking the

[42] See Martines, *The Social World*, pp. 39–50, on the social significance of public office-holding.

[43] There was a small but steady inflow of new families into the *reggimento* from 1382 at least to 1453 (Kent, 'The Florentine *reggimento*' 615–16).

[44] Rubinstein, *Government of Florence*, Appendix XI, esp. p. 323, and pp. 214–15; I have used his translation of the last sentence.

fine social sense which allowed contemporaries to achieve a delicate balance of the complex criteria involved, have formalized their reliance on the Priorate as the surest and stoutest yardstick for social measurement, and have employed with some success a scheme emphasizing certain watersheds in the city's political development.[45] The first followed the great banking failures of the early 1340s and the Black Death later in the decade. The consequent shake-up at the top of the social pyramid and the wave of immigration from the surrounding countryside contributed to the entry into Florentine political life of a large number of citizens very different in social character from the thirteenth-century families who had nearly all made their début in the Priorate before 1343. Different again were those who had taken no part in the tensions and conflicts of political life in the mid-fourteenth century, and had entered the ruling group only after the re-consolidation of an aristocratic establishment in 1382. Although these dates should not be too rigidly employed, especially since Guicciardini's comments do not suggest that contemporary social evaluations necessarily corresponded precisely to these dividing lines in the city's political history and the experience of its *reggimento*, they do provide a certain standard for measuring social age in Florence, and for sketching in a rough, but hopefully helpful and suggestive social profile of the ruling class.[46]

When measured in these terms, the Medici partisans are revealed as a socially disparate group. Contrary once again to the crudest tradition, the party contained a solid block of members of a number of old and distinguished houses who had regarded control of state affairs as part of their patrimony for a century or more. Notably, however, almost half the Miceans came from much newer families, who might reasonably have been regarded as upstarts and described by their more distinguished fellows in the *reggimento* as men with 'very little status'.[47] Its peculiar social composition affected not only the party's external image, but also

[45] Cf. Kent, 'The Florentine *reggimento*' 594–5.

[46] The importance of distinctions in social age within the Florentine ruling class was first realized and demonstrated by Gene Brucker and Marvin Becker, and the schema here outlined is essentially theirs. See Brucker, *Florentine Politics*, esp. pp. 20–1, and Becker, 'An Essay on the "Novi Cives" '; it has been most fruitfully applied in practice by Martines, *The Social World*.

[47] Fifty partisans belonged to families which gained the Priorate before 1343; 46 were from houses which entered the ruling group after that date, and of these 20 or so belonged to the post-1382 period.

its aims and internal structure. We have already seen something of the way in which the social status of partisans determined the nature of their relationships with the Medici and the bonds which linked them to the party, and now through the consideration of some particular partisans we may observe the specific contributions of citizens from differing social strata to the tone and function of the whole.[48]

It is important to stress that despite their general poverty, divisiveness, and the embroilment in unpopular and unsuccessful political adventures which had limited their influence on government in the later fourteenth century, the Medici family, by virtue of age and traditions, of the wealth, and political and personal charisma of its leaders, was in a highly favourable position to dominate and direct that half of their party which consisted of men from families comparatively recently risen into the ruling class. While, as we have seen, many of their associates from older families enjoyed the equalizing relationships of *parenti*, only one of their newer partisans married a Medici. Conversely, while most of their more prestigious supporters came from other quarters of the city, about half the newer men were neighbours whose circumstances probably reinforced their dependence upon their more established patrons.[49] They were subject to that pervasive influence which, in a face-to-face society, a large and powerful lineage might exert in the crowded city districts, and even more in the country, where the realities of power were in practice less trammelled by principles and regulations concerning its distribution. There were a number of partisans who originated from the Mugello and maintained their ties there, and strongly pro-Medicean families like the Della Casa and the Ciai from Scarperia, the centre of the district dominated by the Medici estates, may well have accorded the Medici something much more like the inevitable allegiance of rural retainers than the negotiated and contingent support of many urban partisans.[50]

[48] These portraits in the round also provide a more comprehensive picture of some of the leading Medici supporters who have hitherto only been mentioned in connection with particular aspects of the party structure.

[49] The only partisans resident in the three Medici *gonfaloni* belonging to the inner circle of the *reggimento* were Nerone di Nigi Dietisalvi and Giovanni di Lorenzo di Ugo della Stufa. Only 15 of the 45 Medici neighbourhood partisans came from families who had gained their first Prior before 1343.

[50] Cf. the observations of Jones concerning relationships of urban patricians based on rural land tenure, quoted above, p. 8 n. Niccolò Cavalcanti, though officially

More specifically, most citizens sought a powerful protector in their own district, to defend their interests in the scrutinies and the distribution of taxes,[51] and there is some evidence to suggest that the interests of many of the newer partisans in these two crucial areas may well have been in need of defence. Although some pro-Medicean *gente nuova* had achieved economic success well before 1434—in 1427, for instance, Ser Martino di Ser Luca Martini was 120th on the list of the richest citizens of San Giovanni—almost all of those Medici partisans (over a quarter of the total) whose expenditure so exceeded their incomes that there remained no surplus on which to levy a normal tax, belonged to newer families like the Ciai, Guiducci, Cocco-Donati, Martelli, Masi, Del Nero, and Pucci, and most of these were from the Medici *gonfaloni*.[52]

As no complete scrutiny list survives for the years between 1411 and 1433, the period in which the Medici began the promotion of their supporters to power, it is difficult to interpret the remaining figures. Many of the newer Medicean families, especially those in the Medici *gonfaloni*, like the Masi and the Martelli, were rather favoured after the Medici triumph in 1434;[53] a notable improvement in the position of others between 1411 and 1433 may or may not have been due to Medicean manipulation of the electoral process towards the end of the twenties.[54]

classified under Vipera in the *catasto*, actually lived in Scarperia (Cat. 74, f. 191v). Cf., however, Brucker, *The Civic World*, p. 256, on the Della Casa and the Albizzi in the 1390s.

[51] Cf. Morelli, *Ricordi;* Perosa (ed.), *Rucellai, il Zibaldone*, and various exchanges from the Sacchetti letters, quoted above, e.g. p. 62.

[52] For the 600 wealthiest citizens of Florence in 1427, see the wealth tables published by Martines, *The Social World*, pp. 365–78. Of the total of 25 Mediceans 'composti', only 6 were from pre-1342 families; the other 19 were newer men. It is broadly assumed here, and below, e.g. pp. 140–4, that as indicated by extensive reading of the *catasto* registers, there is a general correlation between a citizen's wealth and the size of his taxable income, and thus between poverty and paying only a nominal tax. However, the original amount of his assets before the deduction of expenses, and the general size of the sums involved, are also relevant to a really accurate evaluation of effective wealth, particularly as a determinant of social status.

[53] See Rubinstein, *Government of Florence*, p. 66.

[54] In general, the electoral gains in the scrutinies made by Medicean new men between 1382 and 1433 resembled those made by the average representative of the *reggimento*; e.g. most more or less doubled their representation between 1411 and 1433, in accordance with the over-all pattern. There are a few examples of outstanding increases (Martelli, 1 to 5; Orlandini, 1 to 6; Della Casa, 5 to 14); it should be borne in mind, however, that given the apparent existence of some sort of absolute

It is clear, however, that few of the newer men commanded sufficient political reputation to carry much weight in the *stato* independently of the Medici. Of the score of Mediceans in the inner *reggimento*, only Niccolò del Benino and Agnolo Pandolfini came from families in the post-1343 wave of admissions to the Priorate.[55] Moreover, being of relatively recent origin, most of the newer families were comparatively small—some two or three households on average; none of them was large enough to constitute a force in itself, or solely with the support of its own adherents.[56] By the same token, they were also comparatively freer of such densely spun webs of customary association as encumbered many of the older families, divided their loyalties, and complicated their choices in the event of divisions within the *reggimento*. The party gained much of its strength from a core of supporters whose partial dependence made them relatively reliable, and whose social status made it natural for them to accept rather than compete for leadership.

A more specific, if more limited, contribution of this group of partisans to the promotion of the Medici was made possible through their occupancy of notarial positions which were peculiarly the prerogative of the *gente nuova* and often the means of their social ascent—about a third of the Medicean new men came originally from notarial families and at least five or six were still practising notaries in this period.[57] Those who were attached to the leading magistracies had unique access to classified information

ceiling of representation (Kent, 'The Florentine *reggimento*' 591–2), it may have been rather easier for new families, often small and with limited initial representation, to increase their majorities than for older, larger, and initially more prominent houses to make the same proportional gains.

[55] The Tornabuoni had their first Prior only in 1445, but as a *popolano* offshoot of the magnate house of Tornaquinci, they were certainly not 'new men'.

[56] e.g. in 1427 there were five or six Ginori households, four each of Pucci and Cocci-Donati, and three Martelli, though it is difficult to be precise about the number of households comprised in each lineage. Counting is complicated by confusion due to the numbers of separate families with the same surname and often, especially in the case of newer families, to the omission of the surname in the *catasto* report or its appearance in a different form—e.g. several of the Ginori described themselves simply as 'di Ser Gino'. Hence the print-out from the computerized study of households from the *catasto* (A.S.F.) is not always a reliable guide.

[57] Those from notarial backgrounds included the Della Casa, Ginori, Pandolfini, Parenti, Dello Scarfa, Serristori, and Di Ser Segna; among those still practising notaries were, in addition to Ciai, Martini, Tinucci, Cepperello, Orlandini, and Benedetto Masi. Another Medici client, Antonio da Villa, though not sufficiently documented to be classed among the partisans, was also a notary (above, p. 89).

concerning elections and other key areas of government; the prevalence of notaries among the Medici *amici*, and the particular intimacy they enjoyed with the leaders of the party, suggest that the latter were well aware of the strategic value of their support. There is some evidence that Niccolò Tinucci, Ser Ciao Ciai, and particularly Ser Martino Martini kept the Medici regularly abreast of the official secrets which they acquired,[58] and Martini was actually convicted in 1429 of interfering with government and leaking confidential information after 1426.[59]

Obviously partisans from newer families had much to gain from association with an increasingly powerful house bent on winning for itself and its followers the larger share in the *stato* which was the natural goal of citizens still in the ascendant, and despite the limitations of their position they constituted a valuable source of support for their patrons. A mutual recognition of the advantages of their relationship is implied in the relatively early commitment of many of the more prominent new men in the party to the Medicean cause.

The Martelli, a family of nine brothers living in Lion d'oro, were among the earliest and most devoted of the *gente nuova* associates;[60] they gained the Priorate quite early, in fact precisely in the year 1343, which we have selected to mark the division between the old and newer families. However, they would seem rightly to belong to the latter group, not simply on a technicality, but by virtue of the fact that they made little social or political headway throughout most of the fourteenth century.[61] A couple of relatively distinguished marriages in this period marked the beginning of their social ascent which coincided with their involvement in 1393, along with several members of the Medici family, in an attempted *coup* against the Albizzi government. In

[58] Below, for example, pp. 224–34.

[59] Giud. Appelli 75, f. 428r; cf. below, p. 225. Martines, *Lawyers and Statecraft*, esp. pp. 32, 50, 54, comments on the strategic political skills of notaries, the corruption which often existed among them, and the fact that in 1434 they were consequently forbidden to hold major offices in future.

[60] There is so much evidence concerning the pro-Medicean connections of most of the brothers both before and shortly after 1434 that it seems reasonable to consider the entire household as supporting them; however, the youngest of the nine brothers has been omitted from the list of partisans for analysis because even by 1433 he was only 14 years of age, and therefore presumably not an effective independent agent (Cat. 78, ff. 70v–72r).

[61] In the scrutinies for the *Tre Maggiori* from 1382 to 1433 they gained 2, 2, 1, and finally 5 majorities.

consequence they were excluded from eligibility to hold office, a fact which might naturally have inclined them to draw closer to their similarly deprived Medici neighbours, even had there been no intimacy between them before the incident.[62]

Although the Martelli are among the few partisans who left no surviving letters to the Medici in the succeeding years, the *Ricordo* of Ugolino, the eldest of the brothers, leaves no possible doubt about the length and strength of Martelli allegiance. From it we may discover that Ugolino himself was the *compagno* of Bernardo d'Antonio da Uzzano, Carlo di Nicola de' Medici, and Messer Donato his brother, that Ugolino's marriage was arranged by Lorenzo di Giovanni, Cosimo's brother, and that the Martelli brothers were heavily involved in business not only with Cosimo and Lorenzo, but also with Bernardo d'Antonio de' Medici and Orlando di Guccio.[63] Indeed several of the Martelli were employed by the Medici bank, both before and after 1434; it was partly in this capacity that they were able to render constant and invaluable assistance to the family during their period in exile.[64] The letters of Francesco di Giuliano di Averardo de' Medici in Venice to his father in Rome record in particular the support of Lotto, Antonio, and Domenico, who accompanied the Medici into exile; it was Antonio Martelli whom Cosimo sent to Florence in the early days of September 1434 to seek confirmation of their recall by the government.[65] The diary of Ugolino contains a vivid record of the events of the crisis of 1434, in which he described how his brother Bartolomeo was one of the first to warn the *Signoria* of the anti-Medicean revolt against them, and how after its virtual collapse the defeated rebels attempted to set fire to the Martelli houses in recognition of, and reprisal for, their identification with the Medici interest.

In a not dissimilar position were the Ginori, who had their first Prior in 1344, and began to establish themselves in the *reggimento* before the beginning of the fifteenth century. Between 1411 and 1433 they increased their majorities in the scrutiny for the *Tre Maggiori* from two to five, by 1427 the three sons of Francesco di

---

[62] For the history of the Martelli family before 1434, see Martines, 'La famiglia Martelli', which includes a partial edition of Ugolino's *Ricordi*.

[63] C.S. 5ª ser. 1461, f. 3r.

[64] De Roover, *The Rise and Decline*, pp. 377-9; cf. M.A.P. XI, 611, Roberto Martelli to Cosimo, 4 Feb. 1432 (1431 *s.f.*).

[65] See, e.g., M.A.P. V, 706; Cosimo, *Ricordi*, p. 101.

Ser Gino were among the wealthier citizens of the quarter of San Giovanni, and by the 1430s they had made some respectable marriages with families like the Albizzi, Cavalcanti, and Dietisalvi.[66] It seems likely, however, that they owed their ultimate success to the Medici; the association began some time in the mid-fourteenth century, when as notaries to the *Signoria* the Ginori also did some work for their powerful neighbours in Lion d'oro.[67] They lived virtually on the Medici doorstep, and co-operated with them in the acquiring of land for the site of the new Medici palace. By 1432 Giuliano Ginori was writing to Averardo de' Medici rejoicing in the successes of the *amici*,[68] and some evidence of the degree of Ginori identification with the Medici interest by 1433 is Cavalcanti's claim that Piero Ginori was the only man in Florence to protest openly at Cosimo's arrest, and that he 'quite fearlessly roamed the city, shouting out, and virtually showing himself to be utterly lacking in wisdom, and in fact quite mad'.[69] The family was rewarded on the Medici return, and after 1434 finally acquired the political and social prestige which had previously eluded them. In the scrutiny of 1440 the Ginori, though still quite a small family, were among the best represented in their *gonfalone*, and as the century went on a series of very distinguished marriages confirmed and crowned their social success.[70]

The rise of the Pucci seems to have been the consequence of a particular combination of personal talent and Medici support. They lived in Via de' Servi, in the *gonfalone* of Vaio, and were neighbours to a number of the Medici family, including Cosimo's cousin Averardo, whose crucial role in the promotion of the party has already been described. Their involvement in the political activities of the family began early in the century; in 1412 Antonio di Puccio Pucci and his son Puccio were banished, along with several Medici, Alberti, and one of the Ricci,[71] and by 1427 Puccio was already corresponding with the Medici concerning the affairs of 'nostri amici'.[72] Still artisans in the early 1430s, and

---

[66] L. Passerini, *Genealogia Ginori*, Tav. III, VIII; Brucker, *The Civic World*, p. 256.

[67] F. W. Kent, *Household and Lineage*, p. 216; see also his general observations on the relations between the Ginori and the Medici, esp. Ch. 4.

[68] M.A.P. V, 201, discussed below, p. 288.

[69] *Istorie*, pp. 279-80; cf. Tinucci, *Examina*, p. 413.

[70] Rubinstein, *Government of Florence*, p. 66; Passerini, *Genealogia*, loc. cit.

[71] Acqu. e Doni 301, Ins. I.   [72] M.A.P. II, 69; below, p. 227.

unable to pay more than a token tax in 1427,[73] the brothers
Puccio, Piero, and Giovanni d'Antonio had only limited access
to major offices and the status which they conferred, and a considerable way to rise to the upper echelons of the ruling class.
However, by this time both Puccio and Giovanni enjoyed a
sizeable share of those offices open to *minori*, and their frequent
appearances in the *Consulte* indicate the degree of their political
influence;[74] indeed Puccio must on these grounds be considered
at least a minor member of the inner *reggimento*. The fact that
Cosimo regarded him as one of 'my most valued friends'[75] may
have been either a cause or a consequence of this fact; certainly
he was known in Florence to be Cosimo's right-hand man in the
conduct of the party and thus some citizens even named the *amici*
'Puccini' after him. That his reputed role in the Medici party was
more than popular gossip is demonstrated in the exile of Puccio
and Giovanni shortly after the expulsion in 1433 of the Medici
themselves. After 1434 the Pucci were enrolled in the *Cambio*
guild, it is said by the favour of their prestigious patrons,[76] and
having naturally been absent from the scrutiny of 1433 were
represented there by no less than fourteen members in 1440.[77]

The Medici also helped to promote the careers of the Masi and
Orlandini, two families who had the advantage of being enrolled
in the major guilds, but did not in fact hold the Priorate until
1416 and 1420 respectively.[78] The Orlandini brothers lived in the
parish of San Lorenzo, in the heart of Medici territory, where
they counted among their neighbours two of the Pucci. Bartolomeo Orlandini was denounced as a Medici partisan shortly after
their expulsion in 1433—quite appropriately, since he was one
of those who had written after the death of Giovanni di Bicci
pledging his loyalty to Averardo.[79] He was closely involved with

[73] Cat. 81, ff. 35r–v, 47v.

[74] e.g. between 1429 and 1434 Puccio had been an artisan representative in such
prestigious magistracies as the officials of the *Monte* (Tratte 80, f. 393r), *Catasto*
(ibid., f. 409r) and *Conservatori delle Leggi* (ibid., f. 416r); he also took part in twenty-
seven *Consulte* in that period. [75] *Ricordi*, p. 100.

[76] Litta, *Famiglie Celebri* x, Tav. III. [77] Rubinstein, *Government of Florence*, p. 9.

[78] MSS. 253, ff. 1314, 1325; the Orlandini of Drago San Giovanni would appear
to be the family of the Medici partisans, although there is another Orlandini family
with whom they might be confused; see Kent, 'The Florentine *reggimento*' 629.

[79] See Tinucci, *Examina*, pp. 408–9; M.A.P. II, 167; cf. ibid. 191, 287; III, 242,
14. Since his family contained five adult co-resident brothers, it is possible that all
were Medici sympathizers. On his own political role pre-1430, see Brucker, *The
Civic World*.

Mediceans and their affairs in the intervening years; his creditors were nearly all from Medicean families, including Giovanni di Bicci and Cosimo,[80] and his brother had married in 1424 a daughter of the Davanzati,[81] a distinguished family which had similarly acknowledged Giovanni's death with renewed promises of support. Bartolomeo considered himself sufficiently important to the Medici to expect that they would want to keep him off the *specchio* by paying his taxes for him;[82] since on one occasion he agreed to satisfy a request of Averardo's even though it meant defying the orders of the *Signoria*, he was probably right.[83] He was to play a major role in the upheaval of 1434; Cavalcanti describes how as commander of the citizen army he came to the aid of the pro-Medicean Priors and 'under the guise of doing his duty as Captain, blocked off all the entrances to the *piazza*'.[84] In the late twenties and early thirties he had made some appearances in the *Consulte*, and during the years between 1427 and 1433 obviously prospered financially, since his assets increased tenfold over a period when the tax returns of most citizens recorded a decline.[85] By 1441 he was considered sufficiently distinguished to be appointed an ambassador to accompany Pope Eugenius on his journey from Florence to Rome.[86]

The Masi of Lion d'oro were notaries to the *Signoria* from 1386 on into the mid-fifteenth century.[87] Although we know little more of Benedetto di Guido than what appears from his letters,[88] Antonio di Ser Tommaso and his four brothers are better documented. They lived in Via della Stufa only a block or so away from the main Medici houses in Via Larga. In 1427 they were *compagni* of Zanobi di Salvestro Serristori, the brother of Antonio Serristori, Averardo's wealthy son-in-law, though they were not themselves particularly well-off, and indeed in 1433 their liabilities exceeded their assets by the considerable sum of 1,395 florins.[89] Antonio was deeply involved in the Medici efforts to improve their position in the *stato* through the control of major offices, and during a term as Prior in September 1430 he was the organizer of an attempt by the Medici to stack the election of the *Dieci di Balìa* with Medici partisans in order to ensure the success

[80] Cat. 498, ff. 75v–78r.   [81] Ancisa, AA, f. 655v.   [82] M.A.P. V, 14.
[83] Ibid. II, 242.   [84] *Istorie*, p. 311.
[85] Cat. 79, f. 151; cf. ibid. 498, ff. 75v–78r.   [86] MSS. 253, f. 1325.
[87] Ibid., f. 1314.   [88] Above, pp. 102–4.
[89] Cat. 49, ff. 948, 1632r; 497, ff. 68r–71r.

of their favoured candidate.[90] He was the enthusiastic friend who, after the drawing of the pro-Medicean Priorate in September 1434, came to Cosimo in Venice, 'sent there by many citizens to urge us to start out for Florence, offering when they should hear that we were nearby, to provoke a rising and to install us within';[91] he was also one of the *Priori a mano* hand-picked by the *Balìa* less than two months later.[92] Although in the scrutiny of 1433 only one of ten members of the family nominated received a majority, in 1440 seventeen Masi qualified; they enjoyed the highest representation in Lion d'oro in that year and were second only to the Medici in 1449.[93]

Although the careers of some of these more successful and outstanding of the newer men among the *amici* are particularly representative of that group of partisans, there were others from families of similar age and background whose relationship to the Medici resembled that of their more socially distinguished fellows. Perhaps the most notable example is Antonio di Salvestro Serristori, whose family received the Priorate only in 1392 and was not represented in the *Signoria* again until 1428.[94] However, at the age of only 32, he was in 1427 the second richest citizen in the quarter of Santa Croce, with a taxable income of over 28,000 florins.[95] Presumably his wealth accounts for the fact that he was the only partisan from the newer group of families with whom the Medici connected themselves by marriage, and certainly his union with Averardo's daughter Tancia in the twenties would have had the effect of binding him and his money to the service of Medici concerns. By the end of the decade he appears literally as one of the family in the letters of Cosimo, Averardo, and Giuliano, who seem to have sought his advice on most matters of importance.[96] As one of the major creditors of the commune during the war with Lucca, along with Cosimo and Andrea Pazzi, he increased the Medicean financial stake in the *stato*, and when with the expulsion of Cosimo their enemies tried to break the bank which threatened to give them the controlling interest, Serristori was able to put his own bank and his business acumen at their disposal

---

[90] M.A.P. II, 508.   [91] *Ricordi*, Fabroni, p. 101.
[92] Balìe, 25, ff. 44v–45r. On the suspension of normal sortition and the procedure of election *a mano*, see Rubinstein, *Government of Florence*, pp. 6–7, 10–16.
[93] Rubinstein, *Government of Florence*, pp. 9, 66.
[94] MSS. 252, f. 1217.   [95] Cat. 72, ff. 26r–39r; cf. 492, ff. 53v–59r.
[96] See, e.g., M.A.P. II, 23, 27, 141; III, 51, 206.

in order to save it.[97] Several other newer men who, like the Del Benino family, the Carducci brothers, and Agnolo Pandolfini had declared their support for Medici political manœuvres by the early thirties, but expressed in the pattern of their more general associations and activities a certain independence from the leaders of the party more characteristic of the older families, were similarly citizens of considerable wealth or personal political influence.[98]

It is clear that the Medici party did represent to some extent the specific interests of the newer sections of Florentine patrician society, that its success was partly due to their support, and that they were among the chief beneficiaries of that success; in all these respects their prominence was an important determinant of the tone and quality of the Medici party and its significance as a phenomenon in Florentine political life.

On the other hand, their presence and influence were balanced by those of an almost equal number of citizens from more socially established families whose adherence to the Medici cause shows that the interests which it represented were not exclusively those of the *arrivistes*. As a group, the partisans from older families were comparatively wealthy; by contrast with the new men, only half a dozen had insufficient surplus assets to merit the normal tax. Almost a third of them belonged, like Cosimo and Averardo de' Medici, to the inner circle of the ruling group, and most were attached to the leaders of the party by bonds of *parentado* and business association appropriate to citizens of similar status.[99] Conversely, partisans from older families tended to attach themselves less exclusively to the Medici, and to enjoy a much wider range of associations with other members of the ruling group than their fellow *amici* more recently risen into it.

[97] M.A.P. V, 699, 702.

[98] Niccolò d'Andrea del Benino, Filippo di Giovanni Carducci, and Agnolo Pandolfini were all members of the innermost circle of the *reggimento*. The Carducci brothers, Bartolomeo, Niccolò, and Lorenzo di Giovanni, ranked 33rd on the list of the wealthiest taxpayers in Santa Maria Novella in 1427; Pandolfini was the seventh-richest man in San Giovanni. Both the latter families enjoyed close associations with their Strozzi *parenti* (Pol. Gar. 497; Vespasiano da Bisticci, *Vite* iii. 139); for their other connections, see 'Ricordanze di Filippo di Giovanni Carducci', C.S. 2ª ser. CXXVIII. See also Brucker, *The Civic World*, esp. p. 256.

[99] Above, Ch. 1 (iii) and (v). About half of the partisans from older families were either *parenti* of the Medici or their business associates, and some were both; of those with such close ties, over half were members of the inner *reggimento*.

Such partisans made valuable allies by virtue of the wealth, influence, and general prestige which they could place at the service of the party. For example, the role of several as financiers to the state during the Lucchese war was a crucial one in establishing the early ascendancy of the Mediceans over their opponents, and the more prominent members of this group, like Luca degli Albizzi and Piero Guicciardini, made a vital contribution to the Medici victory in 1434 by leading the swing within the ruling group away from the prevailing regime and towards the support of the absent Medici.[100] But if their greater capacity and opportunities for independent action made some more distinguished partisans less dependent on Medici patronage than many *gente nuova*, nevertheless one of the more interesting features of the composition and structure of the Medici party remains the absence within it of any other family fitted to compete with the Medici themselves for its leadership.

For while the *gente nuova* were limited by their lack of social prestige, many of the older citizens suffered from such various disabilities as the lack of a large and powerful family for support, unpopularity with the pre-1434 regime, or the politically debilitating effects of a magnate background or tradition. Among the older families as among the newer there was a contingent (though a rather smaller one) from the Medici *gonfaloni* which had much in common with its newer neighbours. Of the dozen or so partisans in the older group, only one, Berto Carnesecchi, declared assets in 1427 of a value as substantial as 6,000 florins; most of the rest were of very moderate means, and indeed four of the six citizens from the older families whose expenditure at that time exceeded their assets were Medici neighbours—Pigello Portinari, Matteo Cerretani, Battista Arnolfi, and Giovanni della Stufa.[101] Nor did this group of partisans enjoy the support of large or influential *consorterie*. Most of their families consisted of one, two, or three households; and none with the possible exception of the Della Stufa could be described as playing a major part on the Florentine political stage in the years immediately preceding the Medici rise to power.[102]

[100] Below, p. 324.

[101] A fifth, Niccolò Cavalcanti, was assessed for the *catasto* in Vipera, but actually lived in Scarperia (Cat. 74, f. 191v).

[102] For the role of particular individuals and families in politics in the twenties, see Brucker, *The Civic World*, Ch. 7.

Several families who had fallen from positions of former power in the thirteenth and fourteenth centuries must, by the beginning of the fifteenth, have had strong inducement to hitch their creaking wagons to the Medici star in the hope of turning decline into recovery, and those in most need of the promotion and protection of their already powerful and ambitious Medici neighbours were usually among the first to align themselves with the party. For example, an attempt by the Medici in 1427 to interfere with the scrutinies in their own interest was helped along by the co-operation of Battista di Doffo Arnolfi, from a smallish San Giovanni family which gained its first Prior in 1318 but had enjoyed little prominence in Florentine affairs more recently. As he assured Averardo early in 1428, Battista had played the part allotted him as faithfully as he could, and hoped that the results would soon be apparent in government.[103]

Also among the family's earlier associates were members of the Alberti and the Ricci, two large and formerly very powerful families with highly distinguished traditions who found themselves outside the *reggimento* in the early years of the fifteenth century.[104] Their appearance among the Medici partisans may constitute some limited support for a once-popular view that the Medici–Albizzi confrontation of the early 1430s was essentially a continuation of the Ricci–Albizzi feuds of the later fourteenth century.[105] Some members of the Medici family had been associated with the opposition to the Albizzi at that time, and the rehabilitation of the Alberti after 1434 gives some reason to believe that the connection with them was a continuing one.[106] Certainly the

---

[103] Below, pp. 233–4; cf. Neri di Domenico Bartolini-Scodellari, whose family gained the Priorate in 1299, but had only one Prior (in 1409) between 1386 and 1428 (MSS. 248, f. 327). Neri appeared only three times in the *Consulte e Pratiche* between 1429 and 1434, although he held several major offices in the same period and was notably one of the pro-Medicean Priors in September 1434 whose appointment heralded the Medici victory. The Bartolini-Scodellari were neither large nor wealthy; in 1427 they consisted of only two households, and in 1433 Neri boasted assets of only 1,068 florins (Cat. 498, ff. 514v–516v). A neighbour of the Medici in Drago San Giovanni and in the Mugello (ibid.), Neri was by 1430 one of those *amici* who co-operated to elect their fellow partisans into office (M.A.P. II, 373, 508), and his appointment as *Accoppiatore* between 1434 and 1439 indicates that the Medici considered him a particularly strong and reliable supporter (see Rubinstein, *Government of Florence*, pp. 9, 24).

[104] Brucker, *The Civic World*, pp. 173–4, 337–40.

[105] Pellegrini, *Sulla repubblica*, pp. 12–13. Conversely, some Ricci were associated in various ways with the exiles; e.g. below, pp. 160, 163.

[106] Balìe 25, f. 10r–v; cf. Rubinstein, *Government of Florence*, p. 124. Conversely,

partisanship of members of both these families illustrates the tendency of the Medici party to attract behind it the support of individuals and families currently on the outskirts, socially or politically, with something obviously to gain from any challenge to the *status quo*.

The same might perhaps be said of three families with members who in their business enterprises had joined their fortunes, quite literally, to those of the Medici well before the political divisions of the ruling group in the mid-twenties became explicit: the Bardi, Pazzi, and Portinari. The Medici partisans from these families were among the richer citizens of Florence in 1427, but all these houses lacked political influence commensurate with their wealth. The Bardi, an enormous clan which had played a leading role in the history of the republic in the thirteenth and early fourteenth centuries, were mostly magnates with only a single majority in the scrutiny of 1433; while many of its leaders opposed the Medici at this period to support the explicitly pro-magnate conservatives, the branch of the Conti di Vernio, related to Cosimo by his marriage to Contessina de' Bardi, were among the major supporters of the more populist alternative which he represented. None of the Pazzi or the Portinari was successful in the scrutiny of 1433; although Andrea de' Pazzi was a prominent member of the inner *reggimento*, many of his *consorti* were still magnates in the early fifteenth century, and the family as a whole seems to have suffered for its traditions.[107]

There were a number of Medicean partisans whose prominence in the current *reggimento* might have made them an independent political force of some significance, but as it happened, while on the one hand many of these had by the late twenties been too long or too closely involved with Medici interests to distinguish them easily or effectively from their own, many of the remainder

the complexity of alignments within the *reggimento* makes any simple equation between the two groups quite impossible; for example, in the fourteenth century there were Medici supporters among both factions (Brucker, 'The Medici' 17).

107 On the Bardi at the height of their power and influence, see Becker, *Florence in Transition* i, IV; on the definition of magnates and the significance of their traditions, below, pp. 146-9. There were 15 Bardi households among the top 150 in the quarter of Santo Spirito in 1427, and the Medici bankers, Andrea di Lippaccio and Lippaccio di Benedetto, declared assets respectively of 10,068 and 17,577 florins; Andrea Pazzi was sixth in San Giovanni with 31,000 and a Portinari eleventh with over 18,000.

assumed a major role in the Medici party only after the political situation had crystallized and the indisputable leadership of the Medici was firmly established. Perhaps the best examples of the former group are Averardo's sons-in-law, though even they were handicapped in the struggle for power by specific weaknesses which they may well have sought to offset by virtual integration into the Medici family; their letters reveal them as a major source of advice and support for its leaders in the decade before 1434.[108]

Giannozzo di Stoldo Gianfigliazzi, who married Tita di Averardo in the early twenties, belonged to one of the largest and most powerful lineages in Florence; he was not, however, one of the more influential figures within it, and indeed, his association with the Medici and their ambitions put him on the opposite side of the partisan fence from the majority of his *consorti*, several of whom were among the leaders of the anti-Medicean faction. Both Alamanno Salviati and Francesco Tornabuoni were major figures in the inner circle of the *reggimento*, and appeared continually in the *Consulte* of this period,[109] but they too lacked family backing. The Salviati, who had first gained the Priorate in 1297, also found themselves politically divided in the thirties. While one of his *consorti* was exiled on the Medici return in 1434, Alamanno had been Averardo's son-in-law since 1408, and his own daughter married Andrea Pazzi, Averardo's *compagno* and another leading figure in the Medici party, though one who also had close ties with the old and wealthy families of the conservative group, and was married in 1429 to the daughter of Bindaccio Ricasoli.[110] Soon after, Salviati married another of his daughters to Lionardo di Filippo di M. Castellano Frescobaldi (whose kinsman was privato in 1434), though not without some misgivings, which he expressed in a letter to Averardo at the time.[111] Salviati was heavily involved financially, not only with Cosimo, Lorenzo, and Averardo, but also with the latter's fourth son-in-law, the wealthy Antonio di Salvestro Serristori.[112] The Tornabuoni in 1427 comprised only a single household which Francesco's father

---

[108] See, e.g., above, pp. 231–2; below, pp. 279–82.

[109] Both frequently led the discussions on issues of major importance, and while Salviati appeared at 51 *Pratiche*, Tornabuoni's attendance was among the very highest at 77.

[110] Ancisa, BB, ff. 673r, 671v.

[111] Ibid., ff. 675r, 1431; cf. Pellegrini, *Sulla repubblica*, clxi.

[112] Cat. 493, ff. 35r–37r.

had separated from the magnate house of Tornaquinci in 1393,[113] though they continued to reflect some of the lustre of its distinguished traditions, and Francesco enjoyed the added advantage of an enormous personal fortune, being the second-richest citizen in the quarter of Santa Maria Novella in 1427 with a net capital of over 46,000 florins. He was several times related to the Medici through members of his immediate family over several generations, and his daughter married the son of another of the Medici partisans, Pagnozzo di Bartolomeo Ridolfi.

Almost as closely identified with Medici interests in the eyes of observers as these *strecti parenti*[114] was Nerone di Nigi Dietisalvi; his family had gained the Priorate in 1291, but had had no members in the *Signoria* since 1402,[115] although Nerone himself was an influential member of the inner *reggimento* in the late twenties and early thirties. The family was a small one; in 1427 it comprised only three households which were far from affluent. Nerone himself had to compose a nominal tax with the *catasto* officials in that year. According to Tinucci, he was one of the leading Medici henchmen; certainly he was elected along with Cosimo as an *Accoppiatore* for the scrutiny of 1427–8 through the organized co-operation of the *amici*.[116] Residents of Lion d'oro, the Dietisalvi had been one of the eight families to combine with Giovanni di Bicci in the early plans to rebuild San Lorenzo, and Nerone was closely associated with the Medici and their friends in several spheres of his personal life. Between 1418 and 1421 he shared a company with Simone di Francesco and Giovanni di Piero Ginori, and in 1427 had investments in a mercantile enterprise under the direction of Giovanni Orlandini, father of another of the Medici partisans.[117] His son Dietisalvi was the *compagno* in 1434 of Bartolomeo Corbinelli, brother of Giovanni di Tommaso, and had married in 1429 the daughter of Benvenuto di Zanobi Ginori; after her father's death she became the ward of

[113] Litta, *Famiglie Celebri* vii, Tav. I. M.A.P. V, 5, II, 331, 396, illustrate the close family relationship between the households of Averardo, Alamanno, Antonio di Salvestro, and Francesco Tornabuoni; for example, the latter wrote to Averardo while away from Florence: 'Ti rachomando le cose mie e la mia famiglia, e se ti paresse avessono a piglare più uno partito che uno altro, gli chonsigli chome se fussono tuoi' (II, 396).

[114] They are so described by Francesco di Giuliano di Averardo de' Medici in the *Ricordo* concerning his marriage (M.A.P. CLVIII, 30 ff. 32v–33v).

[115] MSS. 248, f. 240r–v.   [116] Below, pp. 228–31.
[117] Cat. 78, ff. 159r–160r.

the brothers Piero, Giuliano, and Simone di Francesco Ginori, who shared the expenses of her dowry on the occasion of the Dietisalvi–Neroni marriage.[118] Nerone became an *Accoppiatore* again for the Medicean scrutiny of 1434 and was subsequently much favoured in the scrutinies.[119]

Probably less totally committed to Medici advancement, certainly less intimately and exclusively linked to them in either the personal or the political sphere, were two men whose families had boasted great statesmen for many years; Bartolomeo Ridolfi and Niccolò Valori.[120] The latter was wealthy, and had commanded great personal political influence throughout the twenties, although his family was small, and had never been particularly well represented in the scrutinies.[121] Three of his daughters were married to Medici partisans—Piero Guicciardini, Giovanni Giugni, and Donato di Niccolò Cocco-Donati.[122] Ridolfi's son, Pagnozzo, became the husband in 1418 of Lisa, daughter of Messer Simone Tornabuoni and the sister of Francesco.[123] A frequent correspondent of Averardo's, Ridolfi assured him in a letter of 1428 that theirs was a single will;[124] that this was more than rhetoric is implied by Cosimo's hope for an amelioration of their exile under his Gonfalonierate in November of 1433, and by Giuliano's praise some years before for his efforts on behalf of the *amici*.[125]

Although the private letters on which much of this chapter is based reveal a good deal about the structure and membership of the party before the expulsion of the Medici in September 1433 led to an open division in the *reggimento*, the precise relationship to the party in the years preceding of some of Florence's foremost citizens who led the consequent movement for the Medici recall

[118] MSS. 85, f. 97r.

[119] Rubinstein, *Government of Florence*, pp. 47, 236–43.

[120] See Brucker, *The Civic World*, esp. Chs. 5, 7.

[121] The family consisted of three households in 1427; their majorities for the *Tre Maggiori*, 1382 to 1433, were 1, 1, 3, 2. For the Medici appreciation of Valori's friendship see the letter of Cosimo to Averardo, written 21 Oct. 1430, published Fabroni, *Cosmi vita* ii 31–2.

[122] Litta, *Famiglie Celebri* vii, Tav. I.   [123] C.S. 2ª ser. LVI, p. 644.

[124] M.A.P. III, 126, 14 May 1431.

[125] Ibid. II, 145, 22 Jan. 1430 (1429 *s.f.*); below, pp. 311, 316–17. In the first month of the Medici return, the *Balìa* passed an act in favour of Ridolfi (Balie, 25, f. 49v). In the late twenties he was also, however, a friend of Rinaldo degli Albizzi (*Commissioni* iii. 24), and one whom Matteo Strozzi could describe as 'cierto amicho' (*Ricordi*, C.S. 5ª ser. XII, f. 26r).

remains unclear. Circumstantial evidence leaves little doubt that both Luca degli Albizzi and Piero Guicciardini had committed themselves to the Medici by the mid-twenties; the former perhaps lest he find himself in a politically vulnerable position, the latter from a position of considerable strength both in personal reputation and family traditions. But while the Albizzi marriage to the daughter of Nicola de' Medici would certainly appear to have been part of a general turning-away from family traditions and the creation of alternative connections, and the wedding of Guicciardini's daughter Costanza to Averardo's grandson Francesco in 1433 one which publicly set the seal on a lengthy association and friendship, no correspondence survives to enable us to explore their relationships with the Medici before 1433 with any precision.[126]

More limited still is the evidence concerning Agnolo Acciaiuoli; his commitment by 1434 to the Medici was obviously apparent, since he was exiled in February, as Cosimo explained, 'on account of some news which he had sent to Puccio and to us'.[127] The letter which he wrote to Lorenzo shortly after his dismissal from Florence, confirming his continued support for the Medici, implies a friendship and sympathy of considerable depth and fairly long standing.[128] Perhaps his partisanship arose out of personal friendship dating from the time when he and Cosimo had studied the classics together in the circle of Ambrogio Traversari; both continued to be prominent in the avant-garde humanist circles of this period.[129] At the same time there were other reasons why Agnolo might have drawn closer to the Medici in the later twenties and early thirties which saw the beginnings of a polarization of the ruling group between them and some associates of the Albizzi. The Acciaiuoli were an old and distinguished family from the *gonfalone* of Vipera, who had had a Prior in 1282 and who had been prominent in the politics, not only of Florence, but of Italy in general in the fourteenth and early fifteenth centuries.[130] However, since a crisis concerning the leadership of the oligarchy in 1393 had resulted in the victory of Maso degli Albizzi

---

[126] See above, pp. 55-6, 133.

[127] *Ricordi*, p. 100. According to Cosimo, these letters 'in vero non erano d'importanza, nè da esserne cacciato'.

[128] M.A.P. LXVIII, 610, 25 Apr. 1434.

[129] Holmes, *The Florentine Enlightenment*, pp. 92–8.

[130] Martines, *The Social World*, p. 335.

over a group led by Donato Acciaiuoli, who was subsequently
exiled, Agnolo may have felt it prudent to align himself with the
Medici when a new crisis seemed imminent. It is significant that
in 1420 Donato's daughter Bartolomea married Nicola di Vieri
di Cambio de' Medici, and another daughter, Laudamia, had been
the first wife of Piero Guicciardini. Certainly by 1433 Cosimo
felt able to describe Agnolo Acciaiuoli as one of 'my greatest
friends', and the Venetian Francesco Barbaro wrote to Acciaiuoli
that he had heard how 'you defend Cosimo's innocence with no
less fervour than wisdom'.[131]

Benedetto Dei, writing some years later, named Neri di Gino
Capponi, along with Agnolo Acciaiuoli and Cosimo himself, as the
three real leaders of the Medici party,[132] and indeed Neri headed
the group of leading citizens within the *reggimento* who in 1434
rejected the conservative regime and planned the Medici recall.
But the first evidence of support for the Medici is his letter of
September 1433 commiserating with Averardo on his exile, and
the corroborative anxiety of the conservative *Signoria* which
banished the Medici to have Capponi also out of Florence at that
time.[133] Since the correspondence of Rinaldo degli Albizzi and that
of the Mediceans strongly suggest that in the early thirties Capponi
was an independent force in the ruling group, uncommitted to
either party,[134] his name has not been included among those of
the *amici*, who essentially represent the Mediceans as a partisan
group before the resolution of events made them the alternative
regime.[135]

The attempt to describe the social status of the Mediceans, to
define and distinguish between their relationship to the current
ruling group and to the traditional ruling class, has resulted in
a complex picture, but one which perhaps resolves some of the
apparently insoluble conflicts between various of its characteristics and between elements of contemporary descriptions. The
Mediceans as a group sprang from families established in the
ruling class of Florence, though many of those individuals who
became partisans of the Medici found themselves outside the

---

[131] Fabroni, *Cosmi vita* ii. 87.   [132] *Chronica*, f. 14r.
[133] Below, p. 297.   [134] Below, pp. 229, 264-6.
[135] There were, however, generally close links between the Capponi and the Medici; Giovanni di Mico appears to have been a partisan since 1430 (M.A.P. II, 232,
22 Feb. 1430; 1429 *s.f.*), when he recommended his *consorto* of the related Vettori
family with the careful assurance that he was completely faithful: 'è tutto mio'.

reggimento as constituted by the scrutiny of 1433. Conversely, they were prominent in the innermost circle of the informal leaders of the ruling group constantly consulted by the Priors; the discrepancy may be due either to discrimination in a partisan scrutiny, or to a difference in the nature of the influence measured by these two indices.

The fact that almost half the Mediceans were *gente nuova* relatively recently established in the ruling class was an important determinant of the interests which they represented, and of the tone and structure of the party, since the comparative dependence of many of these newer men on their Medici patrons or neighbours for advancement, protection, and defence helped to reinforce the centralization of the party under Medici leadership. The sizeable group of men of considerable wealth and political influence who belonged largely to the older and more established families must have added lustre to the party in the eyes of the political and social establishment; conversely, distinctions of social and political status should not be so strongly stressed as to obscure the fact that many of the 'older' partisans came from families as seriously disadvantaged in the continuing competition for a slice of the *stato* as were the new men, by being either too small, too poor, too divided, or too unpopular with the prevailing regime. Above all, the Medici party represented a fruitful union under Medici auspices of citizens drawn from a relatively wide range of the Florentine social and political spectrum, but all, like their leaders, with something substantial both to offer and to gain in the promotion of the Medici *amici* to a position of greater power.

2

Reactions within the Ruling Class

(i) THE EXILES AND THE RULING CLASS

AFTER the Medici returned to Florence in October 1434, the *Balìa* which had ended their exile proceeded to banish in their stead a large number of those citizens who had been responsible for the Medici expulsion, who had ruled Florence during the year of their absence, and who had resisted the authority of the *Signoria* which threatened to recall Cosimo and his family. Thus the list of those exiled by the pro-Medicean *Balìa* set up in September 1434 may be assumed broadly to represent the party or parties which constituted the opposition to the Medici, and as such provides a useful starting-point for its investigation which was absent in the case of the Mediceans. The essential problem in this case is to establish whether the group exiled in 1434 had any social reality as a unified party in the sense of that led by the Mediceans, and if so, by what ties its members were bound together, by whom it was led, and what interests it represented.

The precise number of political proscriptions in 1434 is rather difficult to determine, since it is not always easy to distinguish between these and normal criminal charges, and in some cases the records are incomplete. In all, about ninety citizens appear to have been exiled by the end of 1434 or early in 1435 on account of their opposition to the triumphant Medici, and at least another eighty or so were fined or made magnates, and thus deprived of the right to hold office, either permanently or for a specified period.[1] The statement concerning the proscriptions in a

---

[1] Otto di Guardia 224, ff. 21r–71r. The grounds for condemnation are not given here. The great bulk of the 93 exiles, however, were sentenced by the end of November and dealt with *en bloc*; after that date the few remaining anti-Medicean exiles appear to be interspersed with others, and have been identified by comparison with Balìe, 25, ff. 21v, 55r–65v, and in terms of their general reputation, background, and activities in the preceding years. Since there is no trace of the original condemnation of some of those listed as rebels against their sentences, obviously not all these are

Pratica of 1 November 1434, by the spokesmen of the new regime—Luca degli Albizzi, Neri Capponi, Niccolò Valori, and Cosimo himself—stresses their representative and admonitory function:

The error which commenced in 1433 in the month of September is now evident, and this error gave rise to another—that of those who desired to act against the *Signoria* and the authority of the government. Those who erred in both cases will be punished, so that they may serve as an example to others not to commit similar crimes, and in order that the authority of the *Signoria*, and the peace and good order of the city and its dominion, may be secured against every reasonable risk; and because those who took up arms against the Palace, those who instigated and supported this action, are so numerous, we will not concern ourselves with the great mass of them, as this would be too extensive a process, but the leaders will be punished, albeit with mercy.[2]

The leaders of the anti-Mediceans as identified by their punishment were fairly numerous; the Bardi, Brancacci, Castellani, Gianfigliazzi, Guadagni, Guasconi, Peruzzi, and Strozzi all had several members exiled, and the fact that in addition to these, whole lines of the Albizzi, Barbadori, Castellani, Gianfigliazzi, Guasconi, Peruzzi, and Rondinelli were made *magnati*, suggests that a number of leading families shared the essential responsibility for the opposition to the Medici. This was certainly the view of contemporary observers, although there is some variation in the particular names which they singled out. For instance, the anonymous author of a *Priorista* described those who gathered in the Piazza Sant' Apollinare to oppose the new Priors in September 1434 as 'primarily Messer Rinaldo degli Albizzi and Ridolfo Peruzzi with a great number of their close friends'. Among these were 'part of the Albizzi family and part of the Peruzzi, and Guasconi and Rondinelli and Castellani, and one of the Bardi with a lot

recorded. Not all those whom the *Balìa* of 1434 deprived of the right to hold office as an alternative to banishment have been included in the groups to be examined in detail. In the case of the exclusion of whole families, insufficient genealogical material exists to enable us to establish accurately the number and identity of individuals involved, although it is important to observe that they may have been as many as 100; see particularly the scrutiny of 1433, MSS. 555, and the genealogies of Passerini, both published and unpublished (B.N.F.). However, the 16 individuals singled out for such punishment have been included with the aim of making this list more broadly representative of the opposition to the Medici.

[2] C.P. 50, f. 204r–v.

of their supporters'.[3] Neri di Gino Capponi wrote in his Commentaries of 'about 600 men, and their leaders were the Peruzzi, Messer Rinaldo, the Guasconi, Raffacani, Arrigucci, and some of the Bardi, Serragli, Gianfigliazzi, and Castellani'.[4] Benedetto Dei, describing the confrontation, explained that 'the leaders of one party were Messer Palla degli Strozzi and Messer Rinaldo degli Albizzi and Ridolfo Peruzzi with other worthy and eminent citizens',[5] while at the head of the list of Medici opponents Palmieri placed the Peruzzi, the Bardi, and Rinaldo degli Albizzi.[6] Despite some individual divergences, observers generally agreed on a core of leading families in opposition to the Medici which corresponds with that apparent in the official condemnations.

However, just as the policy statement in the *Pratica* had mentioned a multitude of followers who were not included in the proscriptions, so contemporaries prior to 1434 quite often described as well-known opponents of the Medici citizens who were not subsequently punished; others, writing after the event, mistakenly included in their accounts of the exiles men whose known sympathies and associations had apparently prompted the erroneous assumption that they appeared in the official lists. Estimates of the number of those punished, ranging from 300 to 500, obviously reflect an awareness of the total number of citizens, including not only the heads of households, but also their families and friends, affected by the hostility of the new regime towards its former opponents and their associates.[7]

[3] MSS. 229, p. 167.
[4] *Commentarii*, col. 1182.
[5] 'Chronica', f. 12v.
[6] Matteo Palmieri, *Annales, Rerum Italicarum Scriptores*, new edn. (Città di Castello, 1917–34), xxvi, I, 138–40.
[7] According to Benedetto Dei, 'Chronica', MSS. 119, f. 14r, 'fu chacciato fuori e frategli e figliuoli e padri di modo che si fa chonto che 500 cittadini e più uscissino fuori di Firenze'. But in his *Memorie Storiche*, Cod. Monac. Ital. 160, Bayerische Staatsbibliothek, f. 97v, he gave the number as 300; cf. Palmieri, *Annales*, p. 138, whose estimate was also 300. See also Cavalcanti, *Istorie*, pp. 317–19; Giovanni Cambi, *Istorie*, in *Delizie* xx, p. 199. There are several families like the Serragli, whose members are so closely intertwined with the exiles that they obviously formed part of the same patronage and party network. Piero di Paolo Serragli was originally deprived of the right to hold office for ten years but was almost immediately 'restituito' (Otto di Guardia 224, f. 69v). Since he and others in a similar situation were not in fact exiled they have been omitted from our list of anti-Medicean partisans for the purposes of comparison with the Mediceans, but their associations with the exiles have been indicated where they seem relevant to a more complete picture of the group. Also included in the discussions of circles of patronage below are three

The 109 citizens specifically named in the records of the *Otto di Balìa* as either exiled, fined, or deprived of political rights, constitute a group comparable in size to that of the Mediceans as identified in their letters, but their position within the ruling class, and their relation to the current ruling group, was rather different. By the criterion of eligibility to hold major office the exiles were, according to the scrutiny of 1433, much better represented in the *reggimento* than were the Mediceans. Though their numbers were roughly comparable, only 31 of the latter gained majorities in that scrutiny, while 74 of the exiles were successful. However, even apart from the possibility of discrimination in this scrutiny, the figures for attendance at the *Consulte* in this period are probably a more immediate indication of effective political influence. Among the group whose regular appearance at these meetings shows that they were generally influential in governing circles were a little over half the exiles, compared with a little less than half the Mediceans; the difference is hardly significant. In the innermost circle of the *reggimento*, however, there were only 10 future exiles, compared with 17 Mediceans and 2 members of the Medici family itself. Even if, in order to represent more realistically the strength of the anti-Mediceans before 1434, we add the names of Niccolò da Uzzano, the leader of this group who died in 1432, and of Messer Giovanni di Messer Luigi Guicciardini, who was saved from exile by the intervention of his brother Piero, the Mediceans would still appear by the early thirties to be gaining the advantage at the centre of unofficial but effective power.

Moreover, these slight differences acquire greater significance over a longer perspective of time. In the ruling group of the first quarter of the fifteenth century, presided over by Maso degli Albizzi and his associates, the leading Mediceans of the late twenties and early thirties were comparatively inconspicuous; virtually the only outstanding figures were Giovanni di Bicci himself, Agnolo Pandolfini, Bartolomeo Ridolfi, and, towards the end of this period, perhaps Nerone di Nigi Dietisalvi. The future exiles of 1434, however, constituted the very core of the

---

prominent conservative leaders who were not proscribed: Niccolò da Uzzano and Bernardo Guadagni, both dead by November 1434, and Giovanni Guicciardini, exempted from exile through the influence of his pro-Medicean brother, Piero. See Francesco Guicciardini, *Memorie di famiglie*, p. 11.

regime; the seven houses with more than one representative
in the élite of seventy-six citizens whom Gene Brucker has identified as the virtual rulers of the republic in this period, the Albizzi,
Gianfigliazzi, Strozzi, Castellani, Guasconi, Ardinghelli, and
Guadagni, provided most of the leaders of the anti-Medicean
party, and were all severely punished in 1434.[8]

The impression that while the Mediceans were a force in the
ascendant, the exiles as a group had passed the peak of their
power and prosperity, emerges similarly from a careful analysis of
their comparative economic circumstances.[9] The two groups
contained a roughly similar proportion of outstandingly wealthy
men; to set against the Medici themselves and their affluent
friends, the Bardi, Pazzi, and Serristori, were Piero Panciatichi,
Ridolfo Peruzzi, Domenico Lamberteschi, Niccolò Bordoni,
Piero Ardinghelli, and Palla Strozzi, all of whom declared in 1427
a net capital of more than 10,000 florins, and indeed the last,
with a taxable income of 101,422 florins, was the richest man in
the city at the time of the assessment.[10] The Mediceans as a group,
however, were very much better off, with a larger number in
the middle-income range and many less at the lower end of the
scale; 45 exiles, compared with only 25 Mediceans, fell into the
category of citizens with insufficient assets remaining to be levied
a regular tax, and therefore obliged to agree upon (*comporre*) the
payment of a nominal sum to the officials in order to retain their
full political rights.

There is a significant difference, moreover, in the type of people
'composto' in each. The Mediceans were from families like the
Carducci, Ciai, Guiducci, Cocco-Donati, Martelli, Masi, Del Nero,
and Pucci, men who had not yet really made their fortunes in
either business or politics, but who were to do both in the near
future. Among the exiles forced to make a token payment, together with the expected artisans and shopkeepers, were members
of such illustrious houses as those of the Aldobrandini, Altoviti,
Dall'Antella, Arrigucci, Baldovinetti, Belfradelli, Castellani,
Guasconi, Lamberteschi, Da Panzano, and Peruzzi. The exiles

---

[8] *The Civic World*, esp. Ch. 5, p. 268.

[9] Of course in characterizing the anti-Mediceans before 1434 as a party of eminent citizens on the verge of decline, one must beware of concluding the case too
strongly in the light of hindsight; presumably a victory over the Medici would have
altered the course of their development.

[10] Martines, *The Social World*, pp. 365–78; Cat. 27–85 (1427).

who were poor in 1427 were scions of families who in trade and commerce had once been among the richest and most powerful in Florence. The Dall'Antella and the Spini, for instance, are two of the few thirteenth-century companies whose records survive.[11] The latter owed their greatness partly to their operations for the papacy; with an irony which may well have been bitterly felt, when in the early twenties they were declared bankrupt, their privileges as current papal bankers were transferred to the Medici.[12] Among the other great Florentine companies already operating internationally on a major scale before 1300 were the Altoviti in France, and in England the Bardi, Frescobaldi, and Peruzzi.[13] These families were already closely linked with one another; the *socii* of the Peruzzi bank in the thirteenth and fourteenth centuries included several members of the Baroncelli family, and of their *parenti* the Raugi, also exiled in 1434. Members of these families and of the Aldobrandini served as representatives of the Peruzzi bank abroad, and those families whose connections with the company endured over half a century include the Baroncelli, the Raugi, and the Bencivenni.[14]

Just as the majority of the colossi who created this golden age of Florentine commerce were families prominent among the opponents of the Medici in the early fifteenth century, so they were the most numerous among the victims of the disastrous failures of the 1340s which ended it.[15] Of course by the early fifteenth century the fortunes of these families had undergone considerable fluctuation, but even within those families who could still boast several extremely wealthy members, the 1427 figures on the financial position of Mediceans and exiles do highlight some signs of comparative decline. Certainly there is evident among the exile families, even before the failure of their political gamble in 1434 and the Medici victory dealt them an effective *coup de grâce*, a powerful, if actually disproportionate sense of failure and decay.

[11] S. L. Peruzzi, *Storia del Commercio e dei Banchieri di Firenze dal 1200 al 1345* (Florence, 1868), esp. pp. 143, 174.
[12] Villani observed that 'erano mercatanti di papa Bonifazio, e del tutto guidatori' (Fiumi, 'Fioritura' cxv. 413); G. Holmes, 'How the Medici . . .' 377–8.
[13] Fiumi, 'Fioritura' cxv. 407; Peruzzi, *Storia del Commercio*, p. 227.
[14] Peruzzi, pp. 233, 250 ff., 282–4, 475.
[15] Ibid., p. 287. Among the more prominent victims of the crash were the Bardi, Peruzzi, Dall'Antella, Da Uzzano, Castellani, and Acciaiuoli, the last the only family to support the Medici in 1434.

In the early 1430s Alberti expressed his sympathy for the misfortunes of families such as the Peruzzi and the Spini, 'who once abounded in great, and indeed, in measureless wealth, but suddenly, struck down by fortune, fell on hard times and even, in some cases, into dire necessity'.[16] Doffo Spini seems to have been impelled by a pervasive sense of mortality to take up his pen and write in 1429 'of the stock of the house of Spini, and of their generations from the day that they were first called Spini to the day on which I, Doffo di Nepo degli Spini, should draw my own last breath'. He went on to 'pray God may maintain our house of the Spini in faith and devotion to him and in a condition of confidence, liveliness, and the increasing affection of the people of Florence, if that be his will towards our clan'.[17]

In 1427 Ridolfo di Bonifazio Peruzzi, leader, with the wealthy Bartolomeo di Verano, of the Peruzzi lineage, was the sixth-richest citizen of Santa Croce with a net capital of 20,542 florins. By 1433 his assets had fallen to 12,130, a notable drop despite the general decrease.[18] His real financial situation cannot be determined from his tax declaration, a notoriously unreliable source concerning absolute, as distinct from comparative, wealth. But for all that attempts to enlist the sympathy of the officials were a common tactic, and that Peruzzi, with a taxable income of 12,000 or so florins, was still a relatively rich man, the concluding note at the end of his 1433 report has the ring of genuine despair. His position aggravated by defaulting debtors, among whom were the Ricasoli and Benizzi, to be fellow exiles in 1434, he declared that

I have no more capital remaining in the shop; it is all in the wool manufacturing, and indeed both businesses are ruined. I have made nothing or very little in the last two years because all our capital is tied up in debts which can't be called in, because the times are so hard, and properties are being renounced . . . I can't consider myself as worth anything but my Monte shares, and yet the family will need plenty on account of their age. I find myself reduced to nothing and without much capacity for recovery.[19]

[16] *Libri della Famiglia*, in *Opere volgari*, i, ed. C. Grayson (Bari, 1960), p. 143. Of two dozen Peruzzi households in 1427, two-fifths had to compose with the tax officials and another third had assets of under 1,000 florins remaining after deductions had been subtracted.

[17] 'Ricordanze di Doffo di Nepo degli Spini', C.S. 2ª ser. XIII, f. 15r–v.

[18] Martines, *The Social World*, p. 365; Cat. 492, f. 439r.

[19] Cat. 451, f. 288r; for the list of his 'debitori chattivi', ibid. 35, f. 1342v.

A similar picture of the failure of enterprises in which he and other exiles were concerned is presented in the *catasto* report for the same year of Piero di Messer Vanni Castellani, head of the clan after the death of his father in 1429.

I am owed something from a company with Ramondo Manelli and Matteo Benizzi, and from another company in Avignon with Ramondo Manelli and Iacopo Castellani which both failed . . . I've got what I could back from them; what little still remains we may consider as lost, in view of their ill-fortune. They are ruined on account of those involved, and of the king of France who will not pay them, and other bad debtors, so that I would give away my share for a mere 150 florins.

In this case, the figures clearly support his tale; in 1427 he was already down to a net capital of 2,540 florins, and by 1433 was forced to make an accommodation with the officials, as his expenses exceeded his assets by 45 florins.[20]

Even Palla di Nofri Strozzi's net capital dropped from 101,422 florins in 1427 to the still substantial sum of 39,192 in 1433.[21] Again, part of the difference was no doubt due to his increased skill in the art of economic self-defence, but in fact a great part arose from the unfortunate chance that most of the Strozzi money was in real estate, and with the imposition in 1427 of the new and more efficient tax system of the *catasto*, followed almost immediately by a spate of levies at the rate of several per month during the worst years of the war, Palla lacked the ready cash to pay his taxes. He was forced not only to sell up his land where possible, but also to borrow heavily to meet the immediate demands. As his son-in-law, Giovanni Rucellai, observed later, 'in a very short time, his wealth was consumed for two reasons; the first, that in a period of ten years, that is, from 1423 to 1433, he paid to the commune in normal taxes, on account of the wars being waged at that time, 160,000 florins'.[22]

The second reason, of course, was his banishment from Florence in 1434. It may perhaps have been partly Palla's increasing problems which inspired the strange letter of his kinsman, Lionardo d'Antonio Strozzi, to his cousin Matteo di Simone, bemoaning 'the injuries which are suffered every day by our house on account of our lack of men', but reflecting with resignation that God himself must have willed 'the misfortunes which

[20] Cat. 28, f. 813r; 68, f. 146v; 491, f. 370v.   [21] Ibid. 68, f. 146v.
[22] Perosa (ed.), *Rucellai, il Zibaldone*, p. 63.

have beset our house for the last four years'.[23] His fears would certainly appear literally groundless in view of the fact that the Strozzi were at that time almost the largest lineage in Florence with fifty-four separate households in 1427;[24] possibly he referred figuratively to a lack of men of worth and quality. What is clear is that the Strozzi family felt themselves to be seriously in danger of losing their place among the city's most powerful and influential families, and whatever the relationship of the feelings expressed by them and other exiles to the real facts of their situation (and there are a number to bear them out), their pessimism contrasts strikingly with the optimism of the Mediceans; to judge at least from the most vocal of the partisans of each group, they perceived their prospects, as governed by the turning wheel of fortune, in a very different light.

However, the chief and most obviously measurable difference between exiles and Mediceans lies in their social origins. While the Medici party was almost equally composed of older families and *gente nuova*, eight out of every eleven exiles came from the more ancient Florentine houses, and belonged to that proud group of patricians whom Poggio, and indeed most Florentines, would have described as the noble citizens of Florence. Measuring by the standard of the Priorate, 72 were admitted into the *reggimento* before 1343, and, like the Tornabuoni among the Mediceans, there were 8 more who gained their first Priorate rather later, but were not in fact *gente nuova*. Only 19 exiles were certainly members of genuinely new families, although another 10 whose families' reception of the Priorate cannot be dated were probably on that account of relatively recent origin. Certainly half those identifiable as new men were very new indeed, being among the post-1382 admissions.[25]

Within the exile group the *gente nuova* were insignificant, not merely numerically but also, apparently, in their influence on its structure and policies, by contrast with the corresponding sector of the Medici party which contained a number of their most important and prominent supporters. None of these representatives of the newer families was included in the ranks of the leaders

[23] C.S. 3ª ser. CXXXI, c. 20.

[24] This figure is based on the computer print-out of the results of the study of the *catasto* of 1427, in the A.S.F.

[25] See *Priorista Mariani* (MSS. 248–54), and Kent, 'The Florentine *reggimento*', Table II.

of the exiles, and indeed the only member of the group to distinguish himself particularly was Stefano di Salvi di Filippo Bencivenni, who on account of his frequent, if not commanding, appearances in the *Consulte* must be considered a member of the inner *reggimento*. He was also 114th on the 1427 list of the richest men in San Giovanni, with a comparatively modest fortune of 3,265 florins; the rest of the new men in the exile group were relatively indigent and at least half a dozen of them found that their expenditure exceeded their income when these were calculated for the tax returns.[26]

The newer men of both parties had in common the fact that they were generally less politically influential than their more established associates; however, despite their comparatively greater poverty and obscurity, in the degree of their social dependence on the latter the exiles do appear to have been less disadvantaged. Although several were residents of the quarter of Santa Croce where over a third of the party originated,[27] and Tano Fenci and Lorenzo del Forese lived literally in the shadow of their eminent Castellani and Strozzi neighbours, from whom they rented their houses,[28] as with the majority of the exile group, it was the ties of marriage which bound new men like Bernardo della Casa, Piero Ciampegli, and Stefano Bencivenni to eminent exile families like the Ricasoli, Baldovinetti, and Altoviti.[29]

As we have observed, beyond the convenient criterion of the Priorate, Florentines continued to recognize and revere the distinction of noble and aristocratic traditions established before 1282, dating back to the early thirteenth century and beyond, and despite the notorious difficulty of verifying many claims to absolute antiquity these traditions continued to influence the way in which Florentines regarded themselves and others. Although we

[26] These included Bernardo di Filippo della Casa, Corso, Simone and Tommaso di Lapo Corsi, Tano d'Antonio Fenci, and Lorenzo di Stefano del Forese.

[27] The three Corsi brothers lived in Bue and rented their house from the Bischeri, an older exile family (Cat. 69, f. 244r–v); in the same *gonfalone* were Ser Niccolò Biffoli and Bernardo di Ser Lodovico Doffi, whose neighbours included the Scolari and the Pepi, an exile family which shared a tower with the Baldovinetti, also proscribed (ibid. 29, f. 91r).

[28] The former, a butcher of the *gonfalone* of Carro, explained in his *catasto* report of 1427 that he was 'sanza aviamento o esercizio alchuno' and declared that he rented for eight florins a year a house from the heirs of Vanni di Stefano Castellani 'posta da Chastellani' (ibid. 28, f. 949r). Del Forese, of Lion Rosso, was the tenant and neighbour of Messer Palla di Nofri degli Strozzi (ibid. 76, ff. 166r–168r).

[29] Ancisa, AA, f. 809v; Pol. Gar. 591, 253.

are confronted with difficulties similar to those experienced by contemporaries in determining the precise age of any family, there are some guide-lines which can be employed as a general indication of antiquity, and measuring by these standards, it would appear that the patricians of the anti-Medicean party were, on the whole, a more aristocratic group than their pro-Medicean counterparts.

The lists of twelfth- and early thirteenth-century consuls provide some index of families early established in Florence,[30] and whereas the only really eminent Medicean family to appear there is the Ridolfi,[31] a number of leading families among the exiles and their associates dated back to the consular period, including the Altoviti, Ardinghelli, Arrigucci, Baldovinetti, Guadagni, Lamberteschi, and Rossi. The same is true of the lists which recorded the damages sustained to the property of leading Guelf families in Florence at the hands of the Ghibellines in 1266; while only five Medicean families, including the Medici themselves, claimed damages, the exile families important and established enough to invite the Ghibelline vengeance included the Aldobrandini, Barbadori, Altoviti, Arrigucci, Bardi, Benizzi, Bucelli, Guadagni, Cavalcanti, Raffacani, Spini, Solosmei, and their associates the Adimari.[32] While the evidence ascribing towers and palaces of the early thirteenth century to various families of either party may well be unreliable, it is far more abundant for those families exiled in 1434 than for the families who supported the Medici, and the only fully documented case of this kind concerns the tower owned in 1209 by the Baldovinetti, of whom two members were exiled in 1434, in common with a number of other *socii* including the Manelli, who were constant associates of the exile group in the fifteenth century.[33]

The parties also differ markedly in their relation to the technical nobility of Florence—the magnates. It is rather difficult to establish the personal legal status of many individual members of magnate clans at this time since the only relatively complete lists are those in the statutes of 1415 and in the laws of 1434, which

[30] *Delizie* vii, pp. 135–44.

[31] The Ricci, Cavalcanti, Tedaldi, and Vecchietti were also consular families, but the fifteenth-century representatives of the first two were only minor members of the party, and Luigi Vecchietti, though among its staunchest supporters, was never among the party's leaders.

[32] *Delizie* vii, pp. 203–86.   [33] Below, pp. 160–2

effectively destroyed the magnate class by making *popolani* of almost all of its members who were not anti-Mediceans.[34] The list of 1415 records the exemption of some individual members of a lineage from the prohibitions relating to some offices; no doubt others received similar exemptions in the succeeding years.[35] However, while only three or four of the Mediceans came from older families who had been classified as magnates within the preceding century,[36] no less than eighteen of the exile group were either magnates themselves or descended from families who had for much of the period between 1282 and 1434 been included in this class. The significance of a magnate tradition persisting into the fifteenth century lies not only, or even perhaps primarily, in the antiquity which it usually implied, but much more essentially in the fact that citizens were relegated to the ranks of the magnates precisely because they had set themselves apart from the rest of society by their arrogant, lawless, and often violent behaviour; as a result they were generally excluded by the commune from participation in government at its highest levels.[37] The traditions of the magnates implied social and political attitudes which were reflected in the position of the anti-Medicean party in which they were influential.[38]

On the basis of what we have been able to establish about the leadership structure of the exile faction, the magnates, although not so very great in number, were among the more prominent of the opponents of the Medici. Among the exile magnates were five members of the Bardi, inevitably named among the principal families in opposition to the Medici. Though not as old as some of the magnate clans, the Bardi were already great and powerful in the early thirteenth century, and a century later, in 1340, felt themselves strong enough to join with a number of other magnates

[34] *Statuta Populi et Communis Florentiae* (3 vols., Friburgi, 1778–83), i. 444–6; Delib. Sig. e Coll. (speciale) 25, ff. 210v–214v.

[35] For instance, it is purely by chance that we know from a letter of Andrea de' Bardi to Averardo de' Medici (M.A.P. IV, 192, 5 Sept. 1431), concerning the pro-Medicean branch of the family that 'fummo fatti de' popolo sanza alchuno riserbo senon del divieto de' 3 ufici, una cosa ci è suta di buon . . .'

[36] The Pazzi, Bardi, and Gianfigliazzi were the only magnate families with members among the leaders of the Medici party, and the majority of the last two were anti-Medicean.

[37] See M. Becker, 'A Study in Political Failure: The Florentine Magnates: 1280–1343', *Mediaeval Studies*, xxvii (1965), 246–308. On the details of magnate office-holding in the fourteenth and fifteenth centuries, see MSS. 440.

[38] Below, pp. 211–21.

in an attempt to overturn the state.[39] Among these were the Frescobaldi, notorious for their participation in wars and rebellions, and also represented in the exiles of 1434.[40] The five exiles and several *privati* from the Gianfigliazzi belonged to the only line of that family within the *stato* in the fourteenth century— Messer Luigi di Neri and his descendants had been exempted from the general ban and made *popolani* in 1355.[41] The Arrigucci, who were mentioned by Dante as one of the older families surviving into his own day, and appear in a document of 1257 as feudatories of the bishop of Fiesole,[42] were made *popolani* in 1343;[43] they were among the leaders of the 1434 revolt. The Ricasoli, whose friends, relatives, and henchmen, as Buonaccorso Pitti's description of them indicates, were a formidable power in the patrician world of the 1420s, had maintained their warlike traditions into the fifteenth century, and Bindaccio, one of the two Ricasoli exiles, fought for many years in the pay of the Church.[44] Made *popolani* in 1393, the branch of the family to be exiled adopted the name of Fibindacci, but the Ricasoli were perhaps the oldest of all Florentine aristocratic families, and the first notices of their appearance, at the beginning of the eleventh century, reveal them as rich, powerful, and already for some time lords of a vast domain.[45] Indeed Carlo and Bindaccio themselves still lived on their ancestral lands at Brolio in their ancient 'tower with a palace attached'.[46]

In addition to the magnates actually exiled there were a number of others intimately associated with the anti-Medicean group, like the Manelli, Adimari, and Scolari, who were not punished. Possibly the Medici opponents from the magnate class were less completely represented in the exile lists than those within the *reggimento*; the former could more simply be exempted from the general legislation which readmitted most of their fellows to the ranks of the *popolani*.[47] Moreover, having only very limited

[39] Peruzzi, *Storia del Commercio*, p. 148; Becker, *Florence in Transition*, i. 97–8.

[40] Martines, *The Social World*, p. 222.

[41] *Statuta* i. 445.

[42] *Le Opere di Dante Alighieri*, ed. P. Toynbee (Oxford, 1894), p. 126 (*Paradiso*, xvi, l. 108); MSS. Pass. 185, Ins. 19.

[43] *Statuta* i. 446.

[44] L. Passerini, *Genealogia e storia della famiglia Ricasoli* (Florence, 1861), pp. 149–51.

[45] On the origins of the family, ibid., Introduction, pp. 1–11.

[46] Cat. 72, ff. 85v–89v (Carlo); cf. ibid. 72, ff. 68r–76v (Bindaccio).

[47] See Balìe, 25, ff. 61r–63r; Delib. Sig. e Coll. (speciale) 25, ff. 210v–214r.

official access to effective political power, magnate families did not constitute a major threat to any regime, and armed violence, as the events of September 1434 were to demonstrate, was no longer in the fifteenth century an effective political tactic.

Nevertheless, the presence of a comparatively large number of magnates among the opponents of the Medici is an important key to the nature of the opposition party. The independence with which the powerful magnate clans conducted themselves had in the past made successive governments fear them as a formidable threat to the republican commune. By the fifteenth century growing support for the re-entry of magnates into the *stato* was linked to an aristocratic ideal of the governing class, and it was on this, perhaps more than on any other issue of actual policy, that the Mediceans and their opponents differed. Both parties indeed contained a significant group of patrician *popolani*, but whereas the Medicean group admitted large numbers of newer families to their ranks, and were, if not hostile, at least indifferent to the issue of magnates in government, the exile group, in which older families preponderated, was almost devoid of influential newer men and generally in favour of the readmission of magnates into the *reggimento* in the hope of bolstering a tradition of government by older and more aristocratic families.[48]

An exploration of the affairs and associations of the exiles reveals a network of ties of neighbourhood, friendship, and marriage relationships very similar to those which bound the Mediceans together, but with the important distinction that the exiles comprised several such groups of patronage and association, which centred around several predominant families who corresponded generally to those named as the leaders of the opposition to the Medici. Moreover, although the followers of great families inevitably constituted political pressure groups, due to the extent of the operation of patronage in politics, there is no evidence similar to that relating to the Medici party to suggest that these groups were intentionally created for the purpose of specifically political action. Since we lack collections of private letters for each of the exile families comparable to the Medici correspondence,

---

[48] Cf. Donato Giannotti, *Opere politiche e letterarie*, ed. F. L. Polidori (2 vols., Florence, 1856), i. 89–95; he believed that there had always been in Florence a party of the *popolo* and of the *grandi*, which he identified in this period with the Medici and their opponents.

which provides the essential key to their explicit motives, we run the risk of arguing from an absence of evidence. On the other hand, although the extensive Strozzi correspondence of this period reveals a network of patronage very similar in its structure and functions to that over which the Medici presided, there is no hint in the letters of comparable political calculation and ambition.[49] Moreover, the web of relationships linking the exiles was neither so dense nor so exclusive as that which resulted from the comparatively systematic creation of the Medici party over several decades. The nature and number of the connections between them express rather the existence of common concerns and a broad similarity of outlook over an extended period of time which provided the basis for co-operation when ultimately the need to make common cause against the Medici became apparent.

In any case, the comparatively greater antiquity of most of the anti-Medicean families meant that they had naturally built up a more complex web of associative ties over the generations than their newer pro-Medicean counterparts; this made it more difficult for them to give their loyalty to a single group. It would also have been more difficult for many of the greater clans with ancient and distinguished traditions of their own to ally themselves with others in the position of semi-dependent co-operation which provided much of the cohesion between members of the Medici party.[50] They may also have felt less impelled to join together for mutual protection than some of the Mediceans, on account of their sheer size and the man-power at their disposal; while most of the leading Medici partisans belonged to families which, whether new or old, seldom consisted of more than half a dozen households, the families most prominent in the exile group were among the largest in Florence. The Albizzi, Altoviti, Castellani, and Peruzzi all contained between 20 and 30 households; the Gianfigliazzi and Della Casa had 14, the Rondinelli and Spini 17,

⁴⁹ Cf. below, pp. 223–34. Of course political conspiracy and the serious opposition of private interest to that of the commune are difficult to define (cf. above, pp. 98–9); while the private ambitions of the Mediceans focused on illegal interference with the scrutinies (below, pp. 223–34), members of the Strozzi family also took an interest in certain official procedures which was not strictly legitimate; see, e.g., Matteo Strozzi's *Ricordi*, C.S. 5ª ser. XII, f. 32r, 1431: 'Richordo ch'io ebbi da chi si trovò al segreto dello squitino si fe' d'aprile 1431 all'arte della lana che Simone Filippo e Piero mia figliuoli ottenono il partito.'

⁵⁰ Indeed the dangers of the disunity between them is a major theme of expressions of the aristocratic, anti-Medicean point of view (below, pp. 212–18).

and the Strozzi and Bardi were giants of respectively 54 and 60 households.[51] The absence of such particular and intimate evidence as we have for the Mediceans leads to some difficulties in comparing the importance of particular ties within the two groups. However, on the basis of similarly uniform evidence obtained from the *catasti*, and with the aid of letters and *ricordi* relating to the affairs of the exiles, it would seem that while *parentado* served to bind only the uppermost level of the Medici party, it was probably the very foundation of co-operation between members of the exile group; there were at least 35 marriages contracted after 1400 linking members of exiled families, and at least 19 of these involved those actually exiled, or their immediate relations, on both sides. Conversely, while neighbourhood provided the solidest framework for the Medici party, that of their opponents, cemented by unions between illustrious families throughout the city, was not exclusively based in any one area. Nevertheless, there are discernible clusters of families with particularly close associations centred on prominent houses in particular districts which would seem to have constituted the nuclei from which the party finally formed for action.

(ii) THE CIRCLES OF PATRONAGE[1]

The highest density of exile families is to be found largely in the quarter of Santa Croce, but these were part of a group which extended physically down the river into the neighbouring Santa Maria Novella *gonfaloni* of Vipera and Unicorno. This was the territory of the Peruzzi, Castellani, Gianfigliazzi, and Ricasoli, families closely associated with the old oligarchy, the most conservative opposition to the Medici, and all severely punished in 1434. The Bardi, Barbadori, and, before his death, Niccolò da Uzzano, presided over another such group in Santo Spirito,

---

[51] These are minimum figures based on the print-out of the *catasto* index, A.S.F. The Acciaiuoli were one of the larger families of pro-Medicean leanings with 8 households; the Pitti and Ginori had 6, the Pucci and Cocco-Donati about 4, and the Martelli, Dietisalvi-Neroni, and Valori each had 3; there was only a single household of Tornabuoni.

[1] Non-specialist readers particularly may wish to read this section quickly, and in close conjunction with Appendix II, which provides a ready reference to the names of partisan families and individuals; unfortunately it is impossible to convey the density and variety of associations between the members of the exile group in any simple tabular form.

closely linked to the 'Santa Croce group', but showing some features of internal independence and unity. The exiles of San Giovanni, though more dispersed over the quarter, seem also to have clung particularly to one another, possibly in defence against the domination of that area of the city by their opponents, while the Albizzi and the Strozzi, two of the largest single families in Florence at this time, seem despite their close association with other exile families throughout Florence to have attracted their own, to some extent separate and independent followings of *amici*.

The power of the circle of leading families from Santa Croce and Santa Maria Novella exiled in 1434 is apparent in Buonaccorso Pitti's account of the feud in which he was involved at the beginning of the century; as he wrote in his *Ricordi*, 'I didn't see what defence could be sustained against such might as that of the Gianfigliazzi, the Castellani, the Peruzzi, and of the other relatives and friends of the supporters of the Ricasoli and their followers and henchmen.'[2] Some decades later, the quarter of Santa Croce was a particularly anti-Medicean enclave; at least a third of those exiled came from this area, while only a sixth of Medicean partisans were resident there. Contemporaries thought of it as such; Cavalcanti, giving the names of those appointed *a mano* to the police magistracy of the *Otto di Guardia* immediately after Cosimo's expulsion in 1433, remarked that it was the pair from Santa Croce, though neither of them was exiled the following year, who wanted Cosimo strangled and thrown from the Palace tower rather than merely confined.[3] Not only did the area of Santa Croce and the adjoining *gonfaloni* of Vipera and Unicorno represent the greatest physical concentration of anti-Mediceans; the district also provided a directive focus for the opposition. Many of those named as its leaders came from there, and most of the more obscure members of the party were men who sheltered under the patronage of this group. However, while they constituted a formidable local power bloc, the elevated status of many in the ruling class made them figures of importance on the wider stage of Florentine society, and their influence radiated outwards through marriage and friendship to encompass many of the exile families from other districts in the city.

[2] *Ricordi*, p. 172, cf. p. 241.
[3] *Istorie*, p. 281; they were Guido di Bese Magalotti and Priore di Iacopo Risaliti.

By the twenties the Peruzzi were probably the most powerful family of the district, and certainly the dominant force in their own neighbourhood, which centred on the parish of San Romeo to which most of them belonged. In 1420 a process initiated by Antonio Rustichi against Simone di Buonarotto Buonarotti was settled by an assembly in the church of San Romeo, where it was decided that Simone should ask pardon of Antonio in the presence of his relatives and friends; the meeting was organized and presided over by Vanni di Stefano Castellani, Buonsignore di Niccolò Spinelli, and Giovanni di Rinieri Peruzzi.[4] Their pre-eminence is reflected in their punishment; eight Peruzzi were expelled in 1434, constituting the largest number of exiles from any single family, and at least another nine or ten were deprived indefinitely of the right to hold office. Moreover, those punished came from five different branches of the family, which meant that almost the entire lineage was involved.[5] This was unusual; in the case of other large families who had opposed the Medici there were often several branches who, either because they had positively supported the Medici or because they had remained relatively neutral, were not punished, and survived politically intact to revive the fortunes of the house later in the century. By their sentences in 1434, however, the Peruzzi were virtually wiped off the political and social map of Florence, and were not to recover during the fifteenth century.[6]

Undoubtedly this severity against the Peruzzi reflected their strength as a source of possible opposition to the new Medicean regime. They were a numerous and physically united clan, long and firmly established in the heart of Santa Croce in the enclave of the *piazza* which already bore their name, clustered together in the surrounding houses which stood next to or opposite one another around the square; almost all of the exiled Peruzzi named other members of the family as their immediate neighbours and most frequent associates.[7] By the late twenties a number of the Peruzzi were comparatively poor, and not particularly prominent

[4] 'The Diary of Antonio Rustichi', C.S. 2ª ser. XI, f. 26v, from G. Brucker (ed.), *The Society of Renaissance Florence: A Documentary Study* (New York, 1971), pp. 119–20.
[5] See MSS. Pass. 41. One whole branch of the family was exempted from punishment—that of Rinieri di Luigi and Rinieri di Niccolò (Balìe 25, f. 55r).
[6] Ridolfo di Bonifazio was Gonfalonier of Justice in 1432; there were no more Peruzzi in the Priorate until 1495 (MSS. 248, f. 91r-v).
[7] Cf. below, pp. 1 [1–2.

in affairs of state. However, they retained the proud traditions of a once-great commercial and political family; they still boasted a couple of extremely wealthy households in 1427, and were one of the eight families to have two members in the inner *reggimento* in this period, Ridolfo di Bonifazio and Bartolomeo di Verano.[8] Ridolfo di Bonifazio Peruzzi was invariably included in contemporary descriptions among the leaders of the opposition to the Medici, and many observers saw him as in fact more important to the party even than Rinaldo degli Albizzi, who took charge of government after Cosimo de' Medici's exile, and of the actual rebellion against the Priors in September 1434. Certainly the greater significance of the Peruzzi and their associates as an anti-Medicean block seems confirmed by the lists of exiles and *privati*; of the Albizzi only Rinaldo and his sons were punished, while within the Peruzzi and Castellani families alone, at least thirty males were involved. The powerful opposition to the Medici centred on Santa Croce clustered most thickly around the Peruzzi, and drew in smaller families or individuals from elsewhere in Florence who appear to have made their entry into the group via associations with them.

No doubt the marriage early in 1434 of Costanza, daughter of Giovanni di Messer Luigi Guicciardini, to Bernardo di Bindaccio Peruzzi, exiled later in the year, set the seal on the involvement of Giovanni Guicciardini with the Medici opponents,[9] although his business dealings by 1427 were already mainly with families like the Rossi and Baroncelli, and by 1433 his creditors included members of the Benizzi, Peruzzi, Bischeri, and other exile families.[10] A similar case is that of Terrino di Niccolò Manovelli,

---

[8] See Cat. 34, ff. 220r, 260r; 72, f. 56v; 72, f. 34v; 35, f. 1342v; 72, f. 211r. Economic strength and political influence seem to have been concentrated in two or three households, which were those of the exiles. Ridolfo di Bonifazio had assets of over 20,000 florins in 1427 (Cat. 72, f. 211r), and appeared almost a hundred times in the *Consulte* of our period. Bartolomeo di Verano's net income was only 1,822 florins in 1427 (ibid. 72, f. 56v), but he attended more than 60 *Consulte*. These two, however, were the only members of the extensive Peruzzi clan to appear in the *Consulte* at all, though the wealth of some others was also substantial (see Cat. 34, 35, for *portate* of less affluent Peruzzi).

[9] Pol. Gar. 1530. The precise date of the marriage is not given, but in view of Giovanni Guicciardini's subsequent position in Florence, it is almost impossible that it should have taken place after the events of September. On Giovanni Guicciardini's role in the divisions of these years see also above, pp. 90–91, and below, pp. 332,334.

[10] Cat. 65, ff. 482v–488r; 488, ff. 200v–202v.

a resident of the quarter of San Giovanni, and also exiled in 1434. Although he had a share in a company with Baldassare di Niccolò Carducci, his own debtors and creditors were preponderantly from exile families and their associates like the Panciatichi, Rondinelli, Baldovinetti, and Serragli.[11] In 1431 he married the daughter of Berto di Bonifazio Peruzzi, who was himself apparently dead by 1434.[12] Some of the Peruzzi marriages in the fifteenth century were with exile families with whom they had been traditionally associated. In 1414 Ridolfo di Bonifazio's daughter Marietta married Piero di Giovanni di Messer Bartolomeo Panciatichi, exiled in 1434.[13] The daughter of Bartolomeo di Verano, Lisabetta, was married by 1439 to Piero di Filippo di Messer Biagio Guasconi[14] (*privato* 1434), and Filippo di Messer Amideo (*privato* 1434) to Bonda di Amari Gianfigliazzi.[15] Another of Ridolfo's brothers, Donato (also *privato*), became the husband in 1417 of Dragoncina degli Strozzi,[16] and Maria di Giovanni di Rinieri Peruzzi was married in 1426 to Piero di Iacopo Ardinghelli.[17]

Ridolfo di Bonifazio Peruzzi was a close associate of Messer Biagio Guasconi,[18] and did business on a large scale with the Ricasoli, the Benizzi, and the Bischeri, all exile families.[19] He also had strong connections at this time with the Buon Busini, a newer family of Santa Croce who according to Cavalcanti supported the exiles, but somehow escaped proscription themselves, although their later fifteenth-century electoral record suggests that they may have been under the shadow of Medici disfavour. In 1433 Francesco di Betto Busini still owed Ridolfo money 'for the dowry of his wife, my kinswoman'; perhaps this is one reason why the Busini appeared as *mallevadori* of the sons of Bindaccio Peruzzi after their exile.[20] Those who pledged security for the

---

[11] Cat. 475, f. 671r ff.; 55, ff. 519r–521r.
[12] C.S. 2ª ser. XIV, ff. 17v, 18v. By 1432 Ridolfo Peruzzi had become responsible for the payment of the remainder of the girl's dowry. In the negotiations, the arbiter acting on her behalf was Bindaccio di Granello Ricasoli, and her daughter, born 7 September 1433, was baptized by Strozza di Smeraldo Strozzi and Bernardo Giugni.
[13] Pol. Gar. 1529.
[14] Ibid. 1531 (this marriage may have taken place after 1434).
[15] MSS. Pass. 188, Ins. 23.   [16] Pol. Gar. 1530.   [17] Ibid. 1529.
[18] Ibid.   [19] Cat. 35, f. 1342v, ff.
[20] Cat. 492, f. 439r; Otto di Guardia, 224, f. 57v. On the Busini record see Rubinstein, *Government of Florence, passim*; Tratte, 49, ff. 13r–14v; 53, *passim*; 397, f. 74r, ff.; 1151, ff. 393r–395r.

exiles' bonds were usually either close friends or relatives, often neighbours, or men heavily involved in business with them. Apart from other members of the Peruzzi family, the Peruzzi *mallevadori* included, besides the Buon Busini, *amici* and *parenti* like the Ricasoli, Benizzi, Bischeri, Strozzi, Panciatichi, Salviati, and Da Uzzano.[21]

Buonaccorso Pitti's account of his enemies draws attention to the fact that the Peruzzi had long been associated, in marriage and in their other activities, with the Ricasoli, a branch of the ancient clan of the Firidolfi, who had been magnates in Florence for most of the fourteenth century;[22] in the fifteenth century, although officially *popolani*, and entrusted with a number of important communal embassies, they were still not really within the *stato*.[23] In the later fourteenth century they belonged predominantly to the quarter of Santa Maria Novella,[24] but in 1427 the brothers Carlo and Bindaccio di Granello, exiled in 1434, were taxed in Lion Nero, in Santa Croce. However, both seem to have regarded the palace and tower at Brolio as their essential home, though in 1427 Carlo also rented a house in Borgo San Iacopo, in the quarter of Santo Spirito. Bindaccio had apparently no Florentine residence.[25] Both were squires of the pope Giovanni XXIII and for some period attached to his itinerant court; as knights and men of the sword they occupied much of their time with fighting under various banners.[26] Their Florentine associations, however, were almost exclusively with the major exile families. Among their general creditors were Giovanni di Messer Donato Barbadori, whose daughter Francesca had married Carlo in 1417, and Antonio di Ghezzo della Casa, whose brother Giovanni married the daughter of Bindaccio di Granello Ricasoli.[27] Bernardo di Filippo, nephew of Giovanni and Antonio di Ghezzo, was exiled

[21] Otto di Guardia, 224, ff. 36r, 56v–59r. Brucker, *The Civic World*, p. 25, comments on the profound significance of the commitment to stand surety for a fellow citizen.

[22] Jones, 'Florentine Families', esp. 193; both the Da Panzano and the Ricasoli were descended from the twelfth-century feudal house of the Firidolfi.

[23] For their embassies see Passerini, *Genealogia Ricasoli*. However, neither Carlo nor Bindaccio was even nominated for the scrutiny of 1433, and neither appears to have held any major office between 1429 and 1434. Nor do they appear in the *Consulte* of this period.

[24] Brucker, *Florentine Politics*, pp. 32–3.

[25] Cat. 72, ff. 68r–76v; ibid., ff. 85r–89v; 492, ff. 165v–170v. Citizens were normally assessed in the *gonfalone* where they owned most of their property.

[26] Passerini, *Genealogia Ricasoli*, pp. 149–53.

[27] Ibid., Tav. XII; Cat. 72, ff. 68r–76v.

in 1434, and Antonio was erroneously believed by many to have been banished also. Bindaccio's largest creditors were Berto and Ridolfo Peruzzi, for the considerable sum of almost 2,000 florins.[28] Giovanni di Ghezzo della Casa was obliged for a part of this sum, but the Ricasoli were mainly responsible, as Bernardo di Bindaccio Peruzzi made ruefully clear in his *catasto* report of 1427. He recorded the loan made by his father some twelve years before, but observed that since the brothers were poor, 'as it happens, however, we can't get anything back, and it doesn't seem worth even considering more than half'.[29] In 1433 he repeated that he did not expect the Ricasoli debt to be repaid 'and I'm not sure that they could even do it'.[30] Apart from these major links with the Florentine exiles, the Ricasoli were also connected by marriage with the Guasconi, and with the Pistoian branch of the Panciatichi, whose Florentine relatives were important members of the Medici opposition. Bindaccio di Granello married Niccolosa di Bandino Panciatichi;[31] it is interesting that Maso, son of Messer Rinaldo degli Albizzi, had married Giovanna, another of Messer Bandino's daughters, in 1420. Matteo da Panzano, a member of a breakaway *popolano* branch of the Firidolfi–Ricasoli clan, does not appear to have been in close contact with his former relatives, but he was, like them, an exile and a resident of Santa Croce; he lived in the Piazza Sant'Apollinare where the group gathered in defiance of the *Signoria* in 1434. His business dealings in 1427 were primarily with future exiles.[32]

The Peruzzi houses ringed the *piazza* off the Borgo de' Greci which ended at the back wall of the Priors' palace. Resident in and around the great house on the river directly south of the Palazzo Vecchio, sometimes called Castello d'Altafronte after the Ghibelline family believed to be the original owners, the Castellani of Bue were at the centre, figuratively and also literally, of the web of associated exile families in Santa Croce and the adjoining *gonfaloni* of Santa Maria Novella.[33] Another great banking family

---

[28] Cat. 72, ff. 68r–76v.   [29] Ibid. 34, f. 260r.

[30] Ibid. 32, ff. 210r–214v.

[31] Passerini, *Genealogia Ricasoli*, Tav. XII. Cf. the Albizzi marriage connection, below, pp. 179–80.

[32] Cat. 31, f. 706; 447, f. 143r. For earlier associations between the Da Panzano and other exile families, see 'Frammenti della Cronaca di Messer Luca di Totto da Panzano', ed. P. Berti, *Giornale storico degli archivi toscani*, v (1861), 62–8.

[33] Naturally not all of the extended family lived in the major palace; concerning the others, see, e.g., Cat. 28, ff. 836r, 993r.

of the early fourteenth century, they had failed in 1343, but recovered again by the middle of the century to become one of the wealthiest and most prominent houses of the period. They enjoyed the most important embassies, and wore the insignia of the *Parte Guelfa*. The establishment of the oligarchic regime in the 1380s found them at the height of their social and political influence, but after 1400 they had begun steadily to decline.[34] Not one of the five Castellani exiles or the dozen other *privati* in 1434 was outstandingly, or even comfortably wealthy. With the exception of Matteo di Michele, who had died in 1429, but had had in 1427 assets of over 13,000 florins,[35] the highest Castellani *catasto* assessment in 1427 was that of Piero di Messer Vanni, who had a net capital of 2,540 florins. Matteo di Michele and Messer Vanni Castellani had been eminent statesmen of the twenties, but there was no representative of the Castellani house in the inner *reggimento* of 1429–34.

Nevertheless, their fifteenth-century marriages reflected the strength of their former position and illustrated their continuing importance as a social force among the opponents of the Medici. Vanni di Messer Michele had married Francesca, daughter of Bettino Ricasoli, an old ally of the Castellani. Matteo di Michele Castellani had made one of the many marriages over the years linking them to the Peruzzi; his wife was Giovanna di Giovanni di Rinieri di Luigi Peruzzi. The Castellani were joined by marriages over two generations to another house hit heavily in 1434, the Rondinelli of Lion d'oro. The daughter of Niccolò di Michele Castellani, Maddalena, married in 1410 Arrigo di Alessandro Rondinelli, and in 1433 Nanna di Spinello Castellani became the wife of Romigi di Piero Rondinelli. Castellani marriages also associated them with less prominent Santa Croce families involved in opposition to the Medici, who were probably drawn into the group through their Castellani connections.[36] One of the daughters of Messer Vanni married a Pepi, and the marriage of another, Cosa, to Luigi di Ser Lodovico Doffi may even have been the cause of the implication of Luigi's brother Bernardo in the opposition to the Medici, and of his subsequent exile.[37]

[34] See Brucker, *Renaissance Florence*, p. 94; Martines, *The Social World*, pp. 199–210.

[35] Martines, *The Social World*, pp. 365–8.

[36] Cf. the butcher, Tano Fenci, above, p. 145 and n.

[37] MSS. Pass. 186, Ins. 88.

As one would expect, the Castellani did much of their business with *amici* and *parenti* like the Peruzzi, Ricasoli, Rondinelli, and Barbadori.[38] Piero di Messer Vanni was in business with two other exiles from Santa Croce and the leading member of a magnate house closely involved with the exile group—Matteo Benizzi, Iacopo Castellani, and Ramondo Manelli. Theirs were the companies described above as having failed and left the Castellani almost ruined by 1433.[39] The intricacies of the exiles' financial involvement with one another are illustrated by an entry in the 1433 *campione* of Piero di Messer Vanni Castellani; among his properties he listed 'possessions which used to belong to the Ricasoli'; they seem to have been ceded to him on account of some money owing from the Ricasoli to Antonio di Giovanni Barbadori, perhaps because at that time Antonio Barbadori owed Iacopo di Vanni Castellani a considerable sum for the dowry of his wife.[40] The branch of the Castellani descended from Messer Michele may also have been bound up economically with other exile families, as their *mallevadori* included members of the Bardi, Cavalcanti, and Bucelli families; Piero di Messer Vanni's *mallevadori* were, on the other hand, a mixed group.[41]

Quite close to the palace of Altafronte, in the Via Vacchereccia which runs between Por S. Maria and the Palazzo Vecchio, were the houses of the Baroncelli and the Raugi families,[42] linked to each other and to the Peruzzi not only by comparative proximity, but also by their prominent position in the great Peruzzi company of the early fourteenth century. These two families had apparently been *parenti* since before that time, and still lived next to each other in the street where the Baroncelli had originally had their 'torre e chasamenti'.[43] Contrary to the expectations of some, the Baroncelli, unlike the Raugi, were allowed to remain in Florence, though their associations with the great exile families were strong, and their traditions very similar.[44] In this small square of territory behind the Via Vacchereccia and bordered on

[38] Cat. 28, ff. 562r, 813r, 836r, 886r, 993r; 68, ff. 102v, 146v, 269r, 300v, 309v; 444, ff. 31r, 567r, 660r, 759r, 767r; 491, ff. 215r, 276r, 308r, 314r, 370v.
[39] Ibid. 28, ff. 813r–819r.   [40] Ibid. 491, ff. 215r–216v, 281r.
[41] Otto di Guardia, 224, ff. 38v–39v.   [42] Cat. 28, f. 899r, ff.
[43] MSS. 248, f. 177r.
[44] For associations with the Bischeri, Lamberteschi, and Da Uzzano, see Cat. 491, ff. 192r–193v (*campione* of Iacopo di Piero Baroncelli, a member of the inner *reggimento*). He, and his sons and brothers, did in fact lose their political rights in 1444 (Rubinstein, *Government of Florence*, p. 18).

two other sides by Por S. Maria and the Arno, is the church of S. Stefano al Ponte. Next door to this church lived the Lamberteschi, a consular family, of whom two members were exiled in 1434. Among the *debitori* and *creditori* of the wealthy Bernardo, father of the exiled Domenico, were other families from Santa Croce—the Baroncelli, the Castellani, the Peruzzi, and members of the magnate houses of the Degli Agli, Adimari, Manelli, and Ricci.[45] In 1420 Bernardo Lamberteschi had married Francesca di Bernardo di Vieri Guadagni, linking his house directly to that of one of the leaders of the opposition to the Medici.[46]

In the same *piazza*, living in a house which he rented from Bernardo Lamberteschi, was Manetto di Tuccio Scambrilla, one of the poorer of the exiles and *composto* with the *catasto* officials in both 1427 and 1433.[47] In spite of this, however, Manetto had made a prestigious marriage into another old and distinguished house involved in the proscriptions of 1434; his wife was the daughter of Ugolino di Giovanni Spini.[48] She in fact owned a property in her family's *gonfalone* in Santa Maria Novella which they rented to one of the Serragli, another family which apparently escaped exile by good luck or good management.[49] Manetto Scambrilla's associations were very much with the exile group; his son Tuccio had shares in a venture with Antonio and Piero di Tommaso de' Rossi and his own debtors and creditors included Bernardo Lamberteschi, Giovanni Barbadori, the Da Uzzano, and the Della Tosa.

Just across the Via Por S. Maria from the church of Santo Stefano began the *gonfalone* of Vipera, in the quarter of Santa Maria Novella. Here, in its main street, the Borgo SS. Apostoli, were the houses of the Baldovinetti. One of their ancestors had been named among the rectors of the 'tower and society of the Lion' in a document of 1209.[50] In 1427 the Baldovinetti still owned the Torre del Lione, by then in common with Valorino di' Barna, Attaviano de' Pepi, 'and with other of our *consorti*, and with the Manelli'.[51] The latter, an ancient magnate house very

---

[45] See Cat. 27, ff. 198r–205v; 491, 42r–46v (both in the father's name).
[46] Ancisa, EE, f. 230v.
[47] Cat. 28, f. 703r; 491, f. 240r. His son Tuccio was also exiled.
[48] C.S. 2ᵃ ser. XIII, f. 15v.   [49] Cat. 444, f. 494r.
[50] See P. Santini, 'Società delle torri in Firenze', *A.S.I.* xx (1887), 186–91.
[51] Cat. 74, f. 162v; cf. 38, f. 313r, ff., and the entries in reports of other part owners of the tower, ibid. 74, ff. 58v, 97r–98r, 145r.

closely connected with the exile group, had been *socii* of the Torre del Lione, situated at the head of the Ponte Vecchio on the north side of the Arno, and directly opposite the main Manelli houses on the south bank, in 1222;[52] this long-standing intimacy had been recently reinforced by the marriage of Guido di Soletto del Pera Baldovinetti, exiled in 1434, with Caterina di Matteo de' Manelli.[53]

Attaviano Pepi was also exiled in 1434. He does not seem to have been one of the early *socii*, but presumably bought a share in the tower property later; his own houses were in the *gonfalone* of Lion Nero.[54] The Baldovinetti rented out their shares of the Torre del Lione to various families, among the most prominent being the Castellani. Their dealings were in general almost exclusively with other exiled houses like the Altoviti, Serragli, Della Casa, Adimari, Manovelli, and particularly the Cavalcanti, that powerful magnate clan scattered over the ancient centre of Florence, part supporting, and part among the opposition to the Medici and their friends. The Cavalcanti were major creditors of the Baldovinetti, and Mariotto di M. Niccolò, one of the family's exiles, rented his warehouse from 'Domenicho Chavalcanti e fratelli'.[55]

The exiles Mariotto di Niccolò Baldovinetti and Tinoro di Niccolò Guasconi, of the *gonfalone* of Lion d'oro, were in fact half-brothers; on the death of her first husband Mariotto's mother, Costanza de' Mancini, had married Niccolò Guasconi. The marriage of Soletto del Pera, father of the exiled Guido, linked the Baldovinetti to the Strozzi,[56] and when the exiled Mariotto di Niccolò married in 1418, Messer Palla di Nofri Strozzi and Messer Michele di M. Vanni Castellani were leading participants in the ceremonies.[57] Also among their *parenti* was Piero di Giovanni di Domenico Ciampegli, son of a new and minor family

---

[52] P. Santini (ed.), *Documenti dell' Antica Costituzione del Comune di Firenze, Documenti di Storia Italiana*, x (Florence, 1895), pp. 535–7; the illustrations of the Palazzo Baldovinetti and the Torre del Lione from a fourteenth-century MS. in the B.N.F. are reproduced by R. Davidsohn, *Storia di Firenze* (repr. Florence, 1973), iv, 2, Pls. 9, 10.

[53] MSS. Pass. 185, Ins. 29.   [54] Cat. 72, ff. 257v–258r.

[55] Ibid. 454, f. 330r; also 38, ff. 481r, 313r, and 455, f. 176r. Piero Cavalcanti was exiled in 1434. Other associations with exile families in the fourteenth century are recorded in 'Le Ricordanze Trecentesche di Francesco e di Alessio Baldovinetti', ed. G. Corti, *A.S.I.* cxii (1954), 109–24.

[56] Litta, *Famiglie Celebri* v, Tav. VI.   [57] Acqu. e Doni 190, 3 (not foliated).

from Carro in Santa Croce, whose embroilment with the exiles might well be explained by his residence in the neighbourhood of the Castellani, the Cavalcanti, Lamberteschi, Baroncelli, Dall'Antella, and Baldovinetti.[58] In the same *gonfalone* of Vipera, further along the Borgo SS. Apostoli towards the church of Santa Trìnita, were the houses of the Altoviti, an old-established family of Santa Maria Novella who were connected closely by marriage to several exile families of San Giovanni, including the Barbadori and the Albizzi themselves. Sandro di Vieri, exiled in 1434, had married the daughter of Alessio di Iacopo degli Albizzi.[59] The Altoviti did business with families of various political persuasions, but they were traditional supporters of the Albizzi family.[60] The third of their San Giovanni marriages linked them with Stefano di Salvi di Filippo Bencivenni, an exile from Chiavi *gonfalone* whose brother married an Altoviti girl.[61] Probably in or around Borgo SS. Apostoli, apparently next door to Giovanni di Simone Altoviti, who had married into the Bencivenni, lived Oddo di Francesco Franceschi, another of the Vipera exiles who rented a house between 1427 and 1433 from yet another of the Altoviti.[62]

At its furthest end the Borgo SS. Apostoli opened up into the Piazza Santa Trìnita, around which were the houses of two great, old, once-magnate clans of the *gonfalone* of Unicorno, the Spini and the Gianfigliazzi.[63] Along with the Peruzzi and the Castellani of Santa Croce, the Gianfigliazzi had been members of the group which had persecuted Buonaccorso Pitti in 1400, and they were also among those most affected by the punishments meted out by the *Balìa* of 1434; there were five Gianfigliazzi exiles and two *privati*. Those involved were mainly the descendants of Messer

[58] Pol. Gar. 591.

[59] L. Passerini, *Genealogia e storia della Famiglia Altoviti* (Florence, 1871), Tav. VI. The Altoviti had always been closely associated with the *Parte Guelfa* (Fiumi, 'Fioritura', cxv, 407).

[60] A. Rado, *Maso degli Albizzi e il partito oligarchico in Firenze del 1382 al 1393* (Florence, 1927), p. 2; cf. B.N.F., Magliabechiana, II: III: 434 (letters to Maso degli Albizzi and others).

[61] Pol. Gar. 253.

[62] Cat. 38, f. 319r. By 1433 he was renting a house from the Redditi, of the same *gonfalone*; he had to leave the Altoviti house when it was sold to one of their *consorti* (Cat. 455, f. 380r).

[63] The Gianfigliazzi were members of the tower nobility; in 1280 they owned a tower in the Porta S. Pancrazio with the Mazzinghi (Santini, 'Società delle torri' 33, 189).

Rinaldo who, according to the chroniclers, after a wild youth had settled down as a great *cavaliere* of the commune and a close personal friend of Maso degli Albizzi.[64] The exiled members of the family were connected directly through marriage with many of the leaders of the Medici opposition. Giovanni di Messer Rinaldo in 1433 still owed part of the dowry involved in the marriage of an unnamed female relative to Filippo di Matteo de' Bardi, whose father was exiled in 1434.[65] Giovanni's sister Tita was the wife of Albertuccio Ricasoli,[66] and he married his daughter Agnola in 1434 to Domenico di Bernarba degli Agli, a magnate and constant associate of the leading exiles.[67] Giovanni's brother Rinaldo had a daughter, Sandra, married in 1419 to Luigi di Palmieri Altoviti,[68] and a son Baldassare who married Tommasa di Piero Frescobaldi, a relative of Stoldo di Lionardo, *privato* in 1434.[69] Another brother, Iacopo di Messer Rinaldo, had married in 1407 Lena di Giovanni di Bartolomeo Panciatichi; her brother was exiled in 1434.[70] A more distant female cousin of the exiled Gianfigliazzi was married to the son of Andrea di Vieri Rondinelli, head of that exiled house.[71] The *mallevadori* who stood surety for the Gianfigliazzi in 1434 reflect their associations— among them were the Cavalcanti, Panciatichi, Rossi, and Ricci, all houses with magnate traditions.[72]

The great thirteenth-century palace of the Spini stood across the road from the Gianfigliazzi houses, opposite the church of Santa Trìnita.[73] The Spini were a banking family pre-eminent in the late thirteenth century, when one member of the family had been a close friend of Boniface VIII.[74] After the failure of their banking firm in the 1420s they had been ousted from their position as papal bankers by the Medici themselves. The Spini were associated with the *Parte Guelfa*, and many of them had been among the

[64] Cavalcanti, *Trattato*, pp. 189–90, 131; also *Istorie*, p. 40. For his subsequent career as one of the leaders of the élite, see Brucker, *The Civic World*, passim. In 1427 his sons Giovanni, Iacopo, and Francesco, with their sons, lived together in a fraternal joint family in a house in the Piazza Santa Trìnita (Cat. 40, ff. 951r–954r).

[65] Cat. 458, ff. 621r–624r. [66] Ibid. 40, ff. 951r–954r.
[67] Ancisa, AA, f. 766r. [68] Ibid., f. 767r.
[69] MSS. Pass. 188, Ins. 23. [70] Ancisa, AA, f. 767r.
[71] MSS. Pass. 188, Ins. 23. [72] Otto di Guardia, 224, ff. 36v–37v.
[73] Bartolomeo di Bartolomeo, punished in 1434, lived in the parish of Santa Trìnita; among his neighbours were the Gianfigliazzi and Spini (Cat. 75, ff. 97v–99v).
[74] Fiumi, 'Fioritura' CXV. 413. According to Del Lungo (ed.), *Dino Compagni* ii. 94, the Spini were a 'famiglia guelfa popolana, ma di parte magnatizia'.

prestigious order of 'knights of the golden spur';[75] they had been members of the oligarchy after 1331 when, in Doffo Spini's words, 'the great families regained control of the government'.[76] Their known marriages in the fifteenth century were almost all to exile families. In 1401 Antonio di Giovanni degli Spini married Nicoletta di Neri di Messer Bindaccio de' Ricasoli, whose relatives Carlo and Bindaccio were exiled,[77] and a Spini woman in the twenties married Giovanni di Guglielmo di Bindo Altoviti.[78] The marriage of Ugolino Spini's daughter to the exiled Manetto di Tuccio Scambrilla has already been mentioned, and while Lisa di Cristofano Spini married Bernardo di Messer Biagio Guasconi who was among the *privati*, the marriage of Doffo Spini's daughter Costanza to Andrea Sertini in 1428 was arranged by Bartolomeo di Verano Peruzzi.[79]

Also in the parish of Santa Trìnita lived Piero di Neri di Francesco Ardinghelli, a wealthy exile from a former consular family, who in 1427 was the fourth-richest man in Santa Maria Novella with a net income of 29,965 florins.[80] His father had married the daughter of Messer Iacopo Gianfigliazzi, of the main exiled branch of that family; he himself in 1419 married Caterina di Niccolò di Nofri degli Strozzi, niece of Palla di Nofri.[81] He associated almost exclusively with the members of old, prominent, wealthy houses, most of them families who suffered by the proscriptions of 1434. This pattern is apparent in his report for the *catasto* officials in 1427.[82] After declaring his *debitori* as Orsino Lanfredini, Donato Adimari, Tommaso di Piero Velluti, and Carlo di Marco Strozzi, he went on to explain a rather unusual debt due from Domenico di Bernardo Lamberteschi, a fellow exile in 1434, 'which he owes me for a game I won from him'. Clearly Piero di Neri and Domenico di Bernardo moved in the same social orbit before they met together in the Piazza Sant'Apollinare to oppose the Medicean Priors. A number of other *debitori* are grouped together by Piero as those from whom he did not expect to receive any money because in each case 'he is my relative'. Included in this list are Stoldelino de' Rossi, and Bernardo

---

75 MSS. 248, f. 111r–v.

76 C.S. 2ª ser. XIII, f. 15v; cf. Martines, *The Social World*, pp. 72–3.

77 Passerini, *Genealogia Ricasoli*, Tav. XII.

78 C.S. 2ª ser. XIII, f. 16r.   79 Ibid., ff. 15v, 68v.

80 Martines, *The Social World*, p. 372.

81 C.S. 2ª ser. LVI, p. 645.   82 Cat. 41, ff. 565r–581v.

di Vieri Guadagni, the head of a leading exile family who died just before the return of the Medici to Florence in 1434. There is also money owing from Lorenzo di Messer Palla degli Strozzi, who rented part of a *banco* owned by Piero di Neri in the Mercato Nuovo. He also mentioned the sum of 142 florins owed to his father by Ruberto di Simone Spini, but explained that he had lost the documents referring to this and did not really want to pursue the matter in any case. The Ardinghelli were great landowners, and it is interesting to note that Orsino Lanfredini and Bernardo Lamberteschi, mentioned above as his *debitori*, were also Piero di Neri's neighbours at his farm at San Miniato al Monte. Orsino Lanfredini appears again in the list of Piero's *mallevadori*, along with Riccardo Fagni, Niccolò Adimari, and Giovanni di Guglielmino Altoviti.[83]

Other exiles resident in Santa Croce included men from four newer families, the Biffoli, Corsi, Doffi, and Fenci, whose comparatively dependent relations with the older exile families have already been observed. There were as well members of two old Florentine families living in the *gonfalone* of Bue, Francesco di Giovanni Bucelli and Antonio di Lionardo Raffacani; both numbered among their neighbours such prominent exile families as the Peruzzi and the Castellani.[84] The Dall'Antella, from whom two brothers were exiled, were also a Santa Croce family whose origins date back at least to the early thirteenth century.[85] Associations between the exiles of the Santa Croce–Santa Maria Novella district were particularly strong and vital, but they were also linked, as we have seen, to most of the other important exile families elsewhere in the city. If these *gonfaloni* can be thought of as in a sense the physical and spiritual heart of the exile group, it was nevertheless a body with important concentrations of activity in all quarters, and all its parts were ultimately connected with the whole.

Across the river in Oltrarno, in the *gonfalone* of Scala, was the main exiled branch of the Bardi, often described as a leading family in the opposition to the Medici, and neighbours of that

---

[83] For Piero di Neri's *portate* and *campioni*, 1427 and 1433, see Cat. 41, ff. 565r–581v; 75, ff. 161r–169r; 459, ff. 363r–369r; 494, ff. 353r–358v. For his *mallevadori*, see Otto di Guardia, 224, f. 40r.

[84] Cat. 29, f. 188r; ibid., f. 30r.　　　　[85] Jones, 'Florentine families' 185.

bulwark of anti-Medicean aristocratic conservatism, Niccolò da Uzzano. In Drago Santo Spirito were the Brancacci, and in Nicchio the Barbadori, the latter included in the half-dozen families to be punished at large, as well as two important older families, the Frescobaldi and the Belfradelli. Niccolò da Uzzano would have been among those exiled in 1434, but he had died in 1431, until which time he was at the very centre of the exile group and the spearhead of opposition to Medici activities. His personal associations were overwhelmingly with the exiled families, and especially those of Santo Spirito, or with other Santo Spirito families whose allegiance at that time is uncertain. His mother was Lena di Alessandro di Riccardo de' Bardi; his brother Angelo married Bamba di Zanobi di Messer Piero de' Bardi, and his sister Caterina, Alessandro di Messer Riccardo de' Bardi.[86] He did business with the Bardi, Da Panzano, Ardinghelli, and Giovanni Guicciardini; his personal *debitori* included the Peruzzi and the Buon Busini.[87]

The Bardi themselves were an old and independent family, and probably the largest *consorteria* in Florence at this time; in 1415 they were still magnates, but a law of 1431 restored some of them to the ranks of the *popolani*.[88] Like the Peruzzi, the Bardi clustered closely together; the majority resided in the area known as 'casa de' Bardi'.[89] From the branches which had assumed the title of Conti di Vernio in the fourteenth century came Cosimo de' Medici's wife, Contessina, and her relatives the descendants of Messer Iacopo, who played such an important role before 1434 as friends of the Medici and associates in the bank.[90] By the 1430s the exiled branch was closely associated with other exile families. The daughter of Bardo, banished in 1434, had married in 1431 Lorenzo, a son of Palla di Nofri degli Strozzi. Another exile, Lionardo di Ridolfo Bardi, married in 1434 a girl from the Bucelli, an exile family resident in Bue, Santa Croce. A third of the Bardi exiles, Matteo, was related by the marriage of his sister Lisabetta in 1415 to Niccolò d'Antonio Serragli, one of those citizens closely associated with the exile families and erroneously believed to have been exiled himself.[91] Bernardo di Cipriano

[86] Litta, *Famiglie Celebri* xi, Tav. I.   [87] Cat. 64, ff. 65v–75v.
[88] *Statuta* i. 444; M.A.P. IV, 192.   [89] Below, pp. 191–2, 195n.
[90] See the partial genealogy of the Bardi in de Roover, *The Rise and Decline*, p. 386.
[91] Ancisa, BB, ff. 795v, 184v, 799v.

shared in a goldsmith's business in Guido Velluti's name,[92] and Lionardo di Ridolfo's *mallevadori*, in addition to other members of the Bardi family, included Belfradelli and Bucelli.[93]

Some of these ties with other exiled families were of comparatively recent origin in the mid-thirties, and may even perhaps have been formed consciously to counterbalance the weight of earlier associations in business with the Medici. For although the latter's major Bardi business associates and friends came from a single branch of the family which did not include any of the exiles, the Bardi were still virtually the only one of the exile families to have had close connections with the Medici in the recent past. Bardo di Francesco di Messer Alessandro recorded in his *portata* of 1427 a debt of 2,185 florins owing to him from 'a partnership in the name of Francesco my father at Barcelona and Valencia, two-thirds of which belongs to Averardo de' Medici and co. and one-third to Francesco';[94] his relative Matteo di Bernardo di Giorgio, speaking for himself and his brothers, submitted in his *portata* of 1433 'that all their possessions, both real estate and personal property, are in the hands of Cosimo and Lorenzo de' Medici and Messer Andrea and Ubertino de' Bardi and Bardo di Francesco de' Bardi, who are their creditors for a thousand florins'.[95] Whether these obligations were connected is not clear, but their business dealings may perhaps have provided some reason for bad feeling between the Medici and former Bardi associates, which in turn may have contributed to the estrangement of those Bardi actually among their *amici* at the time.

Among those houses of similar age and traditions which had been the Bardi's natural associates since the fourteenth century were the Frescobaldi, who had joined with them in a violent but abortive attempt at a *coup d'état* in 1340.[96] The Frescobaldi too had been a great banking house of the thirteenth century and were also magnates, with a reputation for lawless and anti-social behaviour. They had from the mid-thirteenth century been noted for their participation, not only in wars and disturbances, but also in political competition and conspiracy, and were known for their sympathy with restricted government.[97] Before the crisis of

[92] Cat. 64, f. 58v.   [93] Otto di Guardia, 224, f. 31r–v.
[94] Cat. 64, ff. 36v–40r.   [95] Ibid. 487, f. 315v.
[96] Becker, *Florence in Transition* i. 97–8.
[97] V. Niccolini Spreti, *Enciclopedia Storico-Nobiliare Italiana* (6 vols., Milan, 1928–32) iii. 279–80; MSS. 248, f. 127r–v.

1433, the *catasto* report of Stoldo di Lionardo Frescobaldi reveals that he was doing business with the Pazzi and with the Manelli, another Santo Spirito magnate house,[98] and in 1434 he joined himself explicitly to the Peruzzi by his marriage to Ginevra di Conte di Rinieri Peruzzi.[99]

The Frescobaldi houses were in the *piazza* which now bears their name, immediately across the Arno from Piazza Santa Trìnita on the Santo Spirito side of the Ponte Santa Trìnita. The Manelli houses were in a corresponding position on the Santo Spirito side of the Ponte Vecchio, opposite the tower on the north side of the river in Vipera which they shared with the Baldovinetti. Between the Ponte Vecchio and the Ponte Santa Trìnita in the *gonfalone* of Nicchio, Santo Spirito, runs the Borgo San Iacopo, and in this street were the houses of two prominent exile families, the Barbadori and the Belfradelli. The Belfradelli had been well established in this area since before 1260; after the defeat of the Guelfs at Montaperti in that year, their houses had been ruined by the Ghibellines and their towers in Popolo San Iacopo d'Oltrarno were mentioned in the 'rifaciemento del danno' of 1266.[100] Two members of this family were exiled in 1434, Zanobi di Adovardo and Bernardo di Salvestro. Bernardo's brother Agnolo was the husband of Costanza di Filippo di Messer Castellano Frescobaldi.[101] Among the Belfradelli *debitori* and *creditori* of 1427 and 1433 were several exile families, mainly from Santo Spirito—the Bardi, Da Uzzano, Ardinghelli, Della Casa, and Baroncelli.[102] The Belfradelli *mallevadori* in 1434 were their exiled neighbours, the Barbadori, and members of the Guicciardini and Bardi, also Santo Spirito families.[103]

The Barbadori, another of the families punished *en bloc* in the proscriptions of 1434, were also related by marriage to the Frescobaldi. Those proscribed were Niccolò di Messer Donato and his sons and descendants; Messer Donato's wife had been Caterina di Matteo di Dino Frescobaldi,[104] and Cecca, the daughter of his son, Giovanni, was married in 1417 to Carlo di Granello Ricasoli, exiled in 1434.[105] Niccolò himself was the husband of Vaggia di Piero di Corso Adimari, a leading member of a San Giovanni

[98] Cat. 488, ff. 369r–370v.   [99] Ancisa, FF, f. 112v.   [100] MSS. 250, f. 539r.
[101] Cat. 17, f. 288r.
[102] Ibid.; also 65, ff. 128r, 258v; 434, f. 531r; 435, f. 195r; 500, ff. 76v, 421r.
[103] Otto di Guardia, 224, ff. 34r, 41v.   [104] Ancisa, AA, f. 191r.
[105] Passerini, *Genealogia Ricasoli*, Tav. XII.

magnate house strongly associated with the opposition to the Medici.[106] The Barbadori *mallevadori* included the Strozzi and the Benizzi.[107] The latter family, of whom two brothers, Iacopo and Matteo di Piero, were exiled, lived just round the corner from the Ponte Vecchio, off Borgo San Iacopo, in Piazza Santa Felìcita. Another brother, Antonio di Piero, had a banking company with Battista and Giovanni di Niccolò Guicciardini, who stood surety for Matteo di Piero in 1434; Ramondo Manelli and Biagio di Ser Nello, a relative of Rinaldo degli Albizzi, were also involved in the affairs of this company. A fourth brother, Carlo di Piero, was the *compagno* of Ridolfo Peruzzi.[108]

Another Nicchio resident soon to be exiled was Donato di Piero Velluti, one of several brothers involved in a company with Giovanni Rondinelli, scion of a Lion d'oro house included in the families most severely punished. His business associations were mainly with exile families—the Della Casa, Albizzi, Baroncelli, Panciatichi, Bardi, Strozzi, Rossi, Barbadori, and Lamberteschi.[109] The last remaining exile family of importance in Santo Spirito was somewhat isolated in the *gonfalone* of Drago, but of its four members exiled, two were joined directly in marriage with two of the leading houses in opposition to the Medici. Felice di Michele Brancacci married Lena di Messer Palla di Nofri degli Strozzi, and Ser Branca di Buonfigliuolo Brancacci's sister Antonia married Giovanni di Tinoro di Messer Niccolò Guasconi; his father was exiled and Giovanni himself was *privato*.[110] The Brancacci did business with the Castellani, the Spini, the Bardi, and the Fagni, although their creditors also included both Cosimo and Averardo de' Medici.[111]

In the quarter of San Giovanni, the stronghold of the Miceans, there were no great residential enclaves of opposition to them, except in the *gonfalone* of Chiavi, the home of the Albizzi; in general, the exiles were dotted throughout the quarter, and most had strong ties with exile families elsewhere in Florence. When bonds of marriage, neighbourhood, and friendship were not

[106] Pol. Gar. 186.   [107] Otto di Guardia, 224, f. 50r.
[108] Cat. 65, f. 37r; 500, f. 13r; Otto di Guardia, 224, f. 42v.
[109] Cat. 65, f. 105r, cf. ibid. 17, f. 503r; 433, f. 326r; 488, f. 100v.
[110] MSS. Pass. 186, Ins. 50.
[111] Cat. 67, ff. 46r–48v, 374v–375v; 490, ff. 145r–147r, 306r–v.

mutually reinforcing, as they had been for the Medici partisans, they may have presented exile families with some sharp and conflicting alternatives similar to those described by Dino Compagni over a century earlier. There appear to have been few obviously neutral families in San Giovanni; as both parties by 1434 had their focus in that quarter, its residents probably felt the need to manifest a decided allegiance to one group or the other. Apart from the Albizzi and the Guadagni in Chiavi, two of the families disqualified almost *en bloc* from the *stato* in 1434 were residents of Lion d'oro itself—the Guasconi and the Rondinelli. Also belonging to San Giovanni were several of the great old houses, mainly magnates, who were among those most closely involved with the opposition to the Medici. These included the Rossi, Arrigucci, and Panciatichi, who were exiled, and the Adimari, Degli Agli, and Scolari, who were not. Another prominent anti-Medicean from San Giovanni was Ser Paolo di Ser Lando Fortini who, like Niccolò da Uzzano, may have died before the conflict became an open one.[112]

The Guasconi and the Rondinelli, the leading exile families of Lion d'oro, were twice linked by marriage in the decade or so before 1434. Giovanni di Filippo Rondinelli married Tommasa di Messer Biagio Guasconi, aunt of one of the exiles,[113] and in 1431 another of Tommasa's nephews married Nera di Arrigo Rondinelli.[114] Andrea di Rinaldo Rondinelli also appears among Biagio di Iacopo di M. Biagio's *mallevadori* in 1434.[115] The Guasconi were also connected with a number of exile families outside San Giovanni, including the Strozzi[116] and the Spini. It was the marriage of Bernardo di Messer Biagio Guasconi to Lisa di Cristofano Spini, which, according to Doffo Spini, set the seal on the financial ruin of their house; certainly Bernardo seems to have taken over much of the Spini property and business interests.[117] Another daughter of Messer Biagio had married into the Altoviti, while Piero di Filippo di Messer Biagio was by 1436 the husband of Lisabetta di Bartolomeo Peruzzi, whose household was second in importance within the Peruzzi family only to that of Ridolfo di Bonifazio himself.[118]

However, the Guasconi also had some associations, especially

[112] Cf. Kent, 'The Florentine *reggimento*' 606.   [113] Pol. Gar. 1726.
[114] MSS. Pass. 188, Ins. 44.   [115] Otto di Guardia, 224, f. 60r.
[116] MSS. Pass. 188, Ins. 44.
[117] C.S. 2ª ser. XIII, f. 15v; cf. Cat. 48, f. 385v.
[118] MSS. Pass. 188, Ins. 44.

in business, with pro-Medicean families who were their neighbours. Tinoro di Messer Niccolò Guasconi rented his shop from
Andrea, the son of Ser Paolo di Ser Lando Fortini,[119] but the
brother of Biagio di Iacopo di Messer Biagio had had a company,
'many years ago', with Andrea Pazzi. This association, like that of
the exiled Bardi with the Medici themselves, seems to have been
productive rather of ill-feeling than of common interest. Biagio's
brother, Girolamo, had died in 1425, without having been able
to show his brothers the accounts. Biagio wrote in his *catasto*
report of 1427 that Andrea Pazzi had assured him that nothing
remained to Girolamo; on the contrary, he still owed money to
the company. Biagio was clearly dissatisfied with this report, but
explained that he was unable to take action: 'We, because up until
this very day we have seen neither the account, nor indeed any
statement, cannot make any judgement about it, and so we will
say nothing about it, neither for nor against.'[120] Another interesting suggestion of tension in this quarter appears from the 1427
catasto report of Bernardo di Messer Biagio Guasconi, *privato* in
1434. According to Bernardo there had been an attempt shortly
before, on the part of a Giovanni di Messer Forese (probably
Salviati), to have him made one of the *grandi* on the evidence of a
false document. This had occurred when 'Giovanni di Giannozzo
[Gianfigliazzi] was one of the *Signoria*';[121] he belonged to the
one branch of the Gianfigliazzi which supported the Medici.
This incident may well have been due, or at least attributed by
Bernardo Guasconi, to the growing tension between the two
parties in this area.[122] Notably in the proscriptions of 1434 the
Guasconi were among the most severely punished of all families.
Only three members were exiled, but at least another twenty-one
were deprived of the right to hold office.

The Rondinelli too were included in the wholesale 'family'
punishments, but only one member of the family was exiled; another seven were *privati*. Apart from the Guasconi marriage, the
Rondinelli *parenti* included the Castellani by a marriage of 1431,
and the Dall'Antella; Cilia d'Ugolino di Vieri Rondinelli, whose
father was *privato* in 1434, married Piero di Nofri dall'Antella in

---

[119] Cat. 49, f. 1282r.   [120] Ibid. 48, f. 421r.   [121] Ibid., f. 393v.
[122] Conversely, these sorts of quarrels and litigation were of course quite common
between *amici* and within quite unified *consorterie*, and the ill-feeling arising from
them might be either enduring or very transient indeed.

1428.[123] The exiled member, Andrea di Vieri, did business with the Adimari, Serragli, Guasconi, Spini, and Della Casa; his *parenti* included the Dall'Antella, and his creditors the Medici.[124] His *mallevadori* were a mixed lot, most of them neither Mediceans nor exiles.[125]

As well as these two leading families among the opposition to the Medici there were several other exiles in the heart of Medici territory in Lion d'oro. Nuccio di Benintendi Solosmei and his uncle Matteo di Nuccio were neighbours of the Ginori and of Nicola di Vieri de' Medici.[126] The Solosmei had represented the Guelfs of the district (*sesto*) of Duomo in 1280 at the signing of the peace of Cardinal Latino, and a Bencivenni Solosmei and his son Nuccio had property in that area destroyed by the Ghibellines in 1260.[127] In 1427 Nuccio di Benintendi was doing business with the Medici, Tornabuoni, and the Serristori, as well as the Peruzzi, Adimari, and Della Casa.[128] Nuccio di Benintendi's sister Cecca was the wife of another Lion d'oro exile, Giovanni di Piero Bartoli, whose only other close connections seem to have been with the Rucellai, with whom he owned land 'not to be divided'.[129] The last of the Lion d'oro exiles, Piero di Giovanni Ciampegli, from a new and relatively obscure family, was primarily linked not to other exiles in his own *gonfalone*, but to the Santa Croce–Santa Maria Novella group by his marriage with the Baldovinetti.[130]

Outside Lion d'oro, most of the San Giovanni exiles, except for those in the Albizzi *gonfalone* of Chiavi, were single representatives of distinguished families whose chief associates seem to have been chosen from other families of similar status without regard to *gonfalone* or quarter. Michele di Alessandro Arrigucci, exiled in 1434, had married Lisa di Buonaccorso Adimari in 1425.[131] The Arrigucci were a consular family of feudal traditions; they and the Adimari had both lost enormous amounts of property— houses, palaces, and towers—in the Ghibelline depredations of the 1260s.[132] Both families had been magnates for considerable periods of time over the centuries. The Arrigucci did business

[123] Pol. Gar. 1726.   [124] Cat. 49, f. 1622r; 468, f. 131r; 497, f. 66r.
[125] Otto di Guardia, 224, ff. 37v–38r.   [126] Cat. 78, ff. 157r–158v.
[127] Pol. Gar. 1910; *Delizie* vii, p. 269.
[128] Cat. 78, ff. 157r–158v; 497, ff. 561v–563r.   [129] Ibid. 49, f. 1297r.
[130] Pol. Gar. 591.   [131] MSS. Pass. 185, Ins. 20.
[132] Ibid. 185, Ins. 19; *Delizie* vii, pp. 139, 142, 245.

mainly with other old families like the Strinati, or the Baronci and Lamberteschi, both exiled; however, they also included the Ginori among their creditors, and the exiled Del Bulletta, who were artisans, and neighbours of the Arrigucci in San Giovanni.[133] Lodovico di Giovanni Rossi, of Vaio, belonged to a thirteenth-century banking family who soon became magnates;[134] from the 1427 tax return made out in his name it appears that Lodovico had to earn his living as a mercenary: 'He says he is in the pay of the Marchese, with four horses which he says are pledged to the Marchese for a debt, and he has no other property.' He had borrowed money recently from Baldinuccio Adimari and Piero di Neri Ardinghelli, to whom he was related by marriage.[135] He was also related to the Peruzzi; Agnolo di Francesco Rossi had married Filippa di Amideo di Attaviano Peruzzi, whose kinsmen were to be exiled in 1434, at the beginning of the century.[136]

A supreme example of the existence of powerful bonds between those throughout the city who opposed the Medici is provided in the associations of Piero di Giovanni Panciatichi, a resident of Drago San Giovanni, who was fined 1,000 gold florins for his part in the events of September 1434.[137] Piero was directly related by marriage to two of the leaders of the exile group. He himself had married Marietta, daughter of Ridolfo Peruzzi; his sister Maddalena was the wife of Iacopo di Messer Rinaldo Gianfigliazzi.[138] Other marriages within his immediate family created bonds with exile families and their friends; in 1394 his sister Agnese married into the Del Palagio, who were prominent associates of the exiles and *parenti* of Rinaldo degli Albizzi. Piero's brother Antonio married a girl from the Bucelli family in 1421; ten years later another brother, Zanobi, became the husband of Benedetto Strozzi's daughter, Margherita.[139] Both the Albizzi and the Peruzzi had made marriages with the Pistoian branch of the Panciatichi; the latter during the fifteenth century were engaged in a feud with the Cancellieri of Pistoia, a family

[133] Cat. 54, f. 441r–v; 79, f. 517r; 475, f. 230r; 498, f. 441r.

[134] Martines, *The Social World*, pp. 108, 155, 265.

[135] Cat. 65, f. 488r; 434, f. 49r; cf. bid. 41, ff. 565r–581v.

[136] Ancisa, CC, f. 1r.   [137] Otto di Guardia, 224, f. 40r.

[138] Pol. Gar. 1529; cf. L. Passerini, *Genealogia e storia della famiglia Panciatichi* (Florence, 1858), Tav. V; according to Passerini, Piero's wife was Bandecca di Filippo Peruzzi. Gargani's information straight from the records of the *Gabelle* may perhaps have been more accurate.

[139] Passerini, *Genealogia Panciatichi*, Tav. V.

which strongly supported the interests of Neri Capponi, who after 1433 came over to the Medici side.[140] The Panciatichi were a powerful feudal family who came from the hills outside Pistoia; one branch obtained citizenship in Florence in 1376, but were effectively excluded from the *stato*.[141] Piero did business with various families, both Florentines and others; he had a shop in the city but maintained a rural dwelling in the *contado* of Pistoia and a house for his use in the town itself.[142]

In Drago San Giovanni, besides the Panciatichi and the Arrigucci, were two other exiles who were in fact related to one another by marriage, Michele di Galeotto Baronci and Terrino di Niccolò Manovelli. Baronci's sister, Lena, was the mother of Terrino Manovelli.[143] These families were among the earliest residents of that area; there is an entry concerning the Baronci in the *Capitolo del Duomo* for the year 1137. The Manovelli were responsible for the building of the principal gate of Santa Maria Maggiore, which was there in Dante's time;[144] in the fifteenth century Terrino's own house faced on to the *piazza*. He married one of the daughters of Berto di Bonifazio Peruzzi, brother of Ridolfo; in the arrangement of this alliance Bindaccio di Granello Ricasoli acted for the family of the bride.[145] Manovelli's *Ricordanze* contains a firmly anti-Medicean description of the events of 1433 and 1434.[146] Among his *debitori* were the Rondinelli, the Baldovinetti, and the Serragli, and he rented a house to Bartolomeo Panciatichi in 1431,[147] though his *mallevadori* in 1434 were Mediceans—Bernardo di Domenico Giugni and Bernardo di Cristofano Carnesecchi.[148]

Only one member of the Della Casa family of Drago San Giovanni was exiled—Bernardo di Filippo di Ghezzo. Several contemporary commentators believed that his uncle and business

---

[140] See below, p. 266.   [141] Martines, *The Social World*, pp. 55, 63–4.
[142] Cat. 79, ff. 118r–133v; 498, ff. 334r–344v.
[143] 'Ricordanze di Terrino di Niccolò Manovegli', C.S. 2ª ser. XIV, ff. 10r, 16r.
[144] MSS. 250, 585r–v; MSS. 248, f. 63r–v; cf. F. Carmody, 'Florence: Project for a map, 1250–1296', *Speculum*, xix (1944), 44.
[145] 'Ricordanze', ff. 14, 17 ff. His first wife, who had died even before he took her to his house, was the daughter of Niccolò Buon Busini, and the arbiters were Andrea di Rinaldo Rondinelli for him, and Lionardo d'Antonio Strozzi for her.
[146] See below, p. 246.
[147] 'Ricordanze', C.S. 2ª ser. XIV, ff. 17r, 18v. In 1432 he stood surety for Tinoro di Niccolò Guasconi to Lionardo di Filippo Strozzi.
[148] Cat. 55, ff. 519r–521r; 475, f. 671r, ff.; Otto di Guardia, 224, f. 33v.

partner, Antonio di Ghezzo, had also been confined, but this was not the case. Bernardo was closely connected through his immediate family to the families of fellow exiles. Another uncle, Giovanni di Ghezzo, a *compagno* of the Adimari, had married in 1415 Cecca di Bindaccio di Granello Ricasoli, exiled in 1434. Bernardo's cousin, Lionarda d'Agnolo di Ghezzo, was married two years earlier to Niccolò d'Alesso di Iacopo degli Albizzi, and Ghezzo di Talduccio, probably Bernardo's grandfather, had been the husband of Niccolosa di Aglio degli Agli, of a prominent magnate house of San Giovanni which was closely associated with the exiles.[149] Bernardo himself did business with both exiles and Mediceans of his quarter;[150] one of his more distant relations, Antonio di Ser Lodovico della Casa, was in fact a Medicean supporter.[151]

The Guadagni were the only other important exile family in the Albizzi *gonfalone* of Chiavi, home of some of the most prominent statesmen of the city, and of several Mediceans. Like the Della Casa and several other exile families from San Giovanni, the Guadagni made their marriages mainly with other exile families, but had some important connections, especially in business, with Mediceans. In his *Ricordanze* of 1434 Carlo di Pepo Buondelmonti discussed his *procuratore*, Pippo di Bernardo Guadagni, and how 'we made our agreement in the name of Messer Giovanni di Messer Luigi Guicciardini and Bernardo Lamberteschi and Iacopo di Giovanni Bischeri . . . they are all relatives of Pippo's'.[152] All of them too, like Filippo himself, were exiles or closely related to those exiled. The Guadagni were a consular family who fought at Montaperti in 1260, and many of their marriages linked them to old and distinguished families. Filippo's father, Bernardo di Vieri Guadagni, took as his first wife in 1396 Francesca di Andrea di Messer Bindo de' Bardi; his second wife, whom he married in 1401, was the daughter of Filippo Ardinghelli. The Lamberteschi connection was forged by the marriage of Filippo's sister to Bernardo di Lamberto Lamberteschi, father of the exiled Domenico; Dianora di Giovanni Guicciardini was Filippo's own wife. Another of the exiled Guadagni, Francesco di

[149] Ancisa, AA, ff. 809v–810r; Pol. Gar. 511.
[150] Cat. 79, f. 448r–v; 474, f. 591r–v.
[151] They belonged, however, to separate branches which had not shared a common ancestor since the end of the thirteenth century (MSS. Pass. 197).
[152] C.S. 2ª ser. CXXVII, ff. 10, 25v.

Vieri, had married in 1420 the daughter of Messer Matteo di Stefano Scolari, of a magnate clan of San Giovanni; her sister married one of the sons of Rinaldo degli Albizzi. Francesco di Vieri's mother had been Margherita di Messer Manno Donati, from a magnate family with many exile friends. His sister Niccolosa married Giovanni di Tedice degli Albizzi in 1429 and another sister was the wife of Bernardo di Iacopo Arrighi, of an exiled Santa Maria Novella family.[153]

Although Filippo di Bernardo di Vieri and Francesco di Vieri were closely bound to the exile group by marriage and tended also to have their business connections in this area,[154] the third of the Guadagni exiles, Migliore di Vieri, was a slightly different case. His mother had been Francesca di Simone Tornabuoni, aunt of the Lucrezia Tornabuoni who married Cosimo de' Medici's son Piero; as her husband was dead, she still lived in Migliore's house in 1427. Migliore himself in 1428 married the daughter of Neri Fioravanti, one of the Medici *amici*. Migliore's *compagno* in his *bottega* was Fruosino di Luca da Panzano; one member of this family was exiled, but others supported the Medici.[155] This ambiguity of Guadagni associations may partly have been due, paradoxically, to their residence in the same *gonfalone* as the Albizzi. The Guadagni lived at the Mercato Vecchio end of the Corso; the Albizzi lived in the same street, now called Borgo degli Albizzi, further east towards the Piazza San Piero Maggiore.[156] This may well have been a case of neighbourhood fostering enmity rather than friendship; Cavalcanti commented on 'the great and continuing enmity nourished by Migliore Guadagni against Piero di Filippo degli Albizzi', and the fact that 'in addition neither Bernardo nor Vieri were ever friends of the Albizzi', although in the end Messer Rinaldo 'consigned all this to oblivion, and Albizzi and Guadagni made common cause against Cosimo'.[157] Indeed, however, neither Rinaldo degli Albizzi and his sons, nor the four members of the Strozzi family originally

[153] *Delizie* vii, p. 145; L. Passerini, *Genealogia e storia della famiglia Guadagni* (Florence, 1873), pp. 1–6, Tav. II.

[154] Cat. 57, f. 881r; 80, f. 531; 479, f. 771r; 499, f. 290v.

[155] Ibid. 499, f. 904r; Passerini, *Genealogia Guadagni*, Tav. II.

[156] Limburger, *Die Gebäude*, p. 222.

[157] *Istorie*, p. 266, cf. pp. 267–70. Conversely, Cavalcanti may have been wrong about their relations; Rinaldo received help from Guadagni over a tax assessment in 1429 (Brucker, *The Civic World* 7, v); cf. Guasti, *Commissioni* ii. 85, 89, 278.

exiled in 1433, seem to have been as closely or exclusively entwined with other exiles as most of those we have been considering.

There is some evidence of tension between the Strozzi and Albizzi themselves; in 1429 Antonio di Lorenzo di Lando degli Albizzi brought a petition against Matteo di Simone Strozzi, later one of the exiles, and in this disagreement over a business affair Matteo saw his opponents as a group of specifically Albizzi *amici*, including particularly Cristofano di Niccolò del Chiaro, whom he described as 'very intimate with all the Albizzi'.[158] Similarly, Buonaccorso Pitti's account of his feud with the Ricasoli and their *parenti*, the Gianfigliazzi, Peruzzi, and Castellani, draws attention to another instance of enmity or at least conflict of interest between the Albizzi and their close associates, and other of the exiles. In his fight against these families, aided especially by the Baroncelli and the Barbadori, Pitti observed:

There came out in my favour, to aid me, many relatives and friends, among whom were Giovanni Carducci, Migliore di Giunta Migliori, Rinaldo di Messer Maso degli Albizzi, Piero di Luca degl'Albizzi, Messer Cristofano degli Spini, Messer Francesco Machiavelli, Nofri Bischeri, Sandro di Vieri Altoviti, Currado Panciatichi, Guidetto Guidetti, Francesco Canigiani, and many other similar citizens, and my excellent godfather, Roberto de' Rossi . . .[159]

Here, thirty years before, but already including many of those to be exiled in 1434, or their fathers or uncles, was a predominantly San Giovanni group in which the Albizzi were prominent, in opposition to the nucleus of traditionally associated families which we saw to be the inspiration and focus of a group of exiled individuals and families from Santa Croce and part of Santa Maria Novella, with a concrete base in neighbourhood and intermarriage. These earlier enmities with future allies in the opposition to the Medici, and the fact that Rinaldo's own most intimate associates even in the late twenties and early thirties seem to have been a predominantly local group, not closely connected with those which clustered around the Strozzi, or the Peruzzi and their friends, may help to explain why Rinaldo was a less effective

[158] C.S. 5ª ser. XII, 'Ricordi di Matteo di Simone di Filippo Strozzi', f. 26r.
[159] *Cronica*, p. 176.

leader of his party than the Medici; possibly those who supported him in his opposition to the Medici nevertheless resented a claim to authority which was relatively abruptly and artificially imposed upon them, and did not grow naturally out of a whole web of customary relationships of a more tangible sort.

As often in Florence, neighbourhood fostered both enmity and friendship; most of Rinaldo's *amici* were from San Giovanni families, particularly from his own *gonfalone* of Chiavi. In 1430 his daughter Susanna married Bartolomeo di Antonio Nelli, a very rich merchant whose Florentine residence was in Lion d'oro but who also, as Rinaldo noted in 1427 'had a house and bank in Pisa'.[160] During his absence from Florence on communal business, Rinaldo's correspondents included his next-door neighbour, Piero della Rena, and Bartolomeo Nelli. On one occasion he asked his son Ormanno to seek the latter's advice on a matter of importance, since 'the goodwill of our Bartolomeo Nelli matters a great deal to me'.[161] Another son, Giovanni, was the husband of Francesca di Matteo Scolari, whose father was also a neighbour of the Albizzi in Chiavi, and had connections with several other exiled families;[162] after the death of Matteo, Rinaldo continued to correspond with his widow.[163] The Fortini, of the same *gonfalone*, were regarded by Rinaldo and his sons as trustworthy friends; Ser Paolo di Ser Lando was well known as an opponent of the Medici in the twenties.[164]

Also on intimate terms with Rinaldo, at least during the period when he was commissioner to the Lucchese camp and one of the *Dieci* in command of the war, was Ser Martino di Ser Luca Martini.[165] This relationship is a particularly interesting one because by the early thirties Ser Martino was clearly one of the Medici *amici*.[166] Moreover, during this period Averardo procured a position on the galleys for Ormanno degli Albizzi at the urging of both father and son, though this act of patronage clearly did not imply partisanship and was rather in the nature of a favour extended to respected equals. This was in keeping with the general tone of the relations between them, and while the nineteenth-

---

[160] Guasti, *Commissioni* iii. 337.

[161] Ibid. 347, also 258, 262, 268, 280, 313, 379. Rinaldo's 1427 *catasto* report is published 624–41.

[162] Cat. 499, ff. 317v, 625r–626v.

[163] *Commissioni* iii. 41, 83.

[164] Ibid. 342.

[165] See, e.g., *Commissioni* iii. 342, 347, 351.

[166] Below, pp. 225–8.

century view of the Medici and the Albizzi as personal friends driven apart by the enmity of their associates is belied by the evidence concerning the growth of the Medici party, it is true that Rinaldo had more in common with the Medici, in terms of family age and traditions, and of personal political style, than he had with many of the leading exiles or than the Medici had with many of their own *amici*.[167]

Although very little is known about the attitudes and behaviour of particular members of the enormous Albizzi family in the crises of 1433 and 1434, it is notable that Rinaldo and his sons were the only exiles; his brother Luca was a leading Medici partisan and several other lines of the family prospered politically under the Medicean ascendancy.[168] Their qualification in such numbers in the anti-Medicean scrutiny of 1433 suggests perhaps that Rinaldo hoped and expected his *consorti* would function as a family block in his support.[169] However, it may well be that he and his immediate family were the only ones to throw in their lot with the opposition to the Medici, although the Albizzi name was still heavily associated with Rinaldo's father Maso and the oligarchical regime of generally conservative and aristocratic temper over which he had presided as perhaps the foremost citizen of Florence in the early decades of the century. Certainly Maso's personal reputation and the connections forged in consequence furnished some traditions on which Rinaldo could build in cementing an accord with fellow conservatives.

The Panciatichi, mentioned by Pitti among his supporters, were a family closely associated by marriage with the Peruzzi, Gianfigliazzi, Strozzi, and Bucelli, but also particularly with Rinaldo degli Albizzi and his friends. Rinaldo's son Maso married in 1420 one of the daughters of Messer Bandino Panciatichi of the Pistoian branch of the family; her sister had married another leading exile, Bindaccio di Granello Ricasoli. Rinaldo corresponded frequently with the Panciatichi, and especially with Matteo. Piero di Giovanni di Messer Bartolomeo, an exile of the Florentine Panciatichi, had a sister married to Antonio di Conte del Palagio, a member of a San Giovanni family with which Rinaldo and his

[167] Below, esp. Ch. 4.

[168] For their appearance in the Priorate throughout the fifteenth century, see MSS. 248, f. 49.

[169] With 22 majorities, they were among the half-dozen most successful families in the scrutiny of 1433 (see MSS. 555).

sons were also associated; Rinaldo's sister Selvaggia was the wife of Uberto di Giovanni d'Andrea del Palagio, and Antonio del Palagio was a close friend of Ormanno's.[170] Ormanno's own wife was Leonarda di Lionardo Frescobaldi, whose brother was *privato* in 1433. Another of Rinaldo's sisters had married Messer Biagio di Piero Guasconi; most of their children and grandchildren were either exiled or *privati*.

Judging by their association with his father, many of Rinaldo's supporters among the exile group would appear to have been almost literally inherited. Messer Matteo di Michele Castellani had been a leading figure in Maso degli Albizzi's day, and according to Cavalcanti strongly supported his son Rinaldo.[171] Stoldo Altoviti had also been 'a faithful partisan of Maso degli Albizzi',[172] and the exiled Sandro di Vieri Altoviti had married in 1404 Eletta di Alessio di Iacopo degli Albizzi.[173] Maso degli Albizzi's surviving correspondence includes letters from the Peruzzi and Gianfigliazzi families,[174] who furnished Rinaldo with his leading henchmen between September 1433 and September 1434.[175]

Second only to the Albizzi in their representation in the scrutiny of 1433 were the Strozzi, another very large family with distinctive and independent traditions. They had two representatives in the inner circle of the *reggimento*, Messer Palla di Nofri, who was exiled in 1434, and Messer Palla di Palla, who was not. The former was perhaps the most eminent member of the family; one of the republic's leading statesmen,[176] one of the more humane and learned members of Florence's highly civilized and cultured patriciate of the early Renaissance, and in 1427 the richest man in the city. The wealth and size of the lineage in general, and the personal and scholarly reputations of individuals

---

[170] Litta, *Famiglie Celebri* xi, Tav. XIV; Guasti, *Commissioni* iii. 345.

[171] *Istorie*, pp. 54–5.   [172] Rado, *Maso degli Albizzi*, p. 2.

[173] Passerini, *Genealogia Altoviti*, Tav. V.

[174] B.N.F., Magl. II: III: 434.

[175] Above, pp. 153–6, 162–3. The three exiled Corsi brothers may well have been committed to the Medici opposition by the marriage of Corso di Lapo to Bartolomea di Piero di Filippo Albizzi, although the Corsi were also resident in the heart of exile territory in Bue and were associated in business with other exile families.

[176] He appeared 77 times in the *Consulte* held between 1429 and 1434; his contributions to the discussions of 1 Dec. 1429 (C.P. 48, f. 114r), 16 Apr. 1430 (C.P. 49, f. 33r), and 15 Apr. 1431 (C.P. 49, f. 141v), are fairly typical of the mildness and good sense which he customarily displayed. Cf. below, pp. 204–5, 326, 333–4.

like Palla di Nofri and Matteo di Simone, earned them a wide range of influential acquaintance, not only in Florence, but throughout Italy.[177]

The pattern of Strozzi personal associations and patronage ties within the city is complex and ambiguous, though on balance their obligations to the exile group, to whom they were particularly closely bound by marriage, would seem to have weighed most heavily. However, although their *parenti* were almost invariably distinguished, they were not invariably opponents of the Medici. The Strozzi cultivated their own circle of friends, and constituted the focus of a patronage group containing both pro- and anti-Medicean partisans, and some citizens who apparently were neither. They also had a strong and extensive local following, of which only a part attached itself to the anti-Medicean faction. In 1427 they were one of the largest clans in Florence, and one of the few with a significant number of residents in more than one *gonfalone*, comprising some fifty-four households spread over Lion Rosso, Lion Bianco, and Unicorno, and well represented in the scrutinies in each.[178]

The number and nature of the marriage connections between the Strozzi exiles and other citizens banished in 1434 may almost suffice to account for their embroilment with the anti-Medicean faction. Originally, four members of the family were exiled; Palla di Nofri, his son Nofri, Smeraldo di Smeraldo, and Matteo di Simone. Palla di Nofri's own wife was a Strozzi; his was perhaps one of the few families large and distinguished enough to provide a bride of suitable status for such a man from within its own ranks. His daughter Maddalena became the wife of Felice di Michele Brancacci, a fellow exile in 1434. Palla's uncle, Francesco, had married Elena di Ridolfo Bardi, whose brother was also proscribed. One of Francesco's sons, also called Palla, married Francesca di Giovanni Adimari; another, Giovanni, was the husband of Francesca di Iacopo Guasconi, whose father was exiled. Palla di Nofri's own father married Alessandra di Scolaio Cavalcanti, and his niece Caterina was the wife of a future exile, Piero di Neri Ardinghelli. Palla's daughter Ginevra married

[177] See, e.g., Perosa (ed.), *Rucellai, il Zibaldone*, pp. 54–5, 63–4; Vespasiano da Bisticci, *Vite* iii. 5–34.

[178] Kent, 'The Florentine *reggimento*' 631. The family had its first Prior in 1302 (MSS. 248, f. 94). According to Fiumi, 'Fioritura' 1957, 414, the Strozzi at that time 'furono discepoli e fattori delle compagnie Bardi e Peruzzi'.

Francesco Castellani; his son Lorenzo, Alessandra di Bardo Bardi.[179] Smeraldo di Smeraldo Strozzi's wife Margherita belonged to the exile family of the Aldobrandini. Smeraldo's father, Smeraldo di Strozza, had married the daughter of Simone dall'Antella, and his brother wed Contessa di Messer Domenico Guasconi, both of exiled families.[180] Matteo di Simone's mother was Andreina di Vieri Rondinelli; Vieri's sons and descendants were all exiled. Matteo's aunt Lena was the wife of Giovanni Bischeri, and his uncle Lionardo married Leonarda Guasconi; both of these families had members exiled.[181] The marriages of other Strozzi not so immediately related to the exiled members linked the family directly to other leading exiles; to Soletto del Pera Baldovinetti, whose son was exiled, to Francesca di Iacopo di Messer Biagio Guasconi, whose father was exiled, and to Giovanna di Giannozzo Gianfigliazzi, whose brother was banished in 1434.[182] The number of these marriages, and the closeness of the relationships which they created, make the Strozzi of all exiled families one of the most heavily intermarried with the exile group, of whom they would appear to have counted a larger proportion among their *parenti* than did any other single family in Florence.

Of the exiles from the Strozzi neighbourhood, most were closely associated with them. Lorenzo di Ser Stefano del Forese was a member of a newer family who rented his house from Messer Palla di Nofri, and was also his near neighbour;[183] a certain Zenobius, without a surname, described simply as 'chiavaiuolus', rented both his house and his *bottega* from Messer Palla.[184] A third exiled neighbour of the Strozzi was Niccolò di Paolo Bordoni, whose family had had a reputation since the thirteenth century for violence. However, the Strozzi also had important local connections with families who were not among the exiles, such as the Federighi, the Della Luna, the Mazzinghi, the Rucellai, the Davizzi, and the Davanzati, who formed with the Strozzi quite a strong neighbourhood group whose members' relations to the two major parties coalescing in Florence are various and unclear.[185]

179 Litta, *Famiglie Celebri* v, Tav. IX; Perosa, pp. 158–9.   180 Ibid., Tav. III.
181 Ibid., Tav. XVII, XVIII.   182 Ibid., Tav. VI, IX, XVI.
183 Cat. 76, ff. 166r–168r.   184 Cat. 77, ff. 155v–156v.
185 Cat. 76, ff. 139v–140r, 169v–202v; 494, ff. 422r–423r; 495, ff. 337v–391r, 382r–401r. See also Litta, *Famiglie Celebri* v, for marriages with these families, and most importantly C.S., esp. 3ᵃ ser. CXII, CXIII, for their letters.

The Strozzi relationships with some of these, and also the variety of their personal friendships, are most clearly illuminated in the rich collection of Strozzi correspondence belonging to this period, a considerable proportion of which is addressed to the three leading Strozzi exiles; the letters to Matteo di Simone are among the most interesting of the late twenties and early thirties. They reveal the existence of a web of *consorteria, parentado, amicizia,* and *vicinanza* perhaps more clearly even than do the Medici letters,[186] although those to the Strozzi are generally more personal and less political, more learned and less conspiratorial, and by contrast with the Medici correspondence, they illustrate a comparatively limited coincidence between patronage and partisanship.

The Strozzi were *amici* and *parenti* of the Manelli, the leading magnate family of Santo Spirito who had shared a tower with the Baldovinetti in the thirteenth century, and were closely associated with some other exiled families. Ramondo Manelli fell out with Paolo di Vanni Rucellai (who appears to have been a Medicean sympathizer though other members of his family were closely bound to the Strozzi) over official duties in connection with the galleys. He wrote to Matteo Strozzi to entreat that 'it may please you for God's sake to see by your efforts and those of your friends that I am not wronged'.[187] He also recommended his case to the Strozzi neighbourhood circle, 'to Lionardo, to Francesco della Luna, and all your good relatives and friends'.[188] Another future exile, Andrea di Vieri Rondinelli, wrote to Matteo in support of Manelli,[189] and at his suggestion the latter's problem was referred to Niccolò Valori, a Medici partisan who appears to have defended Manelli's interests in this matter out of friendship for Matteo.[190] Some time after 1434 Ramondo Manelli's daughter married Gino di Neri di Gino Capponi, but the two families had long been associated in various ways.[191] As we have seen, Neri di Gino after 1433 was perhaps the most powerful, and therefore the most

---

[186] See, e.g., C.S. 3ᵃ ser. CXII, c. 126, Neri Viviani to Matteo: 'Ben ti priego che operi insieme cho' gli amici nostri . . .'; ibid. CXXXII, c. 33, Palla di Nofri to Simone di Filippo degli Strozzi: 'certissimo non bisognia distendersi in raccomandarti alcuno amico di costì, intimo d'alcuno nostro stretto parente'; ibid. c. 21, Palla to Simone, recommending one 'il quale è stato sempre amico di tutti noi, è stato a me, e a mmi raccomandato un suo parente'.

[187] C.S. 3ᵃ ser. CXIV, c. 10; see also ibid. CXII, c. 184.

[188] Ibid. CXIV, c. 21. [189] Ibid., c. 11. [190] Ibid., c. 24.

[191] Goldthwaite, *Private Wealth*, pp. 202–3; Kent, *Household and Lineage*, pp. 95 6, 195.

valuable, of the Medici supporters, but he does not seem to have
been a Medici partisan in the early thirties, and indeed in this
period appears to have commanded his own personal following
independent of the pro- and anti-Medicean factions. However,
his close friend Matteo di Simone Strozzi was the recipient of
almost all of Neri di Gino's surviving letters before 1434; it is
clear from these that Neri di Gino included himself in some sense
among the Strozzi *amici*. On one occasion he wrote to Matteo
asking him 'for friendship's sake to put up with a little hard work
with your friends to whom I recommend and offer myself . . .'[192]
Andreuolo Sacchetti, whom Rinaldo degli Albizzi described as
Neri di Gino's faithful henchman,[193] was also attached to the
Strozzi circle through his friendships with Matteo and with
Ramondo Manelli, and by the bonds of *parentado*; Messer Palla di
Nofri's daughter was the wife of Tommaso di Tommaso Sac-
chetti.[194]

Also among Matteo's frankest correspondents in this period
were future exiles and their *consorti*, like Antonio di Giovanni
Barbadori and Biagio Guasconi; the latter's reference on one
occasion to Matteo's failure to 'come into line with the rest of our
friends',[195] may well have been a rebuke concerning the ambiguity
of Strozzi allegiances, which is perfectly embodied in Matteo's
friendship with the Guicciardini brothers, Piero and Giovanni di
Luigi. That the Strozzi did not always choose their friends in
consideration of their support or opposition to the Medici is
evident from the fact that by 1432 Giovanni was embroiled with
the anti-Medicean group while Piero was an open partisan of
theirs. In this period both wrote letters to Matteo which reflected
an intimate personal friendship and considerable agreement concerning the conduct of Florentine governmental affairs.[196]

Furthermore, the Davanzati family, who were firmly committed
in the twenties to Medici support,[197] were also neighbours and
associates of the Strozzi, and while Giuliano Davanzati wrote to

[192] Bencini, 'Neri Capponi', *Rivista delle biblioteche e degli archivi*, xvi (1905), 149;
for other letters of this period see 146–54, 158–60.
    [193] Guasti, *Commissioni* iii. 339. For Andreuolo's letters to Matteo Strozzi, see
C.S. 3ª ser. CXII, cc. 173, 174, 178.
    [194] Litta, *Famiglie Celebri* v, Tav. IX.
    [195] C.S. 3ª ser. CXII, c. 71; cf. Antonio Barbadori, ibid. c. 28.
    [196] See, e.g., from Piero, ibid. CXXXII, cc. 159, 160, 294, 295; from Giovanni,
ibid. CXII, cc. 24, 164.
    [197] M.A.P. II, 92.

Matteo mainly of Cicero's Philippics and the borrowing of books,[198] Mariotto Davanzati asked his help in obtaining office, and begged Matteo to intercede for him in the matter with one of the sons of Messer Rinaldo Gianfigliazzi, who was at that time a Prior.[199] Domenico Martelli, one of the family of nine brothers who had long been closely associated with the Medici cause, corresponded with Matteo from Bologna, where he was studying law, throughout the upheavals of 1433 and 1434, and some months after Cosimo's exile wrote in Latin to Matteo in the humanist manner, praising his virtue and nobility, and his contribution to the rule of the republic.[200]

These latter friendships of Matteo's may have been essentially personal or intellectual, existing above and beyond the framework of instrumental friendship which we have identified as an essential determinant of partisanship in this period; certainly they demonstrate that patronage relationships could be less exclusive than the partisanship which arose from them. Conversely, the role played by Palla Strozzi in the events of 1433 and 1434, and his response to the political authoritarianism of Rinaldo degli Albizzi,[201] suggest that he may have been exceptionally opposed to partisan politics, holding himself intentionally aloof from the divisions within the *reggimento* as far as and as long as possible. Nevertheless, and perhaps inevitably in view of their close links of *parentado* with the exile group, at some time between September 1433 and September 1434 the Strozzi position hardened in favour of opposition to the Medici, and once they had joined this group their very status and position in the city placed them amongst its leaders.

(iii) THE FACTIONS AND THE RULING CLASS

Our examination of the personal associations of those exiled in 1434 reveals a pattern similar to that discernible in the Mediceans; the same preponderance of connections with one another, and the same comparative absence of many important relationships with the opposing party. This supports the impression gained from the evidence of letters and diaries that personal bonds were a fundamental determinant of individual political behaviour, and therefore of the composition of factions. However, that evidence

[198] C.S. 3ª ser. CXII, cc. 78, 79. [199] Ibid. c. 142.
[200] Ibid., c. 139; cf. cc. 131, 141. [201] Below, pp. 326, 333–4.

also suggested that the obligations implicit in one association might well conflict with those arising from another, and even that the practical implications of any single relationship might be ambiguous. The partially systematic creation of such ties to form a Medici party helped to obviate conflicting obligations; many partisans were members of newer and smaller families not yet bound by a complex web of traditional associations within the city, and the local and centralized qualities of the group meant that *vicinanza*, *amicizia*, and *parentado* were often mutually reinforcing. By comparison the exiles, although enabled and probably in some cases impelled to act as a group because they were generally linked by a variety of personal bonds, were more likely to have been confronted with a choice of allegiance to one or another traditional association. This situation is most clearly illustrated by the examples of the Albizzi and Strozzi families, despite the fact that they were to some extent atypical by virtue of their size, which gave greater scope for complexity in their associative patterns, and the fact that no doubt the ambiguities appear more obvious in these cases where most evidence exists to explore them in detail. The connections between members of these two families and other exiled citizens are quite sufficient to explain their co-operation with the opponents of the Medici in terms of natural obligation to *parenti*, *vicini*, and *amici*, but do not appear to have been so exclusive as necessarily to determine an anti-Medicean response to a division of the *reggimento*. It seems likely that the essential factor in their decision to align themselves with the opposition to the Medici was probably the impossibility that the leaders of two such large and powerful houses could tolerate or be tolerated by a group as aggressive and ambitious as the Mediceans in the competition for *stato*.

However, as the leaders of the *reggimento* observed in 1429, 'it is said that almost all our citizens are embroiled in this division'. Since the exiles, and those identifiable as Mediceans, amount at most to no more than a few hundred men from a ruling group of some 2,000,[1] almost all of whom were similarly entwined in such webs of patronage and association, the crystallization of the parties preparing for confrontation would have presented most

---

[1] Conversely, although only about one-sixth of the individuals with majorities in the scrutiny of 1433 were partisans, these involved altogether about one-third of the *reggimento*'s 325 families.

prominent citizens with some sort of choice; between one party or the other, between partisanship or neutrality, between ideological considerations or the pull of practical personal imperatives. As yet, the hard information concerning the precise position of the remainder of the *reggimento* in relation to the two parties of pro- and anti-Mediceans is comparatively limited, but there are some indications concerning the range and terms of this choice and the considerations which might have affected it.

It is certainly important to observe that around the fringes of the parties which we have defined by fairly rigid criteria there are a number of individuals concerning whom there is evidence to suggest association with one or other party, but not quite sufficient to identify them clearly as partisans. In the case of the anti-Mediceans, we have noted in our examination of the circles of patronage of which they were part a number of citizens firmly enmeshed in a web of friendship with the exile group but not themselves proscribed. The subsequent treatment of some of these at the hands of the Medicean regime suggests that there was sufficient public evidence of their association with the opponents of the Medici to render them suspect. For example, we observed numerous connections between the exiles and certain magnate clans; notably, although only a relatively small number of magnates were exiled, a rather larger number were excepted from the provision of 1434 restoring most of the traditional magnate class to the ranks of the *popolani*.[2] Palla Strozzi's son-in-law, Giovanni Rucellai, whose *consorti* were said to have declared themselves in support of the pro-Medicean Priors in 1434, nevertheless remained 'not accepted, but suspected by the regime' for almost thirty years, until the betrothal of his son Bernardo to Cosimo's granddaughter, Nannina de' Medici, signified his readmission into the ruling group.[3] Moreover in 1444, when the sentences of a large number of the anti-Mediceans punished ten years before

[2] Delib. Sig. e Coll. (speziale), 25, ff. 210v–214r; cf. also those whose public reputation gave rise to the erroneous belief that they had in fact been punished, above, p. 138.

[3] Perosa (ed.), *Rucellai, il Zibaldone*, pp. 121–2; Rubinstein, *Government of Florence*, p. 45. The respect of the Medicean regime for the size and strength and distinction of the Strozzi patronage group is indicated, not only in the successive prolongations of the exile of Palla di Nofri (see Vespasiano da Bisticci's biography, *Vite*), but also in actions like the removal from the ballot bags by the *Accoppiatori* in 1455 on political grounds of Marco Parenti, brother-in-law of Filippo, one of Matteo di Simone Strozzi's line then in exile (Rubinstein, *Government of Florence*, p. 45).

were due to expire, and a new *Balìa* was created which not only extended some of the sentences of 1434, but also deprived some additional citizens, not previously punished, of political rights, the latter group included members of several families whom we saw to have been closely connected before 1434 with those exiled in that year; among them were most of the Serragli family, Iacopo di Piero Baroncelli and his sons and brothers, Bartolomeo di Ser Benedetto Fortini, and the sons of Ser Paolo di Ser Lando Fortini and their sons.[4]

Similarly, there were several categories of citizens who were probably Medici supporters, but for whom unambiguous evidence of partisanship has not yet been found. These might include some in whose favour the *Balìa* of 1434 passed acts of personal legislation,[5] or who were subsequently notably favoured by the Medicean regime,[6] some of those who stood surety for members of the Medici family at the time of their exile in 1433,[7] and some either among those named by Tinucci in his denunciation of Medicean conspirators against the state,[8] or among those whom the anti-Mediceans allegedly planned to assassinate or exile in 1434 in order to ensure the security of their own regime.[9] Among the more likely candidates is Andrea Nardi, who was favoured by the *Balìa* of 1434, among those hand-picked by the Mediceans for the politically sensitive office of the first *Signoria* installed after the Medici recall, also an *Accoppiatore* in the forties, and whose kinsman Francesco Nardi was named by Tinucci as a Medici partisan. Another probable partisan is Alessandro di Ugo Alessandri, who appeared among the Medici *mallevadori*, and

---

[4] Rubinstein, *Government of Florence*, p. 18.

[5] Balìe, 25, *passim*; most of those favoured were Medici partisans or their kinsmen, and altogether about a fifth of those identified as *amici* would appear to have been rewarded in this way.

[6] See Rubinstein, *Government of Florence*, e.g. pp. 8–10, 66.

[7] Otto di Guardia, 224; among the Medici *mallevadori* of particular interest were Agostino di Gino di Neri Capponi, brother of Neri, and kinsman of the Medici partisan Giovanni di Mico, and those friends of the Medici also associated with the bank, like Giuntino Giuntini and Andrea and Lippaccio de' Bardi.

[8] *Examina, passim*; in addition to those whose status as partisans can be confirmed, many others named by Tinucci were *consorti* of those we have identified, like Tommaso Ginori, Giovanni Martini, Lodovico da Verazzano, and Orlandino Orlandini.

[9] Below, pp. 319–21; most of these have been identified as partisans, but among those who have not were Giuliano Davanzati, Berto da Filicaia, Lorenzo Lenzi, and Niccolò Popoleschi.

who together with Niccolò Alessandri was included in those whom the Medici opponents intended to eliminate.

On account of the notorious and sometimes demonstrable unreliability of such testimony, those identified as Mediceans simply by common repute have not been included in our list without some more definite evidence of their partisanship; however, undoubtedly the shrewd guesses of contemporary observers were right as often as they were wrong, and suggestive evidence often exists to support their identifications, even where partisanship cannot be firmly established. Cavalcanti's assertion that 'because he was a great benefactor to those who became his friends, many of the Buondelmonti, and particularly the sons of Messer Andrea, became enthusiastic supporters of Cosimo and his interests', is more convincing in the light of the information in the 1427 *catasto* report of M. Simone di Andrea Buondelmonti and his brothers that they owed Cosimo de' Medici almost 3,500 florins.[10]

A further category of likely Mediceans includes those closely bound to them by particular ties, whose kinsmen were generally associated with the family in some way, or whom we know to have corresponded with them on fairly intimate terms, but who made no statements in their letters which implied specific attachment or obligation. One such example is that of Cambino di Francesco Cambini, a resident of Lion d'oro who was married in 1409 to Bartolomea di Antonio di Giovenco de' Medici, whose family continued to appear among the Medici correspondents throughout the fifteenth century, and enjoyed considerable success in the scrutinies after 1434.[11] As our detailed knowledge of the personnel of the Florentine ruling group and of the sources which illuminate their careers and activities increases, no doubt it will be possible to identify more citizens as Medici partisans. For the moment, however, it is important to stress that such people may have constituted a considerable proportion of what might otherwise be considered as the uncommitted section of the *reggimento*.

Although an analysis of the personal associations of those who were demonstrably partisans confirms and illustrates the importance of bonds thus created in determining partisanship, it is impossible to reverse the procedure adopted and infer partisanship

[10] *Istorie*, p. 263; Cat. 74, f. 88v.
[11] M.A.P. II, 244, to Averardo, 25 Feb. 1430 (1429 *s.f.*); cf. *Inventario*, i, index; Rubinstein, *Government of Florence*, p. 66.

from the existence of such bonds because, as we have seen, these were too complex, and therefore too unpredictable, in their ultimate practical effects. However, we can assume the importance of certain factors which may illuminate the likely position of the rest of the *reggimento*.

The relationship which Florentines saw as the most natural determinant of political action was that of blood, and indeed most other bonds of friendship and patronage were in one sense an extension of that primal tie. This assumption is generally apparent in the laws controlling admission to political office and governing its exercise, and specifically articulated with respect to partisanship in the Medicean treatment of their defeated opponents. A study of the legislation relating to office-holding, the composition of the scrutiny lists, and the implementation of the *divieto*,[12] reveals that the *consorteria* in the fifteenth century was still considered as constituting the most fundamental interest group operating in political life, and the unit which posed the greatest single threat to the maintenance of the public welfare against private concerns. A close examination of the membership of the inner *reggimento* suggests that the individual derived his political eminence essentially from the traditions of his family, and only secondarily or more rarely from his own personal qualities.[13] These were certainly the assumptions underlying the specific legislation arising from the crises of 1433 and 1434. In the case of the victors, members of the *Balìa* of 1434 were accorded the privilege of being allowed to bear arms in the future, 'and they may give the same privilege to one male relative, joined to them through the male line'; in the case

---

[12] The *divieto* disqualified some categories of citizens whose names were drawn for offices from actually assuming them; along with insufficient age, tax debts, or having held the office very recently, a major cause of disqualification was kinship with current or immediate past incumbents of the post. See Rubinstein, *Government of Florence*, esp. p. 4.

[13] Cf. Brucker's formulation, *The Civic World*, pp. 271–2. See also above, pp. 107–9, 197–9. Kent, 'The Florentine *reggimento*' 587–93; 606–7; among the 1,757 citizens from 325 families successful in the scrutiny of 1433, there are very few individuals who were the sole representatives of their house. Conversely, a high proportion of all single individuals eligible for the *Tre Maggiori* qualify for inclusion in the inner *reggimento*, which might suggest that outstanding personal ability was more important at the uppermost levels of government. In descriptions above of the exiles and Mediceans, the former are treated more as families because they emerge in this way from the evidence; the Medici friends, however, are identified almost invariably as single individuals, and are not assumed to be acting collectively as families unless there is evidence to suggest that they did. For the promotion of consorterial interests through *raccomandazioni*, see above, Ch. 1 (vi).

of the defeated, the judicial authorities in 1436 exacted with great thoroughness from all *consorti* of rebels a formal oath in the presence of the *Signoria* and colleges, renouncing their 'rebellious *consorti*' and cutting each of them off from 'any privilege, immunity, or honour enjoyed by the family, house, or *consorteria* to which he belonged at the time of his rebellion'. So natural and powerful were the bonds between *consorti* assumed to be that they were explicitly required to acknowledge, on pain of incurring a similar punishment themselves, that it was not permitted

that any brother, relative or *consorto* through the masculine line of such rebel or rebels should continue to address or favour or regard him as a relative or *consorto*, but rather in every way consider himself to be separated and cut off from him and his sons and descendants, nor ought he to be in the future in any way obliged or bound to them in any quarrel or on any other occasion of injury, any more than he would be to strangers.[14]

It is interesting that a general comparison of the associative patterns of the Mediceans and the exiles with those of the remainder of their *consorti* reveals in almost all cases far more similarities than differences in their personal environment, and more explicitly, most of them appear to have relied for assistance in setting up businesses, arranging marriages, borrowing money, and renting houses, much more often on their own kinsmen than on other contacts.[15] Their physical environment would also have fostered intimacy; in almost all cases members of the same family lived in the same *gonfalone*, usually in the same parish, and very often in the same street. This was true not only of smaller families, by definition more compact, but even more notably of extensive clans; the numerous households of the Bardi and Albizzi, for instance, lived almost without exception clustered together in

[14] Capitano di Parte, 58, insert foliated 1–19, see esp. ff. 1r–2r. Dozens of Albizzi, Peruzzi, Rossi, and Della Casa were required to take this oath along with numerous members of the Brancacci, Dello Scelto, Gianfigliazzi, Dall'Antella, and Barbadori families. Also significant is the blanket treatment of anti-Medicean *consorterie* in the scrutiny registers after 1434; see Rubinstein, *Government of Florence*, p. 9. The Peruzzi and Guasconi, with 20 and 24 members respectively in the scrutiny of 1433, were both unrepresented in that of 1440; the Rondinelli, with 32 majorities in 1433, had only one in 1440.

[15] This impression arises from an extensive study of the *catasto* returns of all households of most of those families associated with either faction, though it is particularly strong in some cases; e.g., for the Bardi (Cat. 64), the Serragli (67), and the Strozzi (75, 76, 77).

great residential enclaves referred to familiarly and perhaps symbolically in *catasto* reports as 'luogho detto chas' gl'Albizzi' or 'posta nel popolo di San Romeo da Peruzzi'.[16] Their general circumstances, the strength and number of the everyday connections between them, would certainly have made consensus and co-operation in political situations more natural and convenient than conflict and division.

The specific evidence suggesting family-wide participation in the factional conflicts of our period is fragmentary but considerable. In a great many cases we find links between the Medici and the kinsmen of their partisans, though the connections are not always sufficiently strong or specific to establish partisanship.[17] Of course some of the pro-Medicean families were so small that almost by definition the whole family was involved in support for the Medici. There was only one Tornabuoni household; the Martelli, though numerous (there were in 1433 eight adult brothers), nevertheless lived under a single roof; the Pucci's three partisans were the heads of three of the family's four households.[18] Moreover, there were some partisans, not only from families of modest size like the Davanzati, but even from extensive clans like that of the Alberti, who in writing to declare their support for the Medici spoke not only for themselves personally, but for 'all the family' or 'the other members of our house' as well.[19] Of course, as the subtle and somewhat enigmatic exposition of the conception of family embodied in the *Della Famiglia* of their noted kinsman, Leon Battista, perfectly illustrates, it is always difficult to say exactly whom the speaker meant to include in this sort of expression; the word 'family' could mean anything from his household, through his own immediate line of descent, to the entire lineage of which he was a part.[20]

[16] Cat. 80, f. 206r; 72, f. 35v. Cf. also ibid. 64, ff. 65r, 419v. All but one or two of the 30 Bardi households who resided in the city named other Bardi as their neighbours (ibid. 60), and 16 Albizzi households, for example, lived either in Borgo degli Albizzi or in the smaller streets intersecting it. Half a dozen appear to have shared the same house, though it is not clear how many of them lived in it (ibid. 80).

[17] By the same criteria which indicated likely additional individual partisans, there is evidence to suggest that families like the Ricci, Corbinelli, Dall'Antella, Da Verazzano, Del Benino, Della Stufa, and Orlandini had generally pro-Medicean orientations.

[18] In a similar category were the Corbinelli, Del Benino, and Dall'Antella.

[19] For example, Luigi di Manetto Davanzati (M.A.P. II, 92); Alberto degli Alberti (ibid. 108).

[20] Kent, *Household and Lineage*, Introduction.

Similarly, observers' descriptions of the composition of the anti-Medicean faction sometimes imply that entire lineages were united in their support; at other times, that only a part of these, or even isolated individuals, were involved. There is considerable uncertainty and divergence between the accounts of various observers of the actual confrontation of September 1434. For example, many singled out Rinaldo degli Albizzi and Ridolfo Peruzzi as the leaders of the opposition, but while some described their followers as 'Bardi, Albizzi, and Peruzzi', others specified only 'a part of' the families of each, or referred to *some* members of some houses, while implying *all* of others.[21] The very fact that some individuals or lines of most of those families with members exiled remained unpunished in Florence shows that *consorti* were by no means inevitably assumed to act in unison. The pattern of the exile provisions admits of several possibilities, keeping in mind the claim of the new regime that as the numbers of those in error were so great, only the leaders had been singled out for punishment, to serve as an example for the rest. Sometimes, though more often when the families concerned were small, only one member was proscribed. However, the majority of those condemned were in family blocks, and though some of these might represent only one or two households, others included most of the leading figures of the family. Further legislation, depriving many of those not actually exiled of the right to hold office henceforth, often drew the best part of the remaining portion of the house into the orbit of the disgraced.[22] Conversely, certain untouched branches of families predominantly excluded flourished in political life after 1434, and only a handful of *consorterie* were effectively wiped off the political map for the entire period of Medicean ascendancy.[23]

The practical implications of shared concerns between members of the extended family for specifically political relationships have yet to be fully explored, and it is essential meanwhile, with reference to any given situation, to beware of uncritical assumptions; either that entire lineages which might comprise up to fifty

[21] Above, pp. 137–8.
[22] Above, pp. 136–7. Notably Uguccione di Mico Capponi waited ultimately to conclude a marriage with the single branch of the Peruzzi without an anti-Medicean reputation until the day after the announcement of the final details of the proscriptions; see below, p. 331.
[23] Below, pp. 344–5.

or sixty households acted as a single soul in the complex and shifting partisan struggles of this period, or that each man made a wholly individual choice without regard to the attitudes and behaviour of his kinsmen, and that his choice affected only himself and his wife and children. The evidence strongly suggests that all else being equal, families, as existent and natural interest groups, would co-operate in the event of a political crisis. However, as we have already observed, though the blood tie was a potent bond, in practice its force might be divisive as well as cohesive, not only through the operation of powerful personal passions, generated in the atmosphere of a strong pressure to conformity, but also on account of the rationally self-interested competition for personal office and honours which resulted from laws designed to limit the family's collective share of power in the *stato*.[24]

The assumption that individuals who opposed their *consorti* were remarkable, but by no means inexplicable, divergences from the norm is nowhere more clearly implied than in observations on these events later like Nerli's that 'there were some who had enemies even in their own families',[25] or Cavalcanti's comment that it was no wonder Rinaldo degli Albizzi was deserted in 1434 by supporters not even related to him, when his own brother—'he who had been nourished in the same womb'—rejected him.[26] The fact that in 1434, as at a number of other moments in the history of the republic, some families furnished partisans of both sides, is often invoked to support arguments that by the fifteenth century families had little sense of solidarity.[27] In the light of the evidence we have been considering, this conclusion would appear to represent the over-simplification of a single facet of a subtle and complex reality. However, the question of split families is a particularly interesting one because it throws light not only on the relation of specifically individual qualities and experience to political behaviour, but directs our attention also to a further range of considerations which may have helped to influence it.

[24] Cf. Kent, *Household and Lineage*, Ch. 4.

[25] Filippo de' Nerli, *Commentarii dei fatti civili occorsi dentro la città di Firenze dall'anno 1215 al 1537* (Trieste, 1889), i. 68–9.

[26] *Istorie*, p. 310.

[27] For example most recently by Goldthwaite, *Private Wealth*, pp. 259–60; cf. Dino Compagni's account of the divisions of Guelfs into Blacks and Whites, above, pp. 18–19.

In fact, of the ninety-three families involved in the conflict through partisans of either group, only ten had members of both. Moreover, what evidence we have suggests that few of these families were utterly fragmented by conflicting partisan loyalties; in most cases, the majority of their members supported one or other side, while one or two possibly alienated individuals, households, or lines, joined the opposing camp.[28] Nor do *consorterie* appear to have been permanently or irreparably rent asunder by these differences; for example, though Piero Guicciardini was a relative and friend of the Medici and his brother Giovanni opposed them, the latter protected Piero from the anti-Mediceans at the time of Cosimo's exile, and when Giovanni in turn became liable to the serious threat of proscription after the Medici recall, Piero personally intervened to save him.[29] Apparently after 1434 Giovanni still reposed sufficient trust in his brother to appoint Piero in the vital role of an executor to his will.[30] Similarly, the fact that many citizens stood surety for *consorti* of different partisan persuasions, a responsibility which implied a major

[28] For example, of the Bardi's 60 or so households, one entire branch, that of the Conti di Vernio, were Medici *parenti* and supporters; the rest were usually described as anti-Mediceans. To judge from the extent of their punishment, of the 6 Barbadori households, who must have constituted most of the lineage, two lines were opposed to the Medici, and only one man was clearly a partisan of theirs. Of the Gianfigliazzi's 14 households, only one entire household was exiled, but the family was in general reputed to be anti-Medicean; Giannozzo di Stoldo, Averardo's son-in-law, is the only known Medici partisan. For a couple of families, including the Cavalcanti, there is insufficient evidence to indicate the main direction of their sympathies; on their diverse behaviour in general see Cavalcanti, *Istorie*, pp. 266, 309, 323-4. The Corsi have not been included among the split families because it is not at all certain that the two partisans of opposing factions of this name actually belonged to the same family: see Kent, 'The Florentine *reggimento*', Table II. The Guicciardini family, of half a dozen households, with apparently only one partisan of each faction, would seem to be a rather unusual case. Although almost all of those individuals or branches who diverged from the general partisan line of their *consorti* had strong associative connections with the opposite party, as with the category of 'probable partisans', the evidence is insufficient to constitute an *explanation* of their divergence. The cohesion of families varies according to the traditions and character of each; on this, and on the question of individuals and lines alienated from their lineages, see Kent, *Household and Lineage*, Chs. 3-5.

[29] Guicciardini, *Memorie di Famiglia*, pp. 11, 15.

[30] M. Moriani Antonelli, *Giovanni Guicciardini ed un processo politico in Firenze (1431)*, Collana di pubblicazioni Cuicciardiniane, xxvi (Florence, 1954), p. 75; cf. Francesco Guicciardini, *Le cose fiorentine*, ed. R. Ridolfi (Florence, 1945), p. 258; Guicciardini does, however, remark on the fact: '[credo] lasciassi Piero tutore, di chi sempre era stato inimico'. Cf. also the complex and ambiguous relationship of both with the Strozzi and the Medici families, above, pp. 90-91; below, pp. 273-4, 332-5.

financial, legal, and personal commitment, suggests that kinsmen of opposing factions continued nevertheless to identify to a considerable extent with a common consorterial interest.[31]

However, just as Dino Compagni, describing the divisions between Blacks and Whites in 1300, remarked how in addition to the formation of consorterial blocks there were those who acted to spite their families, 'on account of disagreements they had with *consorti*', or 'because these had diminished their chances of obtaining honours',[32] so positive hostility, the obverse side of strong family feeling and identification, appears to have been a powerful force determining the divisions of the 1430s, and as Machiavelli observed through the medium of a speech attributed to Niccolò da Uzzano: 'There are many families, even many houses, divided; many are opposed to us through envy of brothers or relatives'.[33] Although most of those who in their partisan affiliations conflicted with their *consorti* were either reinforced in this opposition by bonds of friendship or *parentado* with members of the contrary faction, or else contracted such bonds in order to integrate themselves more securely with that group, the evidence is insufficient to enable us to separate cause and effect; however, the limited material relating to the only relatively well-documented cases suggests that personal differences may indeed have been a major positive factor in such divisions.

In his *Memorie di Famiglia* the historian Francesco Guicciardini, grandson of Piero di Messer Luigi, has left us a portrait of the brothers, neither of whom appears to have been a particularly exemplary or attractive character. While Francesco obviously had a sneaking fondness for his own direct ancestor, Piero, and repeatedly referred to his grandfather's munificent and generous nature, he nevertheless recorded also that he was a 'wayward and disobedient' youth, in the habit, for instance, of stealing objects of value from his father's house.[34] By contrast with Cosimo de' Medici's assessment of Giovanni as 'a little soft, but a good man',[35] the family tradition transmitted by Francesco characterized him rather as 'bold and disrespectful, and so free to speak evil of almost everybody, that consequently he was detested by many'.

---

[31] See, e.g., the Dall'Antella, Gianfigliazzi, and Salviati; see also Brucker, *The Civic World*, Ch. I.

[32] Above, pp. 18–19.   [33] Machiavelli, *Istorie Fiorentine*, IV. vi.

[34] See *Memorie*, p. 8, and in general, pp. 7–13.   [35] Below, p. 274.

The mutual antipathy likely to exist between such abrasive characters was apparently fanned by envy; according to Francesco, there was much rivalry between the two brothers, 'each wanting to be more prominent in the affairs of the commune, and Piero being the elder, he wished to enjoy greater status'.[36] Conversely, Piero was a comparatively poor businessman,[37] a judgement borne out perhaps by the assessment for the *catasto* in 1427, when Giovanni was thirteenth on the list of the wealthiest citizens of Santo Spirito with assets of 18,595 florins, and Piero seventy-third with only 3,748 florins.[38] Here alone was a substantial motive for attaching himself by marriage to the affluent Medici; the fact that Giovanni, on the other hand, had an Albizzi wife and chose to marry his daughters into the anti-Medicean houses of the Bischeri, Peruzzi, and Guadagni, may either have been a reason for their adoption of opposing partisan stances, or else a response to a prior estrangement.[39] Although there is even less concrete evidence regarding the relations between the Albizzi brothers, what does remain suggests a similarly personal rivalry and a consequent orientation towards opposing partisan interests; while each benefited in the bequest of their father's concrete assets, Rinaldo was the heir to Maso degli Albizzi's political patrimony, and his younger brother claimed that their father had so neglected his own education that at the age of 19 he could barely read and write.[40] Whether Luca's division of their property, his marriage into the Medici family in 1426, the virtual exclusiveness of his subsequent association with them and their friends and relatives, were prompted by rivalry with Rinaldo, a desire to reject the traditions which he represented, or even a simple personality clash, is not clear.[41]

Just as clashes of personality might divide members of the same family, so it is possible that considerations of personal and political style may have had some influence in determining the partisan sympathies of members of the ruling group in general. Cavalcanti's account in particular suggests that the very distinctive

---

[36] Guicciardini, *Memorie di Famiglia*, p. 14.   [37] Ibid., pp. 9, 13.
[38] Martines, *The Social World*, pp. 376–7.
[39] Litta, *Famiglie Celebri* iii, Tav. II.
[40] Mallett, *The Florentine Galleys*, p. 195.
[41] Rinaldo and Luca were obviously of very different temperaments; see Mallett, pp. 195–200, esp. p. 198; the latter was most notably a conscientious official; cf. below, pp. 261–9, 319–22, concerning Rinaldo.

personalities of the leaders of the *reggimento* affected their political reputations and their ability to attract a following. Averardo de' Medici's exile was welcomed because he was generally disliked;[42] Rinaldo degli Albizzi could not be trusted to look after his supporters' interests because his inordinate pride made him 'wipe the floor with every man'.[43] Conversely, the spirit which induced Rinaldo Gianfigliazzi to wildness and dissipation in youth made him one of the most formidable statesmen in Florence in his old age,[44] and Niccolò da Uzzano's legendary patience and self-control inspired respect and trust even in his adversaries.[45]

Certainly opinions and attitudes recorded in private letters and diaries, and the transcripts of discussions of political issues in the *Consulte e Pratiche*, express a quality of individual political style closely related to personality, and suggest that similarities and differences of this order may often have determined agreement and dissent between speakers as much as personal associations, or the patronage groups and parties in which they were expressed. For example, on the question of the war with Lucca, a preference for decisive action united the representatives of such disparate partisan interests as Rinaldo degli Albizzi, Averardo de' Medici, and Neri di Gino Capponi, and it was probably a common natural tendency to caution which led to their opposition by Agnolo Pandolfini, a Medicean sympathizer, Niccolò da Uzzano, traditional leader of the anti-Medicean establishment, and the powerful but enigmatic Palla Strozzi.[46] While Cavalcanti declared that the Mediceans favoured the war and the Uzzaneschi opposed it,[47] Giovanni di Iacopo Morelli perceived the conflict as one between the wise and the foolish,[48] and according to Buoninsegni it was a question of the young versus the old.[49]

Their correspondence would suggest that Averardo and Rinaldo maintained some personal friendship into the early thirties; obviously they had more in common than the fact that many of their contemporaries disliked them. The latter, however, never concealed his antipathy to Averardo's son-in-law, Alamanno Salviati, who indeed emerges even from his own letters as a rather

[42] Cavalcanti, *Istorie*, p. 282.
[43] Ibid., p. 206.	[44] Cavalcanti, *Trattato*, pp. 189–90.
[45] Ibid., pp. 188–9.	[46] Below, pp. 258–60.
[47] *Istorie*, p. 164.
[48] Giovanni di Iacopo Morelli, *Ricordi*, in *Delizie* xix, p. 73.
[49] *Storie*, p. 32.

unattractive character.[50] As the inheritor of his father's traditions, Rinaldo degli Albizzi was Niccolò da Uzzano's natural successor to leadership of the anti-Mediceans, but the old man himself is reputed to have observed that he would rather see Cosimo ruling Florence than Rinaldo, an understandable preference since the shrewd and careful Cosimo appears to have had much more in common with that patient elder statesman than did the impulsive and disdainful Rinaldo.[51]

The extent to which considerations of principles and personal judgement might compete with more practical and customary loyalties in determining partisanship can only be evaluated by reference to the rifts which they opened up between those whom we actually know on other evidence to have been united by partisan obligations. The above examples might incline us to wonder, since the leaders and hard-core adherents of both factions could well find themselves at opposite poles in their personal inclinations and ideals, how much more might not the relatively uncommitted members of the *reggimento* be influenced in their attitude to one or other faction by the ideology, or at least the approach to issues which appeared to animate it? Conversely, the same examples suggest that while considerations of principle tended naturally to cut across the interests of the major factions, they were not sufficiently important to undermine the strength of partisan obligation, and consequently that there was little coincidence between principle and partisanship. The differing social composition of the two parties did represent or determine a certain element of ideological alternative which was to be expressed and confirmed in action in the events of 1433–4; it may be, perhaps, that the more aristocratic orientation of the anti-Mediceans influenced the attraction to one or other group of some citizens whom we have not been able to identify either as friends or enemies of the Medici. However, given that both parties were primarily based in personal interest, a concern for the ideological principles implicit in Florentine political attitudes would probably have inclined citizens to absolute neutrality rather than to a choice between one or other of the factions.

[50] See, e.g., *Commissioni* iii. 397–8, cf. 410. Similarly, Antonio di Ghezzo della Casa is described by Cavalcanti as a man who disagreed for the sake of it (*Istorie*, p. 299).

[51] Cavalcanti, *Istorie*, p. 204; cf. pp. 143–5, 205–7.

In view of the very limited evidence relating to the greater part of the *reggimento* it is difficult to speak with either confidence or precision about a 'neutral' group. In the first place, it is essential to observe that although most citizens affected by ideological considerations probably took a neutral stand with regard to the two major parties of pro- and anti-Mediceans, by no means all of those who refrained from joining either would have done so on ideological grounds. The fragmentation of the ruling group in the late twenties and early thirties, and particularly as a result of the war, was extreme; as Pellegrini observed, 'almost every man constituted a party in himself'.[52] This is fairly clearly apparent from the records of the *Conservatori delle Leggi*, the officials entrusted early in 1429 with the ostensible task of ensuring that citizens actually holding official positions upheld the laws of the commune. In fact, the institution of this magistracy provided an opportunity for the leaders of the ruling group to denounce one another before some official body, and the result was a flood of accusations which exposed the lack of general confidence in any single group within the *reggimento*.[53] Although they cannot always be neatly identified with establishable partisans, attitudes of hostility to the positions of both parties are clearly recognizable in the denunciations,[54] and indeed the office seems mainly to have served as a vehicle for the attacks of members of these two groups upon one another. Most of the leading conservative families were represented in charges against Bonifazio Peruzzi, Giovanni di M. Donato Barbadori, Francesco di M. Rinaldo Gianfigliazzi, Giovanni di Simone Altoviti, Michele di Alessandro Arrigucci, and Iacopo Guasconi, and even their more obscure associates, and the relatives of these, like Niccolò d'Andrea Ciampegli and Tuccio di Manetto Scambrilla, were not exempt. Among the Mediceans and their close kinsmen denounced were Ser Martino Martini, Luigi Davanzati, Fruosino da Verazzano, Bartolomeo Orlandini, Piero di Giovanni Ginori, Banco di Niccolò Bencivenni, Niccolò Soderini, and Niccolò Cocco-Donati; the several depositions against minor figures in the party like the Cerretani and even Francesco da Cepperello suggest a specifically partisan

[52] *Sulla repubblica*, p. 74.
[53] Cf. below, pp. 244–5, 272–3. For a sample of the denunciations of this period see Giud. Appelli 75, ff. 724r onwards, *passim*; 77, Pt. I; also Misc. Rep. 117, cc. 24–38.
[54] See below, pp. 272–3.

motive behind the denunciations. Nevertheless, there were quite a few directed against citizens who do not appear to have been identified at this point with either party; no doubt some, at least, of these manifold charges were merely the expression of 'professional' rivalries and personal animus. Certainly, although many may have represented a practical party political point of view, it is none the less impossible simply to subsume all under a straightforward bipartisan division into Mediceans and their enemies.

One obvious and well-documented example of another, at least potentially partisan force within the *reggimento* is that represented by Neri Capponi and his following. As we have already seen, while in the late twenties and early thirties his relations with the Medici were amiable and implied mutual respect, but gave no evidence of the crucial support which he was to offer them after their exile, he was a close personal friend of Matteo Strozzi and must be considered part of the Strozzi circle of patronage among whose more prominent members were Medicean families from their own neighbourhood, like the Davanzati, intimates of the exile group, like the Manelli, and the Sacchetti, who seem also to have enjoyed a special relationship with Neri himself.[55] Early in 1430 Rinaldo degli Albizzi commented on the intimacy between Capponi and Andreuolo Sacchetti, and noted that while they were both members of the *Dieci*, in addition to his official bulletins addressed to the magistracy as a whole Neri wrote separately to Sacchetti concerning certain political and military affairs. He also observed that

Neri runs everything over there, partly with the support of Signore Niccolò [Fortebracci] with whom he can do what he likes, and partly on account of the enormous following he has in the Pistoian mountains, for the entire party of the Cancellieri idolizes him, and they are men worth taking account of. For if it ever should happen that in Florence (may God prevent it) there were some sort of revolution within the *reggimento*, and Neri happened to be over here, with the reputation and the following that he has it would be easy for him to create a major split wherever he wanted to.[56]

A letter from Niccolò Valori to Averardo de' Medici in 1431, concerning Neri's summons before the *Signoria* to answer charges

<hr />

[55] Below, p. 266.   [56] *Commissioni* iii. 339.

laid against him with the *Conservatori delle Leggi,* may be seen as
implying that Neri's partisan sympathies were by that time inclin-
ing towards the Medici,[57] and at the same time there is some
evidence that it was Rinaldo degli Albizzi who engineered his
subsequent exile in 1432 out of jealousy at the extent of Neri's
influence in the direction of the war.[58] However, there is apparently no record of the exile incident apart from the Provision of
May 1432 which restored him without explanation to Florence
after serving a sentence of only two months,[59] and in general his
relations at that time with the two parties then in the process of
consolidation remain ambiguous. His letter of consolation and
advice to Averardo when the Medici were banished in 1433, and
the eagerness of their opponents to have Neri out of Florence, are
positive indications of Medicean sympathies, confirmed by the
observation of his Strozzi friends in May of the following year
that Neri was the leader of the group organizing to procure
Cosimo's recall.[60] However, Cavalcanti's story, while possibly
apocryphal, that before he would accept the invitation of the pro-
Medicean Priors to return to Florence early in September 'Cosimo
imposed the condition that above all other citizens, Neri di Gino
should be happy about it',[61] might imply that the Medici did not
in fact consider him as a committed partisan, but rather as a
generally sympathetic but yet independent force within the *reggimento,* whose opinion could carry decisive weight in determining
the behaviour of other members who might also at that point
have remained still uncommitted.

For while the possible alternatives which we have been examining indicate that it is unwise to assume that all citizens who cannot
be positively shown to be members of either the pro- or anti-
Medicean parties therefore took up a neutral position in relation to
the conflicts within the ruling group, there is evidence to suggest
that however limited the possibility of identifying it precisely,
there was a neutral group within the *reggimento.* The success-

[57] M.A.P. IV, 39, 17 Aug. 1431. On the nature and functions of this office, see
below, pp. 244–5.

[58] C. Bayley, *War and Society in Renaissance Florence: The 'De Militia' of Lionardo
Bruni* (Toronto, 1961), p. 115.

[59] I. M. Bencini, 'Note e appunti tratti da documenti sulla vita politica di Neri
Capponi', *Rivista delle biblioteche e degli archivi,* xx (1909), 15–31, 33–56; see esp. 41–2.

[60] C.S. 3ª ser. CXII, c. 176, Giovanni di Marco degli Strozzi to Matteo di Simone,
24 May 1434; cf. below, p. 324.

[61] *Istorie,* p. 302.

ful avoidance of a complete breakdown in government, which might have resulted in the violent overthrow of the Florentine political system, was largely due to the presence in the *reggimento* endorsed by the *Balìa* of September 1433, and again in that of September 1434, of a basic core of citizens not identified with either of the major parties which had brought about these sudden changes in government, and their presence provided an element of stability.[62] From his fundamental study of the electoral system operated by the Medici after their success in 1434 Rubinstein observed 'a substantial continuity in the names of the families represented on the scrutiny registers of 1433 and 1440', although 'both scrutinies contained strong elements of political discrimination'.[63] The difference between the last 'oligarchical' regime of 1433–4 and that of the Mediceans which followed it consisted essentially in a change in the balance of power held by the exile group on the one hand, and the Medicean partisans on the other. These changes were of course highly significant, and markedly affected the whole complexion and tone of the regimes, but owing to the presence of this hard core of citizens whose position in the *reggimento* was unaffected by partisan manœuvring, the composition of the ruling class in Florence remained substantially the same, and the possibility of dramatic social change in the wake of these upheavals never presented itself.

It is difficult to estimate the extent to which even this neutrality was ideological; that is, based on an explicit aversion to factionalism and a desire to elevate the welfare of the commune above the immediate imperatives of private interest. Just as the avoidance of open conflict between the two majority parties proved to be the essential condition of the pragmatic neutrality of citizens like Neri Capponi, and the direct confrontation between the Medici and their opponents in 1433 and 1434 faced them with the prospect of civil revolution and thus necessitated some choice in the interests of the restoration of civic order, so those who remained neutral on principle would have been similarly obliged by these practical problems to make some positive decision. However, the identity and even the position of the latter are further obscured by the fact that just at the point in time where this choice became necessary, the sharpness of the alternatives was blunted by the logic of events which, owing to the blatant illegality of the

[62] Below, pp. 338–9.   [63] *Government of Florence*, p. 9.

anti-Medicean challenge to the incumbent *Signoria*, by contrast with the scrupulous constitutional rectitude of the Medici in exile, identified the latter's cause with the good of the commune, the upholding of the constitution, and the protection of the representatives of the public welfare against the violence of a group of citizens acting in a purely private capacity.[64] This fortuitous equation in 1434 of communal liberties and the upholding of the *status quo* with the blatantly private, partisan, and anti-conservative interests of the Medici and their friends, nicely illustrates the difficulty, in the absence of more explicit evidence, of establishing the real meaning of neutrality in the Florentine context. It seems likely that for many citizens neutrality was essentially a temporary stance, contingent on the endurance of an outward appearance of unity.

Conversely, an abstract and impersonal impulse to elevate the public welfare above private interest was, as we know, the ultimate ideal of the Florentine patriciate, a fundamental element in the tradition of political thought which its spokesmen created and perpetuated, and a major theme even of its more mundane and practical expressions.[65] Speakers in the *Consulte e Pratiche* refer constantly to the conflict between this ideal and the reality of specific situations, and this is also the basic question of principle underlying and uniting most of the varied complaints laid by citizens against one another before the *Conservatori delle Leggi*.[66] Concern for the good of the commune was a real and powerful consideration determining the actions of the most partisan of citizens. There is no reason to doubt that Cosimo de' Medici, whatever his other calculations, was, as he observed, moved to associate himself with the war against Lucca against his better judgement and the interests of his partisans, 'because the honour of the commune is involved'.[67] The notion of the public good triumphed less ambiguously, and on a higher plane of abstraction, when Palla Strozzi and other conservatives were driven to protest in May 1434 against the arbitrary government of the city in the interests of the faction with which they themselves were associated, in the name of 'reason and justice', and to demand that their

[64] Below, pp. 308–10, 312–13, 338–9.   [65] Above, pp. 20–22.

[66] Above, pp. 22–3; below, pp. 244–5; cf. Brucker's observation of the preceding half-century that commitment to the commune was a real force in its political life (*The Civic World*, passim).

[67] M.A.P. II, 178; cf. below, pp. 277–8.

fellows of the *reggimento* dedicate themselves anew to 'the glory and greatness of the *Signoria*, and the liberty of this city'.[68]

The fact that both Cosimo and Palla were, though in rather different spirits, partisan leaders, need not imply at all that their professed attitudes were insincere: merely that the situation was complex, that such abstract convictions could not always constitute the essential determinant of citizens' actions, and that public and private interest were sometimes contrasting, sometimes almost indistinguishable threads running through the experience of those involved in public life.[69] Palla, for example, though consistently revealed in his letters and in his contributions to the *Consulte* as a moderate inclined by temperament to argue in terms of reason and principle,[70] was eventually obliged if for no other reason than the power which was his by virtue of his wealth and position, to align himself with one or other of the factions or risk destruction by both; even so, having thrown in his lot with his *parenti* and *amici* among the anti-Mediceans, he made his protest in the name of principle, and of the public good. The Medici, on the other hand, obviously believed that the public good would ultimately best be served when their private interest triumphed, and there is at least an argument for suggesting that events proved them right; certainly the alternative concept of the public good implied in Giovanni Morelli's injunctions to his sons was in a sense an equally personalized one, amounting essentially to a profound conservatism or defence of the *status quo* as miraculously and necessarily embodying the precious republican traditions, and one which many citizens would have been not only too self-interested, but also too sophisticated to embrace.[71]

---

[68] C.P. 50, ff. 160r–161r; cf. below, p. 326.   [69] Below, pp. 269–82.

[70] See Brucker, *The Civic World*, passim, for Palla's role in the politica life of the commune before 1430; cf. his letter to Matteo di Simone during the peace negotiations at Ferrara in which both he and Cosimo were involved in 1433, C.S. 3ᵃ ser. CXII, c. 112, and another to Simone di Filippo of 18 Apr. 1422 (ibid. CXXXII, c. 61r), in which he expressed the hope that in judging the merits of his appeal for tax relief, his neighbours in his *gonfalone* would be impelled 'avere più riguardo alla ragione e giustitia che a mal parlare'. However, the Strozzi were by no means entirely remote from traditions of violence; in 1414 Iacopo and Biagio di Perozzo, Palla's father Nofri, and Matteo's father Simone di Filippo Strozzi, on finding Giovanni Guicciardini alone in the church of *San Gallo*, had attacked him with iron bars, at which he and Piero, in the name of the *consorteria*, had demanded that the aggressors be brought to trial by the *Signoria* (Moriani, *Giovanni Guicciardini*, pp. 19–20). Cf. also the examples of Strozzi violence in documents in Brucker, *The Society of Renaissance Florence*.

[71] Cf. the conservative element in the neutrality of Lippozzo Mangioni, clearly

Just what proportion of the *reggimento* can meaningfully be described as constituting an effectively neutral group in opposition to the two major parties is impossible to speculate. It is only the innermost circle of the *reggimento* that we can even begin to break down in these terms, and there, although only half of its members can be firmly identified as adherents of a particular faction, there is some evidence concerning the inclination of many others to the support of one or other group. Nevertheless, it is possible to name some citizens who probably belonged to the neutral group and to identify some specific statements of the position which they represented. For example, the inner *reggimento* contained a high proportion of lawyers who, as Lauro Martines has shown, owed their prestigious position in Florentine ruling circles to their possession of the special administrative and legal skills so pertinent to effective government, especially in a state where a developed bureaucracy was comparatively lacking and most key positions were in the hands of non-experts.[72] Lorenzo Ridolfi is one example of a possible exception to his observation that lawyers, as unofficial bureaucrats committed to the abstraction of efficiency in government, seem to have held aloof from party commitments,[73] but certainly the others within the inner *reggimento*—Messer Carlo di Francesco Federighi, Piero Beccanugi, and Guglielmino Tanagli, had no apparent partisan affiliations, and continued to play the same prominent role in active government after 1434 as before.[74] The contributions of the lawyers to the *Consulte* generally reflect their particular concern either for precise problems in practice or

apparent in his observations to the *Consulte* quoted by Brucker, *The Civic World*, pp. 486–7. Cf. Gino di Neri Capponi who in his *Ricordi*, XXVII, also recommended to his sons that 'ne' fatti dello stato concludo che voi tegnate con chi lo tiene, e pigliatene poco e date favore a chi regge'; the reasons he gave for doing so are, however, far more subtle—'perchè e' si conviene avere maggiore stato e popolani spicciolati. Meglio e più sicura cosa è per la città fare grande agnello che lione, perchè a tirare adrieto l'agnello ce n'è molti atti, ma de' lioni non si può. E però, degl'uomini che sono al presente, favoreggia Bartolommeo Valori, Niccolò da Uzzano, Nerone di Nigi e Lapo Niccolini.' See also the importance attributed by many citizens to achieving a balance between 'le famiglie' and 'i spicciolati' (below, p. 224 n.). Gino di Neri's conservatism was clearly not simply habitual, but rather an example of his belief in the importance of responding appropriately to the particular circumstances prevailing, apparent from his earlier observation (II), that: 'Appena sarebbe possibile co' cittadini del presente fare le cose che son già fatte; o se a fare si avvessino di nuovo, noi perderemmo la nostra libertà prima che e' si faccessino.'

[72] *Lawyers and Statecraft*, pp. 67, 210, 376, 396, and Index.
[73] See Cavalcanti, *Istorie*, pp. 11, 76.
[74] Rubinstein, *Government of Florence*, pp. 24, 236–43.

abstract questions of governmental procedure, as distinct from the articulation of a view of the desired ends of a given regime. There were others like Lippozzo Mangioni, for example, who were among the more consistent exponents in these meetings of a positively anti-factional attitude to the problems of the period, who spoke often and constructively in the name of the liberty of the commune, and of justice.[75] The counsel which Giovanni Morelli gave in the *Pratiche* suggests that he also was ready to pronounce in public what he preached in private in his *Ricordi*.[76] The latter, however, constitute the most explicit statement of his views, and perhaps one of the more typical expressions of the most common version of the neutral position.[77] Based essentially in a conservative impulse to self-protection, it might yet rise beyond this to an abstract concern with the preservation of the communal ideal which we have seen, paradoxically, to be most clearly apparent in the attitudes of those more brilliant and distinguished citizens who were themselves eventually to become partisan leaders. Morelli's basic message to his sons was opportunist; in the event of a crisis, they should play their cards close to the chest:

If within the city, or rather within your *gonfalone* or neighbourhood, one or more factions should seek support, and the affairs of your commune are concerned in it, as indeed happens every day . . . hold to a middle course, and maintain your friendship with all; speak ill of no one, either to please one man rather than another, or on account of your own anger.[78]

However, he was genuinely proud to boast that of his ancestors not one 'had ever plotted against the government of any particular regime',[79] and that his own father was 'never moved to desire or consider anything but the situation and the honour and the glory of the Commune'.[80]

Unsophisticated as it might be, the impulse expressed by Giovanni was a powerful agent in the operation of events in Florence, and not least in 1434, when a concern for legality and the maintenance of the city's republican traditions undoubtedly

---

[75] For example, below, pp. 242, 247.

[76] See, for example, below, p. 242.

[77] Morelli's social position makes him in fact not typical of the patriciate (Brucker, *The Civic World*, pp. 35–7), but he was certainly a spokesman for it.

[78] *Ricordi*, pp. 280–1.   [79] Ibid., p. 377.   [80] Ibid., p. 196.

inclined many of the citizens of Florence to the support of Cosimo, who had scrupulously respected the letter of Florentine law at every point since his banishment by Signorial decree the previous year, and against Rinaldo, who in order to preserve the actuality of the regime, which he in fact directed, was prepared to violate the authority of the *Signoria* which theoretically embodied it.

PART II

THE CONFLICT

3

The Beginnings of Conflict
(1426–1429)

IT seems that the parties of the Medici and their opponents began to consolidate in the mid-twenties; by that time, according to Cavalcanti, the Medici were manifestly the leaders of a personal party, and the opposing party was known as the Uzzani, 'since the patricians had taken as their leader a most eminent citizen named Niccolò di Giovanni da Uzzano'.[1] The major indications of their personnel and positions at this very early stage are to be found in Cavalcanti's own account of an alleged meeting of leading citizens of the *reggimento* in 1426, and an anonymous set of verses, attributed to Niccolò da Uzzano himself, which were discovered one morning in that same year attached to the door of the palace of the *Signoria*.[2] The *prima facie* uncertainty of this sort of evidence might incline us to dismiss these accounts as insubstantial, but for the fact that their description of the parties and their genesis accords very closely on many essential points with the picture which emerges from our analysis above, from current *Consulte e Pratiche*, and with evidence from the Medici letters of their political activities in the years immediately following. Too little is known either of the provenance of the verses or the composition of Cavalcanti's chronicle to enable us to exclude the possibility that one was inspired by, or borrowed heavily from, the other, but even if the vision is a single one, and conceived at some remove from the literal truth, these two accounts together constitute a vivid expression of a perceptive contemporary view of the issues in conflict.

The evidence on which Niccolò da Uzzano is credited with the authorship of the verses is limited; in response to their appearance

---

[1] *Istorie*, p. 4.
[2] G. Canestrini (ed.), 'Versi fatti da Niccolò da Uzzano', *A.S.I.* iv (1843), 297–300.

the Priors issued an edict enjoining anyone who could identify the author to do so for a reward of a hundred gold florins. Niccolò da Uzzano was subsequently subjected to an inquisition by the judicial authorities, but no charge was ultimately sustained. On the basis of surviving contemporary manuscripts of the verses, and of other poetry written under his name, literary historians continued to attribute the verses to him,[3] and indeed the views expressed in them are rather similar to those which he was to air in meetings of the *Consulte e Pratiche*.[4] If not in fact established then, the attribution of the verses to him would be at least both likely and appropriate, especially in view of his position as leader of the aristocratic or conservative wing of the *reggimento*, whose outlook they so forcefully embody.

The conservatism of the author is alternatively apparent in the conventional nature of the images and themes of the verses; they are heavily circumscribed by the traditions of Florentine political and patriotic poetry stretching from Brunetto Latini in the later thirteenth century through Dante and Petrarch to their lesser emulators of the later fourteenth century, like Luigi Marsili and Guido del Palagio. Florence, personified as a woman, is compared, as usual, with Rome, and many even of the phrases referring to the time-honoured concerns of civic unity, and its disruption by the *gente nuova*, are virtually direct borrowings from earlier writers.[5] Nevertheless, this is a *pièce d'occasion*; the real point of the poem is to describe the specific and immediate problems confronting the Florentine ruling group in 1426, and to prescribe measures for their solution. It is permeated throughout by the author's ideal of good government and a rightly constituted ruling group, being addressed in fact to those who 'of old have been the lovers of the virtuous and beautiful [lady of Florence], and are her natural rulers'.

He warns his audience that their mistress is in fact on the brink of decline, 'because she can no longer invoke her ancient

---

[3] Cf. Canestrini, 'Nota ai Documenti che seguono', ibid. 285–8.

[4] See, e.g., below, pp. 242–4, 249–50.

[5] See, e.g., Dante Alighieri, 'La Vita Nuova', *Opere*, ed. Toynbee, pp. 203–33; C. Gargiolli (ed.), *Commento a una canzone di Francesco Petrarca per Luigi de' Marsili* (Bologna, 1863); G. Carducci (ed.), 'A Fiorenza', *Rime di Cino da Pistoia a d'altri del secolo XIV* (Florence, 1862), pp. 79, 597–600. The attribution of this last by Carducci to Guido del Palagio has been questioned; see D. Weinstein, 'The Myth of Florence', *Florentine Studies*, ed. N. Rubinstein (London, 1968), p. 32 n. See also Rubinstein. 'The Beginnings'.

customs'; they, 'naturally so wise and powerful', must sink their superficial differences and act rapidly to revive her. They must, 'by following the ancient norms, re-establish the virtuous regime' and secure its permanence by imitating the example of Venice, whose constitution is the embodiment of the aristocratic ideal, 'and whose rulers have held their places for a thousand years'. Otherwise they will find themselves usurped in government and powerless to control the future destiny of Florence:

> Se no lo fate, tosto con dolori
> Sarete spinti fuor della sua sala
> Da genti nuove e vostri debitori.[6]

Already the situation is serious; these people, 'so ignorant, unpleasant, and thankless, who wish to transform the lady Florence':

> . . . son già tanto forti su nel coro
> Del bel Palagio con le bianche e nere,
> Che poco men che tutto il cerchio è loro.
> E quando va a partito il cavaliere,
> E 'l mercatante, o 'l cittadino antico,
> Va come va la zuppa nel paniere.[7]

This is indeed the central point of the poem. The *gente nuova* have already gained a powerful representation in the inner *reggimento*—'il cerchio'—and with their votes—'the white and the black'—are rapidly increasing this representation while excluding those aristocratic citizens to whom government rightly belongs, thus changing the whole nature of the lady Florence. They have attained this dangerously strong position by exploiting the weaknesses of the constitution and conspiring to use their votes in collusion to their own advantage and to the disadvantage of the aristocrats. If the latter are to be secure, the 'democratic loophole' must be closed with the aid of traditional tools; the conservatives should seek the aid of the *Parte Guelfa*—'la rossa gallina'— against these new Ghibellines, and keep before them the example

---

[6] 'If you fail to do this, then soon, to your sorrow, you will be pushed right out of her halls by those new men who owe everything to you.'

[7] '. . . already have such a powerful voice in the Palace with their votes, that they have almost completely taken over in the inner circles of government; and when a knight, or a great merchant, or a citizen from one of the ancient houses is put to the vote, his fate will be that of water in a sieve.'

of the leader of the oligarchy in its classic period, the great
Maso degli Albizzi:

> Il quale sarebbe stato degno re,
> Per la sua grande e degna vigoria,
> Che spesse volte ci si vede, ed è,
> E' c'insegnò di far la buona via,
> La qual ci convien far d'ogni dieci anni
> Sol una volta, e con piena balìa.[8]

Thus the Gonfalonierate of Justice must be given 'ad uom prod-
otto di famiglia antica, esperto e franco, e che non sia garzone
. . .'[9]

> Acciò che nuova gente sotto i panni
> Non faccin con le fave lor postierla
> Come più volte han fatto con inganni . . .
>
> E dico, che per far la buona borsa
> Che voi facciate arruoti allo squittino
> Col suon del parlamento alla ricorsa.[10]

In possession of a legal mandate from the people, the aristocrats
can gain control of the key to the problem—the electoral purses,
and where the *gente nuova* had sought to increase their share in the
stato through the device of the *rimbotto*, they can themselves be
excluded from the purses by a wholesale and permanent reform:

> Per tal maniera fia dato lor tomo
> Giù per le scale a quella gente nuova.
> Che voglion rimbottare ogni vil uomo.[11]

As yet, it is not too late to save the situation:

> Se voi tirate tutti ad uno scotto,
> La bella donna convien che sia vostra
> Sanza contesa e sanza far rimbotto.

[8] 'Who would have been a fitting king, by virtue of his lofty manner and forceful presence, of which we were so often, and still are, aware. He showed us the right way to proceed, that we should carry out the scrutiny only once in every decade and entrust it entirely to our own *Balìa*.'
[9] '. . . to someone from an ancient family, experienced and bold, and not a mere youth . . .'
[10] 'So that the upstarts do not use their votes under cover as a back door, as they have often done so deceitfully. And I tell you, that in order to make the right sort of citizens eligible for office, you must obtain a mandate from the Parliament to nominate candidates of your own choice in the scrutiny.'
[11] 'Thus those upstarts who want to use the *rimbotto* to favour every common fellow, will be pushed back down the ladder.'

Unless, however, they resort rapidly to such radically conservative measures as suggested above, within a couple of years the aristocrats may find themselves completely overthrown by the new men:

> Se non lo fate, la mia fantasia
> Mi profetizza, e fovvene protesta,
> Che mala fin convien che di noi sia.
> Davanti che due volte fia l'agresto
> Rinnovellato nella nostra vigna,
> Il vostro stato sarà tutto pesto
> Da quella nuova gente che traligna.[12]

Cavalcanti expounds a similar view of the situation in 1426, with the difference that he attributes it specifically to the leaders of the anti-Medicean party, and presents it in the context of a description of a meeting which according to him took place in the church of Santo Stefano al Ponte, in the quarter of Santa Croce, when Lorenzo Ridolfi was Gonfalonier of Justice and Francesco di Messer Rinaldo Gianfigliazzi a member of the *Signoria*, at the instigation of a group of citizens led by Messer Matteo Castellani, Niccolò da Uzzano, and Vieri Guadagni.[13] The speech with which Rinaldo degli Albizzi addressed this meeting began, like the verses of Niccolò da Uzzano, with the assertion that those with a natural right to rule Florence were those present, who represented and embodied her traditional values. Addressing them as 'you who are experienced and have long been accustomed to government, which belongs to you as an inheritance from your ancestors', he set about rousing his audience with the exhortation that 'you are the commune, the glory, and the wisdom of this city'. Like the author of the verses, he introduced many of the customary themes

---

[12] 'If you all pull your weight, the beautiful lady should be yours without any conflict and without a *rimbotto*; but if you do not, and I must stress this point to you, I foresee, in my vision of the future, that we are bound to come to a bad end; that before the grapes have twice more been renewed in your vineyards, your prestige and authority will be trampled underfoot through the corruption of the new men.' *Rimbotto* was the process by which officials added to the name-tickets in the electoral purses, filled in accordance with previous scrutinies, extra name-tickets for citizens who had been successful in the new scrutiny (Rubinstein, *Government of Florence*, p. 41). The verses suggest that this device was crucial to the success of either side in the battle for supremacy in government, as those in charge of the process had such extensive opportunities to determine the balance of interests in the composition of the bags.

[13] *Istorie*, Bk. III, Ch. 2, pp. 46–54.

of Florentine political discourse; he stressed the dangers of disunity, invoked the ideas of 'your Roman forbears', and the traditional Guelf and papal connections of the Florentine aristocracy, against a new breed of Ghibellines. He too saw the danger in the purses, to which such a flood of *gente nuova* had recently been admitted that the old-established citizens were overwhelmed: 'Everyone has carried out a new *rimbotto*, and so many immigrants and workers have been added to the purses that their votes outnumber yours and your will cannot prevail.'

The theme of social conflict is elaborated far more extensively by Cavalcanti; in his disdain for the new men, Albizzi's speech surpasses even the verses in its Dantesque echoes. He pours scorn on those 'peasants and artisans',[14] who are inevitably uncivilized, because they lack experience of city life:

They are naturally ignoble and mean-spirited[15]... One has come from Empoli, another from the Mugello, some came here as our servants, and now we find them our partners in the government of the Republic ... now they take us for the servants, and themselves for the lords ... like all newcomers, they don't really know their business, unless it be to overthrow you ... The ignorant mob should stick to their petty skills and concentrate on earning enough to care for their families, and be kept out of the government of the Republic entirely, like the scandalmongers and creators of discord that they are.

His solution is similar in spirit to that proposed by the author of the verses, but his argument goes further. Not only should they be removed from the purses, and the number of fourteen minor guilds be reduced to seven in order to reverse their preponderance and limit their influence in the Council of the People, 'where all the business of the Commune is ultimately concluded'; they should actually be replaced by the magnates whose traditions, despite their customary exclusion from the government, are by comparison much more in keeping with the city's than those of the *gente nuova* currently being admitted. The proposal of a solution so radical in terms of the Florentine experience is some measure of the strength of the speaker's feeling of crisis, though he too expounds his argument by appeal to traditional values.

---

14 'Villani e artefici.'

15 'Sono per natura vili.' Cf. Paolo da Certaldo, *Libro di Buoni Costumi*, ed. A. Schiaffini (Florence, 1945), pp. 91–2: '"La villa fa buone bestie e cattivi uomini", e però usala poco: sta a la città, e favvi o arte o mercatantia, e capiterai bene.'

The 'barbarous race' from Figline and Certaldo being the true Ghibellines against whom the Guelf standard borne by the aristocrats must be raised, the magnates, usually equated with Ghibellinism, appear desirable and worthy companions in city life and government:

You have included these proven enemies of society, Ghibellines by their very origin, whom you know to be enemies of the Guelf *reggimento*, and have left out the noblest men of the city. You claim to have done this on account of the insufferable pride of their ancestors.

But their pride, he declared, was nothing compared with that of the *gente nuova*, and in any case it was infinitely more justified:

Is it not more appropriate that he who is born a Rossi should have authority over a Stucco, than the latter over him? Or should a post which is given to Stuppino be denied to a Frescobaldi? God only knows that the more noble citizens who are responsible for the government of the Republic, the more noble is that Republic, and nevertheless you have excluded the nobles and taken your enemies as your companions on account of your unbridled wilfulness. And I tell you, that if you want to preserve your privileges, you must see that the purses are emptied of these depraved and accursed men.

A further indication of the extent to which the challenge from the *gente nuova* had thrown into relief the similarities between the magnate and the aristocratic outlook is Albizzi's concluding argument, which goes so far as to equate the will of the aristocrats with law and the liberty of the republic, and the latter with the preservation of past customs, as in the Da Uzzano verses: 'Do you not realize that traditional customs are enshrined in the laws and that he who abandons the law renounces good living and civil liberty?' These circumstances justify not merely the imposition of arbitrary control through the creation of *Balìe*, but also a display of the resources of force which are essentially the prerogative of the aristocratic element of the ruling class. 'For God only knows that all just and effective law is amenable to force, and that ultimately only the sword is competent to judge, and you are the ones who have access to force and authority over the militia.' Why not 'lead them to the great *piazza* to stand guard over all the entrances and stop the mob from causing you any trouble? And he who exercises control can determine what goes on in the Palace and arrange the course of the voting with the aid of the sword, and in this way bring about the desired ends.' Otherwise, and he ends with a warning very similar to that of the author of the verses, 'have no doubt that if you continue in your negligence and put your trust once more in the votes and in the speeches of the cowardly and gullible, you will be destroyed and toppled down from your eminence'.

Whether or not this oration, in the classical mode, was an attempt to express in literary form the attitudes which Cavalcanti discerned in the aristocratic sector of the *reggimento* about this time, or whether he composed it as an explanation in retrospect of the subsequent clashes in 1433 and 1434, his analysis of the aristocratic point of view accords so perfectly with what we otherwise know of their background, circumstances, and role in subsequent events, that it must be regarded as at least a valuable insight into the aristocratic mood of the time.[16]

Certainly, there was every reason for the old guard, the conservative core of the oligarchical *reggimento*, to sense an impending crisis, to feel that as a group their backs were to the wall. The classic period of patrician oligarchy had been a golden age for the aristocratic élite and later in the fifteenth century citizens bemoaned its passing in the conviction that 'in those days the whole city enjoyed the utmost happiness'.[17] Luca della Robbia, in his life of Bartolomeo Valori, wrote in 1466 of Florence that:

Although she always flourished, she thrived most between 1390 and 1433 . . . less by the aid of good fortune than through the counsel of the worthy citizens then at the head of the ruling group, whose abilities were marvellously demonstrated, to the extent that they need not be considered inferior to those wisest Romans so celebrated from antiquity.[18]

Della Robbia extended this golden age up to the threshold of the Medicean ascendancy, but in reality it had already begun to de-

[16] Bayley, *War and Society*, pp. 111–12, regards Cavalcanti's account of the meeting at Santo Stefano as purely fictional because it misrepresents the precise attitudes of individuals as revealed in the *Consulte*, and contains a number of errors of detail. Cf. Brucker, *The Civic World*, pp. 472–8; he expresses serious doubts about whether this meeting ever actually took place, but regards Cavalcanti's account of it as a particularly good general statement of the aristocratic-élitist viewpoint in this and the period immediately preceding.

[17] Manno Temperanni, C.P. 58, f. 73v, 2 Jan. 1466, from Rubinstein, *Government of Florence*, p. 144.

[18] Luca di Simone della Robbia, 'Vita di Bartolomeo di Niccolò di Taldo Valori', *A.S.I.* iv (1843), 239–40.

cline in the late twenties into a period of conflict and uncertainty with the loss of so many of the leading citizens of whom he spoke. His backward-looking idealism is reminiscent of the verses of 1426, whose author had sought at the time to stay the process of change and fixate the old regime as it stood, before it should be entirely eroded.

Symbolic of its passing, but also of the greatest practical significance, were the deaths in less than a decade of so many of its leaders; the first of these blows of mortality was the death of its essential creator, the hero and inspiration of the verses, Maso degli Albizzi, in 1417.[19] Four years later Gino Capponi died,[20] and soon after, Rinaldo Gianfigliazzi,[21] followed in quick succession over the next few years by Vieri di Vieri Guadagni,[22] Bartolomeo Valori,[23] Vanni Castellani,[24] Giovanni de' Medici,[25] Matteo di Michele Castellani,[26] Niccolò da Uzzano,[27] and finally, on the eve of the Medici triumph, Bernardo di Vieri Guadagni.[28] The death or decline into old age of so many leaders of the oligarchy in the course of the twenties had certainly left something of a power vacuum, into which there were always new citizens eager to rush.

Whether or not the meeting at Santo Stefano actually did take place, the *Consulte* of the period bear certain witness that Rinaldo degli Albizzi, Niccolò da Uzzano, and Ridolfo Peruzzi led a campaign at this time against those societies believed to be responsible for civic disunity and the hotbeds of conspiracies against the prevailing regime.[29] Whether or not he was the author of the verses, Niccolò da Uzzano's contributions to the *Pratiche* show that he stood four-square for the aristocratic ideals embodied by the oligarchy at the height of its former powers; he was a leading member of a strong and vocal conservative group within the *reggimento* which by the beginning of the thirties had initiated

[19] Rado, *Maso degli Albizzi*, p. 197.   [20] Cambi, *Istorie*, p. 153 (1421).
[21] Ibid., p. 164 (1425).   [22] Ibid., p. 167 (1426).
[23] Litta, *Famiglie Celebri* vii, Tav. I.
[24] He had recently died in 1427 (Martines, *The Social World*, p. 204).
[25] Cambi, *Istorie*, p. 174 (1429).
[26] 1429 (ibid., pp. 176–7; cf. Martines, *The Social World*, p. 209 n.).
[27] Dainelli, 'Niccolò da Uzzano' 208–9 (1431).   [28] M.A.P. V, 298 (1434).
[29] Guasti, *Commissioni* iii. 5; Brucker, *The Civic World*, Ch. 8. The latter observes, however, that others, including Bartolomeo Valori, were concerned to extirpate societies, and that Rinaldo's own political style was not as aggressive or conspiratorial as the speech attributed to him by Cavalcanti would suggest (pp. 475, 478–9).

a vigorous determination to root out from its ranks the advocates of government according to conflicting principles, and his
fellows were the very citizens named by Cavalcanti and later to
emerge indisputably as the leaders of the anti-Medicean party—
Rinaldo degli Albizzi, Francesco di Messer Rinaldo Gianfigliazzi,
Matteo Castellani, Vieri Guadagni.[30] In general the description
of those who met at Santo Stefano in 1426 accords almost precisely with that of the exile group given above. Like the exiles of
1434, its members belonged to older families who had been the
rulers of Florence in the infancy of the commune and in whose hands
power had until recently almost exclusively resided. They too,
though natural allies on the basis of similar social background and
ideals, were often divided in practice by private inclinations and
enmities within their ranks. The 1426 descriptions of an old
and distinguished group of citizens falling away from a position
of former glory and losing their grip on the *reggimento* with the
admission into the inner circles of government of an equal
number of new men are strikingly similar to our picture of the
exile group as composed of families slightly in decline, though
still possessing attributes of greatness.

The conservative conviction, expressed in Cavalcanti's account, that a resort to force is legitimate in order to defend civil
liberty, defined as their own right to rule, is fulfilled in action in
the armed rising of the exiles against the *Signoria* in 1434. The
conservatives who congregated in Santo Stefano had further
expressed their similarity of outlook with the magnates, defined
by their propensity for violent and anti-social behaviour, in their
proposal to strengthen the aristocratic element in government
through the admission of *magnati*. Notably one-fifth of the exile
group in 1434, and many of their associates, were or had been
magnati; these were among the leaders of the group, and intimately
related by marriage and friendship to the *popolani* within it. When
the exiles achieved a predominant position in the *reggimento* after
the expulsion of Cosimo de' Medici, one of the first acts of the
Balìa which they created and conducted was to pass a series of
laws in favour of the magnates and designed to give them a
larger share in the *stato*. Similarly, while both the author of the
verses and the speaker at Santo Stefano isolate the practice of
rimbotto as at the same time the chief potential weapon of the

[30] Below, Ch. 5.

aristocrats bent upon securing their own supremacy, and the main cause of the admission of new men to the state, and hence of all their troubles, another important act of the *Balìa* of 1433, once it had completed a scrutiny to its own satisfaction, was passed to abolish this practice, and to prevent its further use in the future to control the composition of the *reggimento*.[31]

Turning to the Medicean party, we found that it did indeed contain a significant and unusually large number of the *gente nuova* whom the conservatives feared, and if most were no longer relatively recent immigrants from the uncivilized *contado*, nor precisely the *villanie arteficie* whom Messer Rinaldo so scornfully reviled, at least a sprinkling of these remained. Moreover the Medici, while themselves behaving more like *grandi e possenti* than friends of the people, had undeniably acquired, perhaps through their leadership of the *popolo* of San Lorenzo in the 1340s, partly through the activities of Salvestro during the Ciompi revolution, the reputation for popular sympathies of which Cavalcanti was so particularly conscious. Although the activities of the Medici in the fifteenth century and the attitudes which they expressed in their letters and *ricordi* do little to support this image, they were undoubtedly willing to exploit it in their attempts to create a power base from which to increase their own share in the *stato*. They carefully cultivated a group of friends and clients who were their social inferiors and lent to their party just such a tone as the aristocrats deplored, and their reputation flourished accordingly. The threatening upstarts of the verses and Albizzi's oration merge more easily into the Mediceans in the light of such an observation as made by a Sienese lawyer friend to Averardo in 1428: 'I know and have heard tell how recently you and your friends have deservedly won much confidence among the people, and are able to find out and accomplish a great deal, for which I thank God

---

[31] Below, p. 296. Conversely, as Brucker, *The Civic World*, pp. 476–7, shows, it was predominantly the conservatives who, as late as 1426, were the chief advocates in the *Consulte* of the practice of *rimbotto*, and the councils who opposed it; a *rimbotto* for the *Tre Maggiori* was not approved by the councils until February 1428, when the Mediceans appear to have taken advantage of it to further the interests of their own partisans (below, pp. 228–32). Presumably the significance of the *rimbotto* to different sectors of the political class depended on the current balance of forces within the *reggimento*; the prevailing group could use this device to reinforce its predominance, and thus its social and class meaning altered with the balance of these forces. As we have seen, at some time between 1426 and 1429 the Mediceans would appear to have gained the ascendancy. Cf. above, the verses, and n. 12, p. 215.

along with you, and wish you strength in your work, so does my faith in your paternity flourish and increase.'[32] Their influence in the inner circles of the *reggimento* was increasing in precisely the way which the aristocrats deplored, and most importantly, while the central points of the aristocratic plaint against the *gente nuova* concern their conspiracy to augment their strength in the purses and their collusion to use their increasingly large vote to further their own collective interests, there is evidence in the Medici letters that in the years immediately following, the Mediceans were doing just this.

Indeed the letters throw new light on a number of incidents recorded by observers as the early manifestations of the conflict between the parties, but whose testimonies have been generally neglected or even rejected on the grounds that in the absence of any objective supporting evidence, their assertions seemed too unlikely and far-fetched. This has been the fate of Cavalcanti's more specific claims, but most particularly of a confession elicited before the magistracy of the *Otto* by the Medici opponents in September 1433 from one of their rivals' more humble but committed supporters, the notary Ser Niccolò Tinucci.[33] Turned informant against them, his main charges concerned the Medici involvement in the dismissal of the Chancellor of the republic in 1427 and their interference in the operation of the electoral system. His revelations have been treated with scepticism on the grounds that 'before him dangled the dread threat of the rope',[34] and that in the circumstances he might have said anything simply to save himself. While this is undoubtedly true, and many points, particularly in the second and supplementary confession extorted from him, are characterized by the vague hyperbole which one would expect of inventions at the prompting of his inquisitors, the fact remains that not only are the activities which he attributes to the Medici and their friends in these years almost precisely those which the author of the verses and the speaker at Santo Stefano observed in an unnamed group whose description accords closely with the Mediceans, but also supported, in numerous precise details, from the letters identifying partisans and revealing their political preoccupations in this period.

[32] M.A.P. II, 109, Philipus Andree, 'legum doctor', to Averardo, 29 July 1428.
[33] Cf. above, pp. 119–20; *Examina*, and M.A.P., esp. III, 121, 125.
[34] Capponi, *Storia della repubblica* ii. 207.

According to Cavalcanti, the opening of hostilities between the two factions was precipitated in 1426 when 'the gathering at Santo Stefano became known throughout the city'. Consequently, 'the artisans and a good many other citizens became suspicious, and made Giovanni de' Medici their leader'. The conspirators of Santo Stefano, upon hearing of this,

> decided that their best course was secretly to arrange in every way possible to undermine Giovanni's greatness . . . even though Giovanni in no way agreed to form a party . . . But a nephew of his, son of Francesco di Bicci, called Averardo, an evil and unpleasant man . . . continued to incite Giovanni and his sons, Cosimo and Lorenzo, and beseech them to induce Giovanni to seek worldly glory . . . and indeed he didn't want to lose the distinctive reputation which his ancestors by custom had acquired . . . as they had always been protectors of the common people.[35]

As usual in Florence, much of the attention of the partisans of either side was focused on securing a preponderance of influential offices; thus the periodic drawings and elections became a major preoccupation of those citizens involved, and as Cavalcanti observed, by 1429 the situation was such that 'no sooner were the major offices drawn than the whole city knew how many there were from one party and how many from the other; they would rather see her public offices become the cause of the Commune's collapse than see the Republic triumph on account of their rivals.[36]

It would certainly appear from the letters of Cosimo, Averardo, Giuliano, and their closest friends that the outcome of elections and drawings for office was one of their chief preoccupations; if one of them happened to be out of Florence when the results became known, one or more of the others would write announcing the names of the new incumbents and describing them alternatively as 'not in accordance with your friends' desires' or, if they were, as 'an excellent band'.[37] A letter of Cosimo's to Averardo in Ferrara suggests indeed that as early as November 1427 the Medici were anticipating a contest and privately speculating about the line-up of forces in the ruling group. As he observed:

The knight [the customary nickname for Rinaldo degli Albizzi][38]

---

[35] *Istorie*, pp. 56–8.   [36] Ibid., pp. 263–4.
[37] M.A.P. V, 117; cf. V, 76, XVI, 3.
[38] See Cavalcanti, *Trattato*, p. 167; cf. M.A.P. II, 159, 28 Jan. 1430 (1429 *s.f.*), in which Giuliano, writing to Averardo, refers to 'el chavaliere degli Albizi'.

appears to be full of goodwill and anxious to do all the good in the world; it isn't that many of our friends are not a little frightened of him, but those who understand, commend his actions. The others have also taken fright at him and are following in the footsteps of Messer Giuliano [Gianfigliazzi] in showing that one has to take notice of the great families; and the Albizzi, Medici, Strozzi, Altoviti, and others are joining in, and they will all be intending to achieve a lot; concerning the small fry, etc., they will attach themselves wherever they can do best, and let us hope that all will end well.[39]

Three weeks later Puccio Pucci wrote encouraging Averardo to do his utmost to bring to a successful conclusion the peace between Milan and Florence which he had been sent to negotiate, partly for the good of the city, but 'particularly for the comfort and honour which will accrue to yourselves and those whose loyalty you command'. He concluded, however, that for the moment 'the affairs of your friends are proceeding well, and by the grace of God with every day which passes they will proceed even better, for we are responding to events as the necessity arises'.[40] It seems quite possible that this judgement referred not only to the general progress of the party, but more specifically to the two schemes with which Tinucci claimed the Mediceans were involved at precisely this time: the engineering of the dismissal of the anti-Medicean Chancellor, and the intervention of Medici partisans in the making of the scrutiny to ensure a result more favourable to themselves.

Of the two claims the first is less easily substantiated from other evidence, and indeed poses some nearly insoluble problems, but in the light of what we know of the Medici and their partisans in this period, it rings true at a number of points to an extent which has not been sufficiently recognized. The starting-point of Tinucci's story is not the Medici, but his own enmity with the Chancellor, Ser Paolo di Ser Lando Fortini; he explained how, 'because I deprived him many times of the position of notary of the Ten of War, he persecuted me continually within the Guild of Notaries, and did his best to have my name struck off the rolls

---

[39] M.A.P. II, 57, 19 Nov. 1427. The distinction which Cosimo makes here between the power wielded within the *reggimento* by the great families (*famiglie*) and the small fry (*spicciolati*) is a common one and very important to an understanding of the dynamics of the balance of power between interests in the ruling group. Cf. Morelli, *Ricordi*, pp. 430–1, Capponi, Ricordi, XXVII, Cavalcanti, *Istorie*, p. 205.

[40] M.A.P. II, 69, 12 Dec. 1427.

of the guild'.[41] He claimed this was the reason why, despite his intimacy with Niccolò da Uzzano and his *amici*, he was taken up and made a friend of by Ser Martino Martini, an enemy of Fortini, and a Medici partisan who according to Tinucci had brought him into the Medici circle for the sole purpose of persecuting Ser Paolo. In fact the evidence suggests that the Medici, having realized that strength in the scrutinies was the key to predominance in the *reggimento*, and intimacy with the notaries, who were in an ideal position to know or discover their secrets, of considerable assistance in maintaining that strength, did make a policy of cultivating friends who might work for them in the chancery. Certainly it emerged in a denunciation to the *Conservatori delle Leggi* in 1429 that Ser Martino had been falsifying government records since 1426, and he was summarily dismissed; it seems quite possible that he was acting in the Medici interest.[42] Whether or no, Tinucci's account of how the Mediceans offered him their friendship because of his hostility to an opponent of theirs, while he accepted it out of a need for protection, certainly accords very well with what we learnt from the letters of the *amici* of the Medici method of exploiting existing feuds among their fellows in the *reggimento* in their own manœuvres to gain power.

That the officials of the chancery were, by virtue of their privileged access to classified information concerning the scrutinies and other government business, peculiarly vulnerable to partisanship, and that in fact the chancery was a focus for the battles between factions in this period, was subsequently recognized in the virtual exclusion of notaries from the *Signoria* after 1433.[43] In fact Ser Paolo, unlike either his predecessors or his successors, was in the late twenties a major political figure in the inner circles of the ruling group, and one obviously hostile to the

---

[41] *Examina*, p. 399.
[42] Giud. Appelli 75, f. 428r; while coadjutor of the notaries to the *Signoria*, 'multas provisiones ordinamenta et scripturas composuit dictavit fecit et fieri fecit contra veritatem . . . plures deliberationes rogavit seu partita recipit nulla prius firmata scriptura quas postea servi suam voluptatem et prout sibi visum fuit et non secundum voluptatem et sensum statuentium scripxit', and 'omnia in voluminibus reformationis comunis florentinis inservit in grave dampnum et preiudicio tam dicti comunis quam multorum servitorum tam de civitate . . .' He was also charged with revealing many official and unofficial secrets to the detriment of the *Signoria* and the *Dieci*. However, the additional charges of barattry and corruption may imply a more personal motive.
[43] Martines, *Lawyers and Statecraft*, p. 50.

Medici. Since, as Chancellor of the Republic, he was also Notary of the *Tratte,* Tinucci's claim that Giovanni di Bicci wanted to see him out of office because he lent his favour to the Medici opponents, and that his dismissal was necessary to clear the way for the manipulation of the scrutiny which the Medici were hoping to effect in the following month, makes perfect sense.[44]

According to him, this was finally accomplished by Martini himself and Luigi Vecchietti, another enemy of Fortini's who was conveniently drawn for the new Priorate at the beginning of November, and who actually made the proposal that Fortini be dismissed. Cavalcanti's version is that the Medici, knowing that the Uzzaneschi wanted to drive out Martini, took the opportunity of Vecchietti's appearance in the *Signoria* to get in first and eject Ser Paolo.[45] Tinucci maintained that they were assisted by another of the *Signoria,* Francesco Nardi, and the *Gonfaloniere,* Sandro Biliotti, all of whom, he claims, were offered money by Giovanni di Bicci. Certainly, all were members of the Priorate for that month, and while there is some evidence to connect the Nardi with the Medici, Sandro Biliotti and Luigi Vecchietti were certainly partisans of theirs.[46] All were rewarded by the *Balìa* of 1434; Biliotti was made a *Priore a mano* in the strategic first *Signoria* to take up office in November of that year, after the Medici recall, and Vecchietti did in fact record in his *catasto* report for 1433 a debt for the considerable sum of 250 florins to Cosimo and Lorenzo de' Medici.[47]

---

[44] It was unusual for a chancellor to be so personally involved with internal politics, since his duty was essentially 'mantenere alto il concetto dello Stato' (D. Marzi, *La cancelleria della repubblica fiorentina,* Rocca San Casciano, 1910, p. 15). Of particular interest are the letters addressed to him by leading conservative statesmen like Rinaldo degli Albizzi and Michele Castellani, asking for news of political events (ibid., p. 178). Conversely, at the time of his dismissal Fortini was also involved in a clash with the *Ufficiali della Masseritia* over the apportionment of official duties, and this, in addition to his embroilment with political rivalries, may partly have been the cause of his losing the chancellorship; see Martines, *Lawyers and Statecraft,* pp. 164–5.

[45] *Istorie,* p. 58. Cambi, *Istorie,* p. 172, also declares that the Mediceans used Vecchietti to get rid of Ser Paolo; the accounts of Buoninsegni, *Storie,* p. 31, and Filippo di Cino Rinuccini, *Ricordi storici,* ed. G. Aiazzi (Florence, 1840), p. 62, are more non-committal.

[46] See Tratte, 93; M.A.P. IV, 240. Andrea di Salvestro Nardi was a regular correspondent of the Medici before 1434 (M.A.P., *Inventario,* i); he was favoured by the *Balìa* of 1434, and was one of the *Accoppiatori* to the scrutiny of 1443–4 (Rubinstein, *Government of Florence,* p. 237).

[47] Tratte, 93, f. 14v; Cat. 496, ff. 442r–443v; Balìe, 25.

Conversely, the Medici letters on the subject would seem to exclude the possibility at least that Cosimo, Averardo, or Giuliano specifically or directly arranged Fortini's dismissal; there is no evidence to suggest that these three were ever less than completely open and frank with one another in their private correspondence, and yet both Giuliano and Cosimo described the incident to Averardo as if they had no responsibility for it. In a letter of 27 November Cosimo announced that 'this morning the Priors dismissed the Chancellor; the proposal was made by Luigi Vecchietti. A lot of explanations are being put forward, but I think it's probably hatred and enmity rather than anything else.'[48] In his account of the incident the following day, Giuliano observed that Vecchietti had made the proposal, 'they say on account of an old score he wanted to settle with him; with this, as with everything else, there are some who are displeased and others who are the opposite'.[49] Presumably they would have included themselves among the latter, but however interested, they would appear to have been essentially observers of this incident. As always, it is difficult to draw the line between personal and partisan issues; in view of the marked division of the chancery personnel into pro- and anti-Medicean partisans, who very probably had been promoted or at least cultivated there by either group for partisan reasons, it is inevitable that personal enmities between them should have assumed partisan overtones. It seems unlikely that Martini and Vecchietti were acting specifically on Medici instruction, but their actions would have been very much in accord with certain Medicean aims. Possibly they acted independently to further these aims; probably they received encouragement or approval, if not before, then after the event, from some of the *amici*; obviously the incident had become a partisan one when, as Puccio Pucci informed Averardo a fortnight later, it proved impossible for some time to appoint a successor to Fortini because none of the candidates had been approved by the Council of the People, 'owing to the machinations of his friends'.[50]

The major reason, however, for giving serious consideration

---

[48] M.A.P. II, 62, 27 Nov. 1427.   [49] Ibid. 63, 28 Nov. 1427.
[50] Ibid. 69, 12 Dec. 1427. The Medici appear to have shared in the general relief when Leonardo Bruni was finally appointed; as Giuliano announced to Averardo (ibid. 65, 3 Dec. 1427), 'Ieri mattina fu eletto Messer Lionardo d'Arezo cancelliere con fiorini 600 l'ano . . . Anno lo fatto i signori e collegi; a anchora andare pe' consigli, ma a ciaschuno piace tale electione'.

to Tinucci's claim that the Medici party was behind the dismissal
of Fortini is the amount of evidence which emerges to support his
related account of their manœuvrings to influence the scrutiny,
which took place immediately after the appointment of a new
Chancellor.

This done, then during the term of the next Priorate, which included
Tommaso Ginori and Geri del Testa Girolami and others, when
Giovanni de' Medici saw that Niccolò da Uzzano and his friends were
stronger in the purses than he, he discussed with Ser Martino what
strategy they should pursue in order to prevail. And having found out
from Ser Martino the secret of the scrutinies of 1421 and 1426, and
finding themselves strong in the councils, Giovanni de' Medici,
Averardo, Cosimo and Nerone di Nigi and Ser Martino and Puccio
were able to regulate the scrutiny and *rimbotto* which was made in 1427,
and to create Cosimo and Nerone *Accoppiatori*, to come to an arrangement with the Gonfalonier of Justice in accordance with their interests,
so that then in an instant when the time should come, they would be
strong enough in the voting to do whatever they wanted.[51]

His account accords with the view presented by the aristocrats of
1426 on two essential points; the strength of the *gente nuova* in the
Council of the People, and their use of the *rimbotto* as a means of
further increasing that strength, in order to outweigh the votes
of the aristocratic faction when any issue of importance should
arise. Once again, the conspirators named are either members of
the Medici family or men whom we know to have been their loyal
friends and partisans—Tommaso Ginori, Nerone di Nigi Dietisalvi, and Puccio Pucci.

Most importantly, however, the Medici letters over the months
during which the scrutiny was accomplished, though warily
allusive in their references to events and incidents which cannot
always be clearly identified or understood, reveal glimpses of
activities very similar to those described by Tinucci. From
November onwards, the letters which Averardo received from
Giuliano and Cosimo were chiefly concerned with the results of
the drawings of major offices, the composition of the purses, and
the way in which the new scrutinies were in general to be carried
out. Cosimo had clearly seen the election of a new *Dieci* earlier in
the month as a contest between two opposing camps; when he
wrote to Averardo towards the middle of November, he began

[51] *Examina*, p. 401.

by commenting on their initial success: 'I've just got a letter from you, and see that you have heard about the new *Dieci* and are pleased with the result of the election, which is indeed very satisfactory.'[52] The new group included at least four Medicean partisans—Sandro Biliotti, Giovanni di Mico Capponi, Andrea Giugni, and Francesco Tornabuoni, together with Gino Buondelmonti who, according to Cavalcanti, was also a Medicean sympathizer. But although the outcome proved ultimately 'very satisfactory', it seems that for a time it was a close call:

It was a real skirmish, and finally it got to the point where the fight for the majority of votes was between the Fat One [Giovanni di Mico Capponi] and Neri [Capponi], between Messer Roberto and Iacopo Guasconi, between Tornabuoni and Dino [probably Gucci], between Andrea Giugni and Duccio Mancini, and the rest finished up as you see, for all ended well.

It appears, however, that the Medici and their friends were not merely passive observers of all this activity with which they were so concerned.[53] As Giuliano revealed concerning the making of the Cameral Officials, 'I requested favours (*pregherie*) in this matter from a great many members of the Council of the People'. That is, the Mediceans had instructed their friends in order to produce the collective vote which the law forbade in precisely the way described by Tinucci, the author of the verses, and the speaker at Santo Stefano. On this occasion their efforts would appear to have been only partly successful;

Andreuolo Sacchetti and Niccolò d'Andrea Carducci and Tommaso Corsi and Nicholaio Fagni were all put to the vote over and over again, and first one, and then the other gained the most votes; it was complete pandemonium, and in the end it proved impossible to make a satisfactory appointment . . . and all our prior arrangements turned out to be fruitless. The family was very displeased about this tiresome ineffectiveness of the system of soliciting favours, and talked about pursuing some other method.[54]

[52] M.A.P. II, 57.
[53] Cf. ibid. 63; towards the end of the month Giuliano wrote announcing a change in the method of appointing the *Monte* officials: 'è questo d'imborsare tutti e veduti'. The procedure which he described for the *Provveditori della Camera* and the *Cinque del Contado* may have been designed to limit the opportunities of the aristocratic group heavily represented in the council of 200: 'Si fano per borsa gli aroti, sono 2 per gonfalone della borsa del 200, e gli altri usati non possono squittinare loro medesimi, e d'ognuno si fè borsa di per sè.'
[54] Ibid. 86, 1427, n.d.; by its content it obviously belongs to this run.

As Tinucci suggested, the Medici were in fact closely involved with the scrutiny of January 1427/8, in which Cosimo did take part. The record of the scrutiny in a contemporary *Priorista* helps to clarify the complexities of the process glossed over in Tinucci's account;[55] in fact it consisted of a number of separate and distinct processes, some of which were a matter of routine and others of crucial importance to the composition of the *reggimento*. The January operations included a scrutiny proper of all the internal and external offices, with the exception of the Priorate. It would have been difficult to interfere with this process, and the Medici letters certainly do not suggest that they were in any special position to do so, although the correspondence of Cosimo and Giuliano with Averardo continues to indicate the extent of their interest in the subject. On 30 December Giuliano announced to Averardo the membership of a new magistracy of six, closely concerned with the scrutiny, observing that 'here no one has very much regard for anything but this'.[56] On 1 January Cosimo reported that 'I think we will soon be getting down to the scrutinies; the time is ripe'.[57]

In February, however, there was a *rimbotto*, that process which the conservatives had isolated as the major agent of change in the *reggimento*, and to which Tinucci probably meant to allude. Cosimo himself described the operation in a letter to Averardo on 7 February.[58] He explained that he had been unable to attend to some task or other on Averardo's behalf,

for these blessed scrutinies keep everyone fully occupied ... The procedure which has been accepted is to combine the scrutiny of [14]16 with that of [13]91, and those of '26 and '27 with that of '93 ... new *Accoppiatori* have to be created to replace those who have died ... there will also be a *rimbotto* for the lesser internal offices, so that as you see it's a very mixed-up affair.

This observation would hardly suggest that the *rimbotto* for the *minori* was the central focus of a Medici plan to modify the

[55] Priorista, B.N.F., Magl., XXV: 379 (Francesco di Tommaso Giovanni), entries for Jan.–Feb. 1427 (*s.f.*); 'Adì ... di gennaio 1427 si fè 1º squittino dentro et di fuori eccetto il priorato, e mescolòsi con lo squittino 1407, e con altre borse vecchie, e fessi che 1ª volta si traessi della borsa del 1420 e 1ª di questa borsa nuova. Adì ... di febraio se fè lo squittino del 16, che si rimbottò in sul 1391 ... chi vinse lo squittino 1421 o nel 1426, fussi messo con una poliza nella borsa del 1393 e 1398, che è 1ª medesima.' [56] M.A.P. II, 81, 30 Nov. 1427.
[57] Ibid., 3 Jan. 1428 (1427 *s.f.*). [58] Ibid. II, 22, 7 Feb. 1428 (1427 *s.f.*).

scrutiny in their own interests, and indeed, as Cosimo continued rather ironically, 'this plan was suggested in the council by Niccolò da Uzzano, and where in the beginning no one would agree to have a new scrutiny at all, now they have accepted three of them'. Opinions of this, he observed, 'are varied as usual in such circumstances; there are some who disapprove of the arrangements and others who commend them', but in the end, in fact, 'they leave all the measures to the discretion of the men of experience in the ruling circle'. It is, however, significant that he considered this 'too much of a muddle, because there is no one distinguished or capable', and he concluded with the rather pregnant observation that 'now it may be said that the question of taxes has been taken care of by the *catasto* and that of civic offices by the scrutinies; all that remains is that you should do your job and everything will be fixed'. Interestingly enough, Giuliano's letter to Averardo on the same day announcing the same decision added that the internal offices including the *Tre Maggiori* were to be scrutinized and expressed the opinion that this was good news, and all was working out well.[59]

Moreover, Tinucci's claims begin to seem less far-fetched in the light of Giuliano's announcement to Averardo in a letter of 14 February, that the *Accoppiatori* had been made, and that they were in fact Nerone di Nigi, Carlo Federighi, and Cosimo.[60] Once again, the *amici* had been organized in advance to bring about the desired result, as Antonio di Salvestro Serristori, in a letter to Averardo on the same day, revealed in his description of the voting. The point of Serristori's account was paradoxically to deplore the careless voting of the *amici*, which once again had almost led to defeat.

On the seventh I wrote to you, but haven't yet received your reply ... Our attention is occupied with making the scrutiny and almost everything else is banished from our thoughts. Those who were made

[59] Ibid. 23, 7 Feb. 1428 (1427 *s.f.*). Though he appeared to be rather confused about the electoral arrangements, he declared that three *Accoppiatori* were to be elected, and that apparently the offices of the *Tre Maggiori* might be affected by the revision.

[60] Ibid. 25, 14 Feb. 1428 (1427 *s.f.*). Carlo Federighi was not one of the *amici*, but a lawyer whose political success both before and after may have been due to the neutrality of his behaviour in the struggles of 1433 and 1434. He attended 60 *Pratiche* in the period 1429–34; for his political record after that date see Rubinstein, *Government of Florence*, pp. 24, 236–43.

Accoppiatori were Nerone for the scrutiny of '16, Messer Carlo Federighi for that of '21, Cosimo in '26; although he was accepted, Cosimo
was disgraced with Niccolò Valori, and your friends were responsible,
for much as they put all their weight behind him and Francesco della
Luna, some gave their votes to Giovanni and some to Cosimo, and
they should have been told to give their votes to Cosimo and not to
Giovanni. However, he continued to gain on the other, so that Niccolò
had 103 votes to his favour, and Cosimo 103; they were put to the vote
again, and Cosimo had more than 140 and our friend 104, so that he
was aware to what straits we were reduced by carelessness. You might
well say that they really appeared to have lost any benefit from the
favours they had solicited . . .[61]

Perhaps this was the sort of problem which Cosimo had foreseen
when he wrote to Averardo in Ferrara a fortnight earlier: 'I
wish these blessed peace negotiations could be got over with
quickly, because it's time that they were . . . I wish you were here
to promote your own interests and those of our friends.'[62]

The evidence is not sufficient either to confirm or confute the
details of Tinucci's account of the Medici role in the scrutiny of
1427/8, but their correspondence on several points is highly
suggestive. It is absolutely clear from these letters that the Mediceans at this time were most anxious to promote their own
interests and those of their friends, that they did indeed indulge
in the practice of soliciting favours (*pregherie*) from voters before
elections, which made them technically conspirators against the
commune, and this was to be the brunt of the charges against
them in 1434. Their constant concern to measure and augment
the strength of their *amici* in government is an even greater trans-
gression in spirit against the intention of the constitution and its
harmonious operation. Finally, although here there is no concrete
evidence whatsoever concerning the activities of Cosimo as
Accoppiatore, or any other of the *amici* in the positions of authority
into which they had been manœuvred, the Medici letters, despite
the occurrence of such setbacks as the partial failure of the
pregherie, betray a growing elation concerning the achievements
of the *amici*, and also the suggestion that they gained considerable
ground as a result of the new scrutinies.

On the nineteenth of the month Cosimo wrote to Averardo
that 'yesterday four were sworn in to keep the secret of the exter-

[61] M.A.P. II, 27, 14 Feb. 1428 (1427 *s.f.*).
[62] Ibid. 18, 31 Jan. 1428 (1427 *s.f.*).

nal offices, and they were Messer F. Machiavelli, G. Giugni, Guccio da Sommaia, and Puccio, and they were all according to the plan'.[63] These four were the citizens entrusted with confidential and politically strategic information concerning the contents of the purses; the case Cosimo mentions does not concern the Gonfalonierate of Justice to which Tinucci refers, or even the Priorate, but still many of the *Ufficiali di Fuori* held important and influential positions, and it is highly suggestive that two should be Medicean partisans, one a leader of the party, and that Cosimo should conclude by observing that everything had gone according to plan.

His letter ends with a broader expression of satisfaction concerning the progress of the scrutinies: 'They began to draw up the scrutiny yesterday, and I understand that they are proceeding liberally (*larghe*) and very well, and in every man's case, with God's favour, may the consequences be fruitful.' Cosimo's association of a good scrutiny with one which was *largo*, signifying specifically in Florentine electoral parlance 'democratic', recalls immediately the complaints of the conservatives a year or so earlier against 'those new men who want to favour every common fellow in the purses (*rimbottare*)', and the adding of 'so many of the lower classes and *arrivistes* into the bags'. His words appear to be definite confirmation that the Medici, for whatever reasons of their own, were anxious to promote the addition of new names to the purses and the consequent democratization of the ruling group.

Further evidence on this point is provided by a letter of Battista di Doffo Arnolfi, the last of this series, to Averardo in Ferrara on 19 February 1427/8.[64] Arnolfi's letter reads almost like a report of an undertaking successfully completed: 'It remains only to say that in everything I have done my duty as fairly as I am able, so that on your return . . . you will find things greatly improved, though in fact by the merit of others, etc.' He does not specify precisely the nature of the affairs which have so improved, but he then goes straight on to describe the scrutiny most recently completed and to confirm that 'according to the general rumour it will be very democratic'. It is apparently this prospect of the entry of a more democratic element into the ruling group which prompts his revealing concluding reflection

[63] Ibid. 33.   [64] Ibid. 32.

on the traditional leaders of the *reggimento* : 'Our fellows who have governed us in the past have continued to commit their usual rash and foolish acts. They are accustomed to behave like unbridled horses; now they have an obstinate bit between their teeth; they need their throats cut to stop them from being so stubborn.[65] Certainly his words echo in apparent and ominous fulfilment of the warnings issued to the wilful and disunited aristocrats by their own leaders in 1426; Arnolfi's vision of them as 'unbridled horses' conjures up an image strikingly similar to that invoked by the speaker at Santo Stefano when he referred to the 'unbridled wills' of his hearers.[66] His fear that the constant *rimbotti* had made the new men so strong in the Council of the People that 'your wishes will not be fulfilled' also appears to be confirmed in Arnolfi's prophecy that in the future these aristocrats will have to take greater account of the newer men if they are not themselves to be altogether destroyed.

Just as the affair of the Chancellor's dismissal, however unclear its precise relationship to the Medici plans, had been a public demonstration of the hardening of party divisions, these were also reflected openly in the affairs of the Florentine *Studio* at this time. A number of leading citizens from both parties, including Palla Strozzi, Niccolò da Uzzano, and Cosimo himself, were its interested and distinguished patrons, and inevitably the close associates of those whom they sponsored for positions there.[67] The latter were articulate in their involvement in the conflict; a well-known example is the feud between the humanists Poggio and Niccoli on the one hand and Filelfo on the other, culminating in the latter's exile in 1431, and his replacement by a Medicean candidate. While Filelfo became the author of some of the most powerful anti-Medicean invective of the period, the pro-Medicean humanists like Poggio Bracciolini and Niccolò Niccoli wrote to their friends in support of the Medici during the crises of 1433,

[65] Perhaps he feared this outburst had been too frank; he broke off abruptly with the promise that 'a boccha ti direi più, e basta'.

[66] The desire to keep the aristocratic element of the patriciate on a tight rein seems to have been a powerful one among citizens of varying partisan persuasions, which may help to account for the general swing in favour of the Medici in 1434; cf. Gino Capponi, 'Ricordi', XXVII, and Morelli, *Ricordi*, p. 196: 'non gli piacque tutto il loro reggimento, ma sì in alcuna cosa mescolato, ch'è buono per raffrenare li animi troppo grandi'.

[67] See A. Gherardi, *Statuti della università e studio fiorentino* (Florence, 1881), XLIX, LI.

and were lavish in their formal praise after the triumph of 1434.[68]

There is some indication in the affair of the rebellion of Volterra against Florentine domination late in 1429, that the partisan divisions within the ruling group were clearly apparent even to those outside the city, and exercised a significant influence on its foreign policy. According to Cavalcanti, it was the Uzzaneschi who insisted on the imposition of the *catasto* which provoked the rebellion, and mainly to spite the Mediceans; 'more, I think, to stir up a scandal than with the expectation of any gain for the Republic'.[69] Certainly the account of the incident by an anonymous Volterran chronicler records that:

There were at that time in the city of Florence two powerful factions, one led by Niccolò da Uzzano and the other by Cosimo de' Medici . . . who was very warmly disposed towards our commune. It happened that at that time, since Niccolò della Auzzani took exception to Cosimo de' Medici's benevolence towards us, he urged that the *catasto* be imposed on all our possessions . . . We applied to Cosimo for aid and sympathy and advice, as our refuge and protector in every hour of need. He advised us not to co-operate, as we were being treated unjustly, and persuaded us that we should in no wise pay the *catasto*. When we didn't do so, the *Signoria* of Florence, encouraged by the supporters of Da Uzzano, summoned from Volterra a large number of citizens . . .

These were promptly imprisoned, and

things remained at that point for about ten months; finally, at the instigation of Cosimo, his party, and his followers, it was urged that we should pay a nominal tax . . . and so it was decreed. On account of this there was great rejoicing in Volterra, because everything was settled without impugning the honour of our city.[70]

It is difficult to know how far this account can be accepted, but much is confirmed by official evidence from Florence. It is true that, as the chronicler relates, the two citizens sent to reduce

[68] Ibid. LI; Vespasiano da Bisticci, *Vite* ii. 210 ff.; iii. 84; Fabroni, *Cosmi vita Adnotationes* i. 69; 'Commentationes florentinae de exilio', ed. C. Errera, *A.S.I.* 5th Ser. v (1890), 193–227. See also A. M. Brown, 'The Humanist Portrait of Cosimo de' Medici', *J.W.C.I.* xxiv (1961), 186–221; G. Holmes, 'How the Medici . . .', and *The Florentine Enlightenment*, esp. pp. 14–15, 28, 84, 97–9.

[69] *Istorie*, p. 139.

[70] M. Tabarrini (ed.), 'Chronichetta Volterrana di Autore Anonimo dal 1362 al 1478', *A.S.I.* App. III (1846), 319–20.

Volterra to obedience in November 1429 were Rinaldo degli Albizzi and Palla Strozzi, two prominent conservatives, and that the *Dieci* appointed to direct operations included Niccolò da Uzzano himself, as well as Rinaldo degli Albizzi, Palla Strozzi, Ridolfo Peruzzi, and Giovanni di Messer Rinaldo Gianfigliazzi. On the other hand, Puccio Pucci was also a member of that *Dieci*, and Averardo de' Medici advocated the disciplining of the rebel city, albeit in a paternal fashion, at the *Consulta* called to discuss the matter when it first arose, on 24 October: 'We ought to recommend that citizens be sent to Volterra to subdue it as a father would his son; because it is better to do that than to have to make an example of it'.[71] Nevertheless, it is also true that once open rebellion had been swiftly quashed, the essential question of the tax was quietly settled the following year to the advantage of the Volterrans, and at a time when in the internal administration of Florence, the Mediceans were in the ascendant.[72]

Another incident indicative of increasing partisan tension which occurred about the same time, and was also quietly settled as if by semi-private arrangement, was the abortive attempt to assassinate Niccolò da Uzzano. In view of Da Uzzano's by then acknowledged position as leader of the anti-Medicean conservatives, it is difficult to believe that there was no partisan motive behind the attempt. Again there is no concrete evidence to confirm the involvement of the Medici in the plot; there is, however, some reason to believe that they may have had some connection with it. Niccolò Soderini was accused of, and tried for, the crime; he was apparently a supporter of the Medici by early 1431 and may have been so earlier.[73] Even Tinucci does not claim that he was acting on their instructions; the circumstances would seem to have been somewhat similar to those surrounding the dismissal of the chancellor.

According to Tinucci's account, 'it happened that in the month of December 1429, Niccolò Soderini wanted to have Niccolò da Uzzano assassinated, something which I don't think either Cosimo

[71] C.P. 48, f. 95v.

[72] C.P. 49, f. 193v, 30 Oct. 1431. Representatives of the major offices concluded that 'restitutio fiat et quanto citius tanto melius et meo esse prout erant ante novitatem'. The Mediceans were prominent at this meeting. Cf. *Commissioni* iii. 186.

[73] See M.A.P. II, 311, Niccolò Soderini to Averardo, 1 Mar. 1431 (1430 *s.f.*); he wrote to ask Averardo for help in securing an office with the assurance that 'io sono vostro in ogni chosa, e a voi mi raccomando'.

or Averardo knew anything about'. After the attempt had been made and discovered, however, Tinucci related how Soderini sought out the Medici, 'and commended himself to them, and asked for their favour and advice, and they replied that he should have no fear, that they would help him in every way; and they took counsel with Cosimo and decided to do everything within their power to overthrow Niccolò da Uzzano'.[74] Of those whom Tinucci claimed the Medici employed to help them in this enterprise, and to whom they lent money as an inducement—Tinucci himself, Tommaso Barbadori, and Nastagio Guiducci—the first two were Medicean partisans, and the third associated with them, and Barbadori did record debts in 1433 not only to Cosimo de' Medici but also to Niccolò Soderini.[75] Tinucci claims these plans were finally abandoned by mediation and agreement between the two parties; certainly the official evidence suggests, as in the case of the Volterran rebellion, a settlement by private agreement, perhaps in consideration of the external threat to the *reggimento* from the impending war with Lucca.

Soderini's assassination attempt was made the month before its outbreak, in November 1429, and the case came up for discussion in the *Consulte* of that month. Notably, it was not the subject of a major debate by one of the usual comparatively large gatherings of private citizens called in to give their opinions on issues of importance. It was raised in one of those meetings of the *Collegi*—the *Sedici* and the *Dodici*—in which larger discussions were normally either proposed or summarized. The collective view was expressed by a single spokesman for each magistracy; consequently, it is difficult to assess their relationship to partisan divisions. However, it may not be entirely without significance that while Iacopo di Piero Baroncelli, a leading associate of the aristocratic conservative faction, recommended simply on behalf of the *Sedici* that the *Signoria* should provide 'that the truth should be determined and that those who had erred should be punished', Piero del Benino, a member of a very pro-Medicean family, stressed as the spokesman of the *Dodici* that in addition

if what Niccolò da Uzzano says is found to be true, then whoever has erred should be punished, and if it is discovered that Niccolò da Uzzano has invented all this to defame someone, that he should be

---

[74] *Examina*, pp. 402–3.
[75] Cat. 488, ff. 403r–404r; above, p. 80 n., Appendix I.

punished as he deserves, so that in either case the punishment will serve as an example to others to refrain from doing anything similar.[76]

The introduction into the discussion of the suggestion that Da Uzzano was not necessarily an innocent victim in this incident may well have been an attempt on the part of the Medici to make political capital out of it, as Tinucci suggested.

The result of the official trial of Soderini, who was apparently generally accepted as being the likely attacker because of a vendetta which existed between himself and Da Uzzano, was inconclusive.[77] Soderini was accused of the crime, along with his hired accomplices, apparently professional men of violence with no obvious connection with the Medici or with their friends. However, throughout the trial there was mention of assistance being given to the principal accused by a mysterious group of 'others . . . whose names for the moment are better left unmentioned'; this may have been an attempt in turn on the part of a conservative group to implicate the Mediceans by inference, even if they had had nothing to do with the matter, just as the references to Niccolò da Uzzano as 'a noble man, a worthy citizen, and very well regarded in the city of Florence . . . having a major share in the *reggimento*' may have reflected a determination not to consider or admit the possibility that Da Uzzano had been in any way responsible for the incident.

In any case, although one of his accomplices was subsequently condemned to death, the charge against Soderini was dropped in response to a bulletin from the *Signoria*. In this bulletin the *Signoria* expressed its concern that from the charge laid by Niccolò da Uzzano against Soderini 'there could arise or be engendered serious and irreparable scandal, and strife and differences among the vast majority of esteemed and virtuous citizens of the Florentine *reggimento*, and of the city of Florence, and that from such scandal innumerable troubles might spring'. Therefore 'for the public good of the commune of Florence and in order that peace and concord and perpetual unity may be maintained among the citizens and the government of the city of Florence', they ordered that 'the inquiry should for all time be forbidden to proceed further', and recommended quite firmly concerning Soderini that 'you should fully and finally absolve and acquit him'. The

---

[76] C.P. 48, f. 99r. See also ff. 99v–100r, 112r.

[77] Atti del Podestà, 4423, ff. 1r–4v.

Signoria which quashed the incident was composed almost equally of future exiles and their conservative friends on the one hand, and Mediceans and their sympathizers on the other. Whatever the partisan activities which had found expression in this incident, it seems that by this stage, in the month of the outbreak of the war with Lucca, the leading citizens of the *reggimento* were united, if not in effect, at least in the realization of the danger in which such divisions placed the republic.

The transcripts of discussions of the *Consulte e Pratiche* are a source of unparalleled richness for the scope which they offer for the identification of the leading members of the *reggimento* and the precision with which their opinions are recorded. As those most frequently invited to the *Consulte* in the late twenties and early thirties included many of the leading figures of both the Medicean and anti-Medicean parties, and approximately half the members of each group took part in the *Consulte* at some time, it is possible to gain from them some firm indication of the temper of the *reggimento* and the factions within it around the turn of the decade. Of course these discussions essentially concerned various political issues confronting the regime, and since, as we have already observed, partisanship in Florence was not generally or fundamentally based in ideology, but in personal relationships, divisions of opinion in debates did not occur primarily along partisan lines.[78] However, when the issue in question was the problem of re-establishing civic unity and the extirpation of factions, partisan attitudes and affiliations were more clearly apparent, and although in the numerous meetings on this subject throughout 1429 and 1430 the *reggimento* presented a front united in a universal dread of civic strife, the very partisan interests which they feared can be discerned in operation beneath the surface of patriotic consensus on traditional values which they carefully preserved, often at the price of coming openly to grips with the real issues. The

[78] Thus the *Consulte* cannot of course be used to identify partisanship with the same precision that Gilbert, *Machiavelli and Guicciardini*, and Brucker, *The Civic World*, have demonstrated in the identification of ideas and the analysis of a whole climate of opinion. Conversely, the attitudes and opinions which prominent citizens like Averardo de' Medici, Neri Capponi, and Niccolò da Uzzano expressed in the *Consulte* are often very similar to those which they expressed elsewhere. A particularly good example of this is Rinaldo degli Albizzi's preoccupation with 'grado' in a letter to the *Dieci* (Guasti, *Commissioni* iii. 312); he expressed a precisely similar attitude in a *Consulta* held a few months later (C.P. 49, ff. 32v–35r).

anti-Mediceans were the more vocal, and their diagnosis of the problem is almost precisely that of the author of the verses or the speaker at Santo Stefano; the activities which they deplore are those associated with the Mediceans by Tinucci, by the implications of their own correspondence, and finally by the accusations against them on the occasion of their expulsion by the conservative faction in 1433.

The problem of faction is of course one of the continuing preoccupations of Florentine citizens throughout the history of the republic, but naturally it manifested itself more acutely at some times than at others. The summoning of a series of *Pratiche* to consider the question of the growth of societies, and to provide for unity among the citizens of the *reggimento*,[79] suggests that a new and acute phase of concern with this problem arose in 1426 at about the time when the Da Uzzano verses were written, the meeting of citizens held at Santo Stefano, and when Tinucci declared, and their own letters confirm, that the Medici were beginning to consolidate their group of *amici*.

According to Cavalcanti, the meeting at Santo Stefano was held during the Gonfalonierate of Lorenzo Ridolfi, that is, during the months of July or August 1426. In those two months the *Consulte* are more frequent than usual, and full of complaints and resolutions, particularly for stamping out the societies which were thought to lead to the growth of *sette* or parties. In a *Pratica* towards the end of July Rinaldo degli Albizzi and Niccolò da Uzzano moved on behalf of all those present 'that most importantly, the Priors should be advised to attend to the eradication of the societies'. On 12 August Rinaldo and Ridolfo Peruzzi suggested that the *Signoria* should confiscate and destroy the records of all churches and other places where 'societates' might congregate, and finally proposed a measure which struck at the very root of the developing problem as the aristocrats perceived it. They suggested that when a scrutiny was held, those responsible should be instructed in the future to exclude anyone found to be a member of such a society in the same way as usurers and sodomites were then excluded.[80]

If the aristocrats had actually succeeded in pushing through

---

[79] Guasti, *Commissioni* iii. 1–6; Brucker, *The Civic World*, pp. 478–81, and for earlier action in 1419 against societies, Rubinstein, *Government of Florence*, p. 119 n.

[80] *Commissioni*, iii, p. 5.

such a measure at this time, it might well have furnished them with a device by which to exclude their enemies from the purses. However, they failed, or were prevented from implementing this proposition; shortly after there arose the question of the reform of the taxation system with the introduction of the *catasto*, and other issues like the long-standing war with the Visconti of Milan began to occupy more of the attention of the leading citizens, until open hostilities with Milan were concluded with the Treaty of Ferrara, negotiated on behalf of Florence in April 1428 by Palla Strozzi and Averardo de' Medici.[81] The next major series of discussions in the *Consulte* concerning citizen unity and the problem of the factions began early in 1429. These discussions continued throughout the year, and on into the early months of 1430, by which time they were again superseded by the even more pressing problem of the defence of the commune; the war with Lucca had been officially declared in December 1429, and by the middle of 1430 Florence's position was so perilous as to drive other concerns from the minds of the leaders of the *reggimento*.

This series of major *Pratiche* on unity held at frequent intervals throughout 1429–30 demonstrates that the party divisions within their ranks were increasingly becoming a cause of serious anxiety to citizens of the *reggimento* concerned with the good of the commune. However, although the object of the discussions was to find some means of breaking down these divisions, the opinions recorded by the speakers only serve to reveal the full depth and seriousness of the rifts they were attempting to heal.

The main theme of the major *Pratica* of 25 January 1429 was the need to stamp out the *sette* and reassert the supremacy of the authority of the Priors over all Florentine citizens, and especially those active in government in some official capacity. This was a subject on which everyone could generally agree, without being swept away in any of the undercurrents which already flowed treacherously beneath the calm surface of this patriotic discussion. The important role of initiating the proceedings fell to Lorenzo Ridolfi.[82] This prominent lawyer, of conservative leanings, but

---

[81] Buoninsegni, *Storie*, p. 30.

[82] The order of speakers in the *Consulte* appears to have been strategic and pre-arranged. Those expert on the subject under discussion or currently influential in the regime normally spoke first and made the essential contributions to the meeting; subsequent speakers often simply re-phrased the sentiments of these earlier speakers, or sometimes merely registered agreement or disagreement.

not apparently embroiled with either faction, set the tone of the
meeting by couching his plea for greater respect for the *Signoria*
in pious terms. 'As we should adore one God, so you, Lord
Priors, are to be venerated above all citizens, and those who look
to others are setting up idols, and are to be condemned.'[83] Palla
Strozzi signified his full agreement, and the theme was taken up
again by Giovanni Morelli, who observed that: 'Our Lord
stood in the midst of his disciples and said, "Peace be unto you"!
In the same way you, Lord Priors, etc. . . . He who creates a
party, sells his liberty . . .' This last remark neatly introduced the
perennial theme of liberty, redefined for every occasion, though
on this one Morelli's basic point seems related to that expressed
more crudely by the speaker at Santo Stefano, when he argued
to his aristocratic audience that if any more new men were
admitted into the *reggimento*, 'your wishes will no longer be
fulfilled' and consequently, 'the liberty of the Republic will be
destroyed'.

A sharper note was introduced into the discussion by Lippozzo
Mangioni,[84] who cut across this pious and patriotic rhetoric with
the abrupt remark that 'the causes of faction are twofold; namely,
profit, and honour'. His observation would seem to amount to a
recognition that the essential source of partisan friction was the
inevitable conflict between the various individuals and parties
striving to procure wealth and high office for themselves and
their friends. Notably his suggestion that the Priors should act
positively in seeking out the causes of discontent and remedying
them was taken up by several of the following speakers, including
both Mediceans and their opponents; Averardo himself, Niccolò
da Uzzano, Giuliano Davanzati, Bartolomeo Peruzzi, and Neri
Capponi.[85]

[83] C.P. 48, f. 51r.

[84] Ibid. The attribution of this speech to Luca degli Albizzi seems to be a mistake
on the part of the scribe; Luca had in fact spoken after Giovanni Morelli, and it was
not the custom to speak more than once. Moreover, the next speaker, Stefano di
Salvi di Filippo Bencivenni, praised the advice given by Lippozzo Mangioni, whose
name did not appear among the previous five speakers; almost certainly he had made
the second speech attributed to Luca degli Albizzi.

[85] Ibid., ff. 51v–52r. This was a traditional conclusion of observers of the Florentine political scene; cf. in the later fourteenth century Marchionne di Coppo Stefani,
Cronaca Fiorentina, ed. N. Rodolico, *Rerum Italicarum Scriptores*, new edn., xxx, pt. I,
(Città di Castello, 1927), rubr. 923: 'Tutto ciò che di male è stato nella benedetta
città di Firenze nulla cosa è proceduto, se non da volere gli ufici, è poi auti, ciascuno
a volerli per sè tutti e cacciarne il compagno.'

However, the force of Mangioni's point soon became neutralized by the non-committal tone of the ensuing discussion, and particularly of Niccolò Barbadori's contribution, which rounded off on a rather incongruous note the abstract religious theme introduced by the earlier speakers. 'This is the day the Lord has made; let us be glad and rejoice in it. The Lord Priors should consult closely with the colleges and appoint a number of citizens, and they should provide by their authority a means of doing away with these divisions.' Only at the very end of the discussion was the real issue again squarely confronted by Dino di Messer Guccio Gucci. 'The difference lies between those who in attempting to regain their former position suffer harm, and they who seek the promotion of those who occasioned this harm.' This statement of the issues accords closely with those of 1426; Gucci's was clearly the most perceptive observation of the meeting, but interestingly enough it was completely ignored. None of his points was taken up by the following speakers, and the *Pratica* ended on that general and inconclusive note which was typical of so many of these discussions by the *richiesti* of difficult or sensitive matters, and which caused citizens constantly to demand that 'we should produce deeds and not words', or that 'if words do not suffice, then we should proceed to actions'.[86]

As a result of this discussion, four days later, on 29 January, a *Iuramentum* was drawn up to be sworn on the Bible by as many of the citizens as possible.[87] They promised:

To forgive those both present and absent their wrongs. To abandon all hatreds. To divest ourselves completely of partisanship and loyalty to factions. To consider only the welfare and honour and greatness of the Republic and of the *Parte Guelfa* and of the *Signoria*. To forget every injury received up to this day on account of partisan or factional passions, or for any other reason.

The language of this petition bears a striking resemblance to that of the Da Uzzano verses, in the injunction to 'abandon all your rivalries entirely, and make peace among yourselves immediately'. The final total of signatures to this pledge was little short of 700,

---

[86] C.P. 49, f. 67r (Marco di Goro Strozzi, 3 Aug. 1430); 48, f. 51r (Giovanni di Paolo Morelli, 25 Jan. 1429); cf. 49, f. 97v (Averardo de' Medici, 27 Nov. 1430) and 49, f. 188r (Manetto di Tuccio Scambrilla, 20 Aug. 1431).

[87] C.P. 48, f. 54v; signatures ff. 54v–60v.

approximately the number of citizens whom we calculated to belong to the effective *reggimento*.[88]

However, in February it was considered necessary to create a new magistracy which enabled citizens to give vent to those passions which they could neither forgive nor forget, and in precise accordance with the prescriptions made by Rinaldo degli Albizzi, Niccolò da Uzzano, and Ridolfo Peruzzi in 1426. The chief task of the ten citizens appointed as *Conservatori delle Leggi* was to prevent any citizen who belonged to a society which might give rise to a *setta* from assuming any of the major offices of the commune, 'so that whatever by the laws of the Florentine Republic is justly and legally ordained, should be inviolably observed, and neither through ambition, nor for private obligation, nor through rash presumption, should anyone dare to act against them'. The object of the law was to be achieved by providing that the *Conservatori* should make a thorough investigation 'of each and every one who in the future in whatsoever way should accept or exercise any communal office',[89] and in this they were to be aided by the depositions of citizens which generated such bitterness in the succeeding years, and did so much not only to impede the war effort, but to widen the rifts in the *reggimento* and actually to drive apart some citizens previously united by good sense and goodwill.

It soon became apparent that the denunciations to the *Conservatori delle Leggi*, rather than providing the remedy for factionalism, were themselves to prove the greatest possible source of scandal, and a provocation of existing hostilities. Tinucci suggests that the Mediceans exploited this law to divide and weaken the existing regime and thus pave the way for their own ascendancy.[90] Quite possibly they did; among the welter of accusations which followed the establishment of the office, the names of leading anti-Mediceans were prominent enough. Conversely, there were also a number directed against Medici partisans, and others not associated with either faction; moreover, the denunciations in

---

[88] The unusual action of promulgating a general petition on such a scale is a significant indication of the seriousness of the citizens' concern for unity; cf. Brucker, *The Civic World*, p. 488, on the fact that the oath of allegiance was not a Florentine custom.

[89] *Commissioni* iii. 163–4.

[90] *Examina*, pp. 405–7; cf. the impression of more random denunciation arising from Cavalcanti's account, *Istorie*, Bk. I.

general express attitudes which we have seen to be representative of the differing views of each of the parties. For example, the writer of one deposition addressed himself directly to Rinaldo degli Albizzi, then one of the *Conservatori*, ending his denunciation of Fruosino da Verazzano with the observation that 'Messer Rinaldo didn't want to know anything about this, because he was a friend of his, and to tell the truth, Messer Rinaldo wanted to do as his father had done in 1393, and carry out all his own vendettas, and he wanted to do this by means of this office'.[91]

On the other hand, an accusation against the Salvetti brothers concluded that 'you have here three brothers who have agreed to strive to occupy the offices appropriate to old-established citizens . . . conspirators, who have arranged to usurp offices rightly accorded to you. For your honour and the good of our republic, you should curb (rafrenate) such ambition a little.' Also notable among the early charges was that against Bernardo Canigiani, of belonging to 'the gang that runs to the Medici and their crowd'.[92] Indeed the fact that the law was proposed as a solution to the growth of factions by prominent anti-Mediceans using arguments similar to those reputedly adopted by the conservatives since 1426, suggests rather that it may originally have been aimed more specifically against the Medici; this impression is certainly reinforced by the nature of the charges against them and their friends when in 1433 the conservatives did temporarily succeed in putting an end to factionalism by means of exile.

Buoninsegni briefly ascribed the expulsion of Cosimo to previous 'alterations in the scrutinies and in the purses'; notably, late in 1428 and early in 1429 citizens like the anti-Mediceans Ridolfo Peruzzi and Francesco Bucelli, and the non-partisans Giovanni Morelli and Lippozzo Mangioni, were deploring in the *Consulte* the abandonment of sortition for some offices, and favouring scrutiny practices which would preserve the political ascendancy of those who already 'had the state'.[93] The official condemnation of the Medici contained the injunction that it was necessary for 'citizens who wish to live in liberty to make themselves equal, so that no one should occupy a more important place than anyone

[91] Misc. Rep. 117, ff. 28r, 30v.
[92] Giud. Appelli 75, f. 495r, 21 May 1429, cited Brucker, *The Civic World*, p. 492.
[93] Ibid.

else, nor should anyone shine out on account of receiving so many high offices in the republic', and referred to the Medici as 'citizens who are disturbers of their native city, destroyers of the state, and sowers of scandal'.[94] Apart from a reference to the Salvestro episode in 1378,[95] it was claimed that as early as 1426 the leaders of the family, 'continuing in the audacity of their ancestors', had armed themselves in preparation for a rebellion against the *Signoria*, and that in this Cosimo 'made his partners mostly citizens from the ruling group of the city itself, they being won over by the hope of a better life, and the highest honours he handed out to others of his family'. The Pucci were described as being 'not satisfied with the friendly warnings given them . . . going round by day and by night all over the city, maligning, inciting the people to rebellion, sowing scandal to cause unrest in the city'. Specifically, and possibly in respect of the scrutinies of 1427, 'the said Puccio, who was one of those who were privy to the secret of the scrutiny, revealed many things to create sedition and to open the door to scandal, though only his followers throughout the city supported him'.[96] In addition to these official charges, there is an interesting entry in the personal *Ricordi* of Terrino Manovelli, a leader of the conservative and aristocratic group who was subsequently exiled in 1434. His description of the exiles of 1433 has been scored out, apparently by himself, with thick black strokes of the pen; possibly he became alarmed at the rapid reversal of the situation in the early days of September 1434 and, in anticipation of a Medici return, wished to destroy any concrete evidence incriminating himself as one of their opponents. However, it is possible to make out a few phrases, and to see that he began to explain that the Medici were banished 'for their arrogance and the dishonest methods which they employed together with their party'. The Pucci he described as 'always more preferred than they ought to have been' and of doing 'things inappropriate to their powers'.[97]

As the year 1429 went on, a growing consciousness of the practical implications of the unchecked spread of factionalism is

[94] Fabroni, *Cosmi vita* ii. 75–6; cf. Cap. Pop. Lib. Inquis. 3175, f. 63r.

[95] Salvestro de' Medici played a prominent part in the popular revolution of that year; see Brucker, *Florentine Politics*, esp. pp. 363–6.

[96] Acqu. e Doni 301, Ins. I.

[97] C.S. 2ª ser. XIV, f. 3v. It is impossible to read any further, even with the help of an ultra-violet lamp.

apparent in the more specific content of speeches in the *Consulte*, which reflected increasingly the old fear of interference with the purses, and raised the new spectre of exile. On 29 September Messer Lorenzo Ridolfi was the spokesman for a dozen or so citizens who felt that despite the fear of plague in the city, the scrutiny should be held as planned, but that 'afterwards precautions should be taken to allay any suspicion that anyone might entertain, although he ought not, that someone might touch the purses in any way once they had been prepared'. A proposal to increase the number of votes needed within the *Signoria* to declare a citizen *confinato* had also been brought forward for consideration; clearly the fear that conflict within the *reggimento* might possibly end in the exile of some of its members was beginning to take shape in their minds.[98] In February of the following year Lippozzo Mangioni betrayed the growing apprehension of confrontation in his expression of the hope that 'if justice is done, no one need fear confinement or exile, but on account of the existence of factions, everyone will be defiled and we will all lose our good names'.[99] Some months later Schiatta Ridolfi revealed that his mind had been working along the same lines, in the opinion that 'as it will hardly be possible to dispose of the entire citizen body by means of exile or dispersing them on embassies it is much better rather at this point to hold on to the citizens and gradually to demand of them whatever is possible'.[100]

By 21 November 1429, shortly before the declaration of war with Lucca, certain members of the ruling group felt impelled to speak more plainly, as in the assertion 'that every man, those of great, of small, and of middling rank, should be content with his limitations and live peacefully'.[101] The emphasis on the conservation of the *status quo*, and the quashing of private ambition for social and political advancement, suggests that by this time the aristocrats and conservatives were becoming increasingly willing to show their teeth. The majority of those present at this meeting were members of the exile group, or at least well-known conservatives, while the Mediceans were comparatively poorly represented. It was proposed that a group of citizens should be elected to write down the names, 'in accordance with their conscience',

---

[98] C.P. 48, f. 89v.   [99] Ibid. 49, f. 124v, 21 Feb. 1431 (1430 *s.f.*).
[100] Ibid., f. 169v, 3 July 1431.
[101] Ibid. 48, ff. 106r–107r.

of anyone whom they considered 'as behaving in a scandalous manner or doing anything against the interests of the present regime'. On 24 November the proposal for the election of a group to identify and denounce the *Scandalosos* was reiterated, and the same two major themes were uppermost; that no one should seek 'to be equal or wish to be greater than the *Signoria* . . . but that every man accept his reasonable limitations'.[102] Again on 26 November action was urged on the leaders of the *reggimento* to seek out anyone who 'was not content with his prospects and to live virtuously and honestly'; this time the proposals aroused strong echoes of the words of the author of the verses and the speaker at Santo Stefano. They suggested that 'we should legislate to give full authority to a *Balìa*, as was done in 1372, to a group who were called the fifty-six . . . to get rid of factions and divisions and to restrain and bridle the audacity and might of anyone who should wish to be greater than he ought . . .' Notably the social implications of the desiderata had subtly changed; not only should no one attempt to be greater than the *Signoria*, but neither should anyone entertain aspirations 'beyond his station', which sounds very like an aristocratic prescription directed against the lower strata of the ruling group. The signatories to this proposition did not in fact include a single Medicean partisan; the names are all those of well-known conservative or exile families like the Bucelli, Brancacci, Corsini, Solosmei, Fagni, Manovelli, and Baroncelli.[103]

Finally, on 19 December, the law was passed under the name of *Lex contra Scandalosos*,

to restrain the pride of the great which requires to be subdued and checked, so that no one either relying upon his own judgement or actions, or by trusting in kinship, neighbourhood, patronage, or partisanship, should dare to cause any disturbance to the peace and tranquillity of the city.[104]

In framing the law its promotors boasted that they were 'imitating the practice of the most skilful and careful physicians (*medici*)'. The analogy between the body politic and the human body is a commonplace of medieval political discourse, but nevertheless one wonders whether on this occasion the reference to 'medici' was not a bold hint at a more immediate and explicit preoccupation.

[102] Ibid., f. 108r.   [103] Ibid., f. 112r.
[104] Guasti, *Commissioni* iii. 170–2.

However, the most public acknowledgement of the existence of two major factions of the Mediceans and their opponents, and the clearest indication of their personnel and the issues which they represented, is to be found in a *Pratica* of 16 April 1430,[105] which stands at the very end of the lengthy and difficult discussion on unity held throughout 1429, and took place at a time when the customary practice in the *Pratiche* of restricting the expression of grievances to innuendo and implication may have been beginning to break down under the strain of conflicts greatly exacerbated by the war with Lucca, now in its fifth disastrous month. The first speaker was again Lorenzo Ridolfi, who contented himself simply with praising the *Signoria* 'for introducing the problem of concord which is vital to the preservation of the city', and with asserting that 'the way to solve it, nevertheless . . . is for every single citizen to open his own heart'. Indeed, some of them did; Rinaldo degli Albizzi swiftly acknowledged the real dimensions of the problem by pointing out that none of the measures previously proposed had been effective in stamping out the *sette*, and now 'it is said that almost all citizens are embroiled in this division'. Possibly in the same spirit Filippo di Biagio Guasconi, later supported by Giovanni di Rinaldo Gianfigliazzi, recommended

that anyone who belongs to a society should have his name inscribed in a book and he should be excluded from offices (*divieto*). Those societies or factions have been the cause of divisions, and many unjust things have been done by them; now other citizens perceive themselves to be in the same boat, and thus do not wish to discuss the matter further . . . the *Signoria* should see that the wicked and the guilty are punished.

Palla Strozzi voiced a characteristic plea 'that everyone should resolve to desire the well-being and tranquillity of his city'; his friend Messer Giuliano Davanzati agreed.

However, a rather different note was struck by Niccolò da Uzzano, who brought up the familiar issue of the distribution of offices.

That which disturbs the city is seeing some enjoying greater honours than is appropriate, and others in the leading positions. The first thing is that justice should be done, and the honours should be distributed according to the virtues and merits of families and their relatives.

[105] C.P. 49, ff. 32v–35r.

Reverence for the Priors should restrain the more powerful within limits, and the weaker should be supported. If anyone is greater than the *Signoria*, then all is not well.

This is in fact a clear statement of the aristocratic view of the right distribution of power in the city and within the *reggimento*; it closely resembles the similar statements made in the verses attributed to Niccolò da Uzzano, in the speech at Santo Stefano, and in a *Pratica* of the same month by a future exile, Luigi Aldobrandini, who expressed the conservative ideal that the greater houses should be the more heavily represented.[106] Once the discussion had taken this turn other leading conservatives, many of them soon to be exiles, were encouraged to enlarge upon their grievances in this area, against an opposition which was obviously not the comparatively abstract group to which speakers in earlier *Pratiche* had referred, but a clearly envisaged body of particular citizens whom they wished to see exposed and expelled; the content of their allegations provides some reason to identify this body with the Medici party.

Niccolò Bellacci favoured coercion by authority to maintain control of the electoral processes, suggesting that the Priors

should provide that citizens remain happy within their limitations . . . And the electors should go to their own districts for elections so that they can be recognized, and established as being experienced and of mature age.

Later Andrea del Palagio, in referring to the problem, spoke pointedly in the singular, and chose to introduce the controversial issue of responsibility for the war:

If you seek a remedy, it is necessary to uncover the ailments. The faction arose partly to defame worthy citizens, and to allow nobody to speak out but its satellites, and to appropriate offices unlawfully; so that their wishes would be fulfilled, they brought about war and involved the community in expense and danger.[107]

Niccolò di Gentile degli Albizzi also maintained that 'many undeserving citizens believe themselves to be worthy of offices', while Antonio della Casa pursued the point that the matter should be brought right out into the open with the insistence that 'the *Signoria* knows who these men are, who want to be greater than the Priors, allotting honours, and engaging in wars'. Ser Paolo di Ser Lando Fortini agreed, and Felice Brancacci went on to elaborate on this theme: 'Things which are done in a private capacity by the factions and associations should be restored to the public sphere, and that is the way to correct things.'

The practical solution suggested by Mariotto Baldovinetti was the revival of the practice of *ammonizione,* which had proved such a powerful weapon in the previous century in the hands of the conservative *Parte Guelfa,* bent upon the arbitrary and unchallenged elimination of political opponents.[108] And indeed, in the last great conservative broadside of the day Andrea di Vieri Rondinelli proposed plainly that directive authority should be removed from the purview of the people; the Priors and selected others should create the *Dieci di Balìa,* the *Ufficiali del Banco,* and other offices, 'and then we will see what sort of men will be elected'. Twelve of the speakers who expressed views in the spirit of those summarized above were exiled or *privati* in 1434, or else escaped certain proscription only because they died before that date. Of the 27 citizens who spoke at the meeting, 17 were arch-conservatives or men of markedly aristocratic inclinations; 9 were partisans of the Medici, or their immediate relatives. If the former were in fact engaging in a frontal attack on their enemies, the latter would appear to have adopted the defensive strategy of a taciturn refusal to give anything away; their contributions were brief and conventional. Cosimo himself was the last of the Mediceans to speak, and he too concurred simply that a *Pratica* should be arranged, and some solution found.[109]

Perhaps the most revealing proposal of the day was made by Dino Gucci, who in a meeting of the *Signoria* and its colleges clearly implied that, as the conservatives had suggested, the identity of the partisans within the *reggimento* was indeed well known to the Priors; Gucci recommended that the *Pratica* summoned by the *Signoria* to consider the question of civic unity should consist of twenty-four citizens, 'twelve of whom should not be partisan in any sense, and the other half comprising partisans, in

---

[108] See Brucker, *Florentine Politics,* esp. pp. 170–2.

[109] The report of his speech concludes with the sentence: 'Denique remisit, et remissionem petiit.' The possible implication of this unusual request, that Cosimo proposed either that the meeting disperse or that he be permitted to leave, is an intriguing one.

equal numbers from each faction . . .'[110] However, even such a radical attempt to disarm the factions by according them official recognition and a measure of representation was bound to be too limited and too late. The anti-faction measures of the late twenties and early thirties, initially instigated essentially by the aristocratic group within the *reggimento* in response to a challenge to the *status quo*, had failed; the catalyst of war precipitated not conciliation, but open confrontation between those dissatisfied with the role allotted them in the prevailing regime, and those committed to its preservation.

[110] C.P. 48, f. 32r; quoted Brucker, *The Civic World*, p. 500. The transcript of this committee meeting precedes that of the general audience of citizens on the same day; however, both would have been later compilations from rough notes taken during the discussions, and meetings of the *Signoria* and colleges usually served to summarize and consolidate previous general sessions.

4

The Impact of War

(1429–1433)

B Y the end of 1429 the attitudes and personnel of the two major parties within the Florentine ruling group were already comparatively clearly defined, and the antagonism between them becoming increasingly overt. The outbreak in December of war between Florence and Lucca had important, if ambiguous effects on the development of the partisan divisions which we have traced so far. The ambiguity arose essentially from the conflicting pressures on leading patricians of public loyalties and service on the one hand, and private needs and obligations on the other. This was, as we have observed, a tension always present in Florentine society, but it was greatly exacerbated under wartime conditions.[1]

A considerable proportion of the more eminent members of the *reggimento*, including most of the actual or potential partisan leaders, took an active part in the direction of the enterprise, and their common concern to bring it to a successful conclusion tended to underline the similarities of attitude between them. The cumbersome administrative machinery and the frequent financial crises which hampered their activities united citizens of intelligence and ability in impatience with incompetence and inefficiency, whatever its source. Moreover, as the Florentine position deteriorated, it became clear to responsible citizens that a degree of co-operation was needed even to ensure survival; this consideration became increasingly paramount as the war dragged on, and the Florentine pose altered from the offensive one in which it was undertaken, to the defensive one in which its last years were waged. Their leaders' awareness of the need to refrain from making full political capital out of issues connected with the security of the commune probably served to postpone the open

---

[1] Above, pp. 19–24.

confrontation between the two major parties which might have seemed likely to occur at any time between 1426 and 1429.

The direct responsibility of so many citizens for the conduct of the war encouraged the tendency of Florentine patricians to equate personal honour and advantage with the good of the commune, and certainly the most prominent members of the *reggimento* had a political and financial stake in the state so substantial that their private interest was inevitably closely involved with the public welfare. However, the sheer scale of the operations demanded a co-operation which was even more impossible of achievement amidst the exigencies of war than it had been in peacetime; where inevitably it failed, mutual responsibility being intolerable, the defence of personal honour became the chief consideration. With the multiplication of offices and responsibilities, and the opportunities to gain—and lose—the 'honour and profit' (*onore e utile*)[2] for which citizens competed so strenuously, the need to protect the private interests of self, family, and friends became increasingly pressing. In this sense the war increased the virulence of factions; tensions between citizens became almost unbearable as each sought to defend himself by defaming and discrediting his fellows. Denunciations poured in to the *Conservatori delle Leggi*, and the air hummed with accusations and countercharges. While some were dismissed as malicious gossip, others became the subject of concern even in the councils and in the gatherings of the *richiesti*, where there was constant concern about disunity, mutual jealousies, and dissension between members of the ruling group.[3]

The explicit tension between public and private interest is clearly articulated in the letters of Rinaldo degli Albizzi and in those of the Medici and their friends, which enable us to explore in some detail the developing relationship between the leading protagonists of the crises of 1433 and 1434, and to attempt some assessment of the activities of the Medici party in this period.

[2] Honour and profit were seen as the major benefits accruing from the holding of public office; see, e.g., M.A.P. II, 171; cf. C.S. 3ᵃ ser. CXIV, c. 32; also above, pp. 242, 249–50; below, pp. 280–1. These questions of honour could be exceedingly subtle and complex; Guidetto Monaldi wrote to Averardo (M.A.P. II, 199, 10 Feb. 1430; 1429 *s.f.*), begging him that having once obtained the command of a galley for Ormanno degli Albizzi, he should ensure that the second-in-command was also suitable, 'che dubita non gli fosse tolto el veglio per via indiretta'; cf. below, pp. 267–8, 270–1.

[3] Above, pp. 244–5.

Unfortunately, we know almost nothing of the progress of the hard core of the aristocratic alliance during these years, but it is clear that Rinaldo, its future leader, having initially been drawn to the Medici by a shared concern for the good of the commune and respect for common sense and ability, was eventually and inevitably alienated by the threat which increasingly they posed to his own precarious pre-eminence. The Medici response to the conflicting pressures of this period is more complex and their role in events much less clear-cut; the abundant evidence is difficult to interpret, and not simply because of the proliferation of ciphers to ensure official secrecy.[4] Not only were the partisan conflicts of previous years rendered in fact more complicated by the ambiguous effects of war; their manifestations become far more difficult to distinguish on the one hand from the myriad petty dissensions and enmities in which 'almost every man constituted a party in himself',[5] and on the other from more disinterested differences of principle and judgement concerning the conduct of the war.

In the section of his confessions dealing with these years Ser Niccolò Tinucci accused the Medici and their friends of conspiring to provoke and then to prolong the war as part of their plan for political self-advancement, with the explicit intention of enriching themselves and ruining their enemies. To this end they exploited their friendships with the *condottieri*, manœuvred themselves and their friends into positions of authority, and then slandered their fellow patricians in office. Similar charges were incorporated into the denunciation of the family at the time of the expulsion in 1433.

As we have seen that the Medici letters themselves offer substantial support for Tinucci's account of their ambitions and activities in earlier years, his allegations cannot be lightly dismissed. Once again his claims appear generally plausible in the light of the known facts of the situation, and they probably

---

[4] Both Guasti and Pellegrini made various attempts to decode the ciphers of the letters which they published, but were not able to establish with certainty the identity of more than a handful of persons. See Pellegrini, *Sulla repubblica* clxxxii; Guasti, *Commissioni* iii, notes *passim*. Even if letters were not written in code their meaning was often obscured by an intentionally allusive style and the habitual use of private names for people and places.

[5] Pellegrini, *Sulla repubblica*, p. 74. His own excellent account of this period effectively demonstrates his point.

contain specific elements of truth. However, the attitudes which
emerge from the correspondence of this period epitomize the
ambivalent regard for the claims of public versus private interest
which was characteristic of the ruling group in general, and while
the picture which they reveal is unclear in many details it is
infinitely more subtle in tone than Tinucci's and quite different
in its total impact.

Nevertheless, two things are plain. Whatever their motives,
the Medici and their friends during these years devoted much of
their formidable energies and resources to the service of the
commune, and appear to have co-operated successfully, if superficially, with a wide range of other citizens who did likewise. At
the same time, they contrived to advance the interests of the
amici within the *reggimento*; indeed the greater part of the evidence
concerning their partisans belongs to this period, and suffices to
demonstrate that the conflict between Mediceans and their opponents continued as perhaps the most constant element beneath
the troubled and shifting surface of alignments and enmities
between members of the ruling group. When, after the signing
of the peace, the parties began to move rapidly towards a decisive
confrontation, it became apparent that perhaps the major effect
of the war on their struggle had been to alter the balance of power
between them. The conservatives, while having gained little
positive ground, had lost the benefit of the moderating and stabi-
lizing influence of Niccolò da Uzzano, who had died early in
1432; they were now chiefly reliant on the leadership of the quix-
otic Rinaldo degli Albizzi, whose comparative alienation from his
fellow patricians had only been increased by the disillusioning
and embittering experiences of the previous years. The Mediceans, however, had profited from events, and emerged from this
period with the authority of their leaders confirmed and enhanced
by their role in the direction of the war, and more importantly,
by the revelation of the extent to which the city now depended
on Medicean financial support.

The war with Lucca began in December 1429 and lasted until
April 1433. The issues over which ostensibly it was waged were
on the one side the Lucchese failure to satisfy an old debt with
Florence, and on the other the violation of Lucchese territory in
mid-November by the *condottiere* Niccolò Fortebracci, at the promp-

ting, claimed the Lucchese, of Florentine citizens.[6] Later, when
the disastrous effects of the war on the Florentine commune had
become clearly apparent, it was rumoured also in Florence that
Fortebracci had been encouraged by his intimate friend Neri
Capponi, or by the Medici and their friends. Even Tinucci
absolved the Medici of responsibility for Fortebracci's expedition,
but he did accuse them of exploiting the situation it created;
having seen 'the way open to effect their designs, they took advantage of the opportunity to foster the enterprise . . .'[7] However,
in September 1433, Cosimo and Averardo were officially charged
with having conspired 'to induce the people of Florence to enter
into a war with the Lucchese, which was almost the ruin, not only
of the Florentine Republic, but of the condition of all Italy'.[8]

The reference here to the unfortunate outcome of the war
betrays the general tendency later to impute responsibility for its
initiation in the light of its subsequent effects, chief of which
were on the one hand the grave threat to the Florentine economy
and the stability of its ruling group, and on the other the obviously
unforeseen aggrandizement of the Medici as leading financiers to
the state. Once the futility and foolishness of the undertaking
became apparent, many citizens were naturally eager to dissociate
themselves from it, and the retrospective evasions of those who
had unwisely advocated war help to obfuscate the truth about
their attitudes at the time.

As far as the charge of conspiracy with Fortebracci is concerned,
a number of Florence's leading citizens were, by virtue of their
years of service as military commissioners and diplomats for the
Florentine state, and their personal and financial associations
outside it, on intimate terms with various *condottieri*;[9] any one of
them may well have encouraged Fortebracci to provoke an
incident in the hope that it would lead to war. However, in the
absence of any evidence on this question, there is no reason to
assume either that this was so, or that the Medici in particular
were responsible. In any case, the effect of Fortebracci's action

[6] For a contemporary narrative of the war, see Buoninsegni, *Storie*, pp. 31-46;
cf. Bayley, *War and Society*, Introduction.

[7] *Examina*, p. 403,

[8] Fabroni, *Cosmi vita* i. 76; cf. Rinuccini's observation, *Ricordi storici*, p. 63, that
the war 'fu quasi la ruina di questa terra'.

[9] See Bayley, Introduction, I, and the wartime letters of both the Medici and
Rinaldo degli Albizzi.

depended essentially on the subsequent response of the Florentine government to the diplomatic situation which it created.

The only reliable evidence concerning this reaction is that of the *Consulte* in which the leading citizens of the *reggimento* debated their response to the Lucchese gestures of conciliation between October and December; these suggest that the decision to declare war on Lucca represented the wishes of the majority of the Florentine *reggimento* at the time. During October and November most citizens were prepared to accept the advances of the Lucchese ambassadors for peace, and several even suggested that the Florentine *Signoria* should apologize to the government at Lucca and send a reprimand to Fortebracci.[10] But at the beginning of December the temper of the *reggimento* suddenly changed. Aggressive action was demanded by a whole cross-section of the ruling group, including conservatives like Manetto Scambrilla and Giovanni Gianfigliazzi, citizens who like Carlo Federighi were not apparently aligned with either party, and Mediceans like Giuliano Davanzati and Ser Martino Martini.[11] It was not in fact true, as Cavalcanti suggested, that 'all those of Da Uzzano's party opposed the war';[12] in so far as there were parties of war and peace, these did not really correspond to those of the Mediceans and the conservatives, but were apparently determined by differences of personal and political temperament.[13]

The latter faction particularly, being a disparate group, embraced a variety of styles and attitudes, though it should be noted that a significant number of conservatives were opposed to war from the beginning. Both Palla Strozzi and Giovanni Guicciardini appear to have been essentially honest and principled men who sincerely believed that the war was unjust. It is perhaps notable that Niccolò da Uzzano took no part at all in the discussions, and that another prominent anti-Medicean, Felice di Michele Brancacci, argued that right was entirely on the side of the Lucchese.[14]

---

[10] e.g. Antonio da Rabatta, C.P. 48, ff. 110r–111v, 25 Nov. 1429; cf. ibid., ff. 91r–92r, 92v, 93r–94r, 112v.

[11] See the discussion of 1 Dec. 1429 (C.P. 48, ff. 114r–117r); also 117v–118v (2 Dec.); 119r–120v (3 Dec.); 124v–125v (7 Dec.); 126v (8 Dec.); 126v–129r (9 Dec.).

[12] *Istorie*, p. 164, cf. p. 259.

[13] As Gelli, 'L'esilio' 75, observes, the differences of opinion in the *Consulte e Pratiche* over foreign affairs are so great that it is 'impossibile determinare da quali sentimenti fossero governate le parti'.

[14] C.P. 48, ff. 114r–115r, 1 Dec.

The stance of the more highly centralized Medicean party is perhaps more difficult to gauge; although Averardo and Cosimo were also absent from the councils in which the decision was taken, their friend Ser Martino Martini was among the more prominent promoters of the enterprise, and may have been acting on their behalf.[15] Conversely, Piero Guicciardini, an intimate of the Medici family, wrote home to his friend Matteo Strozzi that Lorenzo de' Medici when in Venice had remarked on the controversy in the *Consulte* over the issue, while observing that the war 'had not found favour with either them or their friends'.[16]

Certainly the outstanding advocates of aggression against Lucca were Neri Capponi and Rinaldo degli Albizzi, neither of whom were at this time inevitably identified with support or opposition to the Medici, but who were later to emerge in the van of opposing parties. Although in his *Commentaries* of 1440 Neri disclaimed all responsibility for the Lucchese war, his account there is flatly contradicted by the record in the *Consulte* of his opinion that 'we should waste no time, but proceed immediately to overthrow their government'.[17] Rinaldo also committed himself whole-heartedly to the contest, and even succeeded in time-honoured Florentine fashion, in transforming it into an issue of principle rather than one of pragmatic advantage. As he exhorted his fellow citizens : 'We must go forth boldly against the tyrant, and if we are obliged to come to a settlement with him, it should be discussed and concluded on the battlements of Lucca.'[18] More honest, perhaps, than Capponi, or enabled, perhaps, to be so more easily in the comparative privacy of his personal correspondence with his own son, Rinaldo later admitted, at least to himself, that after two months the war seemed to him likely to do great harm to the commune, and that those who had favoured it

[15] Ibid., ff. 124v (7 Dec.): 126v (8 Dec.); 131r (14 Dec.).

[16] C.S. 3ª ser. CXII, 38, Piero Guicciardini in Venice to Matteo Strozzi, 7 Dec. 1430. I should like to thank Professor Gene Brucker for bringing this comment to my attention.

[17] C.P. 48, f. 115r; *Commentarii*, col. 1166. See also Cavalcanti's declaration that the four citizens who swayed the ruling class into accepting the war were Albizzi, Capponi, Martini, and Averardo de' Medici. The first three appear as prominent advocates of belligerence in the transcripts of the *Consulte*; the latter did not, whatever attitudes he may privately have expressed or implied.

[18] C.P. 48, f. 128v (8 Dec.). He had also been prominent in earlier *Pratiche* and was later to defend his position with the argument that it had been a war undertaken for the sake of liberty (C.P. 49, f. 42v).

might have to bear the burden of blame.[19] Cosimo, in a characteristically perceptive and tough-minded statement of the issue in
rather similar circumstances some seven months later, turned
this proposition on its head in pointing out in a letter to Averardo
that those in fact to blame were those who opposed the war at the
time when it could have been easily won, 'and may God forgive
those who were responsible for this'. Nevertheless, their respec-
tive observations demonstrate a certain fundamental similarity
of outlook,[20] and make the claims that either or both prolonged
the war for personal advantage seem rather implausible.

The comments of the *richiesti* to the *Consulte* make it clear that
the leading citizens of Florence were generally willing to seize
on the flimsiest pretext for aggression in the hope of profiting
thereby. As Giovanni di Iacopo Morelli observed: 'You create
war, you lead us into war, you suckle those nourished by war.
Florence has never been without war, and she never will be, until
you cut off the heads of four of your leading citizens every year.'
According to his account, when the issue of war was raised in the
Consulte, 'there were some citizens giving their opinions on the
rostrum who greatly favoured a yes vote, and those who advised
a no were not permitted to speak for coughing and clearing of
throats, for stamping and clapping'.[21] War was declared, and
turned out to be a disaster of which the Medici were perhaps
almost the sole benefactors; in the circumstances, it seems emi-
nently possible that the subsequent accusations against them were
made essentially in an attempt to foist the blame upon the ideal
scapegoats for the mistaken ambitions of the entire ruling group.

If the Medici share in the responsibility for involving Florence
in the war is doubtful, they took, along with Rinaldo and Neri
Capponi, a leading part in its direction from the very beginning.
In the *Dieci* elected on 10 December to conduct operations, the
Santo Spirito contingent consisted of Neri di Gino himself, one
of the Bardi, who had always been quite closely associated with
the Capponi in Santo Spirito, and Arrigo di Corso, a shoemaker
who was a faithful follower and *amico* of Neri Capponi. Santa

[19] *Commissioni* iii. 347, 4 Feb. 1430 (1429 *s.f.*).

[20] 4 Sept. 1430, published Pellegrini, *Sulla repubblica* xviii; cf. Rinaldo's argument,
C.P. 45, f. 114r, that 'maius periculum est in mora, et nihil agendo, quam in faciendo'.

[21] *Ricordi*, pp. 73, 86; cf. C.P. 49, f. 39v, 4 May 1430, Lippozzo Mangioni:
'Quando imprehensa Luce facta fuit, illam negantes non intelligebantur, quia tussis
aliorum impediabat.'

Croce was represented by another of Neri's *amici*, Andreuolo di Nicola di Franco Sacchetti, and by Alamanno Salviati, Averardo de' Medici's son-in-law. From Santa Maria Novella came Carlo di Francesco Federighi and Bartolomeo Carducci, the latter also a Medici friend. The San Giovanni contingent was entirely pro-Medicean, and consisted of three Medici *amici*, Ser Martino di Luca Martini, Giovanni di Lorenzo della Stufa, and Giovanni d'Antonio Pucci.[22] This was the group from whom Rinaldo degli Albizzi had to take his directions when he and Astore Gianni were appointed first commissioners at the Florentine camp.

It is fortunate that Rinaldo's correspondence with the *Dieci* and other leading citizens during his period of office has survived; less fortunate that his letters illuminate only the first three months of the war from December 1429 to March 1430. These letters reveal how disorganized was the war effort from its earliest stages, and how divided the ruling group which directed it. In them we can trace Rinaldo's increasing alienation from the *Dieci*, and to some extent from the groups which they represented, although it is clear that at this time the Medici themselves and some of their closest friends were united with Rinaldo at least in their desire to see Florence win the war, and prepared to co-operate with him to bring about this end. These latest surviving letters of the man who was to lead the conservative opposition to the Medici through the upheavals of 1433 and 1434 by far predate his open breach with them, but they do help us to understand it more clearly by what they reveal of Rinaldo degli Albizzi's view of his own role in Florentine political life. It is this revelation which suggests the explanation of his subsequent behaviour, and may bridge the gap between the Rinaldo of early 1430 who sought the aid of Cosimo and Averardo to preserve his family's honour, and the Rinaldo of September 1433 who banished them to maintain it.

By the last week of December 1429 it was clear that Rinaldo was becoming dissatisfied with the *Dieci*'s management of the war. On 21 December he and Astore Gianni wrote pointing out that Niccolò Fortebracci would never win the war for them while his attacks were so ill planned.[23] By 27 December, however, Rinaldo was writing alone, complaining about the departure of

[22] See the list in Buoninsegni, *Storie*, p. 33.   [23] *Commissioni* iii. 222.

Gianni which they had ordered, 'because one is much happier about making decisions when two minds are of the same opinion than when one man has to take the judgement entirely upon himself . . . and from my point of view, I have lost a good companion'. There is a hint of criticism in his suggestion that they themselves should act more rapidly, 'because one hour can be worth a thousand in this business',[24] a hint which sharpened to open irritation when the *Dieci* demanded a fortnight later that he should stop Fortebracci from sacking the entire country without at the same time dampening his zeal for the acquisition of territory. 'I am doing and will continue to do whatever is humanly possible,' he replied, 'and I am bound to do no more.'[25]

This mutual dissatisfaction, probably in reality due to the intrinsic impossibility of satisfactorily conducting a war by remote control and under divided command, soon resolved itself into a question of honour, by which all future communications were to be inevitably complicated. By 11 January Rinaldo was begging the *Dieci* to send him reinforcements and precise instructions which he could carry out to the letter, 'to justify myself before God and the world in any event'; meanwhile, he firmly disclaimed responsibility by maintaining that 'I am risking my person, and you, your honour'.[26] They refused to allow him to dissociate himself thus, and replied, with some derision, that 'these matters concern the reputation of the Commune and of ourselves, and yours as well'. They ordered him on pain of death not to leave the camp, 'even if the heavens and the earth and the whole world . . . should threaten to fall'.[27] Rinaldo was mortally offended, and answered haughtily that their threats of punishment 'might be necessary to those who were compelled to serve, or did so out of fear; but my devotion arises rather out of love and duty to my native city than from fear of any penalty'.[28]

Towards the middle of January Rinaldo once again reported that Fortebracci was proving hard to handle; he requested advice from the *Dieci* as the commanding body. Particularly in view of their customary insistence on absolute adherence to their instructions by commissioners in the field, their reply to him does indeed seem not only unreasonable but deliberately and provocatively insulting. They began with a back-handed compliment; he

---

[24] *Commissioni* iii. 241–2. [25] Ibid. 273–4. [26] Ibid. 286.
[27] Ibid. 288–9. [28] Ibid. 292.

had been chosen to go to the camp because they had judged him
to be

a man of such unique ability and boldness of spirit that there is no one
to compare with you, not only in Florence but in all Tuscany. And
therefore they consider that far from your being troubled by the
necessity of writing to a *condottiere* who is nothing but a paid, or rather
an overpaid hireling, you who are bold enough willingly to turn up
your nose at popes and emperors, that when you perceive something
to be the cause of such harm and shame as this has been to the Commune, and to our magistracy, and to you, you should not merely have
written to him, but rather have sent him packing.[29]

Rinaldo replied with comparative dignity and forbearance; he
repeated his opinion that it was better to handle the situation with
care and tact than so abruptly as they suggested. But it was clear
that the *Dieci* had now alienated him completely, and he concluded
bitterly: 'You speak of my ability and spirit, etc. I can put up
with your giving me a thorough going-over and kicking me
when I'm down. Be that as it may; but if I had half as much virtue
as God has given me courage, I should consider myself a very
fine man.[30]

At the same time as he felt his authority challenged and his
honour impugned by the *Dieci*, Rinaldo was attacked on another
flank; news was reaching him from Florence of 'the serpents'
tongues' spreading malicious gossip about him there.[31] The
Dieci do appear to have recognized this problem and tried, at
least ostensibly, to do something about it. As they had informed
his son Ormanno,

in order to vindicate his honour, and to cut the ground from under the
feet of those who speak ill of him, they had gone before the *Signoria*
and the Colleges, and sought not only to cleanse him of all the charges
against him, but also to punish severely anyone who should slander
him unjustly.[32]

However, Rinaldo had been deeply offended by their own treatment of him, and now saw their response to this problem as an
offence in itself:

You claim, my Lords, to have written to me and issued such harsh
commands in order to vindicate my honour, etc. My Lords, I do not
believe that I have done anything for which I need to be defended, and

[29] Ibid. 304–5.   [30] Ibid. 306–7.   [31] Ibid. 297.   [32] Ibid. 311.

in any case I trust I am able to justify myself, and if by God's will I may return home, I hope I know how to demonstrate the truth to any man, which will be enough for me.[33]

His own impulses were reinforced by the advice of his *amici* and *parenti*; in a letter of 4 February he discussed with Ormanno the opinion of Ser Martino Martini and 'the rest of our friends' that he should return to Florence to repair his position there, and wondered if 'perhaps passions there aren't rather more inflamed than I thought'. His own feeling was that he ought not to leave the camp, 'since things there are looking more hopeful', but he admitted that 'however, I wouldn't want to lose the substance for the shadow, and I ought not to value Lucca above Florence'.[34] But as the war situation became more desperate, the *Dieci* had become more determined that Rinaldo should remain until the situation improved. They replied to his applications for a licence to return with predictions of disaster:

To be absolutely frank with you, if you leave there without succeeding, in view of the way the people are talking, and the temper of those who are urging them on, we can consider our magistracy as good as finished, and we will return to our houses, and you to Florence, not in a blare of trumpets, but to the accompaniment of the jeers and shouts of youths, and perhaps worse.[35]

So Rinaldo remained, but grew increasingly sensitive concerning his own position and reputation, which seemed to be constantly under threat from every new development in this unpromising situation. He was temporarily heartened by the arrival at the camp of Neri di Gino Capponi, which, he told the *Dieci*, 'pleased me very greatly, because he saw at first hand the dangers and disorder of this camp and the causes of its deficiencies'.[36] On 18 February he received advice that another of the *Dieci*, Alamanno Salviati, would be joining them soon.[37] On 20 February he wrote again asking permission to return to Florence immediately, as there was no longer any point in his remaining at the camp now that Capponi and Salviati were there.[38] However, permission was not forthcoming, and his initial pleasure at their arrival seems rapidly to have faded with the dawning realization that they had apparently been sent to investigate and to silence the rumours

---

[33] *Commissioni* iii. 312.   [34] Ibid. 347, cf. 405–6.   [35] Ibid. 294.
[36] Ibid. 302.   [37] Ibid. 310.   [38] Ibid. 312.

spreading in Florence concerning his own malconduct of the camp.[39]

On 22 January the *Dieci* attempted to soothe him by claiming that Capponi and Salviati were there on account of similar rumours which had been circulating concerning Astore Gianni, his earlier companion, 'rather so that we can silence the evil tongues over there and rob your rivals of anything to talk about, than because we ourselves are in any doubt'.[40] Gianni was in fact accused of having embezzled communal funds and supplies, and was later tried on this charge, but Rinaldo was not satisfied, and complained to his son Ormanno that everything was being done at the camp now by the other two, 'perhaps because they didn't believe I was capable of running it'. He spoke of trying to escape from the authority of the two members of the *Dieci*, and hinted darkly that 'envy is a frightful monster, and I don't think I could get much closer to its fiery breath'.[41] He asked Ormanno to pass on his letters and information to Ser Martino Martini, another of the *Dieci*, who was an *amico* of the Medici and also a particular friend of Rinaldo's at this time. Clearly the *Dieci* themselves were divided by the special appeals and interests of members and their friends.

On 28 January the Florentines captured Collodi. This was a major triumph, and perhaps their last great success of the war. However, even this victory turned to ashes in Rinaldo's mouth, as he complained to Ormanno that 'Neri, who stayed back here at the camp, wrote to the *Dieci* that he and Alamanno had been responsible for the capture of Collodi and made no mention of me, though it was I who was in the area, in the midst of all the dangers and difficulties'.[42] This charge is borne out by the commentaries on the war written later by Neri Capponi; no mention is made there either of Rinaldo, and the credit for victory is given to Salviati and to Neri himself.[43]

It is impossible to say how far the *Dieci*, in its negotiations with Rinaldo, expressed the consensus of its members, and how far its treatment of him reflected the attitudes of any individual. There were distinguishable factions within the group, and after this episode Rinaldo's general hostility towards it as a directing body resolved itself increasingly into a particular mistrust of Capponi and Salviati, and a corresponding reliance on the only member whom he felt that he could trust, Ser Martino Martini. In view of what he considered as his betrayal by Neri Capponi, Rinaldo suggested to Ormanno that he pass on to Ser Martino the fruits of Rinaldo's cross-examination of Neri.

He tells me that Ser Martino is the king-pin of the Dieci, although as yet he has behind him only the craftsman of Santo Spirito, who was always utterly committed to him, and he has Andreuolo Sacchetti. Alamanno Salviati he hasn't been able to pin down as yet, for he has been oscillating between one side and the other . . .

As Rinaldo observed, relations between Capponi and himself remained superficially cordial,

but I have given the matter a certain amount of attention, and I note that Neri writes separately to Andreuolo and not to the others, and I have observed that Andreuolo writes separately to Neri, letting him know what the officials are doing over there . . . From what I can see, Neri runs everything over there, partly with the support of *Signore* Niccolò, whom he can do what he likes with, and partly on account of the enormous following he has in the Pistoian mountains . . . Tell Ser Martino that we must keep our eyes open, and that it would be better to have Neri in Florence than over here, for a number of respects and reasons.[44]

Certainly Capponi, at the beginning of the Lucchese war, with the prestige of his father's Pisan exploits fresh in Florentine memories, was a formidable rival; a close friend of such generally influential figures as Piero Guicciardini and Matteo Strozzi, and perhaps already on the point of increasing intimacy with the Medicean group. It is no wonder that Rinaldo, as his morale was sinking, saw Neri Capponi's growing influence as a real threat to his own prestige and power.

But while a concern with his own honour increased Rinaldo's alienation from Capponi and his friends on the one hand, and from Alamanno Salviati on the other, his relations with the Medici themselves remained comparatively cordial, and indeed when Ormanno too seemed threatened with dishonour, they turned to Averardo for assistance.[45] Ormanno had recently been appointed

[44] *Commissioni* iii. 339. On the violence and factiousness of Pistoian political life, and the territory's relations with Florence, see D. Herlihy, *Medieval and Renaissance Pistoia* (New Haven and London, 1967), pp. 198–231.

[45] See, e.g., M.A.P. II, 218, 230, 237, 261, 271, 278.

master of a *galea sottile* and the question arose as to whether or not
the galley should be armed. Averardo, then one of the five
Consuls concerned with the matter, received several letters from
Ormanno begging him to see that it was; then if Ormanno should
meet the enemy he need have no reason for avoiding battle, 'for
I would rather die first, than come back here weighed down with
the burden of dishonour'. He told Averardo that two other of the
Consuls, Banco Bencivenni and Rinieri Lotti, both of whom were
closely associated with the Medici party at this time, had said
'fraudulent things . . . against me. It is all false, and God knows
that nothing but honour brings me here.' Although Ormanno
considered Bencivenni 'a man disposed to stir up scandal', and
expressed to Averardo his opinion that by now 'your friends have
realized anew what sort of man he is', he declared that in Averardo
himself, 'I put my trust . . . as in a beloved father'. He concluded
that since

it was by reason of your efforts that I was elected master of this blessed
galley, I know you want me to derive some honour from it, which I
hope to do by the grace of God, so long as it is well armed, and manned
by experienced and practised men, and the matter isn't decided on the
basis of patronage or favour, as I believe Rinieri and Banco plan
to do.[46]

. The Mediceans appear to have responded in similar spirit to this
appeal for solidarity between leading citizens in time of crisis.
It seems that Averardo at least was not anxious to antagonize the
Albizzi, since Rinaldo wrote to Ormanno in February 1430 that
'Averardo came here to visit me yesterday evening; we spoke
about your affairs among other things. He wants to do you honour, and is very solicitous about everything.'[47] Given the considerable agreement in this period between the Medici and Rinaldo
on practical proposals concerning the conduct of the war, it is
even possible to imagine, considering the correspondence of
these years, that in spite of the aristocratic attitudes which Rinaldo had displayed in the past, a *rapprochement* between the two

[46] *Commissioni* iii. 329–30, 25 Jan. 1430 (1429 *s.f.*).
[47] Ibid. 339. On 3 Feb. Banco di Niccolò Bencivenni, Averardo's *amico* and col-
league in the Consulate of Pisa, wrote again with the instruction that the galleys
would be lightly armed 'solo per levarsi dinanzi certe nebbie' (presumably the importunings of Rinaldo and his son) 'a cui la converrebbe dar loro per forza d'amici e di
parenti' (ibid. 214).

groups might still have been effected. In mid-February he received from Giovanni Pucci what can only be seen as an assurance of the frank support and encouragement of the Medici *amici* should he decide to stay at the camp and continue to prosecute the war; there may have been an ulterior motive behind this note, but both the words and the actions of the Medici at this time suggest the contrary. Pucci acknowledged that Rinaldo might feel moved to return to Florence to silence at first-hand the spreading rumours:

However, because I know what people are saying over there, and that you can do no more, I feel safe in telling you that despite the leave which you have been granted, if you want to please those who wish you well, and to gain the good opinion of the mass of the people, you shouldn't abandon the region round Lucca, but you should make every effort to take Pontetetto if that is possible; this is what I advise and indeed beg you to do myself, and on behalf of all our friends.[48]

But the unavoidable stumbling-block in the path of any lasting accommodation was Rinaldo's view of his own role in Florentine political life. The preoccupation with his own honour reflected in these letters was not mere vanity, but a constant consciousness of his position in the city as his father's heir apparent; this was only sharpened by the fact that in reality he had not himself succeeded in establishing the same authority within the ruling group. Maso was his model and mentor, even from the grave; in 1426, while on a mission to explore the possibility of a pact with Milan, Rinaldo wrote in his diary: 'On the morning of the fifth, just before dawn, my father appeared to me in a dream, and instructed me concerning the peace negotiations.'[49] When he thought of the intrigues of others, he consoled himself with the contemplation of his family's invulnerability: as he remarked to his own son Ormanno: 'My father used to say (may God rest his soul): "Let him cook who will; I shall have soup".'[50] When he felt himself to be overridden by Capponi and Salviati, he entreated the *Dieci*:

Now consider, my Lords, the position I have enjoyed in the past, and how I have been accustomed to conduct myself, and may it please you

---

[48] *Commissioni* iii. 403. See also 406, Rinaldo to Ormanno: 'Vegio quello t'ha detto Nanni Pucci, ch'è segno di buona amicizia; e anche a me ne scrive in pochi versi ... Averardo de' Medici anche me ne scrive da Pisa ... che tutto veggio esce d'un fonte.' See also 407.

[49] Ibid. 76.   [50] Ibid. 354.

therefore above all to have some regard for my honour, that since you keep me here for form's sake, so that I may not be disgraced, that in the meantime I should be in charge, taking account of my rank and age.[51]

Pride in rank and status were clearly major factors in Rinaldo's attitude towards his own society, and he had underlined the essential importance of 'gradus' once before, identifying it in a *Pratica* as the sole determinant of his own associations.[52]

It was hardly therefore to be expected that he could in any circumstances forfeit his special position in Florence by acceding to the advancement of a group of citizens not on the whole his social equals, and already united under the unquestioned leadership of Cosimo de' Medici. If he feared the rival influence of Neri Capponi in 1430, how much more must he have feared the Medici in 1433? Although during the early days of the war Rinaldo had confided to Ormanno his desire to withdraw from intrigues and struggles for power and 'devote all my time to preparing myself properly for death',[53] he had felt himself humiliated and his ascendancy in the ruling group threatened. This experience may well have been the cause of his decision to defend his own position by attacking those most likely to usurp it. When Rinaldo emerged from the comparative obscurity of the war period which had done so much to enhance the Medici reputation, he had finally and decisively assumed the mantle of the deceased Niccolò da Uzzano as leader of the conservative faction.

In any case, the Medici correspondence of this period suggests that in their relations with the remainder of the ruling group, the leaders of the party operated on several levels, however difficult these may be to distinguish precisely in practice. Although they were capable of a comparatively disinterested support of the communal effort and other patricians involved in it, and correspondingly willing to include their own partisans in their frequent criticisms of citizens whose contributions they considered

---

[51] Ibid. 312-13.

[52] C.P. 49, ff. 32v-39r; cf. Cavalcanti, *Istorie*, p. 173, who wrote of 'lo smoderato sdegno del milite Rinaldo'; cf. *Istorie*, p. 206; 'Costui non ha più a grado l'amico che il nimico, ma quel grado dimostra all'uno che all'altro; ogni huomo ha per cencio.' See also M.A.P. III, 183, Alamanno Salviati to Averardo de' Medici. He was probably referring to Rinaldo when he spoke of 'il magiore' who 'credo non arà honore, per cagione delle sete e della superbia'.

[53] *Commissioni* iii. 359.

inadequate or ill judged, these considerations do not appear to have affected their continuing concern to promote the interests of their partisans; relationships and attitudes formed in one sphere were not necessarily transferred to another, though more abstract considerations of private versus public interest were skilfully juggled, and where a direct conflict demanded a choice, the claims of each were carefully balanced.

Throughout most of the war Averardo held important posts as commissioner in Pisa or other areas near to the Florentine field of operations—posts in which he was required to make appointments to a number of offices, and was consequently in a particularly favourable position to dispense patronage. For example, early in 1430 the *Dieci* entrusted him with the task of appointing personnel for the Florentine galleys, in order specifically to relieve themselves of the pressure of demands from *parenti* and *amici*.[54] Jobs on the galleys were generally honourable, and the conditions of service infinitely preferable to those endured by commissioners floundering in the mud of the Florentine infantry camps.[55] A flood of letters—from his own *parenti* and *amici*, and from those of other patricians—with which Averardo was inundated, enable us to observe in detail in one instance the operation of a number of patronage groups, each with its own candidates, concentrating their efforts upon a single goal, and to glimpse the complexity of the conflict of interests which necessarily resulted. The fact that Averardo was generally its ultimate broker enables us to see patronage operating as distinct from partisanship; the friendly but respectful and relatively non-committal requests of various patricians on behalf of themselves or others highlight by contrast the contractual and reciprocal elements of the partisan relationships explored earlier.[56]

[54] M.A.P. II, 170, Banco di Niccolò Bencivenni to Averardo, 3 Feb. 1430 (1429 s.f.). [55] Cf. M.A.P. III, 328, Doffo Spini to Averardo, 23 July 1431.
[56] See, e.g., Mariotto di Francesco di Giovanni di Ser Segna's letter to Averardo in support of the interests of Ormanno degli Albizzi, ibid. II, 196, 10 Feb. 1430 (1429 s.f.); cf. requests for patronage on other occasions from Marcello Strozzi on behalf of his kinsman, Marco di Goro, (ibid. V, 274, n.d., but apparently at some time during the war); also III, 128, Bernardo Anselmi, 14 May 1431. Letters from the Medici *amici* relating to appointments connected with the galleys include those from the Tedaldi (above, p. 93); from the Medici *consorti* themselves, the series from Orlando di Guccio and his sons (above, pp. 93-4), and a note from Giovanni di Zanobi de' Medici rather frankly requesting a position 'perchè il viaggio è bello' (M.A.P. II, 332, 11 Apr. 1430). The correspondence of Rinaldo degli Albizzi and his son with the Medici and their friends concerning Ormanno's appointment is pub-

The letters themselves bear witness to the impossibility of completely impersonal action in a society thus solidly based on the operation of personal relationships, but the Albizzi acknowledgement of the sympathetic consideration which they felt they had received from the Mediceans testifies to the fact that Averardo responded to the situation with something of the objectivity which the *Dieci* had asked of him. Presumably he had rightly judged that the commune would not benefit fully from the cooperation of the Albizzi unless they were wooed with the deference they felt to be their due, and rewarded with appropriate honours. Most of the other letters imply a confident expectation that Averardo would dispose of these coveted posts as the status of the supplicants, and therefore ultimately the interest of the commune, required. A similar consciousness of the dependence of the public welfare on the satisfaction of the private needs of those who administered the state may have encouraged the Medici to maintain good relations with Rinaldo and his son in the face of the growing enmity between the Albizzi and Averardo's son-in-law, Alamanno Salviati. As far as affairs of state were concerned, the Medici party did not necessarily operate as a monolith, and obviously citizens like Rinaldo did not always regard it as such. While on the one hand various Mediceans frequently expressed their respect for the judgement and conduct of those outside their own circle, and occasionally even on the opposite side of the partisan fence, on the other, Averardo in particular received a number of letters from the *amici* which were critical of his behaviour in office,[57] and indeed his cousin Cosimo did not

lished by Guasti, *Commissioni* iii. 393-6, and includes supporting letters from Albizzi *amici* Riccardo Fagni and Mariotto di Ser Segna, and one from Giuliano Davanzati who, under the mistaken impression that Rinaldo did not want Ormanno to be appointed, wrote to recommend a friend of his own instead. Cf. the correspondence of Ramondo Manelli and his *amici*, including Andrea Rondinelli and Andreuolo Sacchetti, with their Strozzi friends and patrons concerning another galleys appointment which became a major issue due to the honour and preferment involved (above, p. 183).

[57] See, e.g., M.A.P. V, 16, 1 Nov. 1431, from Andrea Pazzi, and his conclusion that: 'De' fatto arei fatto che Puccio non arebe giudichato si lunga e di fatti fuori di sua arte.' Cf. also Alamanno Salviati's implicit criticism of Cosimo to Averardo for being among those citizens who abandoned Florence at a crucial moment on account of the plague (ibid. IV, 83; Pellegrini, *Sulla repubblica* clxi-clxii, 25 Aug. 1431), and a very similar letter from Ser Niccolò Tinucci (M.A.P. III, 204, 11 July 1431; Pellegrini, cxliii-cxlv), deploring Cosimo's departure 'perchè veggio quanto vale la presentia loro a Firenze, a bene publico et particulare'.

hesitate to join with the *Dieci* on one occasion in upbraiding
Averardo for his slowness to act in a time of crisis.[58]

In the light of what we know of the Medici leaders from their
letters, Tinucci's unsupported assertions that they and their
friends were responsible for the slander of most of the leading
citizens concerned with the conduct of the enterprise, including
Astore Gianni, Rinaldo, and the unfortunate Giovanni Guicciardini, seem highly implausible. The sheer volume of denunciations
to the *Conservatori* in this period suggest, as contemporaries
believed, that a considerable proportion of the members of the
ruling group were engaged, for a variety of reasons, in defaming
one another; those accused included the whole range of the
ruling group as we have discussed it, including exiles, probable
anti-Mediceans, and apparently neutral citizens, and the Medici
themselves were certainly not exempt from persecution.[59]
Averardo was frequently under attack, to the extent that on one
occasion Alamanno wrote advising him to give up his post and
return to Florence: 'The times are not propitious . . . I think
almost all the time you have been in Pisa . . . there have been a
number of people slandering you in one way or another, so
seeing that there would appear to be little possibility of your
achieving anything worth while, I think it would be best to return.'[60] Just as in February of 1430 one of the *amici* had observed
in a letter to Averardo that the current *Dieci* were more concerned for themselves and their squabbles than for the commune,
referring regretfully to the Florentine problem of 'the unbridled
desire to make mischief',[61] so almost two years later Lorenzo de'
Medici wrote concerning his own recent election to that office
that although the post involved 'a lot of worry and hard work', he
felt at least that he was in good company, and perhaps that all

---

[58] Averardo customarily received much more praise than blame from the *Dieci*,
but on 27 June 1431, they sent one of their rare letters rebuking him; Cosimo wrote
on the same day pointing out how ready some citizens would be to slander him for
dereliction of duty and warning him to avoid bringing dishonour upon the family
(M.A.P. III, 145; Pellegrini, *Sulla repubblica* cxxxii–cxxxiii); cf. a similar and even
sharper communication along the same lines (M.A.P. IV, 246, 3 Oct. 1431; Pellegrini, clxv). Occasionally quite serious misunderstanding and suspicions of disloyalty could arise between the Medici and even their most intimate friends; see,
e.g., the letter of Alamanno Salviati to Averardo, M.A.P. V, 163, 14 Dec. 1431;
Pellegrini, clxxxiii–clxxxiv.

[59] For the details of the accusations and those involved, see Giud. Appelli 75,
77; cf. above, pp. 244–5.

[60] M.A.P. V, 27, 10 Nov. 1431.   [61] Ibid. II, 171, 3 Feb. 1430 (1429 *s.f.*).

might be well, 'if we ourselves don't destroy one another as usual with our tongues'.[62]

Certainly none of the three most prominent victims of this particular Florentine vice belonged at the time to the hard-core opposition to the Medici, and indeed several Mediceans expressed their specific disapproval of the accusations which had been made against them. Early in 1430 Giuliano wrote to his father concerning 'the great uproar over these commissioners', and gave his opinion that 'undoubtedly there are many who would be only too willing to censure them, which is not good; the business is more likely to go badly than well'.[63] Three days later Bartolomeo Orlandini declared angrily to Averardo that the departure of Astore Gianni in consequence of the accusations which had been made had cost the Florentines a valuable strategic advantage, and that 'if only Astore had stayed here another eight days he would have gained everything between Pietrasanta and here by treaties'.[64]

The recent editor of Giovanni Guicciardini's own account of the unjust accusations against him follows Tinucci in holding the Medici responsible, but the discussions of the incident in the *Consulte* on which her argument is chiefly based would seem to be open to an alternative interpretation; Guicciardini's own *Ricordi* describe at length the envy and infamy which he suffered, but give no hint as to the identity of his persecutors, if he knew them.[65] As we have seen, the relationship between Guicciardini and the Medici appears to have deteriorated between 1427 and 1434 from intimacy to opposition, but Guicciardini's ultimate support of the anti-Mediceans can perfectly adequately be explained in terms of strong personal ties with the aristocratic and

[62] Ibid. V, 117, 3 Dec. 1431; Pellegrini, *Sulla repubblica* clxx–clxxii.

[63] M.A.P. II, 159, 28 Jan. 1430 (1429 *s.f.*).

[64] Ibid. II, 167, 31 Jan. 1430 (1429 *s.f.*); cf. Tommaso Barbadori to Averardo de' Medici in Pisa, 3 Feb. 1430 (1429 *s.f.*), printed Guasti, *Commissioni* iii. 349.

[65] Moriani, *Giovanni Guicciardini*, esp. pp. 24, 50, 63–70. Guicciardini's complaints express rather a vague generalized resentment against the ruling group as a whole; for example, 'di continuo n'ero tenuto in infamia; et qui non era chi respondesse per me contro alla 'nvidia' (p. 97), or 'nientedimeno mi furono date molte infamie e false calumpnie, biasimando quel ch'era fatto et me ...' (p. 89). Moriani's characterization of Guicciardini as the 'scapegoat' for the failure of the war (p. 19) and one of the last defenders of communal liberty against the Medici (p. 20), his case a testing ground for the two parties against one another (p. 70), seems essentially to rest on the assumption that the attacks on him were unique; the records of the *Conservatori delle Leggi* show that he was only one, though perhaps one of the more unfortunate, of many.

conservative group, without assuming any personal animus against the Medici or a desire to revenge injury done to himself.[66] On the contrary, his kindness to Francesco di Giuliano in 1434, and a note to Giovanni di Cosimo which must have been written about the same time, indicate that there was no permanent breakdown of relations between them, and that even his political opposition may have been sufficiently qualified to allow of a rapid *rapprochement*.[67] In view of Cosimo's personal judgement of him, recorded in an observation to Averardo some years before the war when Guicciardini had been involved in the negotiations of the peace of Ferrara—'Messer Giovanni Guicciardini is returning; he doesn't feel that over there he was honoured as he deserved, and perhaps he is right; he is rather soft, as you know, but he's a good man'—it is difficult to believe that the Medici would have seen him as a political menace to be hunted down and relentlessly destroyed.[68] Cosimo's general disapproval of those citizens who undermined the war effort by calumniating its leaders is expressed in a letter to Averardo early in 1430: 'There are people here who in order to bring disgrace and harm to others would be willing for the Commune to suffer disgrace and harm, and they do everything they possibly can to bring this about; this is a very evil type of man.'[69]

[66] Above, p. 154.

[67] M.A.P. LXVI, 35, Piero di Cosimo to Francesco di Giuliano de' Medici, 11 July 1434: 'Anchora ò visto la forma buona che pigliasti alla tua giunta per chonsiglio di G. Guicciardini nostro S. che assai mi piace espezialmente colla buona affectione ch'egli t'a mostrato, che al contradio arei creduto.' Cf. ibid. VI, 767, Giovanni Guicciardini to Giovanni di Cosimo de' Medici; the letter is not dated, but must, on internal evidence, belong to the early thirties.

[68] Ibid. II, 3, 1 Jan. 1428 (1427 *s.f.*); Moriani herself represents Guicciardini as quite a just, and essentially apolitical man. However, cf. Francesco Guicciardini's portrait of him, '*Memorie di Famiglia*', pp. 13–14, and his conviction that the Medici and their friends were responsible for ruining him; see also *Cose Fiorentine*, p. 246. While Giovanni Canigiani wrote to his friend Matteo Strozzi (C.S. 3ª ser. CXII, c. 16, 12 Aug. 1430) in terms of enthusiastic praise for Guicciardini: 'e de' buoni in verità si tiene per tutti gl'intendenti che Messer Giovanni ghoverni quel chanpo con tanta prudenza quanto ne fosse mai ghovernato niuno, e veramente non potrà avere se non è grande honore' (a rather ironic assumption as things turned out), Cosimo in fact disapproved of the policies with which Guicciardini was associated (M.A.P. II, 371). But so, for that matter, did the arch-conservative, Niccolò da Uzzano, who wrote to his friend Matteo Strozzi that 'parmi che nell'animo di Messer Giovanni Guicciardini sia entrato che a llui basti salvare le men' gienti, e desi riguardarlo che è il contrario potesse avenire' (C.S. 3ª ser. CXII, c. 20, 15 Aug. 1430).

[69] M.A.P. II, 178, 4 Feb. 1430 (1429 *s.f.*); cf. ibid. VI, 3, Nerone di Nigi Dietisalvi to Lorenzo di Giovanni di Bicci de' Medici, 5 May 1431.

While at least the leaders of the Medici party frowned on the practice of publicly denouncing their fellows for their conduct of operations, they were intensely critical of them in private; such criticism was typical indeed within most circles of friends and associates prominent in the conduct of the war.[70] The increasing participation of leading Mediceans in offices as the war progressed seems to have been partly due to a conviction, not totally ill founded as it appeared, that they could direct the war effort more successfully than could their rivals in the *stato*. For instance, in January 1430 Fruosino da Verazzano wrote to Averardo bemoaning the fact that the war effort had not been proceeding as well as might have been expected, adding that 'however, we must hope that your friends through doing good hour by hour will prevail'.[71] When Averardo, who may have been more tentative than Cosimo at least in this one respect, showed some signs of doubting his own capacity to judge what was best for the commune and to direct the military captains as to precisely what strategy should be pursued in the conduct of the war, his cousin wrote a very brisk letter to rally his confidence and spur him to more decisive action, with the argument that

although we do not possess that experience in warfare of those who engage in it continually, that is no reason why, having seen what others have done, we are unable to judge who is acting more appropriately. I believe that although you are not a great painter, nevertheless you would judge the figures of Giotto to be better than those of Balzanello.[72]

Cosimo's letter epitomizes the strong but ambiguous impulses of powerful patricians consciously or unconsciously to identify the ultimate welfare of the state with their personal successes and failures. On the one hand he was concerned to imbue Averardo with his own confidence that he was peculiarly personally qualified to judge what was best for Florence; on the other, he was

---

[70] For the general disillusionment of members of the ruling group, and their lack of faith in their fellows, see, e.g., Niccolò da Uzzano to Matteo Strozzi, C.S. 3ª ser. CXII, c. 20, 15 Aug. 1430; Neri Capponi to Matteo, ibid., cc. 25, 99; Doffo Spini to Averardo, M.A.P. III, 328; Niccolò Valori to Averardo, ibid. II, 374, 22 Oct. 1430, and in general the letters of the Mediceans published by Pellegrini, *Sulla repubblica*.

[71] M.A.P. II, 154, 22 Jan. 1430 (1429 *s.f.*); cf. Ser Niccolò Tinucci to Averardo, ibid. III, 122, 26 Apr. 1431; Pellegrini, lxxxiii–lxxxiv: 'per certo troppo cattivo governo a mio iudicio è quello, in che al presente noi ci troviamo'.

[72] M.A.P. IV, 246, 3 Oct. 1431; Pellegrini clxv–clxvii.

fearful lest Averardo's inadequacy discredit the Medici and their partisans. A related sentiment is expressed, however conventionally, in Bernardo de' Medici's hope that in office 'by God's grace, I may achieve something for the exaltation of our commune and which may bring pleasure and honour to us'.[73] Cosimo's chagrin at the poor figure cut by the Florentines in foreign eyes may similarly have been due to the identification of personal with public honour,[74] and the same spirit apparently informed a request from Francesco Tornabuoni to Averardo in 1431 that he and Cosimo should use their influence in Venice to maintain the reputation and honour of the Florentine state.[75] It is in this context that a good deal of the Medicean criticism of the official failures of their rivals must be seen, and in particular a most interesting letter from the Medicean partisan, Piero Guicciardini, to his old friend Matteo Strozzi, describing the reactions of Averardo's son Giuliano and their friend Giovanni Carnesecchi when the news of the rout of Florentine troops by Piccinino in 1430 reached them in Venice: 'You never saw such demonstrations of happiness nor heard more poisonous words against the former *Dieci*, without any restraint, in the presence of the Venetians and others.'[76] An incident such as this, which aroused the indignation even of their friend Guicciardini, might well provide a basis in honest observation for allegations such as Tinucci's, but the target of Guicciardini's criticism was almost certainly less disloyalty to the state than a simple lapse of taste, and the Mediceans were roused to no less patriotic distress by the event of the rout than the rest of the *reggimento*.[77]

Nevertheless, where the choice between self-interest and service to the commune was more overt, the Medici did not lightly sacrifice personal reputation and the interests of their partisans to patriotism, and rather than seeing control of the war as a means to control of the state, at least at first they were somewhat fearful of impugning their own honour by associating it with such a risky

[73] M.A.P. V, 140, 8 Dec. 1431.

[74] Ibid. II, 371, 21 Oct. 1430, to Averardo; Pellegrini, xvii: 'Essi fatto beffe di noi da ciaschuno, perchè si chonosce non vi poteva stare'; cf. ibid. II, 390, 10 Dec. 1430, to Averardo; Pellegrini, xx-xxi.

[75] M.A.P. III, 114, 6 Apr. 1431, to Averardo; Pellegrini lvii–lviiii.

[76] Acqu. e Doni, Carte Carnesecchi (taken from Filza CXII, Strozzi Uguccioni), c. 43, 19 Dec. 1430.

[77] Below, pp. 278–9; cf. the letter of a friend to Matteo Strozzi, C.S. 3ª ser. CXII, c. 39, 10 Dec. 1430.

enterprise as they obviously felt the war with Lucca to be. In a letter to Averardo in February 1430 Cosimo asserted in principle his qualified support for the war on the grounds of patriotism, while still uncertain personally of its advisability:

It seems to me that whether or not we approve of this undertaking, things have come to the point where the honour of the commune is involved, so that everyone must give it all the support they can; I shall do so as far as possible from here, and I encourage you to do the same, although I am sure there is no need.[78]

However, by September he was writing again to advise Averardo: 'It doesn't seem to me that the affair of Lucca is going to turn out as successfully as expected, which I regret.' He believed that the Duke of Milan had gained control of the situation, 'and we must assume that the principal strongholds are in his hands, and on account of this, I don't think there's any hope of getting Lucca by agreement' (as in fact some members of the *reggimento* were hoping to do at that time). He concluded that the war was going to be longer than they had anticipated, and consequently suggested to Averardo that the Medici themselves should not be available for the forthcoming election to the *Dieci*, particularly in view of the fact that two of the *amici* could be relied upon to represent them:

As I wrote to you before, we should not attempt to be among the *Dieci* this time; partly to give a share to others, and furthermore because it seems to me that considering the divisions within our city, they can't do very well . . . for this reason I shall write to the Gonfalonier and to Antonio di Ser Tommaso Masi[79] asking that neither Lorenzo nor I should be included in the vote, and I would advise you to do the same.[80]

Cosimo's remarks to Averardo constitute not only an acute judgement on the progress of the war and an accurate forecast of future difficulties; they also betray the unwillingness of the Medici to waste time on insoluble problems or to identify themselves too closely with a hopeless cause.

---

[78] M.A.P. II, 178, 4 Feb. 1430 (1429 *s.f.*).
[79] A friend of the Medici and at that time one of the Priors.
[80] M.A.P. II, 371, 21 Oct. 1430. He was relying on Niccolò Valori and Luca di Messer Maso degli Albizzi to represent Medicean interests; he obviously judged that both were available candidates and likely to be elected.

Nevertheless, it must also be said that the Medici, whatever their motives, were prepared to respond to the needs of the commune. Less than three months after this letter was written, on 2 December, the Florentine forces were routed in an engagement on the Serchio with the Lucchese, reinforced by Milanese troops led by the *condottiere* Niccolò Piccinino, who had previously been in the service of the Duke of Milan. According to a contemporary commentator, 'if it hadn't been for that rout, the commune of Florence would have had Lucca';[81] as it was, the war was to drag on for two more weary and debilitating years. Moreover, it was this defeat which led the Florentines at last to see the war in a different light, and which marked the definitive alteration of the Florentine posture from one of offence to one of defence. The Florentine situation had been deteriorating throughout the year as other north Italian powers began to take sides in the conflict, and it became clear that the Florentines were confronting not only the lord of Lucca, but also their old enemy, the lord of Milan. 'Now', as the commissioners to the camp observed, 'it is no longer a matter of obtaining Lucca, but of preserving our own state.'[82]

Among the more constructive of the citizens who gathered next day to review the situation were Rinaldo degli Albizzi and Averardo de' Medici, who admitted that 'this is a serious misfortune, but nevertheless our spirits should not be subdued'.[83] In a letter of 22 October Niccolò Valori had suggested to Averardo that the *Dieci* who had taken office the previous June had not done everything possible to ensure victory; he believed that 'it would be helpful if some really able men got back into the *Dieci*, men who really want to win'.[84] When the new *Dieci* were announced a week after the news of the defeat, Cosimo himself was among them, together with three other leading Mediceans, Bartolomeo Ridolfi, Agnolo Pandolfini, and Puccio Pucci.[85] According to Tinucci, the rout on the Serchio gave Cosimo the opportunity for which he had been waiting to take over the direction of the war. The Medici letters suggest that despite the tactless triumph of Giuliano and Giovanni Carnesecchi at the discomfiture of

---

[81] Rinuccini, *Ricordi storici*, p. 63.   [82] MSS. 315, p. 16.
[83] C.P. 49, f. 103r (3 Dec.). For the comments of other speakers see ff. 101v–104r.
[84] M.A.P. II, 374.   [85] Pellegrini, *Sulla repubblica* xix

partisan opponents for whom they had little admiration, the assumption of office by Cosimo and other prominent *amici* probably represented rather a decision to rally to the emergency created by the rout in spite of personal misgivings.[86]

The ambivalence of the Medici towards the conflicting claims of service to the commune and self-interest is similarly reflected on a less dramatic plane in their attitude to more routine administrative offices. Averardo had been one of the Consuls at Pisa before the outbreak of hostilities, and subsequently served continuously in positions of authority until 1432, mainly as a commissioner in various camps, and particularly in the strategic area of Pisa. He did not assume responsibilities comparable to those attached to the office of the *Dieci*, but he was closely and continuously involved with the war effort on a more mundane level. His few surviving replies to his son's numerous letters in these years leave no doubt that he was personally committed to the cause of Florentine victory; as he wrote on one occasion, when the customary problems of maintaining the provision of supplies to the camps were particularly acute: 'I am driven half mad by not being able to do any good.'[87] How genuinely he was dismayed by setbacks to the Florentine progress is apparent from a rather whimsical letter of encouragement from Ser Niccolò Tinucci about this time:

The other day I got a letter of yours of the 25th of last month, from which you seemed to me so cast down that I couldn't have hoped with all the savours of Damascus or Capri to have restored your appetite! I thought, however, that you would keep in mind that although there are many things which are alarming, there are few which are actually harmful. I believe that the gains made at Carrara and at Moneta will have settled your stomach a little.[88]

It would seem that Averardo spared neither his energies, nor his own health, which by 1431 was rapidly deteriorating, in his concern to serve the commune. In August of that year his son-in-law, Giannozzo Gianfigliazzi, begged him to take more care of himself, 'for by God I know that you take upon yourself too

---

[86] This apparently was more than many citizens were prepared to do; Antonio di Salvestro Serristori wrote to Averardo six months later concerning the appointment of commissioners that 'n'abiamo fatti due altri; poichè gran maestri no' volgliono, tolgliemo de' mezzani' (M.A.P. III, 349, 29 July 1431).

[87] Ibid. V, 684, 3 Dec. 1431.   [88] Ibid. II, 186, 7 Feb. 1430 (1429 *s.f.*).

many discomforts and too much hard work. It is a fine thing to carry out the business of your commune faithfully, but you must still be willing to look after your health and I beg you to do so.'[89] A certain amount of Gianfigliazzi's concern, and that of another of his sons-in-law, Alamanno Salviati, sprang from the conviction that in his dedication to the commune Averardo was neglecting the interests of the *amici*, which depended on the maintenance of the Medici honour and the avoidance of the scandals and vituperation which most of the commissioners to the field inevitably incurred while they were safely out of Florence; thus they urged him to return. As the former put it:

> It isn't that the good work you have done isn't recognized over here, but as you know, nevertheless there are those here who would not be too regretful at any injury you might sustain . . . you should act in accordance with the profit and advantage of your friends and to hell with the others.[90]

Averardo ignored their advice on that occasion, but when in January 1432 he was drawn for the prestigious but onerous post of *Capitano di Pisa*, and his son Giuliano wrote to him announcing that he had fourteen days to accept or refuse,[91] he had the leaders of the family and of the party call a veritable council of war. Giuliano wrote to him reporting on their decision three times in four days, in case his letters should have gone astray and fail to reach Averardo in time to assist his decision.[92] Notably, about the same time one of the humbler Mediceans, Giovanni Cirioni, had written to ask a favour of Averardo, and observing in conclusion that he had heard Averardo had been drawn for the Captaincy of Pisa, expressed his fear that 'you won't want to accept', although to do so would be greatly to the honour and profit both of himself and of the commune.[93]

In fact he was right; the leaders of the party were not on the whole in agreement with him. Cosimo 'took his time in replying', but finally sent word that 'it is up to you, as it is you who are in the situation'; however, he threw out in conversation with Giuliano later that 'he would have refused twice over'. In a letter

[89] M.A.P. IV, 6; cf. III, 112 from Ser Ciao: 'Meglio voglate ad altri che a voi proprio, che è una pazz[i]a', 23 Mar. 1432 (1431 *s.f.*).
[90] Ibid. IV, 6, cf. V, 27, and above, Ch. 1 (vi).   [91] M.A.P. XX, 81.
[92] Ibid. II, 33, 46, 51; Pellegrini, *Sulla repubblica* cxcii-cxcviiii.
[93] M.A.P. III, 28, 31 Jan. 1432 (1431 *s.f.*).

written on 2 February Giuliano described how that morning 'Giannozzo, Alamanno, and Antonio and I got together in the house'; he then went on to report on the results of their deliberations, 'although Giannozzo and Alamanno are also writing to you about it'. Giannozzo, in accordance with the views he had earlier expressed,

thought that for the benefit of the Commune, it would be best to say yes, and that really each of us ought to be well content to do so in an atmosphere of reasonable goodwill; however, given the way we have behaved, and how little gratitude anyone receives for the good he does, and that there is no shame in saying no, but rather a means of avoiding all danger, and that saying yes will involve difficulties and dangers and regrets, taking all things into account, he replied no.

Alamanno Salviati expressed the opposite opinion,

because he thought it a good thing to consider the needs of the Commune, and that the consequences of this concern were personal honour and the appreciation of the citizenry; he certainly had his doubts, but seeing that things are no more unfavourable to us there than here, he is of the opinion that in sum we shouldn't waste our expertise, since over there any likely solution ought to be tried. Antonio said no altogether, because although you could be of use to the commune, you ought to look carefully at your own interest, and he envisaged some of the irreparable ills which might result from acceptance.[94]

Giuliano, not surprisingly, seems to have experienced some difficulty in distilling the collective wisdom of the Mediceans from this exhaustive balancing of positive and negative considerations, for although his reporting of individual opinions is substantially identical in all three letters, while in that of 3 February he concluded that 'as I understood it, the general opinion is in favour of your accepting rather than not, essentially on the grounds of the public need', two days later he wrote that finally after all three had carefully considered the matter, they agreed that it would be better to say no than to say yes'. Perhaps in his last letter he represented the discussion more in the light of his own opinion that 'in hanging yourself by the neck for the commune you gain neither favour nor goodwill, and in this matter I should examine my own interest'.

It is difficult to imagine these letters being of much material

[94] Cf. the opinion of Nerone di Nigi Dietisalvi, whom Giuliano also consulted that there were a great many dangers involved in accepting.

assistance to Averardo in making his decision, but they do serve to illustrate perfectly the spirit of the leadership of the Medicean party in the war period; although the party and its members were patriotically concerned with the promotion of the war, they were no less concerned than before with their own self-promotion, which operated in a new, in some ways more favourable, context, and it was extremely difficult to balance the claims of each where they conflicted. Nevertheless, whatever they chose to do, the *amici* clearly continued to act as a group and to advance the interests of that group as a primary consideration.

Although the defence of their particular interests might, and no doubt did, conflict not only with the ideal 'good of the commune' but also, in fact, with the opposing interests of a number of its leading citizens, it seems unlikely, as we have observed, that the Mediceans indulged in the random and highly impolitic alienation of the ruling group at large. As far as can be seen from the letters of this period, their chief opponents were much the same during the war as they had been just before it; this is certainly implied in the letters of Benedetto Masi early in 1430 begging the Medici to defend him from the 'unbridled fury' of the Peruzzi, Guadagni, Scolari, and Aldobrandini. Whether, as Tinucci claimed, the Medici were planning an armed *coup* during this period, to impose their ascendancy on the *reggimento*, is doubtful; as usual, a number of the facts fit Tinucci's account, but it is difficult to distinguish with any certainty in their letters the possible hints at a conspiracy from the many enigmatic and allusive references to collusion and conflict which when finally pursued to the point of explanation are revealed simply as descriptions of Florentine military strategy, or of attempts to solve commercial problems through the usual tortuous chains of patronage and negotiation.[95]

[95] See *Examina*, pp. 412–13. Tinucci claimed that when on 1 March their friend Piero Bonciani was drawn Gonfalonier of Justice, Ser Martino Martini and the Medici, fearing a decline in support for their party, had conspired to stage an armed revolution if the major offices drawn in that period should turn out to be favourable to themselves. Tinucci was at the time notary to the *Dieci di Balìa*, a very favourable position from which to acquire information, and Piero Bonciani had given his support to Medici electoral manœuvring in the past. However, such an enterprise would have been out of keeping with the tone of the Medici letters at the time, and with their future behaviour under much more concrete pressure from their enemies; moreover, owing to the rapid rotation of leading magistracies, few of the officials from whom Tinucci claimed they hoped to gain support would have held power concurrently.

If the Mediceans intended to stage a *coup* at this point, it never eventuated; instead we see them in the latter years of the war rising more naturally to a position of predominance over their opponents through the major offices of the *Dieci* and the *Ufficiali del Banco*, by whom the war was substantially directed. Both these offices were elective; whether through the co-operation of their numerous and powerful friends, by the merits of their own undoubted administrative and political abilities, or simply on account of their wealth and general influence, the Medici and their leading supporters became increasingly prominent in the direction of the war.[96] As their personal letters revealed, Cosimo and Averardo quickly grasped the importance of a swift, decisive, and adequate response to the turning of the tide against the Florentines; the latter's insistence that 'we must not be sparing with our wealth, lest this should threaten the success of our cause; we must employ all the men and captains we need', is characteristic of the sort of attitudes which the Medici expressed in *Pratiche* throughout 1430.[97]

In this respect they and their friends were no more conspicuously astute than many others, particularly such experienced campaigners and politicians as Neri Capponi and Rinaldo degli Albizzi.[98] There is no precise correlation between partisanship and opinions concerning military or financial problems, but the positive attitudes of the Medici leaders on these questions do contrast notably with those of some leading conservatives, including figures of such importance as Niccolò da Uzzano and Ser Paolo Fortini. Such men had either opposed the war from the beginning or grown rapidly disillusioned with it, and as hostilities dragged on, became increasingly preoccupied with recriminations and with keeping down expenses at all costs; as Niccolò da Uzzano remarked, 'it is indeed regrettable that we were drawn into this enterprise in the hope that it would be brief and inexpensive'.[99] Stefano di Salvi di Filippo Bencivenni believed that 'a city should be governed like a household; that is, on the basis of what

96 See the lists of these offices in Camera del Comune, Ufiziali del Banco dei Soldati, Inventario, 509, 397; Pellegrini, *Sulla repubblica* xix, cxxxii, clxxx, clxiiii, ccxvi; Buoninsegni, *Storie*, p. 33, and Cambi, *Istorie*, p. 181.
97 C.P. 49, f. 26r.
98 Ibid., ff. 66v, 42v.
99 Ibid., f. 14v; cf. Fortini, ff. 28r, 38v, and Giovanni di Messer Rinaldo Gianfigliazzi, f. 27v.

is paid out and what comes in; otherwise it can't be managed',[100] and Giovanni Minerbetti actually thought that financial provision should be made from month to month, and not a year or eighteen months in advance. He supported his opinion with a homely proverb: 'The tailor cuts his coat to suit his cloth.'[101] Galileo Galilei, putting his trust in God, appears to have been averse to making any provision at all. 'This enterprise is just and reasonable, besides being profitable and honourable', he declared. 'We must believe that God will help us.'[102]

The issue of finance was indeed a burning one, for by the middle of 1430 it was clear that the central problem raised by the war was paying for it. It is not simply that the Medici were among those citizens most capable of grasping the dimensions of the financial problem; they were, more essentially, prominent in the tiny minority capable of providing a solution. Anthony Molho's detailed study of the Florentine financial crises of the 1430s shows that while throughout the war the government continued to rely basically for the fulfilment of its needs on the city-wide exaction of the *catasto*, the sheer length of the operation, coupled with an astronomical rise in the price of mercenary troops, on which Florence was almost wholly dependent, soon produced a deficit in the communal budget which not even the most frequent exactions of *catasti* could manage to repair. A series of desperate *Pratiche* were called to provide some solution to the city's financial problems, with the result that the commune came increasingly to rely on the *Ufficiali del Banco*, a magistracy originally created in the mid-fourteenth century, but revitalized after 1425 to play a key role in the management of Florentine finance. While also taking over general control of finance from the *Dieci*, and assuming responsibility for the assignment, exaction, and collection of forced loans from individual citizens, the members of this magistracy were expected to advance large loans to the state from their own private patrimonies; those unwilling or unable to do so were removed from office. While their duties gave them extensive powers to dispose of citizens' private fortunes and to determine

---

[100] C.P., f. 187v; cf. Lippozzo Mangioni, f. 15r: 'Providendum est ne aliquis audeat facere imprehensas isto modo in privatis domibus.'

[101] Ibid., f. 237r.

[102] Ibid., f. 15r. See also a wartime letter of Giuliano's to Averardo, observing that before the ruling group would agree to the imposition of sufficient *catasti*, 'prima sofferrebbe che pericolasse il cielo alla terra' (M.A.P. III, 31).

the direction of communal policies, they also acquired the status of a financial élite, loaning enormous sums of money at very high rates of interest, which was paid by the ever-increasing exactions of *catasti* from the rest of the citizenry.[103]

The records of the *Ufficiali del Banco* indicate that from 1427 onwards the Medici *amici* were prominent in this office. During the eight terms for which membership is recorded, covering almost the entire period from 1427 to 1433, Antonio di Salvestro Serristori, Andrea di Guglielmino Pazzi, and the Medici themselves each appear five times. Representatives of the Tornabuoni, Valori, Capponi, Carducci, Ginori, and Pucci families appear two or three times each, and several other Medici friends were each appointed on one occasion.[104] Even more interesting are the lists of major creditors of the *Ufficiali del Banco*, for more than 10,000 florins in the period between the end of 1430 and mid-August 1432. Eleven citizens account for over 75 per cent of the sum borrowed by the *Ufficiali del Banco* during this time, amounting to some 560,000 florins in all. The leading creditor was Cosimo himself, who had loaned to the commune 155,887 florins, or 27 per cent of the total amount borrowed. Andrea Pazzi, Averardo's *compagno*, was next with 58,524 florins, and further down the list after the exiled Bernardo Lamberteschi at 34,825, Lorenzo di Messer Palla Strozzi at 33,951, and Pierozzo della Luna, a Strozzi friend, at 27,156, came Antonio di Salvestro Serristori, another leader of the Medicean party, who loaned 26,527 florins. The remaining creditors included two more citizens generally associated with the Medici, then the arch-conservative Iacopo Baroncelli, for the comparatively small sum of 18,362 florins, and at the end of the list two citizens who cannot be identified by any particular partisan attachment.[105]

The degree of the commune's reliance on the supplementary resources of this group was bound to have radical consequences for the financial, and indirectly for the political, structure of the

---

[103] The observations on Florentine finance during the war, and particularly on the role of the Mediceans in this area, are based on Anthony Molho's work, published in *Florentine Public Finances*, Ch. 6, esp. pp. 166–82. I should like to thank him, however, for allowing me to read the earliest draft of this study some years ago, thus enabling me to integrate his findings into the argument of the doctoral thesis on which the present study is based.

[104] Camera del Comune, etc., Inventario, 509, 397.

[105] Molho, *Florentine Public Finances*, pp. 181–2.

Florentine state. The citizens of the *reggimento* were generally aware of the enormous power wielded by the magistracy in time of war, and the prominence in it of the Mediceans and their friends undoubtedly aroused some envy and disquiet; this may have been the reason for the numerous calls during these years for elective offices like the *Dieci* and the *Ufficiali del Banco* to be put into the purses, and thus more equitably distributed among the leading citizens. The limited nature of these proposals, however, might suggest that the full political implications of the financial expedients of these years were not always totally apparent to contemporaries.[106] Conversely, the continuing use of this body as an auxiliary, in time of financial crisis, to the regular machinery of the *catasto*, may have signified some partial acknowledgement of the fact that the need to sustain the credit structure, based on the *Monte*, or funded debt, led necessarily to a reliance on forced loans from individual citizens, and that the political consequences of this situation, however distasteful, were inescapable. Inevitably, the greatest shareholders in the state would be also its most influential citizens.[107]

It may be that Cosimo perceived these truths more clearly than others, and that the enormous financial contributions to the state from himself and his friends were made explicitly with the ingenious intention of manœuvring the remainder of the *reggimento* into a position of financial dependence on the leaders of the Medici party. However, his own observations to his cousin Averardo, and those of the other *amici*, provide no support for such a hypothesis. Cosimo was far too shrewd to have been entirely unaware of the power and prestige which they were, quite literally, purchasing with their loans, but private Medicean comment on financial matters suggests that they, like the rest of the *reggimento*,

---

[106] Cf. Molho, *Florentine Public Finances*, p. 178.

[107] On these questions, see particularly M. Becker, 'Problemi della finanza', also 'Economic Change and the Emerging Florentine Territorial State', *Studies in the Renaissance*, xiii (1966), 7–39; L. Marks, 'The Financial Oligarchy'. Molho (*Florentine Public Finances*) explores in detail the economic dimension of the war with Lucca, and makes some interesting and suggestive observations concerning its political implications (pp. 183–92). The evidence examined in this chapter would not confirm the element of calculation in Medicean financial assistance to the state about which he speculates, and in general the present study emphasizes factors other than financial predominance in explaining the Medici rise to power; conversely, the latter should not be minimized, and hopefully, as Molho suggests, future research may reveal more about its role in these events.

primarily responded to the obvious and immediate needs created by events, and that their vision of the likely political consequences of the financial situation was somewhat less explicit than that which hindsight allows us.[108]

Molho has observed that despite the high rate of interest on his loans, it would appear from the fragmentary evidence available that in purely financial terms Cosimo may have lost money rather than profited by lending such enormous sums to the state.[109] Certainly the letters of several of the leading *amici* during this period are full of moral strictures on the necessity of fulfilling one's financial duty to the commune, and somewhat self-satisfied comparisons of their own assiduity in this respect with the derelictions of others, including some of their more prominent political opponents. In February 1430 Averardo received a letter from the chief partner in his bank, Andrea Bardi, complaining of the enormous *catasto* payment being demanded of them, which in fact, he declared, they were incapable of meeting; he suggested that the commune should look to others better off than themselves, like Niccolò da Uzzano and Bernardo Lamberteschi, two of the wealthier and more eminent members of the aristocratic faction.[110] In July 1431 Niccolò Valori expressed the opinion that the war would by then have been won but for lack of finance, and spoke bitterly of those who 'refuse to lay out a farthing for the defence of liberty, and thus abandon the commune', preferring rather 'to defend their own state with the property of their companions, and indeed they don't realize what straits we are in; it must be driven home to them by reason and by fear'.[111] The following month when both the *Dieci* and the *Ufficiali del Banco* were heavily Medicean in composition, Alamanno Salviati declared in a letter to Averardo that 'those who avoid paying their

---

[108] Several days after the appointment in September 1431 of a group of twenty *Ufficiali del Banco* who included Giovanni Corbinelli, Antonio di Salvestro Serristori, Filippo Carducci (brother of Bartolomeo and Niccolò), Andrea Pazzi, Giuliano Ginori, Puccio Pucci, and Cosimo himself, Niccolò Valori wrote to Averardo that 'our consolation is in these 20 men, for we may hope that they will greatly assist us'; he may well have been speaking to some extent as a partisan, but on the other hand Cosimo, Lorenzo, Alamanno Salviati, and Giuliano Ginori had all expressed the opinion in *Pratiche* that the role of the *Ufficiali del Banco* was crucial to the safety of the commune (e.g. C.P. 49, ff. 100v, 146v–147r, 228v; 50, f. 23v).

[109] Molho, *Florentine Public Finances*, pp. 176–8.

[110] M.A.P. II, 217, 17 Feb. 1430 (1429 *s.f.*).

[111] Ibid. III, 196, 10 July 1431.

taxes are defrauding the commune, and so many do it, that those who are doing their duty wonder whether they should or not, which doesn't seem unreasonable, since indeed I don't know why I should worry about our liberty more than Messer Palla, who hasn't settled either his private debts or those to the commune, and I don't point out only because it affects me that he hasn't paid anything since April, and that nor has Messer Giovanni Guicciardini and a lot of others.'[112] Writing to Giuliano on the same day he emphasized again that 'the leading citizens are the worst'.[113] A week later he repeated that 'nobody pays unless he wants to, and those who do in fact pay are then so completely discouraged that they too fall behind . . . God only help us; I do what good I can . . .'[114]

Although the evidence concerning the enormous Medicean loans to the commune, coupled with their political triumph less than eighteen months after the peace, strongly suggests a connection between the major role which they played in financing the war, and their subsequent ascendancy in government, it is difficult to say at this stage whether, or to what extent, the Medici were recalled in 1434 because the Florentine state could not survive without their financial support. But clearly the strains and stresses of the war intensified factional feelings to the extent that some observers, looking back, believed it had been their essential cause, and it does seem that by 1433 the advantage in the contest between the two major parties within the *reggimento* had passed to the Mediceans. This, even more than the influence of their experiences on the loyalties of individuals, and subsequently on their actions, was perhaps the most profound effect of the war upon the Florentine factions. In March 1432 Vanni de' Medici observed of the Medicean influence outside Florence that 'thanks be to God, we are in green pastures'.[115] Two months later Giuliano Ginori reported on the progress of the party in one of the latest surviving letters written by the Medici and their friends before the exile of Cosimo in September 1433; as he told Averardo, 'your friends really have the wind in their sails, and are navigating in all waters'.[116]

[112] M.A.P. IV, 19, 11 Aug. 1431. [113] Ibid. III, 381.
[114] Ibid. IV, 50, 18 Aug. 1431. [115] Ibid. III, 110, 17 Mar. 1432 (1431 *s.f.*).
[116] Ibid. V, 201, 12 May 1432.

5

The Confrontation

(1433–1434)

ON 26 April 1433 the peace with Lucca was finally concluded. In the months that followed, the composition of the principal offices reflected no sudden and dramatic change in the balance of power between the two major parties within the *reggimento*. However, while during the war years the number of Mediceans in the temporarily swollen ranks of the *Ufficiali del Banco* had been remarkable, of the new and smaller group appointed in May 1433 not one member was a partisan of the Medici family.[1]

Niccolò da Uzzano, leader of the conservative faction and the outstanding representative of its point of view, had died during the second year of the war. Although no evidence remains to illuminate the process of Rinaldo's final alienation from the Mediceans, and his definitive assumption of the leadership of the conservative circle for which he had long been a vocal spokesman on many issues of principle,[2] Cavalcanti assures us that by the time the war was over the Uzzaneschi were following Rinaldo degli Albizzi, and seeking an opportunity by any means to expel Cosimo. Rinaldo's own experience and view of his position in the *stato* predisposed him to seek leadership of the Florentine ruling group at any cost, and certainly in terms of background and associations, the conservative and aristocratic group were his natural allies, though in fact, according to Cavalcanti, Rinaldo hesitated to identify himself fully with either group:

Given that he often behaved like a Medicean, and then at other times like an enemy of theirs, as if utterly in agreement with the Uzzani . . . it was said by many people, and particularly those who were best informed, that he didn't know what he wanted, unless to be recognized

---

[1] Camera del Comune, Inventario, 509. The composition of the office commencing on 30 Nov. 1433 was also heavily conservative.

[2] Brucker, *The Civic World*, Chs. 5, 7.

as the most able man, and I agreed with their view that all these cunning changes of direction that he made so often were because he wanted to be the boss of a party and the leader of the citizens.[3]

But by the end of the war the Mediceans constituted a threat to his position in the *stato* which could no longer be ignored, and the death of Niccolò da Uzzano obviously offered a convenient opportunity to Rinaldo to consolidate his own position with the help of those who had been his father's friends and allies.

The Strozzi, the other leading family which before and during the war had maintained a relative independence in the internal balance of the *reggimento*, may have been similarly motivated in their support of the conservatives between September 1433 and September 1434; they too had innumerable natural ties with that group, and shared some of its general sense of crisis and decline. Although Palla di Nofri, their most eminent and experienced statesman, was likely to have been more idealistic, or at least more objective than Rinaldo degli Albizzi in his evaluation of the relative claims of public and private interest, the two were very closely identified in his own mind, and this fact probably influenced his judgements in the public sphere.[4] Certainly Lionardo d'Antonio Strozzi's letter to his kinsman Matteo di Simone, bemoaning the harm suffered recently by their house on account of a lack of good men, made this connection quite explicitly when he concluded by observing 'the disgrace of our community by the evil men within it' and prayed 'that God might repair this deficiency'.[5]

As early as 1426 the conservative oligarchs had seen their position threatened by the challenge of a faction whose policy was to strengthen itself by widening the base of the regime, while at the same time squeezing many of the old guard out of office. By the beginning of 1433 it may well have appeared to many that the Medici and their friends had succeeded in doing just this,[6]

---

[3] *Istorie*, p. 264. Cf. above, pp. 204–5.
[5] C.S. 3ᵃ ser. CXXXI, c. 20; cf. ibid. CXIV, c. 9, Matteo to Benedetto Strozzi: '. . . istimando l'onorre del chomune assai, ch'è simile del nostro', and above, pp. 143–4.
[6] It is possible that the Medici *amici* were taking more specifically aggressive action against the conservative leadership in the first half of 1433; Professor Gene Brucker has drawn my attention to several accusations resulting in trials for malfeasance which may have represented an attempt to discredit this group. Giovanni di M. Rinaldo Gianfigliazzi was accused of taking a bribe while serving as vicar of San Miniato, but he was absolved (Giud. Appelli 77, pt. 2, ff. 229r–v, 29 May 1433). Giovanni di M. Donato Barbadori was convicted of barattry while serving as

and so it is not surprising, once the war had been concluded and the leaders of the *reggimento* were free to turn their attention to questions other than those of survival, that men of like mind and close associations should coalesce into a concrete party to effect the solution proposed in 1426—to create a *Balìa*, enlist the aid of magnates, abolish the *rimbotto*, and carry out a new scrutiny, with Rinaldo cast in the role for which his father had provided the prototype.

The initial prerequisite for such action was to deprive the opposition of its leadership, and the characteristic Florentine way of doing this was by exile. As early as the beginning of 1431 Lippozzo Mangioni, speaking in a *Consulta* on the need to achieve unity, had raised the spectre of 'confinement or exile' if the divisions among the leading citizens continued.[7] While Florence made peace with the external foe, enmities within the city walls caused increasing unrest. In April 1433 the functions of the police magistracy, the *Otto di Guardia*, were extended to cope with the growing number of disturbances in the city at night.[8] One such incident which occurred in August, shortly before the storm broke, was an attack on Piero Serragli, a scion of one of the leading conservative families, by two citizens without surnames from the Medici quarter of San Giovanni. Piero Serragli had been on his way home from the palace of the Priors when he was set upon, seized by the hair, and struck in the face several times.[9]

Although there is no record of any open moves against the Medici by the conservative faction in the months between April and September, there is evidence that the Medici may have read their approaching fate in these signs of the times. According to Raymond de Roover, in his study of the Medici bank,

the Medici records . . . give the impression that a coup was in the offing and that precautions were being taken to meet any emergency. On

---

Podestà of Montepulciano, and fined 1,500 florins (ibid. ff. 334r–336r, 13 July 1433). Mariotto Baldovinetti was accused of extortion while serving as *Commissario* in Volterra during the rebellion, but the case was dropped (ibid. ff. 303r–304v, 31 July 1433). Conversely, these denunciations, like those of the war years, might well have been made by any number of others, even within the ruling group.

[7] C.P. 49, f. 124v; above, p. 247.

[8] G. Antonelli, 'La magistratura degli Otto di Guardia a Firenze', *A.S.I.* cxii (1954), 3–39. See esp. 16–17.

[9] Cap. Pop. Lib. Inquis. 3170, f. 38v. There is no concrete evidence to associate this incident with partisan conflicts, but the details of the case are suggestive.

30 May 1433, 3,000 Venetian ducats in coin were removed from the former residence of Ilarione de' Bardi and handed over for safe keeping to the Benedictine Hermits of San Miniato al Monte. Another 5,877 ducats were placed in custody at the Dominican friary of San Marco. On the same day, 15,000 florins were transferred by the *tavola* of Florence to the credit of the Medici branch in Venice. Cosimo and his brother Lorenzo sold stock in the Monte Comune, worth 10,000 florins, to their branch in Rome. All these precautionary moves suggest that the Medici were mobilizing their resources and accumulating liquid reserves to ward off any run on their *tavola* in Florence. At the same time, they were storing their specie in places where it would be safe from confiscation by a hostile Florentine government.[10]

The Medici may have made some effort to defuse the situation by withdrawing temporarily from the Florentine political scene. Mediceans played a leading part in *Pratiche* dealing with finance as late as May 1433; on 14 May a report was jointly presented by Cosimo and Puccio Pucci, and their proposition signed by ten more citizens who included Piero Guicciardini and Alamanno Salviati for the *Dieci di Balìa*.[11] But in the succeeding months leading Mediceans became less prominent in the *Pratiche*, and Cosimo himself, according to his own account, retired to the Mugello for several months 'to remove myself from the strife and divisions which existed in the city'. It was there that he received the request from the newly elected *Signoria* for September–October 1433 to return to Florence, which he did on 4 September. On 5 September he was summoned to the palace of the Priors on the pretext of a *Pratica* to be held there in two days' time; on his arrival he was promptly arrested and incarcerated.[12]

There is no specific evidence concerning the genesis and the authors of this *coup*, but these can be quite plainly inferred from the events themselves. The *Signoria* which took office on 1 September was captained by Bernardo Guadagni as Gonfalonier of Justice. A member of a consular family from the *gonfalone* of Chiavi, his father Vieri had been among the leaders of the meeting at Santo Stefano in 1426. He himself had emerged in the *Consulte* of the intervening years as one of the foremost opponents of the Medici, and among his closer *parenti* were the Lamberteschi, the Bischeri, and Giovanni Guicciardini, all of whom were to be

[10] *The Rise and Decline*, p. 54.   [11] C.P. 50, ff. 71v–72r.
[12] *Ricordi*, p. 96.

closely associated with the anti-Medicean regime in the following twelve months. The other two representatives of the Medicean quarter of San Giovanni in the *Signoria* of September were both *minori*, Piero Marchi and Iacopo Luti.[13] Neither belonged to the inner circle of the *reggimento*. The Priors from Santa Maria Novella, Bartolomeo Spini and Mariotto di Niccolò Baldovinetti, were both members of the hard core of the conservative party, and related to other leading families in the group like the Guasconi, Castellani, and Manelli. The Spini family owed its final economic collapse to the loss of the papal banking business to the Medici; the Baldovinetti were a family of great antiquity who still owned part of a tower which they had shared with the magnate Manelli since 1222.[14] Of the Priors from Santa Croce, Jacopo Berlinghieri was not an enemy of the Medici, and after September 1434 was exempted from the punishment meted out to his colleagues. Corso di Lapo Corsi, however, had married into the Albizzi family and was closely associated with the conservative group. From Santo Spirito, Donato Sannini was also excepted from punishment; his fellow representative for Oltrarno was Giovanni dello Scelto, who was ready to play a leading role in the anti-Medicean regime.[15]

According to Cavalcanti, the secret of the purses was by now an open one; he claimed that Rinaldo degli Albizzi knew Bernardo Guadagni was to be drawn, and judging that under his Gonfalonierate the moment had come to move against the Medici, laid aside the traditional enmity between Guadagni and Albizzi and paid Bernardo's tax to keep him off the *specchio*. He then persuaded the Gonfalonier to undertake the banishment of Cosimo, assuring him of the support of the 'old-established members of the ruling group', especially the Guasconi and Rondinelli, and 'all the nobles'.[16] Whether this is true or not, Cosimo himself asserted that as soon as the *Signoria* was drawn and seen to contain such a strong representation from the conservative faction, 'it began to

[13] Tratte, 93, f. 43v. The two representatives to which the minor guilds were entitled in each group of eight Priors were drawn from the quarter to which the Gonfalonier of Justice belonged. In this case the system worked very much to the advantage of the anti-Mediceans; at the same time as they secured the partisan Guadagni as Gonfalonier of Justice they also obviated the possibility of powerful Mediceans from the major guilds being drawn as Priors for the Medici quarter.

[14] Above, pp. 160–2, 163–4.   [15] Tratte, 93, ff. 14v, 25v, 34v.
[16] *Istorie*, pp. 263, 266–70.

be rumoured that during their term of office there the government of the city would be reformed'. He claimed to be surprised by the action against himself as he believed most of the group to be quite friendly to him, particularly Giovanni dello Scelto, 'whom I considered to be a great friend, and he was beholden to me'.[17] However, it soon became clear that the *Signoria* was not acting entirely on its own initiative, but rather co-operating, presumably at the instigation of its anti-Medicean members, with the leaders of the conservative faction soon to become the leaders of the anti-Medicean regime. The *Pratica* under the pretence of which his enemies effected the essential step of capturing and holding Cosimo prisoner contained, besides himself, three outstanding figures of the anti-Medicean regime—Rinaldo degli Albizzi, Ridolfo Peruzzi, and Giovanni di Messer Rinaldo Gianfigliazzi. With them were two more prominent conservatives, Giovanni Guicciardini and Tommaso Corsi, and after them these five drew by friendship, marriage, and association a substantial proportion of the conservative faction. The two Mediceans present, Bartolomeo Ridolfi and Agnolo Acciaiuoli, were outnumbered and obviously outmanœuvred; with Cosimo in the enemy's hands they were in no position to oppose the resolution of the rest that he should be exiled. According to Cosimo, he was retained in custody 'so that they would be able to succeed in the *Balìa* in arranging the government of the city in the way that they wanted; for when their proposals were not accepted, they threatened to have me killed, and for fear of this my friends and relatives in the *Balìa* resolved to accept whatever measures were put before them'.[18]

The exile proposal, when submitted to the *Signoria*, was passed, he claimed, with six out of the nine votes. An ordinance of the *Signoria* issued on 8 September to all rectors and officials of the city condemned to death any of those present who should express in public or in private any opinion on the meetings concerning Cosimo's fate, and no one was able to visit or converse with him without special permission.[19] Although a move against Cosimo had been generally anticipated, the speed and discretion with

[17] *Ricordi*, p. 96. Obviously patronage, even with a partisan tinge, was not inevitably rewarded with grateful service.

[18] Ibid., p. 98.

[19] Gelli, 'L'esilio di Cosimo' 149.

which his opponents acted when the moment came appears to have taken Florence by surprise. Cavalcanti relates that

the word went out through the city that Cosimo was being held in the Palace; at which the citizens were much dismayed, and knew not what to do. But Messer Rinaldo came out with a great troop of men, and rode to the *piazza*, and the Peruzzi, the Gianfigliazzi, and all those who had belonged to Da Uzzano's faction, did the same.[20]

Strategy was underlined by a show of force, and owing, perhaps, to the firmness with which the conservatives as a group took control of the situation, the *Parlamento*, summoned by Guadagni as Gonfalonier of Justice, was held on 9 September 'without any blood being spilt'.[21] Over 200 citizens were nominated to assist the *Signoria* and given *balìa* to reform the government. Two days later 'the Count of Poppi sent us 500 foot-soldiers to protect the *Signoria* and similarly from all over the *contado* came troops who kept guard day and night'.[22]

On the same day the *Balìa* began its work, and in the circumstances the claim, with which it prefaced its deliberations, that it had been constituted because 'the whole city was disturbed, and up in arms', rings somewhat false. Nearer the mark is the admission that the *Balìa* existed to assist the *Signoria* and the *Podestà* in their activities 'so that with God's grace, scandals might be got rid of, and dangers removed'.[23] Their first act was to exile the Medici, described later in the judicial condemnation as 'disturbers of the citizens of their native city, and destroyers of the state, and sowers of scandal'.[24] The entire family, excepting the descendants of Vieri de' Medici, one of whom, Nicola, was at the time among the sixteen *Gonfalonieri di Compagnia*, was deprived of the right to hold office for ten years. Those actually exiled were Averardo to Naples, Cosimo to Padua, his brother Lorenzo to Venice, Giuliano d'Averardo to Rome, Orlando di Guccio to Ancona, Bernardo and Gregorio d'Alamanno to Rimini, and Vanni d'Andrea to Fano.[25] Initially the longest sentences—those of Averardo and Cosimo—were for five years, but were later increased to ten.

---

[20] *Istorie*, pp. 272. [21] C.S. 2ª ser. CIII, f. 110r.
[22] MSS. 229, p. 165; cf. C.S. 2ª ser. 103, Sept.–Oct. 1433.
[23] Balìe, 24, f. 1r. [24] Fabroni, *Cosmi vita* ii. 73.
[25] Balìe, 24, ff. 10v, 23r. Bernardo and Gregorio are wrongly described in the condemnation as the sons of the famous Salvestro; he was in fact their grandfather.

Apart from the obvious desire to remove the Medici from the city in which they had become too powerful, the clearest intention apparent in the terms of the exile was to strike at the financial basis of their power. The bonds demanded from them were enormous, especially by comparison with those imposed on the exiles by the pro-Medicean government a year later. Rinaldo degli Albizzi had to find sureties (*mallevadori*) for 4,000 florins, Giovanni Gianfigliazzi and Palla Strozzi for only 1,000 florins each, and even Ridolfo Peruzzi, meriting the highest assessment, no more than 10,000. Cosimo's guarantee, however, was for 20,000 gold florins, Averardo and Lorenzo di Giovanni 10,000 each, Giuliano 5,000, and even Orlando di Guccio had to guarantee 3,000.[26] Similarly, in view of the provisions which entitled the Tower Officials to confiscate the property of exiles to settle their debts, and the exclusion of credits in their name from the obligations of the *Monte*,[27] it is obvious that the anti-Mediceans were hoping the exile of their enemies would bring economic ruin in its train, and perhaps that they might make some profit into the bargain. Cosimo himself believed that it was the intention of his enemies 'to bankrupt us', but as he observed, 'their plan was not successful, for we didn't lose credit by it, but in fact a huge sum of money was offered to us by foreign merchants and lords, and sent to Venice'.[28]

In addition to expelling those who threatened their security, the *Balìa* instigated by the conservative faction carried out the two other principal prescriptions of 1426. On 8 December it was laid down that there should be no further *rimbotto* of the purses for the Priorate.[29] Earlier, at the beginning of October, some concessions had been made to the magnates as a class by the restitution of certain offices to that group.[30] These concessions were as yet limited; magnates were still not admitted to the key internal magistracies which they had previously been forbidden, but a number of quite important external posts were opened to them. At any rate, the provision was clearly a gesture intended to enlist the sympathy of the magnates for the conservative regime.[31] Of

---

[26] Balìe, f. 11r.   [27] Fabroni, *Cosmi vita* ii. 91–5.
[28] *Ricordi*, p. 99. See also de Roover, 'Cosimo de' Medici' 470.
[29] Balìe, 24, f. 63v.   [30] Ibid., f. 36r–v.
[31] Stoldo Frescobaldi, a magnate prominent in the opposition party, was made a *popolano*, but on the return of the Medici in 1434 he was again *privato*. See also Cavalcanti's account of Rinaldo's attempt at a *rapprochement* with the *grandi* (*Istorie*, p. 288).

course the reward of its supporters was a prominent concern of the new *reggimento*, and the names of those in whose favour acts were passed by the *Balìa* are additional confirmation of the identity of the authors of the *coup* against Cosimo. Among those rewarded for their co-operation were most of the Priors who took office in September, with the notable exception of Berlinghieri. As Cambi commented, after the *Parlamento* of 1433, 'to each of the Priors who were faithful to them, and had summoned the *Parlamento*, they gave some office'.[32] Others similarly favoured included members of the Velluti, Manelli, Gianfigliazzi, Aldobrandini, Strozzi, dall'Antella, Serragli, and Brancacci families.[33]

Apart from these comparatively predictable acts outlined above, the remainder of the provisions enacted reflect a general desire to maintain the *status quo*.[34] This was not a reforming *Balìa*. There is some evidence that, as Nerli wrote much later, Rinaldo was aware of a 'universal discontent' and the presence in the city of 'those who had not really declared which party they belonged to'.[35] For instance, Neri di Gino Capponi was obviously one of the more important of these, and notably the *Signoria* was anxious to have him out of Florence as soon as possible. He had recently been elected one of the *Cinque di Pisa*, and when on 21 September he had not departed, the *Signoria* and Colleges issued a deliberation 'that by the authority of the Priors, Neri di Gino Capponi should be enjoined to leave the city of Florence and go to the city of Pisa to take up his office'.[36] In the absence of really striking innovations, much of the work of the *Balìa* consisted in the transaction of the general business which would normally have fallen to various councils which were temporarily suspended, or to the major offices whose functions the *Balìa* had assumed. However, all members of the *Balìa* were given the right to bear arms for the duration of the proceedings, a new scrutiny was carried out, and it was decreed that no further scrutinies should take place until 1440.[37]

It is surprising that there was no thorough-going attempt to purge the *reggimento* of those who might be hostile to the conservative aristocratic faction. Certainly the decision to hold a scrutiny in 1433, when the next scrutiny of the *Tre Maggiori* was not due until 1436, indicated a desire and an intention on the part

[32] *Istorie*, p. 186.　　　　　　　　　　　　[33] Balìe, 24, *passim*.
[34] Cf. Rubinstein, *Government of Florence*, p. 2.　　[35] *Commentarii* i, 68.
[36] Gelli, 'L'esilio di Cosimo' 151.　　　　[37] Balìe, 24, ff. 11v–12r, 13v–15v, 63v.

of the new regime to strengthen its support within the ruling group through a revision of the lists of those eligible for key office in government. Moreover, the suspension of sortition in favour of the election of the November–December *Signoria* by the then current *Signoria* and *Accoppiatori* represented a striking departure from normal constitutional practice, and set an example in electoral control for the future Medicean regime.[38] However, this unusual procedure was employed on only one occasion; had it been continued throughout 1434 it is unlikely that the Medici would have found an opportunity to return to Florence at the invitation of the Priors. As it was, the composition of a *Signoria* chosen by lot depended generally on the nature of the scrutiny from which the bags had been filled, and the scrutiny of September 1433, apart from the exclusion of the Medici themselves, was not markedly different from those which came before and after, and in effect made even more similar to its predecessors by virtue of the decision to combine the new *borse* based on the new scrutiny with old *borse* dating back to 1391.[39] This was an action which must have surprised many Florentine observers besides Giovanni Cavalcanti and Benedetto Dei, who commented on the foolishness of the conservative leaders in having failed to take the opportunity to destroy the old purses, and with them the political future of their opponents; instead 'they put their enemies into the purses and allowed them to remain there',[40] so that 'after a number of drawings of the *Signoria*, there were hardly any that were in any way different from those which occurred before the scrutiny'.[41]

It is difficult to account for this almost wilful failure to safeguard the new regime from its enemies, especially in view of the existence of precedents for electoral purges,[42] and in the light of the realization, widely expressed in the *Pratiche* of the preceding years, and summed up by Rinaldo degli Albizzi himself, that the cause of civic discord 'is ambition for office'.[43] One must assume either that Rinaldo degli Albizzi and his friends simply underestimated the strength of the Medici party, and overestimated the extent of their own support within the *reggimento*, or else that they recognized the influence of the Mediceans and feared to move

[38] Rubinstein, *Government of Florence*, pp. 5–7.   [39] Ibid., p. 7.
[40] Dei, 'Chronica', MSS. 119, f. 13r.   [41] Cavalcanti, *Istorie*, p. 297.
[42] See above, pp. 213–19; Rubinstein, *Government of Florence*, p. 7.
[43] C.P. 49, f. 124r.

against such a powerful segment of the ruling group. Obviously they expected that most non-partisans would support the *status quo*, which apparently they still envisaged as the oligarchic regime which had ruled Florence for thirty years before Giovanni di Bicci commenced his rise to power, since in the *Balìa* which they appointed, of more than 200 citizens in addition to representatives of major offices, only 54 were so blatantly anti-Medicean as to merit exile the following year, and 13 were in fact *amici* of the Medici.[44] Similarly, the names of those *richiesti* to the few *Consulte* held in the first three months after Cosimo's arrest indicate little change in the composition of the recognized *reggimento*.[45]

However, if the action, or rather inaction, of the new regime did reflect such assumptions, they were soon to prove ill founded. In fact by 1433, when the comparative success of the challenge to their predominance in the ruling group finally impelled the conservatives to a response, the situation they had feared and prophesied in 1426 had almost eventuated; their rivals were already firmly established, not only in the purses, but also by their pervasive influence in the inner circles of the ruling group, in the city at large, and even beyond its walls. If they hoped through the exile of the Medici family to destroy their party by decapitating it, or by undermining its financial support, and thus to re-possess the body of its followers in the name of the new regime, then they misunderstood its nature and quality. The Medici friends were a powerful, extensive, coherent, and ambitious group who, far from collapsing on the arrest of their leaders, rose rapidly to their assistance, and did not rest until the situation was reversed, the exiles reinstated, and their enemies banished in their stead; indeed the Medici owed their recall largely to the manifold activity of their various friends in several spheres. Some of the *amici* offered immediate personal assistance which cushioned the effects of the *coup* on proscribed members of the family, by smoothing their path into exile, by keeping open the channels of communication for the transmission of information and advice on affairs in Florence (despite the dangers of consorting with enemies of the state), by preserving and defending their property and families during their absence. As a result of the close relations between the Medici and leading statesmen of other Italian powers, official diplomatic pressure was brought to bear upon the Florentine government to

[44] Balìe, 24, ff. 2v–5v.   [45] C.P. 50, ff. 100r–110v.

consider their recall, while foreign capital was generously advanced to support their business. At home in Florence the Medici influence was maintained in the electoral bags and thence indirectly expressed in the persons of their followers, in the councils, in the *Pratiche*, in key offices, and finally in the *Signoria* itself.

Even before Cosimo's arrest, his friends were alert to protect his interests; Piero Guicciardini was said to have warned him against attending the fatal *Pratica* in the palace of the Priors.[46] Cosimo records how once he had been seized, the *amici* 'immediately informed my brother Lorenzo, who was in the Mugello, and Averardo my cousin, who was at Pisa'.[47] One of those responsible for this quick-witted action was Ser Giovanni de' Caffarecci, tutor to Cosimo's sons, and a member of his household, who was tried by the *Capitano del Popolo* later in 1433 on the charge that 'knowing Cosimo de' Medici had been detained at the request of the aforesaid Lord Priors in their palace . . . and that they were looking for Averardo de' Medici, who was at Pisa, at his house . . . he revealed to the aforesaid Averardo all that the Priors intended against him, and arranged matters in such a way that Averardo was able to flee to the city of Lucca'.[48] Quite possibly Cosimo owed his life, and the Medici party its survival, to the fact that despite his arrest Averardo, the leading co-ordinator of the *amici*, and Lorenzo, joint heir with his brother to Giovanni di Bicci's bank and fortune, were at large and in a position to revenge any injury done to Cosimo; as the latter observed, 'if all three of us had been taken, we might well have come to harm'.

The *amici* also hastened to convey his situation to Niccolò da Tolentino, Captain of War to the Commune and described by Cosimo as 'a most faithful friend of mine'.[49] Throughout the war with Lucca various members of the Medici family, and particularly Averardo, had worked closely with him; presumably in apprising Niccolò of the attack against Cosimo, the *amici* expected that he might well descend on the city with the Florentine forces under his command, and forcibly re-establish the Medici. This was clearly what their opponents had in mind when, on the day of Cosimo's arrest, they formally notified the Captain of War of

[46] Cavalcanti, *Istorie*, pp. 270–1.   [47] *Ricordi*, p. 97.
[48] Gelli, 'L'esilio di Cosimo' 157; see also de Roover, *The Rise and Decline*, p. 37; Cap. Pop. Lib. Inquis. 3175, f. 84r.
[49] *Ricordi*, p. 97.

their decision to confine Cosimo and Averardo de' Medici 'so that every thought and decision of our republic should be known to your Magnificence'.[50] They declared themselves anxious that he should understand the reasons for their action, and that 'everything is being done in order to avoid greater scandals, and for the sake of the peace and tranquillity of our city and of this government'. In fact, as Cosimo recounted, 'Niccolò da Tolentino, having heard how things stood, proceeded on the morning of the 8th with all his company to Lastra, with the intention of raising a rebellion in Florentine territory'; the Florentine government in alarm ordered him to return at once to Pisa, where he was stationed. Such a demonstration of force at this time by the Mediceans might well have been successful. In addition to the troops commanded by Tolentino they also had at their disposal 'a large quantity of foot-soldiers' who presented themselves to Lorenzo 'as soon as the news of the incident became known in the alps of the Romagna, and in many other places', among them particularly the Mugello, north of Florence (once described by Giovanni Morelli as the home of Florence's finest fighting men),[51] where the Medici clan were strongly entrenched, and where as great landowners they commanded a good deal of personal loyalty from local residents.[52] However, in the end, in Cosimo's words, and obviously to his chagrin,

the Captain and Lorenzo were advised not to stir up a revolt, which might be the occasion of my coming to harm, which they accepted, and although those who gave this advice were relatives and friends, and acting with good intentions, it was not good advice, because if they had gone ahead, I should have been free, and those who were the occasion of my plight would have been destroyed.[53]

Nevertheless, the *amici* were bold enough openly to defy their partisan opponents who had seized control of the government. According to Cavalcanti, Piero Ginori, on hearing the news of Cosimo's arrest, 'quite fearlessly roamed the city, shouting out, and showing himself to be utterly lacking in wisdom, and in fact quite mad'.[54] Nor had considerations of prudence deterred Caffarecci, who in addition to privately warning Averardo of the intentions of the *Signoria*, had held public gatherings in the *contado*

[50] Gelli, 'L'esilio di Cosimo' 157.
[51] Morelli, *Ricordi*, p. 95.
[52] See also above, p. 117; below, pp. 337–8.
[53] *Ricordi*, Fabroni, p. 97.
[54] *Istorie*, pp. 279–80.

inciting his listeners to rebellion against them. It was revealed at his trial that in Lucca 'he made the following conspiratorial speech, designed to stir up scandal, and to do enormous damage to the peace and good order of the state and its rulers: "Messer Rinaldo degli Albizzi and the others with him, and even the Lord Priors of Florence, will rule but a short time in Florence in view of the way things stand"'.[55]

Cosimo's condemnation of the timidity of his friends seems a little ungrateful in view of their profound and emotional concern for the safety of his person; a week after his arrest Bernardo di Antonio de' Medici wrote to Averardo maintaining that 'at the present moment my only wish is that he should escape without injury, and my grief at seeing him in such danger is more inconsolable than any which I have ever experienced or could ever imagine'.[56] On the last day of September Lippaccio de' Bardi, in a letter to Cosimo's son Piero, who had already taken refuge in Venice, could only declare: 'There is no more that I can say concerning the sorrow and regret which I have felt and feel about what has happened . . . there is nothing for us to do but pray that God will inspire those who can to put an end to such cruelty.' In fact the following day he was able to report that 'this evening I heard from Filippo Guadagni that tonight at six o'clock Cosimo will be set free from the Palace to go to Padua; I can't tell you how relieved I was'. However, not having sent off the letter immediately, he added a postscript three days later explaining that Cosimo himself had feared to risk his life in a precipitate departure,

because that night there was a great crowd in the *piazza*, and some wanted one thing and some another, and every one said his piece, and the Gonfalonier of Justice and Mariotto Baldovinetti went to Cosimo and said to him: 'If you want to go we will let you, but look out for yourself'; and because Cosimo was suspicious, as indeed he was right to be, he said 'I would rather stay here than go outside and be attacked'.

Nevertheless, Bardi concluded hopefully: 'But I think that without fail he will be out in two days, and perhaps it may even be tonight.'[57] In fact it was; Cosimo did slip away from the palace that night after dark, and was soon on his way under escort to Venice.

[55] Gelli, 'L'esilio di Cosimo' 159.　　　　[56] M.A.P. C. 160.
[57] Ibid. XVI, 346.

Once Cosimo was out of custody, it rapidly became clear that in resisting the temptation to meet violence with violence, the Mediceans had made the right judgement; as Cosimo observed, 'one might say that it was all for the best, because it led to far greater good, and my honour was greatly increased by it'.[58] For no sooner was the news of Cosimo's banishment made public than his non-Florentine friends began to come forward in his defence, and the extent of Medici support and influence outside the city began to reveal itself. Through their activity as bankers and their increasing participation in the most responsible positions in the Florentine government, the Medici had established friendships with other important statesmen throughout the peninsula, and even across the Alps. They had also made a favourable impression in other cities within Florentine territory; for example, Cosimo had earned the regard of the citizens of San Gimignano while in office there, and in a letter to Averardo a group of them expressed their high opinion of the family in general.[59] Similarly, on the occasion of Giovanni's death, the people and commune of Pistoia wrote conveying their regret; some years before he had been *Podestà* there and 'had always honoured and supported this commune in every way'. Consequently, they felt themselves obliged, not only to him and to his memory 'but to all his family who survive him', and accorded the entire house the honour of using the commune's arms.[60]

Medici influence was particularly strong, however, in the papal states and the Romagna, in the areas further to the north and east of the family's own extensive territorial base in the mountains north of Florence. During the decade preceding their exile, Averardo had frequently been employed by the commune as a commissioner in the Mugello; at Marradi, only a little further up the valley of the Lamone from the Medici-dominated areas of Ronta, Scarperia, and Borgo San Lorenzo, and also particularly at Faenza and Ferrara.[61] Several of the communes on the roads from Florence to Bologna, Imola, and Faenza had paid homage to the Medici with gifts on the occasion of Francesco di Giuliano's wedding only a few months before Cosimo's arrest,[62] and at the

[58] *Ricordi*, p. 97.   [59] M.A.P. II, 125.
[60] Ibid. II, 231; cf. XI, 40, 14 Oct. 1434, to Cosimo from the 'Otto defensori del popolo et Gonfaloniere di Giustizia della terra di Prato'.
[61] See M.A.P., *Inventario*, esp. Filze I–V.
[62] M.A.P. CXLVIII, 30; among them were Santa Maria a Campiano, San Piero

news of that event the men of the Romagnuol mountains were prominent among those who offered their support to Lorenzo. The Medici correspondence reveals the existence of special relationships between themselves and the lords of a number of territories in this general area.[63]

There are letters of the late twenties and early thirties from Lodovico Alidosi and several members of the Manfredi family, in various periods lords of Faenza, Imola, and the surrounding countryside, requesting Medici patronage for their friends or asking for Medici support and intervention in their dealings with the Florentine *Signoria*.[64] During his sojourn in Venice Cosimo received similar requests from families like the Bentivoglio of Bologna asking his intercession in their approaches to the government of the Doge, with whom he was also on intimate terms.[65] One of the Baglioni, lords of Perugia, later wrote to express his great pleasure at the Medici return to Florence, 'since I esteem your reputation and authority as I do my own'.[66] Not only Cosimo but also Averardo and his son Giuliano had, through their solicitude for his affairs, earned the friendship of the *condottiere* Micheletto Attendoli, Duke and Count of Cutigliano, who wrote to Averardo of the 'easy intimacy between us';[67] they had also helped to smooth his path in the transaction of business with the commune. With the Malatesta of Rimini the Medici enjoyed a particularly close relationship extending over a period of some years, and fostered partly through the intermediacy of Florentine *amici* like Filippo dall'Antella; their friendship and respect for Cosimo is especially apparent in one letter from Sigismondo Malatesta in the December after his recall, asking his advice and opinion about a domestic dispute in the territory of Rimini be-

a Sieve, and Ronta. Cf. a letter of Rosso Sassetti to Averardo during the war (Ibid. III, 312): 'Vi pregho fate come avete fatto a Vicho e fate presto e mandaci di vostri da Mugiello qualche trenta o quaranta balestrieri . . . che loro more son persona fidati (*sic*) . . .'

[63] On the great families of this area, see particularly J. Larner, *The Lords of Romagna* (New York, 1965), and P. J. Jones, *The Malatesta of Rimini and the Papal State* (Cambridge, 1974).

[64] M.A.P. I, 91, 94, Gentile Manfredi, Brisighella, to Averardo, 19, 24 Aug. 1425; XI, 7, Guidantonio Manfredi to Cosimo, 7 Mar. 1431; XI, 35, Astorgio Manfredi to Cosimo, 11 Nov. 1434; II, 102, Lodovico Alidosi to Averardo, 26 Apr. 1428.

[65] Ibid. XI, 37, Antonio Galeazzo de' Bentivogli to Cosimo, 5 Sept. 1434.

[66] Ibid. XI, 41, Malatesta de' Baglioni, 7 Oct. 1434.

[67] Ibid. V, 982, to Averardo, 27 Feb. 1434 (1433 *s.f.*).

tween the Bishop of Montefeltro and one of the local communes.[68] Cosimo was able to record with some satisfaction the details of his journey northwards into exile in Venetian territory, a triumphal progress in the course of which, outside Pistoia, he was 'greeted with a warm welcome and provisions as if I were an Ambassador'[69] by the men of the mountains, and escorted to Ferrara, whose ruler expressed his sympathies and observed that Florence 'was certainly going downhill';[70] there were similarly flattering representations from various other rulers along the road to Venice.

It was there, however, that the Medici had their most powerful friends, and enjoyed their strongest support during the year of their exile, in both the personal and the official spheres. The first Venetian branch of the Medici bank had been established by Giovanni di Bicci and Benedetto di Lippaccio de' Bardi in 1398; its partners there in 1433 were Lotto di Tanino Bozzi from Scarperia in the Mugello, and Giovanni Portinari, and its staff included Antonio Martelli, Francesco d'Antonio de' Medici, and Paolo Guasconi.[71] Some months earlier Cosimo and Lorenzo had transferred a good deal of capital from the Florentine *tavola* to Venice;[72] when Lorenzo was exiled there, and Cosimo to nearby Padua, being subsequently allowed the general freedom of the republic's territory, they could naturally make themselves at home and carry on their business, aided also by the substantial sums sent there by 'many foreign lords and merchants'.[73]

The advance party of Lorenzo and the younger members of the family, including Cosimo's sons and Averardo's grandson Francesco, were received royally on their arrival, as the latter proudly related in his correspondence with his father Giuliano, in exile at Rome. The following morning he accompanied Lorenzo to the

---

[68] Ibid. XI, 45, to Cosimo, 28 Dec. 1434; cf. the correspondence of Averardo over the preceding years with Malatesta and Galeazzo de' Malatesti, e.g. II, 295, 301, 303. See also the letters from Antonio Alberico 'Marchio Malaspina de Fosdinovo' (VI, 6), and Ugolino Helias, doctor of law of Rimini (III, 113).

[69] *Ricordi*, p. 98.

[70] M.A.P. V, 704; this comment was reported in a letter of Francesco de' Medici to his father Giuliano describing how he and Lorenzo had met by chance with the Marchese of Ferrara on the road to Venice.

[71] De Roover, *The Rise and Decline*, pp. 240–3. [72] Ibid., p. 54.

[73] Cosimo, *Ricordi*, p. 100. See also the personal letters from other Venetians expressing friendship and support for the Medici during this period, e.g. M.A.P. V, 295 (Iacopello Bufferio); CXXXVIII, 20 (Piero di Vicho).

palace of the *Signoria*, where 'he was accorded the greatest honour,
and everyone bemoaned his misfortune, and that of Averardo,
and I was with Lorenzo, who was deep in conversation with the
Doge, and when he heard of the release of Cosimo he expressed
the greatest possible joy'.[74] He went on to describe the formal
ceremony of welcome with which his cousin was greeted when at
last he was able to join them:

When he arrived, a great number of barges with these noble gentlemen
and their servants went to meet him, and although he arrived here in
the evening, nevertheless many came to visit him. But the next morning
very early he went to call on the Doge, in the presence of all the senate,
in the council chamber. He embraced him warmly, greatly lamenting
his misfortune, and then he sat down between Cosimo and Lorenzo,
as if they had been ambassadors . . . they remained thus for some time,
and all the rest of us went outside, and I can hardly describe the
brotherly affection which all these citizens have extended to them, and
to all our house, and above all my Lord the Doge, who really has
shown and continues to show his friendship in every possible way, so
that one may call him a true friend.

The young man's proud boast was in fact quite justified; the
Medici had received unambiguous assurances of support not only
from the Doge, but also from his kinsman Romeo Foscari. The
latter wrote of his regret on hearing of their expulsion from
Florence, 'which is so much the greater since your misfortune is
due solely to the bitterness of envy and not to any failing of yours
in your duty to your commune'. His own opinion was that their
wealth and reputation entitled them to be considered and treated
as powerful lords, rather than mere merchants; he assured them
that this was the view of all their Venetian friends, and that they
were 'very highly regarded by the Lord Governors of this state'.[75]
In his expression of the attitude of the Venetian government and
'all these noble gentlemen and merchants' to the Medici affair,
Foscari assumed that natural connection between financial and
political power which many Florentine citizens had also perceived, and indeed seen as good reason for the family's expulsion.
The Venetian view was shared by other, even more illustrious
rulers, like the German Emperor who, on learning of their situation from the Venetian ambassadors, had observed ironically that
'the Florentines have driven out those very physicians (*medici*) of

---

[74] M.A.P. V, 703, 14 Nov. 1433.   [75] Ibid. XX, 47, 21 Sept. 1433.

whom they have the greatest need'.[76] No doubt some Florentines were chagrined when the Emperor's pun filtered back to them, but in view of the fact that Venice had traditionally been the city's most valued ally, the Venetian stance was of the greatest possible concern to the ruling group in Florence and a powerful political weapon in the hands of the Mediceans.

Their Venetian well-wishers soon translated their encouraging words into actions. The *Serenissima* dispatched to Florence an eminent envoy, Jacopo Donado, an intimate personal friend of the Medici who had already lent to Cosimo his own luxurious villa for his use in Padua, and as Francesco wrote to his father, 'it is difficult to describe the solicitude which he has shown to all our house with words and deeds . . . if I were to run into him a thousand times a day he would still ask after your welfare every time'.[77] Donado's official attempt to persuade the Florentine government to alter its policy towards the Medici was predictably unsuccessful. Having once raised its hand against them, it could never again feel secure from the vengeance of their powerful friends; the only possible course open to the conservative regime in future was to maintain the severity on which its survival would henceforth depend. The ruling group in general, however, was clearly discomfited by the disapproval of the republic's most powerful friends, and their reply to the Venetian ambassador, though not without a hint of irony in response to such unusual outside interference in domestic affairs, was nevertheless uncertain and conciliatory. The *Pratica* assembled to consider the matter resolved to temporize; they assured Donado that 'concerning the affair of Cosimo, we would be happy to do a far greater favour than this for your *Signoria*; however, because this is a matter which must be submitted to the judgement of many, we cannot give you a definitive answer, but will do whatever is possible'.[78] In the end they agreed to extend the bounds of Cosimo's confinement to the city of Venice itself, and as a gesture of mollification conferred the honorary citizenship of Florence upon Donado himself.[79] However, undoubtedly the lesson was not lost upon the *amici* of the

---

[76] Ibid. V, 703.

[77] Ibid. V, 697, 10 Oct. 1433; cf. 699, 703, 704.

[78] C.P. 50, f. 100r. The preservation of friendship with Venice had been in the preceding years one of the main preoccupations of the Florentine *reggimento*; see, e.g., C.P. 48, ff. 48v–50v, 57v; 49, 7r–10v, 79r–83r; 50, 185r–186r, 132v, 166r.

[79] Balìe, 24, ff. 25v–26r; cf. Cavalcanti, *Istorie*, p. 291.

Medici bent upon bringing about their recall, nor upon the uncommitted members of the *reggimento* strongly concerned with the
city's image in the outside world and anxious to maintain her
standing in foreign diplomatic circles.

Meanwhile Cosimo, Lorenzo, and the younger members of the
family had comfortably established themselves and their business
on the shores of the Adriatic and were free to enjoy there a style
of life inappropriate to the more ascetic republicans of Florence,
and those honours denied them in their native city but considered
their due in Venice. Francesco gives us a vivid glimpse of their
world there in his observation to Giuliano that 'here everyone
dresses very finely, and I often go with Lorenzo to places where
one must cut a distinguished figure, so that at the moment all my
usual outer garments are of silk . . .'[80] The Medici expressed their
gratitude appropriately; the deliberations of the Venetian Senate
contain correspondence between the Doge and the Pope of
January 1434 referring to information concerning Florentine
diplomatic policy which Cosimo had received from a friend at
home and passed on to the Venetian government. This information
was regarded as peculiarly valuable because the Venetians mis-
trusted the foreign policy of the conservative regime, and the
discovery the previous month that Niccolò Piccinino had been
a guest in Rinaldo degli Albizzi's house during a stay in Florence
had greatly increased their suspicions.[81]

Cosimo obviously considered the revelation of such information concerning the rather personal foreign policy of Rinaldo and
his friends as a gesture against his partisan enemies rather than an
act against the Florentine state; concerning the internal affairs of
the commune, the Medici adopted an attitude of scrupulous constitutional rectitude. After his initial regret that his friends had
lacked the temerity to rise against the government and forcibly
reinstate him, Cosimo had the opportunity to re-evaluate his
situation in the mellow light of all the extra-Florentine opinion
so overwhelmingly in his favour. When in mid-November a

---

[80] M.A.P. V, 697; cf. V, 700, 699.

[81] Deliberazioni (Secreta) Senato 13 (1433–1436), ff. 36r, 43r–v, Archivio di
Stato, Venezia. According to a confession of Niccolò Barbadori, obtained after
Cosimo's restoration, Rinaldo degli Albizzi and Palla Strozzi had negotiated secretly
with Piccinino for aid against those who sought to restore the Medici, in return for
the betrayal of the Florentine alliance with Venice and the papacy. See Guasti,
Commissioni iii. 660, and Bayley, *War and Society*, pp. 137–8.

group of Paduan doctors and other dignitaries publicly commiserated with him, Cosimo carefully avoided their invitations to complaint and recrimination against the Florentines with the steadfast reply, reported by Francesco, 'that he has no enemies nor has he ever wished any man ill, and that he and all his have always defended the interests of their native city in every possible way, and now, if it would set the city to rights, he would gladly remain, not simply in Padua, but at the ends of the earth until the day he dies'.[82] It was presumably in the same spirit that Lorenzo refused the invitation of the Emperor to visit him in Ferrara.[83]

By far the most extreme expression of this determination to remain in the constitutional right was Cosimo's reaction to the scandal created by his kinsman Mari de' Medici, one of the younger members of the Talento line, several of whom, including Mari's father Bartolomeo, had previously been employed in Giovanni di Bicci's bank, and had in other ways been closely associated with the main branch.[84] In January 1434 Mari was arrested by the Venetian authorities on a charge of having conspired with the *condottiere* Niccolò Piccinino (at that time in the service of the Duke of Milan) against the Florentine government, and referred to it for sentence.[85] Perhaps Cosimo suspected a connection between this incident and Piccinino's visit to Rinaldo the previous month—that Mari was being used by his enemies as a tool against him. If this was in fact the case, the evidence suggests that Mari himself was not a party to the scheme. There had been some recent minor disagreement over the alienation of family property by his kinsmen without Mari's consent,[86] and in a statement from his confession under torture, reported by Francesco, he did refer to hostility between himself and the rest of his house. Whether or not the two are connected, the central point of Mari's statement was to avow that 'having been the enemy of all his kinsmen, what

---

[82] M.A.P. V, 704.

[83] Ibid. V, 703, 14 Nov. 1433 : 'Erono anche in Ferrara 12 ambascadori di questa Signoria all'omperadore ch'era anchor quivi che assai dimostrono dolersi, e dovettono riportare all'omperadore la venuta di Lorenzo quivi, in forma che 2 volte mandò per llui e molto lo fe' cerchare, ma Lorenzo non vi volle andare.'

[84] De Roover, *The Rise and Decline*, p. 385; Kent, 'I Medici in esilio' 20–1. For an alternative interpretation of official Florentine and Venetian records of the incident, see Bayley, *War and Society,* pp. 130–1.   [85] Gelli, L'esilio di Cosimo 160–1.

[86] Averardo, writing to Giuliano on 15 Dec. 1431 (M.A.P. V, 64), referred to a complaint which had been made by their *consorto* Mari about some property which had been bought and sold without the consent of all 'alle divise'.

he had done had not been done by order or under duress, but to
get back into favour with his *consorti*'.[87]

However, the unfortunate Mari was much deceived if he had
hoped to earn the gratitude of the leaders of his house by procuring their return to Florence with the aid of the Milanese. Cosimo
was far too sensitive to the political climate of Florence not to
realize that for the Medici to attempt a return to the city with the
aid of its greatest enemy would have constituted a disastrous
tactical error, especially from the position of comparative strength
which they had already gained through foreign favour and support; he swiftly averted the danger by utterly repudiating his
kinsman's action. Indeed as Francesco revealed in a letter to
Giuliano, it was Cosimo who had denounced Mari to the Venetian
authorities:

You will have heard how Mari de' Medici turned up here, having come
from Milan . . . He arrived here at Cosimo's house, and told him how
he had been to see the principal advisers of the Duke, naming Niccolò
Piccinino and many others, and that he had arranged with them that
Cosimo might return home with the aid of the Duke, setting off from
here, and many other things which proved to be very harmful to the
League and to this magnificent *Signoria* . . . Cosimo replied that it
should never be said that this intrigue originated with him, and that
he had no wish to return by any other means than that by which he had
left. And he immediately made all this known to the *Signoria* here . . .
The *Signoria* has written explaining the whole incident to our Priors,
and so has Cosimo.[88]

Cosimo saw the affair as an attempt by their enemies 'at a single
stroke to ruin me completely over there, and to put me in disfavour with the *Signoria* here'.[89] The letter of respectful appreciation which he subsequently received from the Florentine Priors
testifies to the sureness of Cosimo's political instincts; presumably
it was indeed with reference to this matter that they wrote, a
week later:

We have received your letter and are fully aware of the importance of
the incident of which you warn us. It seems to us that your irreproach-
able conduct and your candour deserve commendation and praise. We
encourage you to persevere with the same aim, and if anything similar
should occur, to make it known to the *Signoria* in the same way.[90]

87 M.A.P. V, 693.   88 Ibid. V, 690.
89 Ibid.   90 Fabroni, *Cosmi vita* ii. 87.

Obviously the Medici were hopeful, knowing their strength in the unreformed purses, the influence of their partisans in Florence, and the power of pressure from outside the city, that the drawing of a new *Signoria* might soon trigger off a revulsion of feeling within the *reggimento*, impelling it to reverse the policy of their enemies, and effect the Medici recall. Having pinned their hopes on a speedy and legal reinstatement by the Priors, they determined to adopt the public stance of injured Florentine patriots and to do or say nothing which might be seen as directed against the interests of the republic (as distinct from the party of their opponents), and which might subsequently stand in the way of unconditional pardon; hence Cosimo's iron determination not to become associated with conspiracies of the sort which might succeed, where their mere expulsion had failed, in really undermining the family's position in Florence and abroad.

For as early as the beginning of October young Francesco had announced to his father that he needed to go back to Florence 'to look after our affairs, since none of us is there to do so'.[91] His alarmed elders hastened to dissuade him from this impetuous scheme,[92] but in fact it emerges that even Cosimo had entertained some hopes, soon to be dashed by the implacability of the Priors who took office on 1 November, of a change in the political climate sufficiently favourable to allow at least those members of the family not politically influential, and not officially proscribed, to return home. In a letter of 6 November Francesco told his father that

when Cosimo first arrived here, without actually speaking to him, I got the impression that he intended that his young Giovanni and I should return to Florence, and Piero too, when he was better. But then later it began to seem wiser to think it over, for I saw from some letters of Piero Guicciardini's that Cosimo had written to him about it, though he still said nothing to me, except that we should wait and see how Averardo got on about his exile, and if the *Signoria* made any concession to him, and now he says that we shouldn't be in too much of a hurry.[93]

Clearly Cosimo had already taken his cue from the warning of his astute and influential friend and adviser, Piero Guicciardini, even before the proscription in November of several more of the *amici*, including the faithful Caffarecci, Ser Ciao, and most importantly, the Pucci brothers, who had functioned as the chief lieutenants of the Medici in the direction of the party, provided

[91] M.A.P. V, 700.   [92] Ibid. 697.   [93] Ibid. 702.

definite evidence of the continuing ascendancy of the anti-Mediceans in the ruling group.[94]

It was also the *Signoria* entering office in November who rejected Averardo's plea for extra time to proceed to his place of exile. Cosimo had seen the response to this request as an important index of the disposition of the *reggimento* towards the Medici and their party, and regarded Averardo's subsequent failure to comply with the terms of his proscription as a further threat to the legal invulnerability of the family as a whole.[95] For Averardo and his descendants, however, it was the first of a series of personal tragedies which resulted in the extinction of their line within the decade, robbed them of the rewards of the triumph of the party which they had done so much to promote, and consigned them incidentally to historical obscurity.[96]

It seems that Averardo was essentially prevented from reaching Naples within the prescribed time by serious illness, induced partly by the rigours of a very long and difficult journey for a man already old and rather feeble. His enemies (and even perhaps some of his friends) showed some inclination to attribute his tardiness in obeying the Signorial decree to his renowned intransigence; conversely, his own and his family's private statements on the matter are characterized by the same scrupulous respect for its authority that they had demonstrated elsewhere in other contexts.

At the time of Cosimo's arrest, Averardo was one of the Five Sea-Consuls, stationed in Pisa; on receipt of the warning from his friends he fled to Lucca to avoid detention in Pisa by Florentine officials. Neri Capponi, who was currently serving in the same magistracy, sent after him a letter which reveals not only his sympathy and support for the exiled Medici, but also a certain anxiety that Averardo might try to escape his fate. 'I advise you to obey', he wrote,

remembering the experience of Messer Carlo Zene and Messer Donato Acciaiuoli and I myself; we all reconciled ourselves to obedience, and indeed if one does so, all ends well; otherwise everything turns out badly. All of us here greatly regret your misfortune, encouraging you to be patient and obedient, and placing ourselves at your disposal, and we believe that in the end this may prove to the advantage of you and

[94] Balìe, 24, f. 54v; Cap. Pop. Lib. Inquis. 3175, ff. 103r–120v.
[95] M.A.P. V, 706, 19 Dec., Francesco to Giuliano.
[96] See Kent, 'I Medici in esilio'.

yours. Let us know immediately when you make up your mind so that we can inform those who need to know. Christ be with you.[97]

Averardo replied that he had always considered the freedom of the republic to depend on obedience to the *Signoria*, and that 'all their commands must be regarded as just and honourable and reasonable, and one must await pardon and restitution from them'. He did express his regret that it had not been 'the pleasure of the *Signoria* to send me to the same place as Cosimo on account of my advanced age, for I am sixty years old, and likely to die any day now. I should like to die where one of my own family can watch over me in my last extremity and give me the blessing of a holy candle'. But he concluded resolutely that nevertheless, 'even if I have to travel through sickness, I shall take to the road in obedience to them'.[98]

And so he did, but the journey proved to fulfil his most pessimistic predictions. Bernardo d'Antonio de' Medici, while also encouraging Averardo to obedience, 'in order not to make matters worse for yourself or the others', doubted that he would survive the dangerous, if more direct roads by Talamone or Corneto, and advised him to take the longer way round through the Marches and the Abruzzi.[99] Though on 29 September the *Balìa* granted him an extension of one month to reach his destination, 'in consideration of his age and the distance of the place of exile assigned to him',[100] on 3 October Lorenzo wrote to Giuliano that Averardo had got no further than Ferrara and 'is having a bit of pain from his foot, and some fever, so that he can't walk very well'; his request to Lorenzo that no one should commit themselves to stand surety for his fulfilment of his bond suggests that the old man himself was abandoning hope of arriving in time.[101] A note from Begni di Iacopo Strozzi to his brother Niccolò, dated 22 October from Rimini, announced Averardo's arrival there on the eleventh, but added that 'he still hasn't left for Naples to observe his exile, because he says he is very ill indeed'.[102] A second letter of 10 November began with the news that 'Averardo is still here'; he was by then too ill even to ride.[103] Averardo's lack of progress was obviously becoming a *cause célèbre* at home; on

[97] M.A.P. LXXII, 225, 9 Sept.
[98] Ibid. 226, 9 Sept.
[99] Ibid. C, 160, 12 Sept.
[100] Balìe, 24, f. 22v.
[101] M.A.P. V, 696, 3 Oct.
[102] C.S. 3ª ser. CXIII, c. 8.
[103] Ibid., c. 9.

receiving reports of his plight Alamanno Salviati and Andrea Bardi sent on servants to escort him, but as Francesco rather bitterly observed, 'in Florence they don't choose to believe that he is ill, and there are some there who never expected anything else'.[104] In the first week of November Francesco waited anxiously in Venice to hear if his grandfather had received a further stay from the new *Signoria* whose term had just begun, but by the end of the following week he had to inform Giuliano that 'his time has expired, and he has not been granted an extension; you will be notified from Florence of the consequences. We must let God, who knows what is best, determine everything'.[105]

On 28 November Averardo was condemned as a rebel by the *Balìa* on the charge of having defied their edict 'wilfully and with the intention of scorning and degrading the authority of the Lord Priors and the citizens of the *Balìa* and of his entire native city of Florence', and all his property was confiscated by the state.[106] With the aid of the provision which enabled the wives of exiles to sue their husbands for the recovery of their own dowries,[107] Averardo and his family managed to salvage something, and along with the decrees reinstating the family and absolving them of all charges laid in the previous year, the *Balìa* of 1434 granted generous tax concessions on his estate.[108] But their damaged financial position could not be so easily repaired.[109] Moreover, Averardo's condemnation was but the first of their misfortunes. Clearly he had been too old and ill to survive the arduous experience of exile, and his banishment from Florence was in effect a sentence of death. After spending the winter with Orlando di Guccio, who had been exiled to Ancona,[110] he was finally able to rejoin his cousins with whom, as his old friend Piero Guicciardini advised, he would find 'honour and comfort';[111] a letter of another of their intimates, Iacopo Donado, described to Francesco his grandfather's last months as an honoured guest of the Venetian state, and how the Doge himself had spoken 'more highly of him than he had ever been heard to do of any other citizen'.[112] He had at least the satisfaction of seeing his

[104] M.A.P. V, 699, 20 Oct.   [105] Ibid. V, 702, 6 Nov.; 703, 14 Nov.
[106] Balìe, 25, f. 13r-v.
[107] M.A.P. V, 703; LXXXI, 15, f. 48v; also ibid. 17, 94, 205.
[108] Balìe, 25, ff. 29v, 76r-v.   [109] Kent, 'I Medici in esilio' 57-62.
[110] M.A.P. V, 706.   [111] Ibid. XXI, 560, 14 Aug. 1434.
[112] Ibid. XIII, 41, 20 Aug. 1434.

family reinstated almost as rulers of their native city, although he himself died less than six weeks after their triumphant return; his body was laid to rest in Florence with all the pomp and honours of a state funeral.[113] More unexpected was the sudden death of Giuliano in Rome in July or August of 1434, after what had appeared to be a relatively minor illness.[114] Francesco, then eighteen, returned to Florence, but he too died within seven or eight years, having scarcely reached political maturity, and apparently without having succeeded in his efforts to restore the fortunes of his branch. He left no heirs behind him, though his wife Costanza Guicciardini survived him to marry again, and presumably his younger brothers predeceased him, as the inheritance of Averardo's line, including the actual property and the 'house-cum-fortress' of Cafaggiolo, passed to his cousin Cosimo.[115]

All the efforts of friends and family could not stave off these blows of fate which assailed Averardo and his immediate family, but Francesco's letters contain particularly lively evidence of the strong and constant support which they received from the *amici* throughout this period of trials. On the instructions of Cosimo and Lorenzo, he wrote frequently to Antonio di Salvestro Serristori and Alamanno Salviati, 'to ask them to take care of all our affairs, and to let me know if they think there is anything in particular which I should do . . . [Antonio] says I should stay here, and that he will do what he can over there, and he will keep me informed of everything[116] . . . Lotto and Antonio Martelli do what they can to help me'.[117] As Francesco observed, following their precipitate departure Serristori had sent after them all their personal possessions with the aid of Andrea de' Bardi, who was also keeping an eye on the women-folk left behind.[118]

In graver matters, such as the timing of their return to Florence, the entire Medici family as we have seen depended heavily on their friends for information and advice, and despite the dangers of communicating openly with those officially pronounced

---

[113] By the time Cosimo and Lorenzo returned to Florence on 29 September 1434, Averardo was too ill to travel (Cosimo, *Ricordi*, p. 101). On his death see Cambi, *Istorie*, p. 202; for the decision of the *Balìa* to accord him the rare honour of a state funeral, see Balìe, 25, f. 63v.

[114] See Kent, 'I Medici in esilio' 50–1.

[115] Ibid. 62–3.

[116] M.A.P. V, 700.

[117] Ibid. 690, cf. 688.

[118] Ibid. 697. For the role of the *amici* in helping to keep the banks afloat, and their aid with financial problems in general, see Kent, 'I Medici in esilio' 34–40.

enemies of the state, a crime for which Agnolo Acciaiuoli was to be exiled himself, the *amici* continued with messages and letters to assure them of their loyalty, to keep them informed of the state of affairs in Florence, and hopefully to anticipate their return. Among them were Domenico Giugni, who wrote to remind Cosimo's son Piero that 'if there is anything I can do for you, I am entirely at your disposal',[119] Bartolomeo Carducci, who begged Giovanni di Cosimo to assure his elders that 'when it is my turn, I shall not be found wanting';[120] Matteo Cerretani, who promised that 'when there is something I can do for you, you may put my loyalty to the proof';[121] Maso Velluti, who gave his assurance that 'I am more yours than my own, and shall be so as long as I live';[122] and even the humble Cristofano di Gagliano, who promised that 'while I live, as I have always been, so shall I always be faithful'.[123] Clearly the exile of the Medici had not affected their credibility as patrons and party leaders, and in fact, as was soon to be manifest, the conservative attempt to safeguard the oligarchical regime and destroy the Medici party by exiling its leaders succeeded only in providing a stimulus to the action for which the party had long been preparing.

These unpleasant truths may well have become apparent to Rinaldo and his supporters before the year was out. Certainly in the early months of 1434 the records of the *Consulte* reveal a marked change in the mood of the government. Only a few *Pratiche* had been held in the three months after Cosimo's arrest, possibly because for most of this time the *Balìa* was in session, and handled much of the business concerning which the *Signoria* normally sought advice from the *richiesti*. Those summoned to advise were generally those who had been influential in government before the September *coup*. *Balìa* had been given to the citizens appointed with the consent of the *Parlamento* originally for three months; this term had been prolonged by a month in order to enable the 'reformers of the *reggimento*' to complete their work.[124] However, in December the *Pratiche* were resumed with normal regularity, and at once an alteration in the composition of the inner *reggimento* became apparent. The *Signoria* elected *a mano* to take office in November–December had been a safe but not

[119] M.A.P. XIII, 27.   [120] Ibid. C, 16.
[121] Ibid. V, 642.   [122] Ibid. XVII, 3.
[123] Ibid. XIII, 27.   [124] Balìe, 24, f. 43v.

aggressively partisan one.[125] It included one member of a leading exile family, Iacopo di Messer Rinaldo Gianfigliazzi, and several prominent and respected statesmen of generally conservative leanings like Alessandro di Iacopo Raffacani and Andrea di Taddeo Mancini. The Gonfalonier of Justice was Bartolomeo Ridolfi, an associate of the Medici who had also been a friend of Rinaldo degli Albizzi some years before, and whose election may have been intended to conciliate neutrals and Miceans apprehensive of the partisan nature of the new regime.

However, of the four major *Pratiche* summoned by this *Signoria* in the month of December,[126] Messer Rinaldo degli Albizzi, Ridolfo Peruzzi, Palla di Nofri Strozzi, Giovanni dello Scelto, and Giovanni Minerbetti attended them all. The Gianfigliazzi, Baroncelli, Guasconi, Rondinelli, and Della Casa families were heavily represented, and other prominent individuals were Bartolomeo Peruzzi, Niccolò Barbadori, Zanobi Belfradelli, Felice Brancacci, Terrino Manovelli, and Bartolomeo Spini. On 6 December Rinaldo was the spokesman for the rest of the *Pratica*, with the assistance of Piero Pecori. He was the first speaker on the tenth, followed by Palla Strozzi, and, after the brief intervention of Agnolo Acciaiuoli and Giuliano Davanzati, by eight or ten of the other prominent conservatives. On 11 December Rinaldo degli Albizzi, Giovanni Minerbetti, Biagio Guasconi, and Neri Capponi spoke for the other members of the *Pratica*, once again mainly arch-conservatives and future exiles. On 22 December the speakers for the *Pratica* were Rinaldo degli Albizzi, Agnolo Pandolfini, and Giovanni Minerbetti, and the signatories were similar to those mentioned above. In a smaller *Pratica* held later on the same day Rinaldo again spoke first, followed by all the major figures of the anti-Medicean faction—Giovanni Gianfigliazzi, Palla Strozzi, Ridolfo Peruzzi, Giovanni Minerbetti, Andrea Rondinelli, Bartolomeo Peruzzi, Antonio della Casa, Giovanni dello Scelto, Iacopo Baroncelli, and Zanobi Belfradelli. The only Miceans present were Agnolo Acciaiuoli and Agnolo Pandolfini; indeed with the exception of Giovanni Corbinelli, Giovanni Giugni,

---

[125] Its members are listed by Cambi, *Istorie*, p. 187. They were Bartolomeo di Iacopo Ridolfi (Gonfalonier), Alessandro di Iacopo di Niccolò Raffacani, Andrea di Taddeo Mancini, Iacopo di Messer Rinaldo Gianfigliazzi, Domenico di Antonio Allegri, Mariotto di Giovanni di Bartolo dello Steccuto, Bernardo di Iacopo Arrighi.
[126] 6, 10, 11, and 22 Dec.; (C.P. 50, ff. 100v–101v, 102v–104v, 106r–v, 106v–110r).

Giannozzo Pitti, and Niccolò Valori, these men were the only friends of the Medici to appear at two of the four *Pratiche* called in December.

The comparatively unusual procedure of inviting one or more of the *richiesti* to speak for the entire group and recording only the names of the others, instead of allowing each to express his individual opinion, continued to be regularly employed throughout the period until the Medicean return. The *Signoria* for January–February contained three leading conservatives later to be exiled for their opposition to the Medici—Manetto Scambrilla, Antonio di Vieri Altoviti, and Michele di Galeotto Baronci.[127] The composition of the *Pratiche* they summoned—one only in each of the two months—was very similar to that described above for December.[128] The frequency of assemblies increased again in March under a heavily conservative *Signoria* containing three future exiles,[129] though in fact a close look at the gatherings from December to April suggests plainly that whatever the composition of official organs of government during this period, real power resided in the hands of a group who had been during the preceding seven years the advocates of policies to restore power to the aristocratic faction, had united to expel the Medici in order to bring this about, and was soon to throw aside completely all constitutional scruples in an attempt to hold on to this power.

Apart from Niccolò da Uzzano, who was dead by this time, the leaders of the conservative faction since 1426 had been Rinaldo degli Albizzi, Ridolfo Peruzzi, Francesco di Messer Rinaldo Gianfigliazzi, Matteo Castellani, and Vieri Guadagni. Other anti-Mediceans prominent in the *Consulte* of the intervening years were Lippozzo Mangioni, Bernardo Guadagni, Donato Barbadori, Giovanni Guicciardini, Terrino Manovelli, Filippo Guasconi, Giovanni di Messer Rinaldo Gianfigliazzi, Antonio della Casa, Duccio Mancini, and Mariotto Baldovinetti. Finding themselves together in the *Signoria* of September 1433, Bernardo di Vieri Guadagni, Bartolomeo Spini, Mariotto Baldovinetti, Corso Corsi,

---

[127] Tratte, 93, ff. 14v, 25v, 34v, 43v.

[128] 28 Jan., 5 Feb.; (C.P. 50, ff. 112r–114v, 115r–121r).

[129] Tratte, 93, loc. cit. The Priors were Antonio di Lotteringo Boverelli, Francesco di Filippo Castellani, Niccolò d'Andrea Ciampegli, Duccio di Nofri Mellini, Tommaso di Pazzino di Luca Alberti, Antonio di Iacopo di Monte, Cristofano d'Azino Ghinucci, Stefano di Salvi di Filippo Bencivenni, and Lotteringo d'Andrea di Ser Ugo della Stufa.

and Giovanni dell Scelto had conspired with Rinaldo degli Albizzi, Ridolfo Peruzzi, and Giovanni Gianfigliazzi to exile the Medici. This was the group now taking the government firmly into its own hands. Rinaldo himself dominated the majority of the *Pratiche* in this period, with the assistance of his two chief lieutenants, Ridolfo Peruzzi and Niccolò Barbadori.[130] Apart from them, the most prominent *richiesti*, in terms of number of appearances and influence, were Mariotto Baldovinetti, Felice Brancacci, Zanobi Belfradelli, Giovanni Gianfigliazzi, Zanobi, Biagio, and Tinoro Guasconi, Giovanni Guicciardini, Duccio Mancini, Giovanni dello Scelto, Palla di Nofri Strozzi, and Antonio della Casa, with members also of the Baroncelli and Serragli families. Almost without exception, they were to be exiled in 1434.

At the same time most citizens apparently committed only to the good of the commune tended to become less prominent, while those partisans and *parenti* who were personally closest to the Medici—the Pucci, Ginori, Andrea Pazzi, Francesco Tornabuoni, Alamanno Salviati, and Piero Guicciardini—disappeared from the *Pratiche* altogether. Apart from Neri Capponi, who was invited to the *Pratiche* after his return from Pisa almost as often as the leading conservatives, the half-dozen mentioned above as frequent members of the December gatherings continued to be the only Miceans represented at all regularly until the end of April or thereabouts.

During this period for the first time the factional struggle between the citizens of Florence was fought in the open through the official organs of the communal government, and the identity of the partisans, then virtually in direct confrontation, is therefore much more clearly and unambiguously apparent in the evidence concerning their conflict. In a judicial process launched in 1436 by Agnolo Acciaiuoli against the sons of Ridolfo Peruzzi, in which he resurrected his grievances against their father, a document signed by Rinaldo degli Albizzi, Ridolfo Peruzzi, and Niccolò Barbadori was produced to prove that these three had proposed to banish most of the influential supporters of the Medici party along with its leaders. This action was to have been effected while Michele Arrigucci and Biagio Guasconi, both

---

[130] See, e.g., 6 Mar. (C.P. 50, f. 124r); 12 (127r); 17 (127v); 23 (133r); 8 Apr. (141r); 20 (143v); 22 (144v); 24 (145r); 6 May (147v).

prominent conservatives, were members of the Colleges, between mid-December and mid-March.[131] Certainly, the *Consulte* indicate that this was also the period during which the conservative leaders attempted to tighten their control over government. Having realized that they had not in fact destroyed the party along with the Medici, they decided it was necessary to rid the city of the remaining Mediceans within the inner *reggimento*. Those mentioned were Piero Guicciardini, Neri di Gino, Antonio di Salvestro Serristori, Alamanno Salviati, Niccolò Valori, Nerone di Nigi Dietisalvi, Alessandro Alessandri, and of course Agnolo Acciaiuoli.

A similar plan, this time of assassination, is revealed in the confessions of Niccolò Barbadori to the judicial authorities in November 1434.[132] This document declared that an attempt was to be made on the lives of leading Mediceans during the Gonfalonierate of Tommaso di Pazzino Alberti, while Stefano di Salvi Bencivenni, later exiled, was one of the Priors—that is, in March or April 1434. On this occasion the conspirators comprised a much larger proportion of the conservative faction and included Rinaldo degli Albizzi, Niccolò himself, Ridolfo Peruzzi, Luigi Aldobrandini, Rinaldo Gianfigliazzi, Andrea Rondinelli, Biagio Guasconi, Sandro Altoviti, Smeraldo Strozzi, Ormanno degli Albizzi, and Stefano di Salvi Bencivenni. Chief of the intended victims were Neri Capponi, Niccolò Valori, and Piero Guicciardini; these three were to be killed, along with Alessandro Alessandri, Piero Ginori, Alamanno Salviati, Luca di Messer Maso Albizzi, Nicolaio Alessandri, Messer Giuliano Davanzati, and Berto da Filicaia. Eight out of these ten were members of the inner *reggimento*; most have already been identified as leaders of the Medicean party. Several had been prominent in the *Pratiche* of the preceding months, despite their Medicean sympathies. Seven more citizens were to be spared their lives, but confined outside Florence; of these, five had long since declared themselves as Medicean partisans, but could not be classified as statesmen of the first rank. They were Tommaso Barbadori, Niccolò Soderini, Lorenzo Lenzi, Simone Ginori, Giovanni della Stufa, Messer Bartolomeo Orlandini, and Niccolò d'Aginolfo Popoleschi. Clearly the leaders of the conservative regime were beginning to feel gravely threatened by those citizens

[131] The document is published by I. M. Bencini, 'Note e appunti' 29–30.
[132] Gelli, 'L'esilio di Cosimo' 163.

who opposed it, but were too influential to be ignored by a government which still purported to respect republican traditions, and in their fear they began to turn to the weapons of the tyrant. However, in the end these full-scale purges did not take place; only Agnolo Acciaiuoli was exiled on 11 February.[133] According to the document of 1436 it was he whom the regime had seen as its chief enemy, and in fact the general plan to eliminate the other leading Mediceans revolved around his capture, 'since there is not a man in the city but he who would dare to speak out against such an action, and apart from this, you know how many disagreements we have had with him, and how many of our plans he has frustrated . . .' Also included in this diatribe against 'the diabolical Messer Agnolo' was a reference to 'his intrigues with Cosimo, and the letters he has written to him, and received, and in consequence, as soon as he is in your hands, you should send to his house and have all his papers seized . . .' This was obviously done, for according to Cosimo's comment in his *Ricordi*, Messer Agnolo Acciaiuoli was exiled on account of 'some news he sent to Puccio and to us . . . in fact it wasn't anything important, certainly not enough to be banished for'.[134] Nevertheless, presumably their letters betrayed, if nothing more substantial, the intimacy between them, as does one surviving letter which Acciaiuoli wrote from exile to Cosimo's brother Lorenzo, bemoaning the injury to his family caused by his expulsion from Florence, but assuring Lorenzo of his unwavering affection, and begging him to reply soon, because 'there is no one whose letters matter more to me than yours'.[135]

The exile of Acciaiuoli, and other incidents like the inclusion in the ranks of the *popolani* of Lionardo Frescobaldi, one of the leading magnate supporters of the aristocratic faction,[136] serve to confirm the impression arising from the *Consulte* that the regime became more exclusive and repressive in the first months of 1434 than it had been, or intended to be, when it first assumed power in September 1433. The Medici too recognized this change of mood and resigned themselves to the postponement of hopes for an early return. On 20 February 1434 Francesco di Giuliano wrote to his father begging him not to worry; although he had indeed mentioned the possibility of returning to Florence in his letters

[133] Cap. Pop. Lib. Inquis. 3184, f. 21r.
[134] *Ricordi*, p. 100; cf. Cavalcanti, *Istorie*, pp. 292–5.
[135] M.A.P. LXVII, 610.   [136] MSS. 316, p. 309.

to his mother, 'I won't budge a step without the advice of
Cosimo and Lorenzo, so you don't need to worry about me. For
I am not so mad that, seeing how touchy things are for us and for
those who remember us, I should wish to return there under such
conditions.' He concluded philosophically, as he observed, 'after
the style of Sallust in the *Jugurtha*', that 'these are not propitious
times to desire political power or anything else of that nature'.[137]

The apparently unexpected resilience of the Medici party was
only one of the problems threatening the security of Rinaldo's
regime by the beginning of 1434. Equally upsetting, and not altogether unrelated, was the fact that, having become embroiled in
the affairs of the pope and others in the Romagna, the commune
was now almost as desperate for money as it had been before the
conclusion of the war with Lucca. This time the government had
no recourse to Medici wealth. In fact its financial problems could
be seen as a test of whether or not the city could do without
the Medici bank, and as the conservative leaders concluded in a
Pratica of 17 March: 'It seems to us that ultimately the maintenance of our rule depends on solving the problem of finance.'[138]
Moreover, discussions in other *Pratiche* of this period reveal that
it was becoming increasingly difficult for the *Signoria* to get their
provisions through the councils. Time after time, measures were
returned for amendment; this may have reflected the reputed
strength of the Medici *amici* in the councils, or it may simply have
been an expression of dissatisfaction with the new regime on the
part of the *reggimento* as a whole.[139] On 17 February representatives
of the Colleges suggested a meeting of 'all the leading citizens of
the *reggimento*' to enlist their support;[140] any of the *Consulte* of the
succeeding month might have served this purpose, as their
membership was highly selective and highly partisan, and March
was the month of Rinaldo's most inflexible control over the discussions which he almost invariably led, alone or with the aid of
such trusty supporters as Zanobi Guasconi, Niccolò Barbadori,
or Ridolfo Peruzzi.[141]

This situation continued throughout April, by which time the
rifts in the *mariage de convenance* which constituted the conservative

[137] M.A.P. V, 693.
[138] C.P. 50, ff. 127v–129v; cf. ibid., ff. 110v, 115r, 122r–123v, 125r, 126r, 157v,
etc.
[139] Ibid., ff. 123r, 133v–134r, 156r–v, 157r.   [140] Ibid., f. 123r.
[141] Above, p. 319.

alliance were beginning to appear beneath the surface solidarity imposed by the iron controls of its leaders. The turning-point in the fortunes of the regime came in May. The Strozzi and their friends appear to have been most sharply aware of the possible repercussions of the conservative *coup*, and most sensitive to subsequent variations in the political climate. On receiving news of the expulsion of the Medici in September 1433, Tommaso di Giannozzo Alberti had written to his friend Matteo Strozzi expressing his sympathy for all who encountered adversity, but also perhaps a certain fundamental uneasiness at these events in his hope that in the end 'God may provide for all our needs'.[142] Early in February Strozza degli Strozzi, away from Florence for some time as Captain of Castrocaro, begged Matteo to 'keep me informed of any news, either fresh or old, since over here I don't hear anything about what is going on over there, and especially as you, Matteo, have your finger on the pulse of things'.[143]

The Medici *amici* were also keeping their friends well informed. Maso Velluti reported from Pisa to Piero di Cosimo on 21 May: 'Concerning matters here . . . I'll tell you one thing, that things are very bad; may God come to our aid, and establish peace and unity among us, for it is very necessary, and we are not going the right way about it at all . . .'[144] Three days later Niccolò Carducci wrote recommending himself to Cosimo and Lorenzo and 'the whole band of you', and announcing the imposition of a curfew. No one was to be abroad after the bell had sounded, on pain of death. In addition to this measure obviously designed to restrict the opportunities for conclaves and conspiracies, another was passed forbidding citizens to house *contadini* or soldiers or strangers overnight, in order, presumably, to prevent the raising of private armies[145] and to avert the introduction of open force on to the political scene.

Clearly the Medici had sensed the uncertainty of the regime in these and other actions, and soon the Strozzi sensed it too. On

---

[142] C.S. 3ª ser. CXII, c. 131. [143] Ibid., c. 156.
[144] M.A.P. XVII, 3.
[145] Ibid. V, 294. '. . . Andò istamani uno bando da parte de' signori e ghonfaloniere della giustizia che non si potesse andare, sonata la grossa, nè con bullecte soscritte nè con lume nè per veruno modo, sappiendo che la famiglia n'andrà cercando; che piglieranno gliene va la testa; chosì disse il bando, e anchora disse che non si potesse ritenere chontadini in casa nè soldati nè forestieri nè ingniuna altra persona; quello che si voglia dire non so.'

24 May Giovanni di Marco degli Strozzi wrote to Matteo announcing that he had just received a letter from Marco informing him

> how certain of Cosimo's followers have collected a large sum of money to finance a revolt, and furthermore it seems that some have been to Neri di Gino on behalf of the others and offered him the money, and they intend to arm the Gonfalonier and anyone else who will do their bidding; there are more than 300 of them and a number of lords among them. I shouldn't be at all surprised, Matteo, for things are such that if they don't succeed this time, they will another.

Notably Giovanni by then anticipated the success of such a rising and also foresaw that in this event, 'those who have neither sinned nor are guilty will be punished and suffer for it. I am writing to you and Smeraldo because you will be among the worst hit, and so will all our family.'[146]

This letter is perhaps the most immediate and reliable evidence that the Medici *amici*, reinforced by the certainty of strong support both inside and outside the city, were now taking concrete steps to secure their return. It is also the first absolutely unambiguous evidence that Neri di Gino Capponi, who for so long had maintained cordial but comparatively non-committal relations with both sides, had translated his expressions of support to Averardo into action and at last thrown in his lot with the Mediceans in opposition to the conservatives now struggling to retain their grip on government. However, Francesco Guicciardini, who though speaking at second-hand and considerably after the event, had used family documents in his *Memorie*, suggested that Neri Capponi and other leading *amici* had in fact been manœuvring to return the Medici for some months; of Piero Guicciardini he wrote that he 'was waiting . . . together with many others, of whom the leaders were Neri di Gino, who was a close friend of his, and Alamanno Salviati and Luca di Messer Maso, to put into effect the restoration of Cosimo, and their efforts were so effective that the following year the *Signoria* recalled him'.[147]

There were eight major *Pratiche* in May, and most of them were larger than the meetings of previous months; apparently the new

---

[146] C.S. 3ª ser. CXII, c. 176.

[147] *Memorie*, p. 11. See N. Rubinstein, 'The "Storie Fiorentine" and the "Memorie di Famiglia" by Francesco Guicciardini', *Rinascimento*, iv (1953), 173–225. It should be noted that by the Florentine system of dating, the previous year extended up to 24 March 1434.

Signoria found itself increasingly obliged to consult the remainder of the *reggimento* before taking any definitive action.[148] This may have been due to the continuing difficulty of getting its proposals through the councils. On 18 May Gherardo Baroncelli and Bernardo Ciachi were obliged to suggest to the *Signoria*: 'Seeing that the provision proposed yesterday has not been accepted, it seems to us that in the interests of the commune it should go to the Council of the People with five alternatives, and the one which gets the most votes should be effected.'[149] However, three days later they had to console the *Signoria* once more for the fact that the provisions proposed on the previous day had not obtained approval; their advice was to remain undiscouraged, keep trying to push the measure through, and to call a *Pratica* and appeal for the help of their companions in the *reggimento*.[150]

Nevertheless, by now the conservative leaders must have been aware how far their difficulties were due to a lack of unified support within this very group. The first of the May *Pratiche* continued to be dominated by the small and powerful band of conservative leaders; on 6 May Rinaldo spoke first, followed by Palla Strozzi, Galileo Galilei, Niccolò Barbadori, Bartolomeo Peruzzi, and Giovanni Minerbetti. These were again the speakers on 11 May, but a *Pratica* of 9 May had acceded to a proposal put forward by Ridolfo Peruzzi with the help of two conspicuously neutral citizens and one Medicean—Niccolò Valori. The *Pratiche* of both the ninth and the eleventh, and indeed those of the remainder of the month, contained a much larger number of citizens uncommitted to either party than any gathering since the previous November, and in fact the beginning of May saw the re-entry into the effective inner *reggimento* of several Mediceans who had been absent from the *Pratiche* since Cosimo's exile. Among these were Bartolomeo and Niccolò Carducci, Matteo Cerretani, Giovanni di Mico Capponi, Bartolomeo Orlandini, and Alamanno Salviati. At the same time there was a sharp drop in the attendance of several of the conservative leaders, including Rinaldo himself, who had hardly been absent from a *Pratica* since the beginning of December, and also Niccolò Barbadori, Zanobi Belfradelli, Mariotto Baldovinetti, and Giovanni Gianfigliazzi, although

---

[148] 6 May (C.P. 50, ff. 147v–149v); 9 (150v–151r); 11 (152r–153r); 12 (153v–155v); 18 (156v); 21 (157v–159v); 22 (160r–161r) and 28 (161v–164v).
[149] Ibid., f. 156v. [150] Ibid., f. 157r.

Ridolfo Peruzzi and Palla Strozzi continued to be as conspicuous as before.

On 21 May the eminent pro-Medicean statesman Bartolomeo Ridolfi declared firmly that: 'We must provide for the preservation of liberty, and the best way is by achieving unity among the citizens';[151] the following day Palla Strozzi and Giovanni Guicciardini joined with Zanobi Guasconi and Agnolo Pandolfini in making several important propositions to the *richiesti*.[152] These concerned the appointment of 'ten peacemakers', another 'fifty citizens to establish and maintain concord', and the request that the *Signoria* 'restore the six votes now sufficient to exile a citizen to eight'. They insisted that those of the above questions which had already been discussed by the *Signoria* 'should be put into effect rapidly' and that the others should be discussed with the Colleges and effected 'with all speed and solicitude'. Even more clearly indicative of dissatisfaction with the current regime was the request 'that the *Signoria* should ensure that what is done should be just and reasonable, and that the laws are observed', and the proposal that all those present

should swear on the Holy Gospel, and in the hands of Bartolomeo Carducci, who is here at the *Pratica* on behalf of our magnificent Lord Priors, laying his hand on the book of the Holy Gospels, with pure and upright heart, and with perfect faith and true sincerity, to love one another and to behave justly in the interests of the glory and greatness of the *Signoria* and the liberty of this city . . . laying aside all hatred and enmities which have been generated up until now over the question of the *reggimento*.

The demands of the *richiesti*, which would appear to have been made in protest against the arbitrary nature of Rinaldo's regime, may have been either the occasion or the result of an incident described by Niccolò Barbadori in his confession of November 1434. He admitted that during the Gonfalonierate of Aldobrandino di Giorgio Aldobrandini del Nero, in May and June of 1434, 'I, Ridolfo, Messer Palla di Nofri, and many others each went alone to his house when he was ill, and desired and persuaded him to give his vote to Andrea di Vico, a butcher'. Having secured the power to exercise the Gonfalonier's vote, they hoped to call a *Parlamento* and reconstitute the regime. However, they were

---

[151] C.P. 50, f. 157r.
[152] Ibid., ff. 160r–161r, published Guasti, *Commissioni* iii. 590.

opposed by three of the Priors, Giovanni di Francesco Guicciardini, Attaviano Pepi, and Ghirigoro d'Antonio Ubertini, who
threatened to make known the plot, 'and in those days Messer
Rinaldo kept foot-soldiers in the house'.[153]

There were no major *Pratiche* at all in June, and on the fourth
of that month Giovanni di Marco Strozzi wrote another warning
letter to his kinsman Matteo. He had been displeased by the
latter's reply to his earlier message, because it indicated that things
were worse even than he had thought. Again he begged Matteo to
'look and see what is going on, and if you can do anything about
it there, do so'.[154] A third letter from Giovanni di Marco on 16 June
commented on the attempts to provide for the financial crisis.
He had heard that a new and onerous tax was to be imposed on
Florentine possessions, and he feared it would have serious political
repercussions: 'I am concerned that it will cause a great scandal
in our city and indeed no small one has already arisen; may God
put things right, for even the smallest scandal would prove to be
our undoing.[155] Antonio Masi, an *amico* of the Medici, was of a
similar opinion, although he wrote with satisfaction to his friends
in exile that 'there are plenty in the ruling group who are not in
favour of this *novina* and plenty I think who will refuse to pay it'.[156]

Among those accorded the honour of welcoming the pope
when he re-entered Florence on 23 June for a prolonged stay were
Ridolfo Peruzzi, Andrea Rondinelli, Francesco Castellani, Palla
Strozzi, Giovanni Guicciardini, and Aldobrandino d'Aldobrandino del Nero; the only Mediceans included in the ceremonies
were Agnolo Pandolfini and Bartolomeo Ridolfi.[157] Obviously
the conservative faction still dominated the city, but the *Pratiche*
of July contained a growing number of Mediceans and neutrals,
and on the eighth of that month the major speaker was Nerone di
Nigi Dietisalvi, an intimate friend of the Medici who had been
involved with them in their electoral manœuvring in 1427.[158] It
appeared that Giovanni di Marco's worst fears were about to be
realized; the Mediceans were waiting for an opportunity to move,
and their opponents lived in fear of such an action. According to
Niccolò Barbadori, during the Gonfalonierate of Donato Velluti
in July and August the conservative leaders 'spoke in Messer

[153] Gelli, 'L'esilio di Cosimo' 164.   [154] C.S. 3ª ser. CXII, c. 179.
[155] Ibid., c. 180.   [156] M.A.P. XII, 2.
[157] Cambi, *Istorie*, pp. 191–2.   [158] C.P. 50, f. 168v; cf. ibid., ff. 169r–176r.

Rinaldo's room of getting Donato [Velluti] to call a Parliament
. . . many times Donato suggested we should call a Parliament
and what should be said and done, but we didn't trust his judgement, for he seemed to us a man who didn't know how to go
about things'.[159]

Throughout August, Mediceans like the Carducci, the Giugni,
Alamanno Salviati, Francesco Tornabuoni, Nerone di Nigi, and
even comparatively unknown party men like Doffo Arnolfi
flooded back into the *Pratiche*,[160] and before the month was out
it became clear that the conservative leaders had waited too long
to defend themselves against approaching danger. By their own
accounts in the subsequent trials, the Priors drawn in previous
months had not always been sympathetic to their regime, which,
as was now apparent, should obviously have safeguarded itself
with a more drastic revision of the purses. The result of their
omission, in combination with the long-standing concern of the
Medici party to gain electoral qualifications for its members,[161]
was that the draw turned up among the Priors to take office in
September–October no less than four of the most distinguished and
devoted of the Medici *amici*—Luca Pitti, Giovanni Capponi, Neri
Bartolini, Niccolò di Cocco Donati as Gonfalonier of Justice—
and not one prominent conservative.[162] Neri Capponi, in his
Commentarii, described the new Priors as 'almost all suspect in the
eyes of the regime which had admitted them to the purses, and
having seen the results of the drawing, they tried to do something
about it'.[163]

The Mediceans were triumphant; one of the *amici* wrote to
announce to the exiles in Venice that 'the drawing of these Priors
has been greeted with universal satisfaction, especially by those
who desire to live under good government';[164] another, announcing the composition of the group and observing that 'no one
could consider them a nicer little band than I', added: 'May God
inspire them to keep us in mind, although I am certain that they

---

[159] Gelli, 'L'esilio di Cosimo' 164–5.   [160] C.P. 50, ff. 176v–194r.

[161] According to Vespasiano da Bisticci (*Vite* iii. 20), 'avendo quegli del trentatre
serrate le borse, e levata la Balìa, gli amici di Cosimo istavano del continovo a vedere
che fusse fatto qualche priorato al loro modo, per rivocare Cosimo dallo exilio.'

[162] Cambi, *Istorie*, p. 193. The other five Priors were Piero di Piero, *cartolaio*,
Fabriano d'Antonio Martini, *beccaio*, Simone di Francesco Guiducci, Tommaso
d'Antonio di Ser Tommaso Redditi, and Baldassare d'Antonio di Santi.

[163] Col. 1182.   [164] M.A.P. XIII, 24, Anon. 30 Aug. 1434.

will do so.'[165] Cosimo's own reaction was one of hope and relief, and he was convinced that the majority of Florentines shared his feelings: 'When such a splendid group of citizens was drawn, they were encouraged, and took heart, for it seemed to them that the time had come to put an end to the evil regime they had suffered, which they would have done sooner, had they had Priors who had wished to attend to it, because in fact the whole populace, and particularly the worthiest citizens, were very ill content with it.' Certainly a number of them had sent Cosimo's friend Antonio di Ser Tommaso Masi to Venice to persuade him to return immediately as, he observed, 'we were continuously urged by many relatives and friends to do'. However, Cosimo was by now quite confident of his position, and had at that stage no intention of jeopardizing his advantage by precipitate and unconstitutional action; he replied by sending Antonio Martelli to Florence to seek confirmation of their invitation from the *Signoria* itself.[166]

He had, however, allowed the junior members of the family to return home,[167] and about this time, perhaps as an encouragement to his fellow citizens to resolve matters in the Medici favour, offered an extremely substantial loan to the Venetian government in appreciation of their shelter and support; by contrast, the coffers of the Florentine state remained sorely depleted by the conservative regime's rather unwisely extensive participation in the Romagnuol conflict. Presumably Cosimo anticipated that his action might cause at least some of the Florentine ruling group to reflect, like the Emperor of Germany, on their foolishness in having thrust their most prosperous citizens into the arms of others. However, the realization of this fact served only to enrage the author of one contemporary political poem directed against the Medici; he bemoaned the subjection of the new *Signoria* to their tyranny and accused them of defrauding Florence of her great treasures, and 'emptying them into the bosom of St. Mark'. He concluded with an ironic description of the Medici return from Venice and the prophecy that in effect their recall would signify the enthronement of the lion of Venice in the person of the Medicean Gonfalonier of Justice.[168] It also seems likely that

---

[165] Ibid. XVI, 3, Anon., 30 Aug. 1434.   [166] *Ricordi*, p. 101.
[167] See Kent, 'I Medici in esilio' 49, 52.
[168] See Gutkind, *Cosimo de' Medici*, Documenti.

Cosimo was taking out a little insurance against the possibility
that there might well be resistance within the city to an attempt by
the Priors to recall him, and that the authority of the latter might
require some reinforcement from Venetian sources. In this case,
his gesture certainly had the required effect. Iacopo Donado's
letter to his young friend Francesco di Giuliano shows that the
Venetians were most impressed by 'the magnificent offer which
Cosimo and Lorenzo have made to our *Signoria* to lend to them
now for whatever time they please the sum of thirty thousand
ducats'; he expressed the opinion privately that 'when the time
comes, our *Signoria* will demonstrate in action the friendship and
goodwill of all our Republic towards your house'.[169]

Certainly all the evidence suggests that whatever the precise
outcome of these events, once the identity of the Priors of September 1434 became known, the recall of the Medici to Florence
was never in doubt. The news which had provoked such rejoicing
in the Medici camp induced the conservatives, and even their
more moderate associates like the Strozzi, to reveal themselves
finally as autocrats, willing to defend their position by any means.
It later emerged from the inquisition of Donato Velluti that on
hearing the news he, together with Rinaldo degli Albizzi, Barba
Bischeri, Ridolfo Peruzzi, Palla Strozzi, Zanobi Guasconi, and
Matteo Strozzi had met together in the palace of the Priors, 'to
arrange to have twenty-five armed men above in the chamber of
the *Signoria* take and hold the upper part of the Palace, and to call
a new *Parlamento* and to prevent the Priors from entering'.[170]
However, in the last days of August, to compound the effect of
the drawing of the pro-Medicean Priors, came the news of the
devastating rout suffered by Florentine troops in the Romagna
on 26 August. Naturally the conservative leaders were held responsible, and soon realized they had too little credit, and too
many enemies now, to attempt another *coup*.[171]

So for more than three weeks the factions within the ruling
group were gripped in political deadlock, and the city of Florence
remained in a state of suspense. In the days which followed, the
words and actions of many citizens expressed their confusion and
uncertainty, though in general it seems that opinion was swinging
to the prediction of a Medicean victory. On 5 September Pigello

[169] M.A.P. IV, 331, 11 Sept. 1434.   [170] Gelli, 'L'esilio di Cosimo' 162.
[171] See Guasti, *Commissioni* iii. 592.

di Folco Portinari wrote to Giovanni di Cosimo in Venice announcing the death of one of their chief enemies, Bernardo Guadagni, and reporting that 'people are saying that you can see now how God has paid him back for what he did to you and the rest of the family'.[172] In these circumstances there may have been others who, like Uguccione di Mico Capponi, now hesitated to form new associations which might prove prejudicial to their fortunes in the future. On 19 August he had arranged a marriage between his daughter Vaggia and Niccolò di Rinieri di Niccolò Peruzzi. He related in his diary how on 22 September he went ahead with the marriage promise, but that on the following evening, 'she went to dine at his house, and the reason was to put off the final vows on account of certain disturbances in Florence'.[173] Obviously Uguccione had become apprehensive about linking his fortunes to those of the Peruzzi, who had been so prominent in the anti-Medicean regime. In fact the branch of Rinieri di Niccolò had not been active in the opposition to the Medici, and when the sentences of exile against the family were announced by the *Balìa* on 2 October, his line was exempted from the punishments.[174] Consequently Uguccione was able to record on 4 October that the final ceremony had taken place that day.

On 20 September Rinaldo, Ridolfo Peruzzi, and Niccolò Barbadori were summoned before the *Signoria*; they resolved to gamble on a show of force rather than risk in their turn the fate of Cosimo twelve months before.[175] And indeed, as Ugolino Martelli revealed in his *Ricordi*, the Priors,

in view of the bad acts of government over the previous year, that is, in 1433 . . . and how the friends of the Medici and those who desired good government for our city had been treated, . . . having seen to certain needs of the commune, and after taking counsel and advice from the worthiest citizens . . . arranged to call a parliament and to restore those who had been driven out, and those from whom their dignities had been taken without reason, and to set right many other wrongs which had been done.[176]

[172] M.A.P. V, 298.

[173] Conv. Soppr., Monastero di S. Piero a Monticelli, 153, 'Libro d'Uguccione di Mico Capponi, 1433–1488', f. 3r.

[174] Balìe, 25, f. 21v. In fact Luigi di Giovanni di Rinieri was one of Cosimo's *mallevadori* in 1433 (Cap. Pop. Lib. Inquis. 3175, f. 67r–v).

[175] Cavalcanti, *Istorie*, p. 302.

[176] 'Ricordanze d'Ugholino Martelli', published by Martines, 'La famiglia Martelli' 41.

The *Parlamento* was due to take place on Wednesday, 29 September; on the evening of Saturday, 25 September the Priors summoned 'a large number of citizens whom they had taken into their confidence', and informed them of their intention. It was decided to send for the Florentine troops under the command of the Captain of War so that they might be present at the *Parlamento*. But in the course of these preparations, their plans came to the ears of the conservative leaders, who resolved to prevent their fulfilment at all costs, and in fact to forestall them with an immediate assault on the palace.[177]

In a note of 26 September to a member of his household in the country, Giovanni Guicciardini, one of the more moderate forces in the conservative leadership, revealed his apprehension concerning the impending crisis, and his personal resignation to a situation in which the Medicean Priors appeared to have gained the strategic upper hand:

> I must warn you that here there are fears of an uprising, and it could be today; may God preserve us from this evil. I don't intend to allow myself to worry too much, though I am very dismayed at the prospect of revolt, but since when men are thus defeated they are often impelled to unfortunate actions, I should be happy if you would prepare yourself as quickly as possible in readiness to come here with several companions to keep watch over the house; I will let you know when the time comes . . .[178]

However, his first prediction proved correct; even as he wrote on the morning of Sunday, 26 September, the rumour was spreading that the whole city was up in arms.

The aristocratic leaders and their followers, bearing weapons, 'gathered mainly at the houses of Messer Rinaldo and Ridolfo di Bonifazio de' Peruzzi', from whence they finally proceeded to the *piazza* outside the church of Sant'Apollinare, just behind the palace of the Priors in the Via de' Leoni.[179] According to observers, the leaders of the group gathered there included Albizzi, Peruzzi, Guasconi, Rondinelli, Castellani, Raffacani, Arrigucci, Serragli, Gianfigliazzi, and certain of the Bardi.[180] Cavalcanti described how throughout the day 'an enormous number of armed citizens arrived unsolicited to support the knight. The

---

[177] Martines, 'La famiglia Martelli' 42; Cavalcanti, *Istorie*, pp. 300–1; Gelli, 'L'esilio di Cosimo' 165–7.   [178] B.N.F., Magl. II: IV: 375.
[179] Cap. Pop. Lib. Inquis. 3175, f. 142r–v.   [180] Above, pp. 137–8.

whole street was full, from the Camera to the Piazza Sant'Appollinare, behind the palace of the Podestà, and the streets of the Burella, and the Angiullara, right round to the *piazza* again.' Some claimed that five or six hundred men were eventually assembled; according to Martelli the original core consisted of only about 150, but by late afternoon their numbers had increased to almost 1,000.[181]

However, as he put it, 'God did not allow such an evil to befall us'; two of the Medici *amici*, Ugolino's brother Bartolomeo and Luigi della Stufa, hastened to the Palace to inform the Priors that an armed mob was gathering in the streets behind. 'And immediately the great door was locked and those who had already entered the Palace were driven out, and they set about reinforcing it with trustworthy men and with supplies; so that before the hour of vespers there were five hundred men within, ready and prepared with plenty of bows and a great quantity of provisions.'[182] Neri Capponi, in his *Commentarii*, named the leaders of this group as Luca di Messer Maso degli Albizzi, Niccolò Valori, Martelli, Ginori, Nerone di Nigi, Alberti, Antonio di Salvestro, Rucellai, Piero Guicciardini, Capponi, Pitti, and Corbinelli;[183] that is, essentially the more prominent members of the Medici party, and other leading citizens like Piero di Cardinale Rucellai, who accompanied Agnolo Acciaiuoli to the Palace, in the words of a kinsman, 'to come to the aid of the *Signoria*'.[184] For, as another observer put it, the supporters of Rinaldo 'had taken up arms against the *Signoria*, which is something no one ought to do'.[185]

Perhaps it was the realization of the enormity of this act which induced Palla Strozzi at the last moment to draw back from violence against those who embodied the welfare of the commune

181 *Istorie*, pp. 303–4; Martines, 'La famiglia Martelli' 42. See also Petrucci (ed.), *Il libro di ricordanze dei Corsini*, p. 144; 'erano romori e armati quasi buona parte del popolo fiorentino intorno a San Pulinari . . .' Cf. Palmieri, *Annales*, p. 138, who estimated about 300, the author of *Priorista*, C.S. 2ª ser. CIII, who estimated 600 (f. 113r), and Capponi, whose estimate was also 600 (*Commentarii*, col. 1182).

182 Martines, 'La famiglia Martelli' 42.

183 *Commentarii*, col. 1182.

184 Quoted *Della carcere, dell'ingiusto esilio e del trionfal ritorno di Cosimo Padre della Patria, narrazione genuina, tratta dall'Istoria fiorentina MS di G. Cavalcanti*, ed. Domenico Moreni (Florence, 1821), p. 116, from a *Priorista*; the same tradition is preserved, perhaps from the same source, by a late-sixteenth-century Rucellai memorialist (Zibaldone Quaresimale, Archivio Rucellai, Florence, f. 246r; I have used this MS. on microfilm at the Warburg Institute, London).

185 C.S. 2ª ser. CII, entry Sept.–Oct. 1434.

and the liberty of the republic.[186] Cavalcanti relates how after
Rinaldo had several times sent word for him to come to the *piazza*
with his enormous band of private retainers, Messer Palla at last
arrived alone and unarmed, with a single servant, and after mur-
muring his excuses, departed. A runner was also dispatched to
fetch Giovanni Guicciardini, who replied that there was little
point in his coming, since his very existence would in any case act
as a curb to restrain the vigour of his Medicean brother Piero.
'Similarly,' wrote Cavalcanti, 'there were many others who were
obliged by faith and by oath to respond to Rinaldo's call ... who
did not appear to swell his forces',[187] and ultimately even Ridolfo
Peruzzi was seduced from his side at the eleventh hour by offers
of accommodation from the *Signoria*, by whom he was falsely persuaded that he could secure the protection of his interests without
incurring the burden of guilt attendant upon defiance of its
authority.[188]

In the end, however, it did not come to a confrontation; at the
last moment the climax of violence was averted by conciliation.
With the two groups armed and ready for battle, civic order
collapsed.

The streets were filled with peasants, the whole mob of them hungry
for the possessions of others, and thirsty for the blood of citizens ...
At the sight of such an abominable rabble, so powerful a terror was
born in the breasts of the artisans that they all kept their shops shut.
The workers remained silent and ill-content, just like donkeys in a hail-
storm, and thus the whole city was shrouded in gloom.

In these circumstances the pope, still resident in Florence, 'and
realizing the danger and the destruction which might result',
intervened.[189] He sent an envoy to treat with the group gathered
outside Sant'Apollinare, and Rinaldo was finally persuaded to
abandon all attempts to regain the government by force, and to
entrust the matter instead to the papal arbitration.

---

[186] Cf. Averardo's view (above, p. 313) that obedience to the *Signoria* was the
corner-stone of the liberty of the republic, and the stress in the condemnation of the
exiles on the charge that they had acted against the liberty of Florence (Guasti,
Commissioni iii. 666). See also the anonymous sonnet in answer to the anti-Medicean
poem of Burchiello (Magl. II: IV: 250), quoted Gutkind, *Cosimo de' Medici*, p. 415:

> E saria andata a tredici
> la libertà, se che reggeva privo
> non fosse, a far ritornar Cosimo divo.

[187] *Istorie*, p. 304.   [188] Ibid., pp. 306–7.   [189] Ibid., p. 307.

The impetus of the mob was lost *en route* to the meeting with the pope at Santa Maria Novella; divided and disconsolate, they set out from Sant'Apollinare through the dark and rainy night and arrived in the *piazza* outside San Giovanni two hours after sunset. Their last energies were dissipated in an abortive attempt to set fire to the houses of the Martelli since, as Ugolino explained in the *Ricordi*, 'Neri Bartolini was our uncle and had strenuously opposed them, and because we were heartfelt enemies of theirs and friends of Cosimo'. According to Cavalcanti, both those attacking and those defending seized the opportunity to express the pent-up and frustrated impulses of the day in a battle royal, though as he observed, 'no one of either party was really hurt', and in fact Martelli concluded that 'through the boldness of a band of young men who were spending the evening with us, we defended ourselves . . . so that no damage was done to our property, or injury to any person, but we emerged from the incident with great honour'.[190]

Rinaldo's consent to the papal proposal signified in effect the inevitable triumph of the Mediceans. Many of the leading citizens of Florence, including Rinaldo himself, were on intimate personal terms with the pope, but almost certainly the political and economic self-interest of the papacy necessitated his support of the Medici when it came to a choice between them. They were his official bankers, financiers, and financial advisers; he was reliant on their financial support, and there are a number of letters in the Medici collection testifying to the strength of their influence with him.[191] In addition they had many other friends in ecclesiastical high places, like Ambrogio Traversari, Vicar-General of the Camaldolensian order, who protested on their behalf shortly after their expulsion from Florence in 1433,[192] and other secular supporters whose opinions weighed heavily with the Holy See. Prominent among these was the Venetian government whose communications with the pope in the period of the Medici exile contain references to Cosimo's diplomatic co-operation with Venice and the papacy, and imply a certain mistrust on their part of the foreign policy of the conservative regime under Rinaldo's

---

[190] Ibid., pp. 307–9; Martines, 'La famiglia Martelli' 41–3.

[191] Cf. above, also M.A.P. XIII, 48, 68, and Cambi, *Istorie*, p. 183, for the fact that it was Francesco Boscoli, Averardo's partner in Rome, who provided 6,000 fl. to finance the coronation of Eugenius IV.

[192] Gutkind, *Cosimo de' Medici*, pp. 109–12.

direction.[193] At the time of his exile Cosimo was a close associate
of Eugenius himself, and described Giovanni Vitelleschi, the
envoy sent to treat with the rebels outside Sant'Apollinare, as 'an
intimate friend'.[194] Certainly that shrewd observer Cavalcanti saw
the papal intervention as crucial in the defeat of the conservative
faction, and his comment on the subject indicates that others drew
the same conclusion:

By this means, the knight was divested of all his forces, and they made
their way to the Palace to join his rivals. Many citizens who had waited
hidden to see who got the upper hand, came out in favour of the Palace.
And thus the valiant knight was abandoned, on account of the faithless-
ness of men, and the deceitfulness of two priests.[195]

It seems unlikely that Rinaldo himself was unaware of what was
clear to everyone else. Presumably his comparatively submissive
accession to the papal proposition expressed the realization that it
would be wellnigh impossible to successfully establish and maintain an illegally inaugurated anti-Medicean regime in the face of
papal antagonism, in addition to all the other opposition, both
inside and outside the city, which he had encountered in the preceding twelve months. Perhaps Rinaldo realized he was beaten,
as his coalition of family forces began to disintegrate under the
pressure of events, and thought it wiser to give in gracefully at
the opportunity offered by the papal intervention, before he and
his followers were convicted not simply of opposing their wills to
the *Signoria*, but of raising the sword against them in open revolution. Certainly, subsequent appeals to the Medici for clemency by
other leaders of the conservative faction suggest that for some
time afterwards they clung to the hope that, having drawn back
from the brink of bloodshed and civil strife, they might be par-
doned and allowed to resume their former position in the city.

Two days later the *Signoria* felt confident enough to summon a
Parlamento to obtain permission for the constitution of a *Balìa* to

[193] Above, p. 308; see also the letter of Leonardo Dati in Rome to Matteo Strozzi,
27 Sept. 1433, published Gutkind, pp. 112–13: 'Quidquid in Medices gestum sit, iam
diu intellectum est. Quod aut S. P. infensissimus fuerit hoc multi saepenumero
suspicati sunt. Erant etiam qui dicerent eum clam hosti ferre opem concilii nomine.
Id alii disputent.'
[194] Cosimo, *Ricordi*, p. 102.
[195] *Istorie*, p. 310; cf. Niccolò Barbadori in his confession (Gelli, 'L'esilio di
Cosimo' 166): 'Poi venne il vescovo di Richanati e andossi a Santa Maria Novella e
ponemo giù l'arme che fu nostra disfazione.'

reform the *reggimento*, and to determine the fate of the rebels. Throughout the crises of 1433 and 1434 one is aware of the shadowy presence of armed force in the background behind the political manœuvring and the personal pressures. On both occasions the Medici had privately assembled their own troops at Careggi in readiness to defend their interests,[196] and according to the Venetian historian, Sanudo, when they finally left Venice for Florence on 29 September, they were accompanied by 300 Venetian soldiers.[197] Certainly on both occasions observers stressed the role of arms in 'protecting' the *Parlamento* called to provide a mandate for the new regime. In 1433 the firm control exercised by the militia had facilitated a bloodless *coup*; in 1434 the *Signoria*, having assembled 500 men in defence against the conservative arms, sent for further reinforcements; by Cosimo's account, 'they called into the city a huge number of foot-soldiers, and from the Mugello, the Alps, and the Romagna alone there came to our house more than 3,000 troops, in addition to the company commanded by Niccolò da Tolentino'.[198] According to another observer, throughout Monday, 27 September 'troops poured in from the *contado*, from the Mugello, and Pistoia, to reinforce the citizens within, and on Tuesday 28th at the eighteenth hour the bell sounded for the *Parlamento* which had been summoned by Neri Bartolini, one of the Priors, and there were in the *piazza* about 6,000 armed men, or perhaps eight counting the citizens armed, conducting themselves in an amazingly orderly fashion, and at that moment there rode into the *piazza* almost 700 horses carrying armed soldiers of the commune'.[199] Through Cavalcanti's somewhat jaundiced eyes the scene appeared rather more sinister:

All the soldiery, with a huge multitude of wild and fierce peasants, suddenly poured into the *piazza*. The militia of the commune was led

---

[196] See Gelli, 'L'esilio di Cosimo' 78; cf. the letter of 27 Sept. from Piero di Cosimo to Francesco di Giuliano (M.A.P. IV, 332), describing the anti-Medicean attempt to set fire to the Martelli houses, how it was only foiled by the intervention of the Ginori, Masi, and Della Stufa, and urging Francesco to recruit as many men as possible from the Mugello and send them immediately to Careggi: 'Sarebe buono qui in chasa fussino istasera 30 ho 40 fanti, acciò che se lla brighata aversa ci volessi venire ad ardere, ci fussi chi difendessi, che 40 la difenderebono da mille'. He also suggested that in general Francesco should ensure that 'non ci sia si debole di fanti, benchè tutavia ci è ne trapela in aiuto della Signioria'.

[197] Gutkind, *Cosimo de' Medici*, p. 96. [198] *Ricordi*, p. 102.

[199] C.S. 2ª ser. CIII, *Priorista*, Sept. 1434.

by Messer Bartolomeo Orlandini, and in the manner of a good captain, he blocked off all the entrances to the *piazza*; Papi de' Medici was the leader of the mob of peasants, and the whole city was occupied by their two companies.[200]

These troops led by the Medici *amici* Bartolomeo Orlandini and Papi de' Medici obviously functioned partly as a private army of the Medici, albeit with the consent, and officially under the auspices, of the state. Like its predecessor of 1433, the *Balìa* granted to its members the particular privilege of permission to carry arms, though as Nerone Dietisalvi, another of the Medici *amici* currently serving on the police magistracy—the *Otto di Guardia*—observed in his diary, while the *Balìa* was at work, 'the members of the Otto were heavily occupied with the defence of the Palace, and also with importuning the government that the *Balìa* should ensure that where the other had had one weapon, we should have two . . .'[201]

Despite all this, the fundamental fact remains that while the *Parlamento* granted authority to a *Balìa* to reform the state in the presence of force, the evidence does not justify the assumption that this was the essential factor in the transfer of power to the new regime. The *Signoria* took its stand firmly on the legality of its own position and stressed the role of the conservatives as rebels against the commune;[202] the comments of other contemporaries suggest that they too saw the situation in this light. In addition to the charge that Rinaldo had armed himself against the *Signoria*, 'which is something no one ought to do', was the explanation of an observer that by the will of the people the *Balìa* had been entrusted with establishing a new regime, 'since that of the ruling faction seemed to the people unsatisfactory',[203] or of another that 'many citizens were suspicious of the grandeur and ostentation of Rinaldo and his adherents'.[204]

Although the main purpose of the 1434 *Balìa* was to restore the Medici and to banish their opponents, there is no suggestion of a popular revolution effected by a pro-Medicean mass. However

[200] *Istorie*, p. 311.
[201] MSS. 85, f. 101v; cf. Rinuccini, *Ricordi storici*, p. 64: 'venne in piazza tutto il popolo armato e feciono uomini di Balìa . . .'
[202] Balìe, 25, f. 58v; C.P. 50, f. 204r.
[203] C.S. 2ª ser. CIII, ff. 112v–113r.
[204] MSS. 120, *Priorista* of Bernardo Lotti, entry Sept. 1434.

inadequately the *Parlamento* represented the general will of the citizens of Florence, it created the *Balìa* of 1434 in technical accordance with normal Florentine procedure, and the *Balìa* appointed was in fact genuinely representative of the ruling group. It contained rather more of the Medici *amici* than had its predecessor of 1433, and correspondingly less of the leading exiles, but as before, the remainder of the *reggimento*, unaligned with either party, had swung into line behind the *Signoria* as the legal representative of the communal will.

That they anticipated and were prepared to accept the consequent recall of the Medici to Florence under circumstances peculiarly favourable to their predominance in the ruling group is suggested by the comments of Guccio di Cino de' Nobili, who was not a member of the inner *reggimento* but whose family maintained a secure place in the larger governing group. In his *Ricordanze* he described how in September 1434, as if by some objective and inexorable process, the *reggimento* 'was taken' from Rinaldo, and given to the Medici. His account of their return to the city on the day following their official recall is restrained but cordial: 'All the citizens were waiting to greet them for they had been greatly wronged, and it had pleased God and the Florentine people to restore them'; he expressed the hope that their return might prove to be 'the salvation of our city'.[205]

The Mediceans were naturally jubilant; Cosimo described in his *Ricordi* the scene of welcome at Pistoia, where 'the whole populace had gathered at the gate to greet us', and in Florence where 'all the people clustered in the Via Larga, and outside our house to wait for us, and for that reason the *Signoria* preferred us not to enter the city by day in order not to create any more commotion in Florentine territory'.[206] His friends outside the city wrote congratulating him on his return, among them Almoro Donado, who thanked God that justice had prevailed in their restoration, although he had always been convinced in his heart 'that your exile would not last more than a year'.[207]

Meanwhile the fate, and even in some cases the identity of their defeated opponents appear for some time to have remained uncertain, since the *Balìa* constituted in response to their rebellion against the *Signoria* contained no less than fourteen future exiles.

[205] *Ricordanze*, C.S. 2ᵃ ser. LIX, c. 211.   [206] *Ricordi*, p. 103.
[207] M.A.P. XIII, 21.

Five of these were citizens automatically included as incumbents
of major magistraces, but nine were appointees.[208] On 2 October
one of the first acts of the new *Balìa* was to banish Rinaldo degli
Albizzi and his son Ormanno, and Ridolfo Peruzzi with his sons,
and brother Donato.[209] But no further moves were made against
individuals until 15 October, when several citizens soon to be
exiled were replaced in office by others more acceptable to the
new regime;[210] the first full-scale list of *confinati* did not appear
until 3 November.[211]

A note of 28 September from Lippaccio de' Bardi to Cosimo
contained the information that their chief enemies had already
fled from Florence: 'Niccolò Barbadoro is in Barberino, Messer
Rinaldo is here in the pope's palace, and Ridolfo [Peruzzi] with
him.'[212] However, their letters to the Medici family in the weeks
following the uprising against the Priors indicate that some of
those whose commitment to the anti-Medicean forces was less
obviously irrevocable believed they might still escape retribution.
Indeed, even before the conflict came to a head on 26 September,
one anonymous friend who had apparently attended the *Pratica* at
the Palace which was the occasion of Cosimo's arrest, had written
to Cosimo in Venice 'with the intention of cutting short your
complaints, and the excuses of the *reggimento*, and especially mine'.
He wrote in response to 'your letter, which contains some words
which seem to have been written with the deliberate intention of
imputing blame to me', and he went on to give his assurance that
'until the Priors began to distrust you I never did or intended to
do anything to cause you harm . . . and as I have told you before,
I was called there to discuss the matter with the others, and I
simply complied with the will of the government'. He concluded
with the rather unconvincing claim that he had not previously
asked pardon for his part in the affair, because it had seemed to
him a relatively minor matter in a long history of friendship
between two men who had been as close to one another as brother

[208] Future exiles in the *Balìa*, subsequently replaced (Balìe, f. 49v), were Antonio
di Vieri Altoviti (*Sedici*), Bernardo d'Anselmo Anselmi, Mariotto di Niccolò
Baldovinetti, Bernardo di Salvestro Belfradelli (*Sedici*), Giovanni di Simone Biffoli
(*Sedici*), Niccolò di Paolo Bordoni, Felice di Michele Brancacci, Francesco di
Messer Rinaldo Gianfigliazzi, Francesco di Vieri Guadagni, Terrino Manovelli
(*Sedici*), Antonio di Lionardo Raffacani, Piero di Manetto di Tuccio Scambrilla
(*Dodici*), Nuccio di Benintendi Solosmei, Palla di Nofri degli Strozzi.
[209] Balìe, 25, f. 21v.   [210] Ibid., f. 39r.   [211] Ibid., f. 55r, ff.
[212] M.A.P. XIII, 18.

monks, and begged him not to take to heart anything else he had since written merely in jest.[213]

On 8 October Antonio di Ghezzo della Casa wrote to Lorenzo from Santa Maria Novella, where he too had taken refuge, on the grounds that 'more than two of your *amici* have entreated me to do so'.[214] Tinoro Guasconi, writing on 12 October from Castel San Giovanni, made his intentions quite clear; he began by assuring Lorenzo that the recall of the Medici 'was so welcome to me, and of such comfort that there is nothing which could possibly have occurred to give me greater pleasure'. However, after this manifest lie he did go on to admit to 'a certain doubt and fear' that others might interpret unfortunately his own actions of the previous year, and throwing himself in fact on Lorenzo's mercy he begged him to be 'alert to my situation, and if you see anyone attempting to do anything to harm me, to come to my aid . . .', invoking 'what has always been my upright way of life, and that I have never been a partisan . . .', and concluding that 'my only hope is in God and then in Cosimo and in you.'[215]

Rather different in tone from Guasconi's rather pathetic plea was the extraordinarily bold appeal which Bartolomeo Peruzzi made on the same day to Cosimo.[216] He began with the claim that 'I knew nothing of your misfortune until after it had occurred, nor did I even hear about the *Parlamento* called at that time until the very day when I arrived at the Palace'. He had merely followed the lead of his cousin Ridolfo; he himself had always been well disposed towards the Medici, 'and you may be certain that in my heart I always grieved over all your misfortunes . . . since I have always wished you well . . . and also your dear departed father'. He assured Cosimo that all his claims would be verified by 'your friends, including Bernardo Carnesecchi, with whom I have often spoken of these matters', and that they need never fear his opposition in the future, since 'now I am really satisfied and delighted by the prosperity which you enjoy'. Bartolomeo was willing not only to pledge his devotion to the Medici in the future, but even to offer information about his companions in the past; he affirmed that he had been 'coerced by those more powerful than myself, as I will amply demonstrate to you . . .' He actually begged them to ignore the accusations of others, 'and to be pleased to treat me as

---

[213] Ibid. XI, 39.
[215] Ibid. XX, 49.
[214] Ibid. XCVII, 431.
[216] Ibid. XIII, 45.

you do your friends, and to allow me to return openly to my previous path, and to be good enough to include me in the number of your friends'.[217]

There is also a letter to Cosimo and Lorenzo from Matteo Panciatichi in Pistoia dated 26 October, and stating briefly that 'not by words but by deeds you will see if I have not always been your friend, and how greatly and undeservedly I have been tormented'.[218] These letters reflect not only the amazing optimism, or possibly the desperation of their authors, but also an awareness that despite the emphasis given by the new regime to the more immediate and objective charge of rebellion against the *Signoria*,[219] those to be most heavily punished would certainly be those who had taken a prominent part in the anti-Medicean government of the preceding year, and those who, like Matteo Panciatichi, had not been personally active in government but were inextricably involved with the leading figures of the anti-Medicean party by marriage, custom, and long years of association; such indeed was the nature of the group of exiles finally announced. In the event, Antonio della Casa and Matteo Panciatichi were spared, although it is doubtful if even Cosimo could have saved Tinoro Guasconi or Bartolomeo Peruzzi, whose families were more severely treated than any others in Florence.

Later commentators, even those generally favourable to the Medici, were comparatively critical of the government for its confinement of so many good and glorious citizens. Cambi observed that on regaining power the new Priors 'took their full measure of vengeance',[220] and indeed the proscriptions were on a grander scale than any since the thirteenth century. Both Cavalcanti, and later Vespasiano da Bisticci, were anxious to attribute what they saw as the savagery of this vengeance to the Medici supporters rather than to Cosimo himself: 'There were at this time some very bold and rash citizens in Florence, who considered that Cosimo ought to recognize them as the authors of his recall.'[221]

---

[217] 'Mettermi nel numero de' vostri amici'; the phrase implies almost formal recognition in the group of patronage and protection; cf. its use above, p. 99.

[218] M.A.P. XIII, 70. Cf. the interesting appeal for mercy after the event addressed by Branca Brancacci to Cosimo from the *Stinche* (the communal prison) which appears almost to parody a prayer: 'Fiat misericordia tua domine super nos quemadmodum speravimus in te...' (ibid. XII, 189, 6 July 1439). [219] See, e.g., Balìe, 25, f. 58v.

[220] *Istorie*, p. 193; cf. his comment on Averardo's death (p. 202): 'venne a ghodere pocho la ritornata della sua patria, con tanta gran vendetta fatta.'

[221] *Vite* iii. 24; cf. Cavalcanti, *Istorie*, p. 323.

Cosimo too stressed in his *Ricordi* that many of the sentences were passed before he returned to the city, and although he implied ultimate approval of the Priors' actions by including the confinements among the principal acts they performed 'on behalf of the state', he also took trouble to point out that during his own period of office as Gonfalonier of Justice in January–February 1435 'no one at all was exiled or punished'.[222]

Writing some years after these events, Vespasiano argued the injustice particularly of the Strozzi exiles, and declared that others, including two kinsmen of Palla di Nofri, Agnolo Pandolfini and Bartolomeo Carducci, although themselves among the principal *amici* of the Medici, were repelled by this act.[223] The continued appearance throughout October of Palla di Nofri Strozzi in the *Pratiche* which began to meet again on 15 October, when all others shortly to be exiled, with the exception of Cosimo's erstwhile friend, Giovanni dello Scelto, had failed to reappear after 27 September,[224] suggests that his fate may have remained in doubt longer than that of his companions. Possibly this was due to his lifelong reputation for genuine patriotism and a preference for peace, and to his record of conciliation and moderation over the preceding months.[225] Nevertheless, it is difficult to see how the new regime could have felt itself secure while he remained in Florence. Even if the assertions of his fellow conservatives in their confessions concerning his conspiratorial activities are false, Palla di Nofri had belonged to the inner core of the conservative leadership and was only a little less prominent than Rinaldo and Ridolfo Peruzzi themselves. Other members of the family had also taken important parts in the anti-Medicean government, and all of them were supported by a family which was one of the largest, the richest, and the most powerful in Florence. Despite the difficulties of the preceding years, Palla's own personal fortune was still immense, and his influence as a statesman, both in Florence and abroad, was formidable. Whatever the nature of Palla's personal attitudes and ambitions, the Medicean establishment could not afford to tolerate the continued presence of the leader of such a powerful rival interest group.

It may well have been true that the Mediceans, rejoicing in their new-found supremacy, were motivated as much by personal

[222] *Ricordi*, p. 103.   [223] *Vite* iii. 24–5.   [224] C.P. 50, ff. 200v–203v.
[225] Above, pp. 204–5.

jealousies as by consideration for the safety of the state. But the fact remains that, as our earlier analysis showed, almost every single citizen exiled was bound by numerous and interlocking bonds to a party which was loosely structured but solidly based in Florentine society. A large proportion of the exiles had been notably prominent in the anti-Medicean government of the preceding year, and many of them had been open opponents of the Medici party and all it stood for since the twenties. The activities of the Medici party itself from 1433 to 1434 had demonstrated the disastrous consequences to a regime of failing to eradicate underground opposition; in the interests not only of self-preservation but even of peace and prosperity for Florence there was much to encourage the new regime to stamp out this long-standing factional struggle once and for all. Seen in these terms, the claim of its spokesmen at the *Pratica* of 2 November to have shown clemency in punishing only the leaders of those who opposed the *Signoria* was probably more justified than might at first appear.[226]

Finally, the impression that, in the words of a modern writer, 'after Cosimo's triumphant repatriation dozens of old families were politically liquidated',[227] proves on analysis to be incorrect. It is quite true that nearly a hundred individuals were banished, and that their families who accompanied them swelled the exodus from Florence significantly.[228] But the effect on the *reggimento*, and on the nature and composition of the political class of the proscriptions of 1434, has sometimes been exaggerated. Considering all those exiled and deprived of office, still only 58 families out of the 325 who constituted the ruling class were involved. Of these, several contained partisans of the Medicean as well as the conservative group, the most notable examples being the brothers Luca and Rinaldo degli Albizzi, and Giovanni and Piero di Luigi Guicciardini;[229] thus of the 58 families involved in the

[226] Iacopo Donado, writing to Cosimo shortly after his recall, revealed that the Venetians 'from the highest to the lowest' were speculating on the provisions the regime would make against his enemies, and generally advised him to exercise prudence (M.A.P. XIII, 78, 11 Oct. 1434).   [227] Martines, *The Social World*, p. 49.

[228] Our figures would suggest, however, that Benedetto Dei perhaps exaggerated when he wrote ('Chronica', MSS. 119, f. 14r) that 'per la ritornata di Chosimo fu chacciato fuori di Firenze e nominati cittadini e principali e chapi di chasa e oltra lloro fu chacciato fuori e frategli e figliuoli e padri di modo che si fa chonto che 500 cittadinio più uscissino fuori di Firenze da portare arme . . .'

[229] Others were the Barbadori, the Dall'Antella, the Bardi, Della Casa, Cavalcanti, and Gianfigliazzi.

proscriptions, only 21 failed to regain the Priorate under the Medicean regime of the later fifteenth century.[230] Of these 21, several were represented in the *Signorie* of the later republic,[231] and five had been newer families not yet firmly entrenched in the governing class when they were expelled from it in 1433.[232] In addition, of course, many of these families regained a position in Florentine society before the end of the century, despite their failure to satisfy the most stringent criterion of purely political prominence.

What had occurred was an alteration in the balance of power, especially marked within the inner *reggimento*. Of the core of sixty to seventy citizens who constituted the basis of the really effective governing group throughout our period, a quarter had been exiled, or had died and had not been replaced by sons or brothers or cousins because their families were now 'suspect by the regime'. The *Consulte* of the last months of 1434 contained a stronger representation of apparently non-partisan citizens than any of the meetings since the middle of 1433, and give the impression that the exiled citizens were being rapidly replaced by Medici friends who had not previously enjoyed major influence in the state. Among these were such loyal Mediceans as Niccolò Cocco-Donati, Francesco Berlinghieri, Neri di Domenico Bartolini Scodellari, Bartolomeo Orlandini, and Antonio di Salvestro Serristori.[233] All of these, as well as those Mediceans who had formerly been members of the inner *reggimento*, and a number of influential unaligned citizens like Astore Gianni, Giovanni Morelli, and Francesco della Luna, were present at the historic *Pratica* of 2 November, at which Luca degli Albizzi, Cosimo de' Medici, Neri Capponi, and Niccolò Valori led the meeting in condemning 'the error . . . which arose in 1433 in the month of September . . .'[234]

The same changes are reflected, though less sharply, in the broader sample of the *reggimento* represented by the *Balìa* which

---

[230] The Aldobrandini, Anselmi, Ardinghelli, Arrighi, Baronci, Barbadori, Bencivenni, Benizzi, Biffoli, Bischeri, Bordoni, Bucelli, Della Casa, Ciampegli, Fenci, Guadagni, Manovelli, Peruzzi, Raffacani, Raugi, and Solosmei.

[231] *Priorista Mariani*, MSS. 248–54.

[232] The Bencivenni, Biffoli, Della Casa, Ciampegli, and Fenci. On the general problem of cyclical movement within the *reggimento* see Kent, 'The Florentine *reggimento*' 615–20.

[233] C.P. 50, ff. 198r–213v.   [234] C.P. 50, f. 204r–v.

assumed office at the beginning of October.[235] Of this group, containing representatives of most of the prominent political families in the city, 14 citizens originally appointed were later themselves exiled by the *Balìa*, compared with the 46 future exiles who appeared in the *Balìa* of 1433. Again the Medici *amici* were correspondingly a little more prominent than they had been in the previous year's *Balìa*; 36 were included in the *Balìa* of 1434 where only 13 had taken part in that of 1433. However, among a total of almost 350 appointees to the *Balìa* of 1434, in addition to the representatives of major offices, the discrepancies between the two can only be described as a shift in the balance of representation; there was certainly no 'revolution' in the *reggimento*, of however circumscribed a nature.[236] Similarly, the Medicean *Balìa* concerned itself with much the same sort of issues as had its predecessor in 1433; it was merely the emphasis given to particular problems which made it representative of the concerns which had characterized the Medicean party since 1426.

Since the status of the magnates had constituted the only major ideological issue between the two parties, it is interesting that the traditional threat to successive regimes inherent in their existence as a potential force to be manipulated by various private partisan groups was finally banished by the virtual liquidation of the magnates as a genuine social category in the acts of the *Balìa* of 1434. According to Giovanni di Iacopo Morelli, 'all the nobles, except those who had erred in 1434', were made *popolani*;[237] this is perhaps not strictly true, but the 232 individuals from 21 families who were readmitted to political life in Florence must have constituted the greater proportion of the *magnati* as described in the Statutes of 1415.[238] Although the proscriptions of 1434 resulted in the relegation to the category of magnates of a number of *popolani*, many of whom had close ties in the past with older magnate families and shared some of their traditions and attitudes, the essential continuity with the class created by the Ordinances of Justice at the end of the thirteenth century had been broken,

---

[235] Balìe, 25, ff. 2r–6r, 34r–38v, published Rubinstein, *Government of Florence*, pp. 244–53.

[236] Rubinstein, *Government of Florence*, pp. 8–10.

[237] *Ricordi*, p. 125; cf. C.S. 2ª ser. 102, entry Nov.–Dec. 1434.

[238] For details, see Delib. Sig. e Coll. (autorità speciale), 25, ff. 210v–214r. The original acts of the *Balìa* concerning the magnates are recorded in Balìe, 25 ff. 61r–63r.

and the final phase in the transition of the *magnati* from social to juridical class had been accomplished; notably the office of the Executor of the Ordinances of Justice, set up to administer the anti-magnate laws of 1293, was eliminated in 1435.[239]

Like its predecessor, the *Balìa* of 1434 devoted a considerable proportion of its energies to rewarding the supporters of the party whose victory was the occasion of its creation, but otherwise its main tasks were to ensure the financial stability which had obviously by now become a precondition of continued support for any regime,[240] and to safeguard it from attack from opposing factions by means of electoral controls.[241] Both of these concerns had been clearly reflected in the activities of the *Balìa* of 1433, but it is characteristic of the Medicean regime that its provision in both these areas should have been very much more thorough and far-reaching. After all, the Medici party had succeeded in its original aim to make itself and its members a force in the *stato* largely by its preoccupation on the one hand with the composition of the purses and the electoral promotion of its members, and on the other by the unique and fortunate ability of the Medici family and their most intimate friends to rescue the city from the financial problems which in the preceding years had threatened it with ruin. It is not then surprising that the *Balìa* of 1434 should undertake a general review of the financial basis of government and should institute a practice of controlling elections which was eventually to transform the effective nature of Florentine government.

The way in which the pro-Medicean *Balìa* built on and extended the precedent of electoral control laid down by its predecessor in 1433 has been described by Nicolai Rubinstein in his study of the government of Florence under the Medici. Rubinstein goes on to trace the implications of a more marked concentration on electoral controls for the political history of Florence in the latter half of the fifteenth century. His work emphasizes that such changes as did take place as a result of the events of 1433 and 1434 did not occur immediately; the way was laid open for future changes which were to come about only gradually as the shift in the balance

[239] The remainder of his jurisdiction was transferred to the *Podestà* (Martines, *Lawyers and Statecraft*, p. 137); see also Becker, 'A Study in Political Failure'.
[240] For financial legislation see Balie, 25, e.g. ff. 17r, 33r, 38v, 44v, 53v, 54r, etc.
[241] See especially ibid., ff. 24r–25v, 44v, 87r, ff., 90v, ff.

of power within the *reggimento* in favour of the Mediceans became, over a long period of time, increasingly more pronounced.

The object of this study has been to contribute to an explanation of the establishment of a Medicean ascendancy in Florence in 1434 by identifying the parties of the Medici and their opponents and by exploring the social bases of these parties, of whose confrontation Medicean Florence was the outcome. It appears that the major conflict in the city from 1426 to 1434 arose not out of an opposition of fundamental class interests, but between two groups within the ruling class whose subtle differences in social and political background and experience significantly affected their structure and organization, and were also reflected partly, though not wholly, in their differing attitudes to questions of major importance like the financing of the republic, the admission of newer citizens into the ruling group, and the treatment of that supra-political Florentine class, the magnates. Most immediately, however, the two parties were essentially dedicated to the defence of their own private interest in the *stato*; theirs was a clash, not of opposing ideologies, but of the conflicting claims of individuals to the exercise of power. It is in these terms that the explanation of the Medici victory of 1434 must initially be sought, though the outcome of their struggle was affected by larger and more abstract forces acting upon them, and the fact of the Medici victory has wider implications for the understanding of other fundamental themes in Florentine political experience. Some of these represent development in new directions, a changing political climate; others are constants of Florentine social and political life.

Piero Guicciardini at the end of the fifteenth century remarked on the cyclical nature of the rise and fall of families on the Florentine social scale, and his observation is supported by a study of the composition of the ruling group over the preceding century.[242] The fact that the conservative aristocratic faction consisted largely of families who had apparently passed the peak of their prosperity and were moving towards decline, while the Mediceans were mainly men in the ascendant, might lend to our understanding of the events of 1433 and 1434 a little of the inevitability of a natural social process. Moreover, the conservative party had its roots in traditional rather than planned associations between a consider-

[242] Kent, 'The Florentine *reggimento*' 615–20.

able number of large and important families accustomed to the exercise of power, and comparatively equal in wealth, prestige, and influence, only imperfectly united by their comparatively late perception of the need to defend the conservative interest in response to the Medicean challenge. Because the Medici were trying to break back into the governing circle after their relative political isolation in the fourteenth century, they could not rely on the traditional support of their social peers, but were impelled to build up afresh a sphere of influence with less self-sufficient houses, or with individuals only recently risen into the ruling group, as yet uncommitted in their loyalties, and comparatively uncertain of their personal influence. Although there is no sign of anything intentionally new or revolutionary in the Medici approach to the attraction of a party, these circumstances inevitably affected the nature of the group which eventually they created. Because the interests of its members were more directly dependent on their more influential patrons, they were more amenable to direction, more single-minded in their allegiance. As an early-sixteenth-century writer, reflecting on the historical development of the Medici regime, observed, Cosimo defeated his enemies 'with the weapon of a party of faithful friends who identified their fortunes with his'.[243]

Changing conditions in Italy at this time, and particularly the territorial expansion of imperialistic states, were everywhere producing a tendency towards government more centralized than that of the classic communal era; the union in the Medici party of many hearts with but 'a single will'[244] coincided with a currently felt need in Florence, accentuated by the experience of the Lucchese war, for a strong and co-ordinated government which would nevertheless respect the cherished constitutional safeguards of oligarchy. As a result of his experience in directing that war, the Medicean Piero Guicciardini expressed the opinion in a letter to his friend Matteo Strozzi, destined for exile in 1434, that in truth the Florentine people yearned for 'the discipline of the rod',[245] and as Giovanni Rucellai was to observe twenty years later, Cosimo and his sons had indeed proved to rule in Florence 'as if they were its veritable Lords'.[246]

[243] Ghoro Gheri, *c.* 1513, quoted by A. Anzilotti, *La crisi costituzionale della Repubblica fiorentina* (Florence, 1912), pp. 100–1.   [244] Cf. above, p. 132.
[245] C.S. 3ª ser. CXXXII, c. 295, 19 Mar. 1430 (1429 *s.f.*).
[246] *Zibaldone*, p. 57.

If the prevailing political and social conditions determined the framework within which the struggle between the parties was fought, there were also more immediate factors decisive in its outcome. The conflict had been brewing throughout the late twenties and early thirties, and might well have broken into the open at several points during this period; the fact that Rinaldo degli Albizzi and his conservative supporters happened to make the first move meant that they had much less room for manœuvre when their *coup* proved to be a very incomplete and temporary success. The Medici were wise enough to eschew the temptation to resist exile by force, relying upon strong internal support to sweep them to power. They waited instead until the apparently normal and legitimate operation of the electoral machinery produced a *Signoria* who would naturally reverse the exile decision of 1433. Thus Rinaldo and his supporters were forced into the radically unconstitutional action of opposing the ultimate representatives of the commune's interests in order to protect not only their own position in government, but also their persons from the inevitable revenge of a revived Medici faction. Such action offended the renowned and traditional preoccupation of the Florentine ruling class with the strict observance of constitutional prescriptions, and finally alienated the remainder of comparatively passive, but numerically crucial members of the ruling group not irrevocably committed to either party, and already disillusioned with the peculiar combination of authoritarianism and ineffectualness which characterized Rinaldo's regime.

It is somewhat ironic that the Medici were swept to victory partly on a tide of desire to defend public government from private violence, when in fact in several spheres their own personal interests had already, even before their exile, begun to encroach upon the autonomy and authority of the state. Such encroachments were not always wilful or even intentional; the indispensable role which Medici money came to play in shoring up the solvency of the state was the inevitable result of general political and economic factors beyond the personal control of individuals, though the attribution to Cosimo even by his admirers of the conviction that 'if money can conquer, then by heaven, we shall',[247] is far

---

[247] Giovanni Avogadro, text quoted by E. Gombrich, 'Renaissance and Golden Age', in *Norm and Form* (London, 1966), p. 33; cf. Cosimo's maxim to Averardo, M.A.P. IV, 221, 24 Sept. 1431, that 'el povero huomo non può mai far bene'.

from being entirely fortuitous. The same might be said of the Medicean cultivation, partly as a consequence of their wealth, of private relationships with other states with whom, before 1434, they dealt independently of, and sometimes as intermediaries with, the government of Florence. Perhaps more conscious was their perception, and uniquely successful implementation, of the principle that the key to exercising power in Florence was to establish and maintain their friends as a major force within the office-holding group. Previous party leaders had of course elevated their followers to position and prosperity, but the Medici added a new dimension to the art of securing a regime when they embarked upon the systematic exploitation of the paradoxical weaknesses of an electoral system originally designed to preclude the predominance of particular groups in government; by means of this formula they achieved a degree of success in the promotion of partisan interest which initially even they could scarcely have foreseen.

Clearly the experience of the Florentine state, at the beginning of the fifteenth century one of the last real republics in northern Italy, was analogous in spirit to that which other communes had previously undergone; however, if her case is broadly in conformity with the general pattern of development from commune to despotism, the particular quality of the Florentine experience was nevertheless affected by the preservation of the constitutional role, however formalized at times, of the oligarchy from which the rulers of most such states drew their essential support. As Rubinstein has shown, throughout the fifteenth century the evolution of the Florentine state towards despotism was limited by the ultimate dependence of the Medici on the acquiescence of their partisans, and even if the tide of history was turning inevitably against them, the rebellion in 1466 of a group of their most influential former friends within the oligarchy, and the recovery, however brief, of real republicanism after the expulsion of the Medici in 1494, demonstrated that this relentless development could be at least temporarily resisted. In this sense the subtle genius of the Medici family in using the operation of electoral controls to reconcile the survival of powerful republican impulses in Florence with their own ascendancy through the instrumentality of their party created an ingenious and characteristically Florentine solution to the European-wide problem in this period of achieving stability through the adaptation of existing political forms.

APPENDIX I

List of apparent Medici friends and partisans

Acciaiuoli, Agnolo di Iacopo
Alberti, Alberto di Giovanni
Albizzi, Luca di Maso
Dall'Antella, Filippo
Arnolfi, Battista di Doffo
Barbadori, Tommaso di Bartolomeo
Bardi, Andrea di Lippaccio
Bardi, Bardo di Ser Bardo
Bardi, Lippaccio di Benedetto
Bartolini-Scodellari, Neri di Domenico
Benci, Giovanni di Amerigo
Bencivenni, Banco di Niccolò
Del Benino, Niccolò di Andrea
Benintendi, Francesco di Lorenzo
Berlinghieri, Francesco di Francesco
Biliotti, Carlo di Bonaiuto
Biliotti, Sandro di Giovanni
Boni, Stefano di Matteo
Capponi, Giovanni di Mico di Recco
Carducci, Bartolomeo di Giovanni
Carducci, Niccolò di Giovanni
Carnesecchi, Bernardo di Cristofano di Berto
Della Casa, Antonio di Ser Lodovico
Cavalcanti, Niccolò
Cepperello, Francesco da
Cerretani, Matteo di Niccolò
Ciai, Ser Ciaio di Pagolo
Cirioni, Giovanni
Corbinelli, Antonio di Bartolomeo
Corsi, Banco
Davanzati, Giuliano di Nicolaio
Davanzati, Luigi di Manetto
Dietisalvi-Neroni, Dietisalvi di Nerone
Dietisalvi-Neroni, Nerone di Nigi
Donati, Giovanni di Cocco
Donati, Niccolò di Cocco

Fioravanti, Neri di Francesco
Gianfigliazzi, Giannozzo di Stoldo
Ginori, Giuliano di Francesco
Ginori, Piero di Francesco
Ginori, Simone di Francesco
Giugni, Andrea di Niccolò
Giugni, Bernardo di Domenico
Giugni, Giovanni di Domenico
Giuntini, Giuntino di Guido
Guicciardini, Piero di Luigi
Lapi, Salvestro di Michele
Martelli, Antonio di Niccolò di Ugolino
Martelli, Bartolomeo di Niccolò
Martelli, Domenico di Niccolò
Martelli, Francesco di Niccolò
Martelli, Giovanni di Niccolò
Martelli, Martello di Niccolò
Martelli, Ruberto di Niccolò
Martelli, Ugolino di Niccolò
Martini, Ser Martino di Ser Luca
Masi, Antonio di Ser Tommaso di Ser Francesco
Masi, Benedetto di Ser Guido
Michelozzi, Michelozzo di Bartolomeo
Del Nero, Bartolomeo
Del Nero, Neri di Filippo
Niccolini, Giovanni di Lapo
Orlandini, Bartolomeo di Giovanni
Pandolfini, Agnolo di Filippo di Ser Giovanni
Da Panzano, Giovanni d'Antonio
Parenti, Nofri
Pazzi, Andrea di Guglielmino
Pecori, Daddo di Simone
Pitti, Giannozzo di Francesco
Pitti, Luca di Buonaccorso di Neri
Portinari, Pigello di Folco
Pucci, Giovanni d'Antonio
Pucci, Piero d'Antonio
Pucci, Puccio d'Antonio
Ricci, Piero di Giovacchino
Ridolfi, Bartolomeo di Iacopo
Salviati, Alamanno di Iacopo
Sassetti, Rosso
Dello Scarfa, Martino di Francesco di Bencivenni
Di Ser Segna, Antonio di Francesco

Di Ser Segna, Stefano di Francesco
Serristori, Antonio di Salvestro
Soderini, Niccolò di Lorenzo
Della Stufa, Giovanni di Lorenzo di Messer Ugo
Della Stufa, Luigi
Della Stufa, Ugo di Lorenzo
Tedaldi, Bartolomeo di Bartolomeo
Tedaldi, Papi di Tedaldo
Tedaldi, Tedaldo
Tinucci, Ser Niccolò
Tornabuoni, Francesco di Simone
Valori, Niccolò di Bartolomeo
Vecchietti, Luigi di Raimondo
Velluti, Maso
Da Verazzano, Fruosino di Cece
Villani, Papi

APPENDIX II

List of those exiled or otherwise punished by the *Balìa* of 1434

Albizzi, Ormanno di Rinaldo di Maso
Albizzi, Rinaldo di Maso
Aldobrandini, Luigi di Giovanni
Altoviti, Antonio di Vieri
Altoviti, Sandro di Vieri
Anselmi, Bernardo di Anselmo di Giovanni
Dall'Antella, Antonio di Lionardo
Dall'Antella, Roberto di Lionardo
Ardinghelli, Piero di Neri di Francesco
Arrigucci, Michele di Alessandro
Baldovinetti, Guido di Soletto del Pera
Baldovinetti, Mariotto di Niccolò
Barbadori, Cosimo di Niccolò
Barbadori, Niccolò di Donato
Bardi, Bardo di Francesco di Alessandro
Bardi, Bernardo di Cipriano
Bardi, Lionardo di Ridolfo
Bardi, Matteo di Bernardo di Giorgio
Bardi, Simone di Iacopo di Bindello
Baronci, Michele di Galeotto
Bartoli, Giovanni di Piero di Arrigo
Belfradelli, Bernardo di Salvestro
Belfradelli, Zanobi di Adovardo
Bencivenni, Stefano di Salvi di Filippo
Benizzi, Iacopo di Piero
Benizzi, Matteo di Piero
Biffoli, Giovanni di Simone di Ser Matteo
Biffoli, Ser Niccolò di Simone
Bindo di Ciuccio di Bindo
Bischeri, Bernabà di Bartolo
Bordoni, Niccolò di Paolo
Brancacci, Ser Branca di Buonfigliuolo
Brancacci, Felice di Michele
Brancacci, Salvestro di Guasparre

Brancacci, Simone di Guasparre
Buccelli, Francesco di Giovanni
Del Bulletta, Lorenzo di Giovanni
Della Casa, Bernado di Filippo di Ghezzo
Castellani, Iacopo di Vanni
Castellani, Otto di Michele
Castellani, Paolo di Giovanni di Matteo
Castellani, Piero di Vanni
Castellani, Richo di Giovanni di Matteo
Cavalcanti, Piero (*privato*)
Del Chiaro, Piero
Ciampegli, Piero di Giovanni di Domenico
Corsi, Corso di Lapo (*privato*)
Corsi, Simone di Lapo (*privato*)
Corsi, Tommaso di Lapo (*privato*)
Doffi, Bernardo di Ser Lodovico
Doffi, Niccolò di Doffo Bernardini
Fagnoni, Bartolomeo di Francesco
Fenci, Tano di Antonio di Paolo
Del Forese, Lorenzo di Ser Stefano di Rinieri
Franceschi, Oddo di Francesco di Andrea
Frescobaldi, Stoldo di Lionardo (*privato*)
Gianfigliazzi, Baldassare di Francesco di Rinaldo
Gianfigliazzi, Francesco di Rinaldo
Gianfigliazzi, Giannozzo di Giovanni di Rinaldo
Gianfigliazzi, Giovanni di Rinaldo
Gianfigliazzi, Iacopo di Rinaldo
Guadagni, Antonio di Bernardo
Guadagni, Bernardo di Vieri (*privato*)[1]
Guadagni, Filippo di Bernardo di Vieri
Guadagni, Francesco di Vieri
Guadagni, Migliore di Vieri (*privato*)
Guasconi, Biagio di Iacopo di Biagio
Guasconi, Iacopo di Bernardo di Biagio
Guasconi, Tinoro di Niccolò
Lamberteschi, Domenico di Bernardo
Lamberteschi, Ser Goccio di Ser Goccio
Luti, Iacopo di Giovanni (*privato*)
Manovelli, Terrino di Niccolò di Manovellozzo
Montecastelli, Francesco di Filippo di Castellano (*privato*)
Panciatichi, Piero di Giovanni di Bartolomeo (fined)

---

[1] He was automatically included in the sentence against all those who had been Priors in Sept.–Oct. 1433, although he was dead by the time that sentence was pronounced.

Da Panzano, Matteo di Matteo di Luca
Pecora, Ser Benedetto di Ser Lorenzo
Pepi, Actaviano di Chirico
Peruzzi, Amideo di Amideo
Peruzzi, Bartolomeo di Verano
Peruzzi, Bernardo di Bindaccio
Peruzzi, Giovanni di Bindaccio
Peruzzi, Lorenzo di Bindaccio
Peruzzi, Luigi di Ridolfo di Bonifazio
Peruzzi, Mariano di Giovanni
Peruzzi, Ridolfo di Bonifazio
Pierozzo, Ser Antonio di Niccolò di Ser
Da Pino, Cristofano di Agnolo di Giovanni
Raffacani, Antonio di Lionardo
Raugi, Alessandro di Bivigliano di Andrea (*privato*)
Ricasoli, Bindaccio di Granello Fibindacci
Ricasoli, Carlo di Granello Fibindacci (*privato*)
Richoldi, Richoldo di Ser Paolo
Rondinelli, Andrea di Vieri di Andrea
Rossi, Lodovico di Giovanni
Salviati, Iacopo di Simone
Sannini, Donato di Cristofano (*privato*)
Scambrilla, Manetto di Tuccio
Scambrilla, Piero di Manetto di Tuccio
Dello Scelto, Giovanni di Matteo
Solosmei, Matteo di Nuccio (*privato*)
Solosmei, Nuccio di Benintendi (*privato*)
Spini, Bartolomeo di Bartolomeo (*privato*)
Strozzi, Matteo di Simone di Filippo di Lionardo
Strozzi, Nofri di Palla di Nofri
Strozzi, Palla di Nofri
Strozzi, Smeraldo di Smeraldo
Velluti, Donato di Piero
Zanobi di Lorenzo, *chiavaiuolo*

SELECT BIBLIOGRAPHY

ARCHIVAL SOURCES

1. Archivio di Stato, Florence:

   Acquisti e Doni
   Atti del Capitano del Popolo
   Atti del Esecutore degli Ordinamenti di Giustizia
   Atti del Podestà
   Balìe
   Carte Strozziane
   Catasto
   Consulte e Pratiche
   Conventi Soppressi
   Giudice degli Appelli
   Manoscritti
   Medici avanti il Principato
   Otto di Guardia e Balìa
   Provvisioni, Registri
   Signori e Collegi, Deliberazioni
   Tratte

2. Biblioteca Nazionale, Florence:

   Fondo Magliabechiana
   Manoscritti Passerini
   Poligrafo Gargani

PRINTED SOURCES

Buoninsegni, Domenico, *Storie della città di firenze dall'anno 1410 al 1460* (Florence, 1637).

Cambi, Giovanni, *Istorie, Delizie degli eruditi toscani*, ed. P. Ildefonso di San Luigi (4 vols., Florence, 1785–6).

Canestrini, G. (ed.), 'Versi fatti da Niccolò da Uzzano', *A.S.I.* iv (1843), 297–300.

Capponi, Gino, 'Ricordi di Gino di Neri Capponi', ed. G. Folena, in *Miscellanea di studi offerta a A. Balduino e B. Bianchi* (Padua, 1962).

Capponi, Neri di Gino, *Commentarii di Neri di Gino Capponi di cose seguite in Italia dal 1419 al 1456, Rerum Italicarum Scriptores*, xviii, ed. L. A. Muratori (Milan, 1731).

Cavalcanti, Giovanni, *Istorie Fiorentine*, ed. G. di Pino (Milan, 1944).

Da Bisticci, Vespasiano, *Vite di uomini illustri del secolo XV*, ed. L. Frati (3 vols., Bologna, 1892).

Grendler, M., *The 'Trattato Politico-Morale' of Giovanni Cavalcanti, Travaux d'Humanisme et Renaissance*, cxxxv (Geneva, 1973).

Guasti, C. (ed.), *Commissioni di Rinaldo degli Albizzi* (3 vols., Florence, 1867–73).

Guicciardini, Francesco, *Memorie di Famiglia*, in *Scritti Autobiografici e Rari*, ed. R. Palmarocchi (Bari, 1936).

Ildefonso di San Luigi, P. (ed.), *Delizie degli eruditi toscani* (24 vols., Florence, 1770–89).

Mallett, M. (ed.), 'The Diary of Luca di Maso degli Albizzi', in *The Florentine Galleys in the Fifteenth Century* (Oxford, 1967).

Medici, Cosimo de', *Ricordi*, in A. Fabroni, *Magni Cosmi Medicei Vita* (Pisa, 1789).

Morelli, Giovanni di Pagolo, *Ricordi*, ed. V. Branca (Florence, 1956).

Perosa, A. (ed.), *Giovanni Rucellai ed il suo Zibaldone*, i (London, 1960).

Pitti, Buonaccorso, *Cronica*, ed. A. B. della Lega (Bologna, 1905).

Strozzi, Alessandra Macinghi negli, *Lettere di una Gentildonna Fiorentina*, ed. C. Guasti (Florence, 1877).

Strozzi, Palla di Nofri, 'Diario', *A.S.I.* xi (1883), 26–48, 145–56, 293–309; xii (1883), 3–22; xiii (1884), 159–70; xiv (1884), 3–18.

Tabarrini, M. (ed.), 'Chronichette Volterrane', *A.S.I.* App. III (1846), 309–52.

Tinucci, Ser Niccolò, *Examina*, in G. Cavalcanti, *Istorie fiorentine*, ed. F. Polidori (2 vols., Florence, 1838–9).

SECONDARY WORKS

Becker, M., 'An Essay on the "Novi Cives" and Florentine Politics, 1343–1382', *Mediaeval Studies*, xxiv (1962), 35–82.

Bencini, I. M., 'Neri Capponi', *Rivista delle biblioteche e degli archivi*, xvi (1905), 91–100, 136–54, 158–74.

—— 'Note e appunti tratti da documenti sulla vita politica di Neri Capponi', *Rivista delle biblioteche e degli archivi*, xx (1909), 15–31, 33–56.

Boissevain, J., 'Patronage in Sicily', *Man*, i (1966), 18–33.

Brucker, G., 'The Medici in the Fourteenth Century', *Speculum*, xxxii (1957), 1–26.

—— *Renaissance Florence* (New York, 1969).

—— *The Civic World of Early Renaissance Florence* (Princeton, 1977).

Dainelli, A., 'Niccolò da Uzzano nella vita politica di suoi tempi', *A.S.I.* 7th Ser. xvii (1932), 35–86.

Dami, B., *Giovanni Bicci dei Medici* (Florence, 1899).

Fabroni, A., *Magni Cosmi Medicei vita* (Pisa, 1789).

Gelli, A., 'L'esilio di Cosimo de' Medici', *A.S.I.* 4th Ser. x (1882), 53–96, 149–69.

Gombrich, E. H., 'The Early Medici as Patrons of Art', in *Italian Renaissance Studies*, ed. E. F. Jacob (London, 1960), pp. 279–311.

Gutkind, C., *Cosimo de' Medici, Pater Patriae, 1389–1464* (Oxford, 1938).

Heers, J., *Gênes au XVᵉ siècle* (Paris, 1961).

Herlihy, D., 'Veillir à Florence au Quattrocento', *Annales — Économies — Sociétés-Civilisations*, xxiv (1969), 1338–52.

Holmes, G., 'How the Medici became the Pope's Bankers', *Florentine Studies*, ed. N. Rubinstein (London, 1968), pp. 357–80.

Hyman, I., *Fifteenth Century Florentine Studies: The Palazzo Medici and a ledger for the Church of San Lorenzo* (New York, 1977).

Jones, P. J., 'Florentine families and Florentine Diaries in the fourteenth century', *Papers of the British School at Rome*, xxiv (1956), 183–205.

Kent, D., 'I Medici in esilio: una vittoria di famiglia ed una disfatta personale', *A.S.I.* cxxxii (1974), 3–63.

—— 'The Florentine *reggimento* in the fifteenth century', *Renaissance Quarterly*, iv (1975), 575–638.

Kent, F. W., *Household and Lineage in Renaissance Florence: The Family Life of the Capponi, Ginori and Rucellai* (Princeton, 1977).

Klapisch, C., 'Fiscalité et démographie en Toscane (1427–1430)', *Annales-Économies — Sociétés — Civilisations*, xxiv (1969), 1313–37.

Limburger, W., *Die Gebäude von Florenz* (Leipzig, 1910).

Litta, P., *Famiglie Celebri Italiane* (15 vols., Turin and Milan, 1819–1902).

Martines, L., 'La famiglia Martelli e un documento sulla vigilia del ritorno dall'esilio di Cosimo de' Medici, (1434)', *A.S.I.* cxvii (1959), 19–43.

—— *The Social World of the Florentine Humanists* (London, 1963).

Marzi, D., *La Cancelleria della repubblica fiorentina* (Rocca San Casciano, 1910).

Minio-Paluello, L., 'Remigio Girolami's "De Bono Communi": Florence at the Time of Dante's Banishment and the Philosopher's Answer to the Crisis', *Italian Studies*, xi (1956), 56–71.

Molho, A., *Florentine Public Finances in the Early Renaissance, 1400–1433*, (Cambridge, Mass., 1971).

Moriani, M. Antonelli, *Giovanni Guicciardini ed un processo politico in Firenze (1431), Collana di pubblicazioni guicciardiniane XXVI* (Florence, 1954).

Passerini, L., *Gli Alberti di Firenze* (2 vols., Florence, 1869).

—— *Genealogia e storia della famiglia Altoviti* (Florence, 1871).

—— *Genealogia e storia della famiglia Corsini* (Florence, 1858).

—— *Genealogia e storia della famiglia Ginori* (Florence, 1876).

—— *Genealogia e storia della famiglia Guadagni* (Florence, 1873).

—— *Genealogia e storia della famiglia Panciatichi* (Florence, 1858).

—— *Memorie Genealogico-Storiche della famiglia Pecori* (Florence, 1868).

—— *Genealogia e storia della famiglia Ricasoli* (Florence, 1861).

—— *Genealogia della famiglia Salviati* (Florence, 1895).

Pellegrini, F. C., *Sulla repubblica fiorentina a tempo di Cosimo il vecchio* (Pisa, 1880).

Rado, A., *Maso degli Albizzi e il partito oligarchico in Firenze dal 1382 al 1393* (Florence, 1927).

De Roover, R., *The Rise and Decline of the Medici Bank* (Cambridge, Mass., 1963).

—— 'Cosimo de' Medici come banchiere e mercante', *A.S.I.* cxxiii (1965), 466–79.

Rubinstein, N., 'The Beginnings of Political Thought in Florence', *J.W.C.I.* v (1942), 198–227.

—— *The Government of Florence under the Medici (1434 to 1494)* (Oxford, 1966).

—— 'Notes on the word *stato* in Florence before Machiavelli', *Florilegium Historiale: Essays presented to Wallace Klippert Ferguson* (Toronto, 1971), 314–26.

Stradario Storico e Amministrativo della Città e del Comune di Firenze (Florence, 1913).

Trexler, R., 'Ritual Behaviour in Renaissance Florence: The Setting', *Medievalia et Humanistica*, new ser. iv (1973), 125–44.

INDEX

Peruzzi, family (*cont.*):
  Marietta di Ridolfo di Bonifazio
    (Panciatichi), 155, 173
Peruzzi, Ridolfo di Bonifazio, 102–3,
    154, 157, 169–70, 174, 327, 340–1
  associations of, 155–6
  attack on societies, 219, 240
  involvement in conspiracies against
    Mediceans, 319–20, 330
  as leading anti-Medicean, 137–8,
    193, 219, 244–5, 294–6, 343
  in office of *Dieci*, 236
  in *Pratiche* of 1434, 317–19, 322,
    325–6
  role in rebellion against Priors,
    331–2, 334
  wealth of, 140, 142
  Rinieri di Luigi, 153 n
  Rinieri di Niccolò, 153 n
  branch of, 331
Pesaro, 94 n
Petrarch, 212
Petrucci, Manno di Tano di Cambio,
    ricordanze, 50 n
Philippus Andree, *legum doctor*, 222 n
Piazza de' Frescobaldi, 168
Piazza del Mercato Vecchio, 64
Piazza de' Peruzzi, 153, 157
Piazza del Popolo, 124, 295, 302, 337–8
Piazza S. Apollinare, 137, 157, 164, 332
Piazza S. Felicita, 169
Piazza S. Lorenzo, 69–70
Piazza S. Maria Maggiore, 174
Piazza S. Pier Maggiore, 176
Piazza S. Trìnita, 162, 163 n, 168
Piccinino, Niccolò, *condottiere*, 276, 278,
    308–10
Piero, 86, 97
  'al banco', 79 n
  di Piero, *cartolaio*, 328 n
  di Cristofano da Gagliano, 35 n, 86
  da Vico, 305 n
Pietrasanta, 273
Pigli, Francesca di Iacopo di Latino di
    Primerano, 60 n
Da Pino, Cristofano di Agnolo, 68 n
Pisa, 93, 97, 104, 178, 268 n, 270, 272,
    279, 297, 300–1, 312, 323
  Captain of, 280
  sea consuls at, 267. See also *Cinque di
    Pisa*, Consuls of Pisa, Sea Consuls
Pistoia, 173–4, 303, 305, 337, 339, 342
  factions of, 266 n

  mountains of, 201, 266
  Podestà of, 303
Pitti, family, 101–2, 333
  alliance with Strozzi, 52
  Buonaccorso, 59, 101–2, 148, 156, 162,
    177, 179,
  Cronica, 20, 152
  Giannozzo di Francesco, 59 n, 85,
    102, 318
  Luca di Buonaccorso, 59, 102, 328
  Maddalena di Buonaccorso, 59
plebe, in Medici party, 106
Podestà, office of, 94, 295, 347 n
political discourse, customary themes of,
    216
  influence, determinants of, 18
  life, face-to-face nature of, 117
  locus of, 19
  poetry, 212
  power, constitutional distribution of,
    19
  rights, deprivation of, 139, 188. *See
    also* offices, political
Ponte S. Trìnita, 168
Ponte Vecchio, 71 n, 161, 168–9
Pontetetto, 268
pope, 308, 322, 327
  Medici as financiers to, 83
  Boniface VIII, 141, 163
  Eugenius IV, 124
  arbitration between factions by,
    334–5
  coronation of, 335
  palace of, 349
  relations with Medici, 335–6
  Giovanni XXIII, 156
popolani, 115, 119 n, 147–9, 156–7, 166,
    220, 321, 346
Popoleschi, family, 57, 58 n
  Niccolò di Aginolfo, 57, 188 n, 320
popolo, 149 n
  definition of, 7
Poppi, count of, 295
Por San Maria, 159–60
Porta S. Pancrazio, 162 n
portate, passim. See also *catasto*
Portinari, family, 67 n, 74, 80 n, 129
  Accerito di Adovardo, 74
  Bernardo, 74 n
  Folco di Adovardo, 74
  Giovanni di Adovardo, 74, 305
  Nanna (Medici), 74
  Pagolo di Folco, 66 n